BUDDHIST MONASTERIES AND MONASTIC LIFE IN ANCIENT INDIA

Buddhist Monasteries and Monastic Life in Ancient India

(From the Third Century BC to the Seventh Century AD)

REKHA DASWANI

ADITYA PRAKASHAN
New Delhi

First published, 2006

ISBN 81-7742-067-4

Published by Aditya Prakashan, F-14/65, Model Town II, Delhi – 110 009.
email: aditya@bibliaimpex.com

Printed at Rajkamal Electric Press, Delhi – 110 033.

Namo tassa Bhagvatto
Arhato Sammāsambuddhassa.

(Honour to Him, the Blessed One,
the Worthy One, the Fully Enlightened.)

Contents

Preface

The path of Asceticism has been recognized as one of the classical ways of salvation in the religio-spiritual tradition of India. Under the process of institutionalization over the periods of historical development, asceticism became closely connected with monasticism. The latter may be understood as the concretization of the philosophy of asceticism. Whereas asceticism is concerned with the theoretical and practical aspects of the life of an individual spiritual seeker, monastic organization presents itself as a social expression of such a spiritual seeking undertaken by such ascetics who share with each other common ideas and beliefs pertaining to spiritual goal and general conduct considered necessary for its obtainment. In this community form the monastic organizations were bound to evolve certain specific characteristics.

The present work attempts at a systematic reconstruction of some of the principal aspects and peculiar features in the genesis, evolution and functioning of Buddhist monasticism both in terms of an autonomous development and in relationship with the changing conditions of society in India till the seventh century AD.

The first chapter seeks to define the concept of asceticism and monasticism and throws light on the possible pre-Vedic and pre-Aryan origin of the institution of 'wandering almsmen' in India which flowered in the sixth century BC. It discusses the foundational beliefs of Śramaṇism with special reference to the Sakyaputta Samaṇas. It traces the gradual transition of the primitive *Bhikkhu Saṅgha* from a wandering sect to a settled order. It shows how the primitive monk settlements represented by the *āvāsas* and the *ārāmas* gave way, in due course of time, to *leṇas* which became permanent domiciles of the Order.

The second chapter presents the background of Buddhist sects and post-Aśokan developments, highlighting the Mahāsāṅghika-Sthavira schism which was a product of disciplinary and doctrinal issues. The fourth-third century BC was an age of critical transition when numerous sects arose which put forth doctrines varying in meaning, significance and implications, paving the way, ultimately, for the emergence of Mahāyāna.

In deprecation of the old *arhat* ideal, a new ideal—that of the *bodhisattva* was put forth by certain sects. With the radical expansion of world view, a Mahayanic pantheon of Buddhas and Bodhisattvas was evolved who, it was believed, could bestow their grace on firm believers. The mutual relationship of the various sects is discussed on the basis of information derived from literature, epigraphs and accounts of the Chinese travellers.

The third chapter delineates a picture of the life of the inmates in the *vihāras* where key-note of relationship was mutual respect and reverence. The *pabajjā* and the *upasampadā* ordination marking the entry of the novice and full membership in the *Saṅgha* became an elaborate procedure with the gradual lapse of time. Religious life was marked by many features of congregational character like the *uposatha, vassāvāsa, pavāraṇā* and *kaṭhina*. These ceremonies became days of religious observance and celebration for the laity as well.

With the growth of corporate life, the organizational structure of the *Saṅgha* specified status positions with seniority and associated competencies. Office bearers were appointed in order to conduct the multifarious business involved in community life and to procure and distribute the material possessions permitted to the members.

Food, drinks, material possessions, etiquette and the daily

routine of the members have been dealt with in detail keeping in view the transformations in certain spheres in response to the waves of social and cultural change. The Buddhist *Saṅgha* functioned within the scope of *Vinaya* laws which regulated not merely the monk's personal life but also his relations with others and his rights and duties as member of a corporate body. As time went on, old *Vinaya* rules were amended and modified to suit the needs of the members of the *Saṅgha.*

The austere mode of the *āraṇya bhikṣus* has also been considered. The *Bhikṣuni* Order and the status that it enjoyed, finds its due place. Interesting archaeological details are provided about the after death ceremonies of the *Saṅgha* members.

The fourth chapter deals with education and learning as imparted and acquired in Buddhist monasteries. The relationship of the *Saddhivihārika* and the *Antevāsika* vis-a-vis the *Upajjhāya* and the *Ācariya* is unfolded in detail. As the picture emerges, with the gradual lapse of time Buddhist monasteries had become centres for the dissemination not only of Buddhist teaching but also of brahmanical studies and secular branches of learning. Traditional learning was thus progressively liberalized and the curriculum included instruction in arts and crafts, medical science, logic, grammar, astronomy besides the sacred *sūtras* and *śāstras.* As a matter of historical necessity, with the rise of Mahāyānism and the priority given to the laity, the *vihāras* far from being seats of monk life and culture became seats of secular learning.

A new development of monastic education was the growth of specialization in different versions of the *Vinaya*, the *Sūtra* and the *Abhidharma.* The urge for disseminating knowledge among people and preserving it for posterity felt by the Buddhist monk-scholars explains the library tradition in major monastic universities. The catholic spirit of these universities attracted students and scholars from far off places. These universities continued to provide the highest stimulation to independent thinking and reflective meditation.

The fifth chapter, though highlighting monastic celibacy and seclusion in contrast to domestic life and identifying spiritual life with monastic life, seeks to elucidate the general scheme of Buddhistic culture in which mundane social life is considered an integral part. Though the Buddhist bhikkhus naturally enjoyed a superior status by virtue of being active seekers of spiritual progress, the *Saṅgha* included within it the laity as well. It laid down certain norms such as faith, morality, listening to the Dhamma, dāna and the practice of the Brahma-*vihāras*, keeping in mind the potentialities of the faith followers. It may be pointed out that the lay Buddhists also contributed significantly to the growth of Buddhist ideas and practices.

The ideology of merit as conceived by the Buddhists is elaborated upon together with the doctrine of the transfer of merit *(puṇya pariṇāmanā)* which was developed to its logical conclusion by the Mahāyānists. The *Saṅgha* was specified as an auspicious field for potential merit-making and the laity reciprocated in return by regular endowments both in cash and kind.

The Buddhist *Saṅgha* was also able to influence the actions of the state and induce some of the rulers to live up to the ideal of the *Cakkavattī Dhammika Dhammarājā* as is clear from Aśoka's example in whom this ideal of state authority was concretized. The social philosophy of Buddhism is best exemplified in his edicts.

An endeavour has been made in the last chapter to study the gradual evolution of three important structures inevitably associated with the monastic complex, namely, the residential *vihāra* with its essential adjuncts, the *stūpa* and the *caitya-gṛha.* The information provided is primarily archaeological.

If the thesis has seen the light of day, it is mainly due to the unstinting encouragement given at every stage of its preparation by my revered mentor, Late Dr. G.S.P. Misra, Associate Professor, Department of History and Indian Culture, University of Rajasthan, Jaipur. No words can adequately express my gratitude to him for his painstaking guidance and personal interest in my research effort.

The theme of the work was suggested to me by the noted scholar of Buddhism, Prof. G.C. Pande who was also helpful in the preparation of the general scheme of the work. I am extremely grateful to him.

A special word of thanks is due to Dr. K.R. Norman, former President, Pali Text Society, London, for unravelling several knotty queries put up to him as well as for his valuable pointers on many issues. I would also like to acknowledge my indebtedness to Shri R.S. Mishra, Associate Professor, Department of History and Indian Culture, University of Rajasthan, Jaipur, for his helpful and critical suggestions on many vital points.

The valuable assistance extended by the library staff of the University of the Rajasthan and of the Archaeological Survey of India for making available various materials is gratefully acknowledged. I am also obliged to Dr. Jata Shanker Jha, former Director, K.P. Jayaswal Research Institute, Patna, for putting up patiently to my constant pestering of him in my hunt for reference material and for providing me with certain valuable texts.

I am thankful to my brother Surendra Daswani for helping me in the translation of certain French and German passages in this thesis. It is my pleasant duty to express my sincere gratitude to late Shri Pradeep Goel, Aditya Prakashan, Delhi, for kindly undertaking to publish the work and for taking immense pains to bring out the book in its present form.

Jaipur
May 2006

REKHA DASWANI

Abbreviations

AA	:	*Artibus Asiae*
ABORI	:	*Annals of the Bhandarkar Oriental Research Institute*
AI	:	*Ancient India*
AP	:	*Aryan Path*
ASIAR	:	*Annual Report of the Archaeological Survey of India*
ASSI	:	*Archaeological Survey of Southern India*
ASWI	:	*Archaeological Survey of Western India*
BCAP	:	*Bodhicaryāvatāra with Pañjikā*
BDVI	:	*Bauddha Dharma ke Vikās kā Itīhāsa*
BFAC	:	*Buddha and Five After Centuries*
BMD	:	*Buddhist Monastic Discipline*
BMMI	:	*Buddhist Monks and Monasteries of India*
BRWW	:	Buddhist Record of the Western World
BSI	:	*Buddhist Sects in India*
BST	:	Buddhist Sanskrit Texts
BV	:	*Bhāratīya Vidyā*
CII	:	*Corpus Inscriptionum Indicarum*
EBM	:	*Early Buddhist Monachism*
EI	:	*Epigraphia Indica*
EMB	:	*Early Monastic Buddhism*

ERE	:	*Encyclopaedia of Religion and Ethics*
HOR	:	*History of Religions*
IA	:	*Indian Antiquary*
IAR	:	*Indian Archaeology—A Review*
ICTWI	:	Inscriptions from Cave Temples of Western India
IHQ	:	*Indian Historical Quarterly*
JAHRS	:	*Journal of the Andhra Historical Research Society*
JAOS	:	*Journal of the American Oriental Society*
JAS	:	*Journal of Asian Studies*
JASB	:	*Journal of the Asiatic Society of Bombay*
JBBRAS	:	*Journal of the Bombay Branch of the Royal Asiatic Society*
JBORS	:	*Journal of the Bihar and Orissa Research Society*
JBRS	:	*Journal of the Bihar Research Society*
JDL	:	*Journal of the Department of Letters*
JGJRI	:	*Journal of the Gangannath Jha Research Institute*
JIH	:	*Journal of the Indian History*
JMSUB	:	*Journal of the Maharaja Sayajirao, University of Baroda*
JNSI	:	*Journal of the Numismatic Society of India*
JOIB	:	*Journal of the Oriental Institute, Baroda*
JRAS	:	*Journal of the Royal Asiatic Society*
JUB	:	*Journal of the University of Bombay*
LIFE	:	*Life of Hiuen-Tsiang by the Shaman Hwui-Li*
MASI	:	*Memoirs of the Archaeological Survey of India*
NS	:	New Series
PE	:	Pillar Edict
PTS	:	Pali Text Society
QJMS	:	*Quarterly Journal of Mythic Society*

RE	:	Rock Edict
SBB	:	Sacred Books of the Buddhists
SBE	:	Sacred Books of the East
SRE	:	Separate Rock Edict
Studies	:	Studies in the Origins of Buddhism
TOI	:	*Times of India*
WZKSO	:	*Wiener Zeitschrift für die Kunde Südund Ostasiens*
VIJ	:	*Vishveshvaranand Indological Journal*

CHAPTER 1

Historical and Ideological Background of Śramaṇism and Early Development of Monasticism

I

Adoption of homeless life by some, either as individual wanderers or as members of organized ascetic communities *(Saṅghas)* has been since times immemorial a characteristic feature of Indian life. 'It is a tribute to the high metaphysical capacity of the Indian people, says Deussen,[1] 'that the phenomenon of asceticism made its appearance among them earlier and occupied a large place than among any other known people'. Recounting the effect of the example of an ascetic life, Trevor Ling quoting Durkḥiem[2] points out, 'It is necessary that an elite put the end too high, if the crowd is not to put it too low. It is necessary that some exaggerate, if the average is to remain at a fitting level'.

Concept o Asceticism and Monasticism

The term 'Asceticism' is derived from a Greek word, meaning exercise and training for the purpose of strength, skill and mastery in the athletic games. Hence an ascetic may be defined as a spiritual athlete.[3] Asceticism, according to Indian tradition, conveys a connotation which has a deep and

---

[1]Paul Deussen, *The Philosophy of the Upanisads,* p.65.

[2]Quoted, Trevor Ling, *The Buddha,* p.170.

[3]*ERE.,* Vol.II, p.63.

comprehensive bearing in its outlook on spiritual pursuits. It is chiefly concerned with the theory and practice of individual conduct. On the other hand, the term 'Monasticism' means 'alone'.[4] It indicates a mode of life, away from society in perfect solitude—a life traditionally followed by ascetics in their search for salvation from the evils of human existence. But, since man can hardly 'live alone like a rhinoceros', even the pursuit of spiritual life requires organization, though on a different principle.

It was the Buddhists and the Jainas who developed a new context for spiritual quest, namely, existence not apart from the world but from worldly life[5] in communion with one another.[6] Their renunciation of the worldly society led them into a new social state in which the members were bound with each other by spiritual aspiration. Their monastic organization was an expression of their spiritual seeking of which the ascetic tendency is a *sine qua non.*[7] It was this that made the Buddhist *Saṅgha* of particular interest, because there is every indication that the Buddha regarded the monastic life as 'the normative path in the Buddhist community'.[8] Asceticism is a complex of a number of traits. As M.G. Bhagat has pointed out, the principal ones may be distinguished as *Vairāgya,*

---

[4]Solitary eremetical life was common to Hindu *Sannyāsins,* Buddhist *Bhikkhus* and Jaina *Yatis,* though in course of time all the three developed cenobitical life.

[5]To put it in the words of the Pāli Canon, it was 'going forth from home into homelessness'—*Āgārasmā anagāriyaṁ pabbajati (Mahāvagga*, pp.18, 21, 22). The same idea is conveyed in the Ācārāṅga Sūtra *(Jaina Sūtras*, SBE., I, p. xxvii) by the phrase: *'Agārāo anāgāriam pavvaiye'.*

[6]There was a change in the ideal of the ascetic life from peripateticism and solitary life *(eko care khaggavisānakappo—Sutta Nipāta,* 35-75) to monasticism *(Sukhā—Saṅghassa Sāmaggī Samāgganaṁ tapo sukho—Dhammapada*, 194).

[7]Different from the Jaina and the Buddhist approach, there has also existed another pattern of worldly withdrawal in Hinduism. This sprang from the Hindu conception of the four natural stages of life *(āśramas)* allowing an individual to comply both with his ethical obligations to self and society and with his religious obligations to self and God.

[8]Joseph Kitagawa, 'Buddha and the Saṅgha', *Religions of the East,* p.167.

Saṁnyāsa, Tapas and *Yoga*.[9] The ideal of *Vairāgya* is considered to be the fundamental requisite of ascetic life and a worthy objective towards the attainment of self-perfection. The word comes from *vi*, meaning 'apart', 'away', 'without' and *ragā*, meaning 'desire' or 'attachment.'[10] Hence, *Vairāgya* would stand for freedom from all worldly desires and indifference to the worldly objects of life.

The *Jābālopaniṣad* makes *Vairāgya* the only alternative condition for entering *Saṁnyāsa*. Naciketas, in the *Upaniṣads* appears as a true *Vairāgī*, treading the path of *Śreyas* (good) and spurning all wealth, heavenly as well as earthly.[11] Mahāvira and his followers are called *'Nigganthas' (Nirgranthas)*—'the unfettered ones'. The term *Nirgrantha* conveys a literal as well as figurative sense: 'Outwardly unclothed and inwardly unfettered'.[12] The whole apparatus of Jaina monastic code speaks of dispassion or detachment—a state which could be attained by mastery over body and mind.[13] In Buddhism too, freedom from *taṇhā* (desires) is considered essential for eliminating suffering.[14] One who has to go forth and retire from the world has to break the fetters of *taṇhā*, says the Dhammapada.[15]

Saṁnyāsa, an essential concomitant of asceticism and monasticism, implied complete renunciation *(sam+nyās)* of the world and its attachments.[16] In Buddhism, the object and purpose of world-forsaking and becoming almsmen is said to

---

[9]M.G. Bhagat, *Ancient Indian Asceticisim*, p.60.

[10]Monier Williams, *A Sanskrit English Dictionary*, p.1029.

[11]*Kaṭha Upaniṣad*, I.2ff; see, *Maitri Upaniṣad*. I.2-4.

[12]B.C. Law, *Mahavira: His LIfe and Teachings*, p.5.

[13]Haripada Chakraborti, *Asceticism in Ancient India*, pp.367ff.

[14]*Mahāvagga*, p.3.

[15]*Dhammapada*, 335-43.

[16]*Na karmaṇā, na prajayā dhanena. tyāgenaike amṛtatva-mānusuḥ*—'Not by work, not by offspring, or wealth; only by renunciation does one reach life eternal'—*Kaivalya Upaniṣad*, I.2.

be nothing more than *Brahmacarya* (the higher life).[17] The Buddha exhorts his followers: 'Go along in accordance with what has been enjoined, having soon realized—that supreme goal of the Brahma-faring, for the sake of which young men of family rightly go forth from home into homelessness'.[18]

The Sanskrit noun *Tapas* has divergent meanings. Central to all such meanings, however, is the notion of heat or warmth—heat generated by austerities, rather to the practice of asceticism itself.[19] It is used sometimes to comprehend all forms of the pursuit of self-control.[20] The austere life is one which is given to abstinence and discipline, hence *tapas*. The term is used in the ascetic literature of the Brāhmaṇas and the Jainas to convey self-torture or self-mortification.[21] *Brahmacarya* (celibacy) became an integral part of a life of *tapas*[22] and this trait found a place in Jainism and Buddhism

---

[17]The term *brahmacarya* meant the perfect, the best, the highest life (I.B. Horner, *Book of the Discipline*, I, Intd. p.lv), a life synonymous with righteousness (*'Dhammacariyaṁ brahmacariyaṁ, etad āhu vasuttamaṁ ...' Sutta Nipāta*, 54) possible only for a person who entered the Order *(Brahmacariaṁ Sugata cāramase' 'bramacarivaṁ carissāma, Bhagavā, tava santike'. Sutta Nipāta*, 32, 165). In the *Saṁyutta Nikāya* (IV, p.8), the Buddha himself is represented as explaining that holy life *(brahmacariya)* is led by his followers for the sake of the complete understanding of pain *(dukkha-pariñña)* and there is only one way to this—the noble Eight-fold path. Nagasena *(The Questions of King Milinda*, SBE., I, p.31) states that the object of renouncing the world to live in the Order is for the sake of 'being able to live in righteousness and spiritual calm'. G.S.P. Misra *(The Age of Vinaya*, p.39) explains it as living a particular system of life which was conducive to the attainment of the highest truth.

[18]I.B. Horner, *The Book of Discipline*, IV, p.13; *Mahāvagga*, p.12.

[19]Upon whom the seers of yore, that created the beings, brought forth with their songs the cows, they the seven active (priests), by means of the sattra offerings, the sacrifices, and (their) creative fervour (tapas)—*Atharva Veda*, XII.1.39; 'By austerity, knowledge and meditation we obtain Brahman'—*Maitrī Upaniṣad*, IV.4; 'By austerities he cuts off karman'—*Uttarādhyayana Sūtra* (SBE.), XLV, p.166.

[20]S. Radhkrishnan, *The Principal Upaniṣads*, p.375.

[21]*ERE.*, II, p.87.

[22]See, Walter O. Kaelber, 'Tapas, Birth and Spiritual rebirth in the Veda, *HOR.*, Vol.15, No.4, May 1976, pp.362, 366; *Atharvaveda*, XI.5.17-19; The *Upaniṣads (Muṇḍaka* 1.2.11; *Chāndogya* 5.10.1-6) say that one may realize the self by practising *tapas* in the forest, free from passion.

among the five great vows of monastic conduct.[23] It became a condition necessary for the attainment of the highest spirituality. In the Upaniṣads, *tapas* means knowledge—the creative moulding power.[24] It comprehended all forms of the pursuit of self-control as a means to self-knowledge.[25] *Tapas* as self-mortification finds no place in the Buddhist monastic code.[26] In this respect, Buddhism strikes a cordial note with the *Gītā* which denounces all kinds of penances and practices which involve the torture of the flesh.[27] True *tapas* involves the discipline of the body, speech and mind.[28] In Jainism, *tapas* is not merely self-mortification but also the cultivation of a positive spiritual insight. This is clear from the distinction made between physical or external *tapas* and mental or internal *tapas*.[29] The former is of six types: fasting, decreased diet, collecting alms, giving up delicious diet and mortification of flesh. The latter consists of expiation, humility, service, study, renunciation of body and meditation.[30] It is clear that *tapas* in the sense of self-mortification has been regarded a necessary constituent of a larger, comprehensive pathway to realization, though generally, it was not considered an independent and isolated category of spiritual quest. Every

---

[23]T.W. Rhys Davids, *Buddhism,* p.139.

[24]*Muṇḍaka Upaniṣad,* 1.1.9: 'For the real knower, knowledge is tapas'; *Maitrī Upaniṣad,* 4.3: 'If one does not practise tapas. there is no success in (attaining) the knowledge of the Ātman.'

[25]*Chāndogya Upaniṣad*, 2.23.1.

[26]Buddha undoubtedly practised *tapas* for six long years to attain the highest wisdom but realizing its futility sat in meditation. See, G.C. Pande, *Studies,* pp.379-80.

[27]*Bhagavad Gītā,* XVII.5-6.

[28]Ibid., XVII.14-16. In the 'Sihasenapativatthu' of the *Mahāvagga* (pp.250-51) the Buddha explains, how he can be termed as a *tapasi* ('a burner up')? He speaks of 'evil wrong states which are searing: misconduct in body, speech and thought'. He for whom, 'evil wrong states that are searing are destroyed, cut off at the root, made like a palm tree, so utterly done away with that they can come to no future existence—he I call one who is a burner up:' I.B. Horner, *The Book of Discipline,* IV, pp.321-22.

[29]Dayanand Bhargava, *Jaina Ethics,* pp.182ff.

[30]Haripada Chakraborti, op. cit., pp.367-69.

ascetic code of morality definitely formulated systematic and hierarchic stage of development in which *tapas* was an integral element and formed part of a positive moral ideal.

Yoga, a profound discipline, represents in its highest phases absorptive concentration and deep meditation. It is regarded as a technique for the realization of final wisdom. The roots of *yoga* can be traced to pre-aryan antiquities. This receives additional confirmation from the statues or figures unearthed at Mohenjodaro and Harappa. One of the most remarkable of these figures is that which is considered as a representation of *Paśupati* Śiva in a *yogic* posture.[31]

In the *Kaṭha Upaniṣad* we find reference to *yoga* as a 'firm grip on the senses' *(sthira indriyadhāraṇāṁ)*.[32] The first appearance in Vedic literature of ' anything resembling *yogic* practices is in those passages of the *Upaniṣads* which advocate meditative worship.[33] Meditation and contemplation came to occupy a central place in the way followed and taught by the Buddha.[34] The early Buddhist literature mentions Sāriputta, Moggalāna and Nanda as adept in *dhyāna*.[35] A fully developed *yoga* technique is found in later Buddhist literature.[36]

Origin of the Śramaṇic Trend

Scholars have expressed various views regarding the origin of

---

[31]J. Marshall, *Mohenjodaro and the Indus Valley Civilization*, I, p.49.

[32]*Kaṭha Upaniṣad*, II.3.11. *The Chāndogya Upaniṣad* (VIII.15) refers to the practice of establishing all the sense organs in the *ātman—'ātmanī sarvendriyāṇi sampratiṣṭhāpya'*.

[33]*Chāndogya Upaniṣad*, I.1.1ff; 2.2.1ff .

[34]In early Buddhism there is an elaborate theory of different stages of meditative cognition. See, Anāpāna Satti Suttaṁ, Kāyagatā Sati Suttaṁ, Cula-Sūnyatā, Uddesa-Vibhanga of the *Majjhima Nikāya.*

[35]G.C. Pande, op. cit., p.513.

[36]See, E. Thomas, *History of Buddhist Thought,* pp.44ff; E. Conze, *Buddhist Meditation,* pp.11-41. In the Yogācāra school of thought Buddhistic ideas were combined with the practice of *Yoga.* Even in Zen Buddhism there is an increasing stress on *dhyāna.*

Śramaṇism in Indian culture.[37] Kern[38] traces the origin of the ascetic to the Vedic *Brahmacārin.* His view is totally unconvincing because on the basis of rules prescribed for the *brahmacārin* he draws a generalization that the life of a *bhikṣu* was modelled on it. Jacobi[39] has suggested that the *Brāhmaṇa* ascetic served as a model for the Buddhist and the Jainas. In support of his view, he has pointed out the resemblance between the Jaina and the Buddhist rules of discipline with the Brāhmaṇical ones. This view is convincingly refuted by G.C. Pande who remarks, 'that the resemblances consist in the main of rules of a very general character... if there was a borrowing, it was not so much of particular regulations as the ideal of the ascetic'.[40]

Jacobi further states that 'the germs of dissenting sects like those of the Buddhists and the Jainas were contained in the institute of the fourth āśrama'.[41] A careful perusal of the Upaniṣads shows their acquaintance with mendicancy[42] but there is no clear distinction between the third and the fourth *āśramas.*[43] Within the orthodox Brahmaṇical circle itself, we find the so-called fourth *āśrarna* regarded with disfavour. It is the second *āśrama* that is extolled and exalted and regarded as the root and mainstay of the other stages.[44] In no way the fourth *āśrama* could have provided any incentive to Jainism and Buddhism since the fully developed theory of the four *āśramas* itself, belongs to the later period of Dharmasūtras and

---

[37]For a survey of various theories about the origin of *Śramaṇic* cult, See G.C. Pande, *Śramaṇa Tradition,* pp.4-5; S.B. Deo, *History of Jaina Monachism,* pp.48-56; S.R. Goyal, *A History of Indian Buddhism,* pp.35ff.

[38]H. Kern, *Manual of Indian Buddhism,* p.73.

[39]H. Jacobi, *Jaina Sutras* (SBE.), Pt.I, pp.xxiv-xxxii.

[40]G.C. Pande, *Studies,* p.322; See, S. Dutt, *EBM.,* pp.39-40.

[41]H. Jacobi, *Jaina Sutras*, Pt.I, p.xxxii. But Jacobi's view has been controverted by S. Dutt, *EBM.,* pp.39-40 and G.C. Pande, *Studies,* pp.321-22.

[42]*Bṛhadāraṇyaka Upaniṣad,* III.5.1.

[43]*Ibid.,* IV.4.22, IV.5.2: *Muṇḍaka Upaniṣad,* 1.2.11.

[44]*Gautama Dharmasūtra,* III.1.35; *Baudhāyana Dharmasūtra,* II.6.29ff; *Manu,* III.77, 80, VI.87, 89, 90.

Dharmaśāstrās. It seems more reasonable to believe that the Jainas and the Buddhists received their idea of ascetic not from the Brāhmaṇas but from previously existing heretical sects.[45]

Keith,[46] Griffith,[47] Das[48] and Gḥurye[49] hold the Vedic *Muni*[50] as the prototype of the wandering almsmen by tracing certain common traits like celibacy, austerity, concentration and ecstacy but assign no motives or conditions influencing the formation of the ascetic 'complex' in the Vedic environment. The *Ṛgveda,* except for stray references to *Munis,* delineates the picture of a society which took keen pleasure in material prosperity, living a life full of zest and vigour.[51] There is no evidence of an ascetic *Weltanschauung* in the early Ṛgvedic society.[52]

The most plausible suggestion, however, comes from G.C. Pande who assigns a pre-Vedic and pre-Aryan origin to the *Munis and Śramaṇas*[53] (wandering almsmen) having a distinct religious and cultural tradition like the orthodox Aryan tradition in the Vedic Age.[54] Close contact of the Aryan tradition with these *Munis and Śramaṇas* appears to have

---

[45]G.S.P. Misra, op. cit., p.107.

[46]Macdonell and Keith, *Vedic Index*, Vol.II, p.164.

[47]R.T.H. Griffith, *Hymns of the Sāmaveda,* p.50.

[48]A.C. Das, *Rigvedic India*, p.11.

[49]G.S. Ghurye, *Indian Sadhus*, p.12.

[50]*Ṛgveda,* X.136.2, 4, 5. In verse 1 he is described as 'long haired'. VIII.17.14 (Indra is termed as friend of the *Munis*); *Atharvaveda*, VII.74.1 refers to *deva-muni.*

[51]*Ṛgveda*, I.104.8; I.114.7-8; I.13 6.15; X.14.8; X.59.6.

[52]J. Van Troy, 'The Origin of Asceticism and of the Aśrama Dharma, *Bharati,* VIII, Pt.I, 1964-65, p.10.

[53]G.C. Pande, *Studies,* p.261; J. Marshall (op. cit., p.49), affirms the existence *of yogic* practices in India on the basis of some seals depicting a deity in *Dhyāna-yoga posture.* Even S. Dutt *(BMMI.,* p.41) suggests that the custom of world-forsaking was not of Vedic Aryan provenance.

[54]The great antiquity of the *Śramaṇic* cult has received less attention from scholars due to the fact that in historical times the Brāhmaṇa cult appeared to be more influential and widespread. 'The *Śramaṇa* tradition already existed in the Vedic period as an independent though little known tradition'; See, G.C. Pande, *Śramaṇa Tradition*, p.3.

taken place when towards the close of the later Vedic period the Brahmaṇic values underwent a change.

This change affected only a few thoughtful souls who were willing to consider seriously the apparently pessimistic world picture which the doctrine of *Saṃsāra* entails.[55] 'Vedic religion had advanced from pursuing the world to transcending it, from propitiating the Gods to seeking the self.'[56] A silent revolution was being ushered in by the doctrine of *karman* which tended to undermine the indispensability of the priest and the sacrifice. Since bondage within *Saṃsāra* resulted from *kāma* and *karman*,[57] proclaimed the *Upaniṣads,* it was necessary to abandon them.[58] 'To obtain immortality' one had only to 'know the self',[59] to turn back from the world.[60]

Sixth Century BC *and the Śramaṇic Movement*

The age of Buddha is characterized as an age of acute religious consciousness and of social distress which combined to result in the ascetic upsurge.[61] The social and political situation was

---

[55]Two closely linked ideas are in the foreground, transmigration or the flow of existences, *Saṃsāra*, and the moral principal determining the successive existences, *karman* or retribution for actions. These ideas are immediately related to the belief that it is possible to escape from the chain of existences and to attain liberation. See, Louis Dumont, 'World renunciation in Indian religions', *Religion, Politics and History in India,* p.43.

[56]G.C. Pande, *Studies,* p.265.

[57]*Bṛhadāraṇyaka Upaniṣad*, 4.4.5.

[58]Ibid., 4.4.6-7; *Kaṭha Upaniṣad*, 2.2.7-8.

[59]Ibid., 4.4.14, 17; Ibid., 6.14-15; *Śvetaśvatāra Upaniṣad,* 6.6; 3.8 *(tam eva viditvā atimṛtyum eti nānyaḥ panthā vidyate ayanāya; Muṇḍaka Upaniṣad*, 2.2.5 *(amṛtasya setuḥ).*

[60]The *Upaniṣadic* literature in a few places thus conceals in an embryonic form such a world negating attitude. It was in connection with this teaching of the *Upaniṣads* that there developed a view of the material world as something to be rejected and renounced in the interests of *ātman* or true self. It is this spirit which is expressed in Maitreyi's statement to her husband Yajñavalkya, *'yenāhaṁ nāmrta syaṁ kimahaṁ tena kuryaṁ* ('What shall I do with that which does not give me immortality')?—*Bṛhadāraṇyaka Upaniṣad,* 2.4.3.

[61]G.C. Pande, *Studies,* p.327; G.S.P. Misra, *Development of Buddhist Ethics,* pp.2ff.

characterized by an element of intense crisis and insecurity. The rise of imperial Magadha was threatening the very existence of a number of other states both monarchical and republican.[62] Economic life was experiencing a virtual revolution with the development of currency as a medium of exchange and the consequent growth of trade and commerce.[63] Proliferation of industries and emergence of guilds were other noticeable features of the age. These changes in economy led to the emergence of new classes, the *Gahapatis* and the *Seṭṭhis.*[64]

The transition which many people were then experiencing from the familiar small scale society of the old tribal republics to the strange, large scale and consequently more impersonal, bleaker life of the new monarchical state, was accompanied by a psychological malaise, a heightened sense of dissatisfaction with life as it had to be lived.[65] Rival Schools and sects professing different religious doctrines ranging from materialism to mysticism further fed the flame of spiritual quest.[66] Even the traditional account of the 'four signs' *(Nimitte)* seen by Sidhārtha prior to his renunciation can be interpreted as reflecting the changing social scene. 'The first three may be taken as portents of the sense of anxiety from which the old society, now on the verge of transformation was suffering while the figure of the recluse was the traditional answer to the challenge of the times.'[67]

---

[62]Ibid., pp.311-13; G.S.P. Misra, op. cit., pp.204-05; Trevor Ling. op. cit., pp.60, 71.

[63]K.R. Subrahmanyan, 'Appearance and spread of iron in India', *JOIB.*, Vol.13, No.4, 1964, pp.349-57. For early Buddhism and the second Urban revolution, See, S.R. Goyal, op. cit., pp.205-07.

[64]D.D. Kosambi, *The Culture and Civilization of Ancient India in Historical Outline,* pp.100-02; G.C. Pande, loc. cit., p. 314; Trevor Ling, loc. cit., pp.51-52; G.S.P. Misra, loc. cit., p.240; Romila Thapar, *Ancient Indian Social History*, p.44.

[65]Trevor Ling, loc. cit., p.75, See, A.L. Basham, *The Wonder That Was India,* pp.246-47, Thomas Hopkins, *The Hindu Religious Tradition,* pp.52-53.

[66]*Infra.*

[67]B.G. Gokhale, 'The Buddhist Social Ideals', *IHQ.,* Vol.XXXII, June-Sept. 1956, p.141, See, S. Dutt, *BMMI.,* p.36.

These changes, however, should not be taken as the cause of the *Śramaṇic* movement of the sixth century BC. They only created the suitable atmosphere in which the *Śramaṇic* ideology could emerge as an important and dominating phenomenon. The ascetic tradition was already present in the soil waiting for suitable circumstances which it got now ready at hand.[68] The more thoughtful and sensitive persons became inclined to withdraw from the world and enlisted themselves as members of the homeless community.[69] The recruits to this new community are called by different names in Indian literature, viz., *Parivrājaka*[70] (Pali, *Paribbājaka*)—'goer-forth', one who has gone from home into homelessness, *Bhikṣu* (P. *Bhikkhu)*[71]—almsman, *Śramaṇa*[72] (P. *Samaṇa*)—literally labourers in spiritual life, *Yati*[73]—one who has restrained his senses and *Saṁnyāsin*—one who has cast off worldly ties. The last term is commonly used in Brahmaṇical literature to designate men of this type.

---

[68]See, G.C. Pande, *Studies,* p.328; G.S.P. Misra, op. cit., p.35.

[69]Distress with the world and the worldly life, for one reason or the other is, in fact, the starting point of *Śramaṇic* conviction. The various vicissitudes necessarily involved in the life of the world lead one to be convinced about the desirability of the life of worldly renunciation. The fact is clearly recognized in the *'Rathapāla Sutta'* of the *Majjhima Nikāya* (II, pp.290-93) where one finds an enumeration of four factors which ordinarily impel people to adopt the monastic life—(a) *Jarāhani,* old age, decrepitude, (b) *Vyadhīhani,* fatal disease, (c) *Bhogahani,* loss of fortune and (d) *Jñatihani,* loss of relations. Contrary to this A.K. Warder (*Indian Buddhism,* p.47) says. 'this alternative way of life was embraced by many who wished to escape the need to work, or the responsibility of family life, not to speak of conscription, forced labour or slavery, and was a carefree existence very different from the life strenuous asceticism, complicated discipline and intensive study required of members of most of the organized sects afterwards'.

[70]This was a common denomination for all ascetics—rather a condition of life represented by men who may not have gone through different *āśramas* (stages of life) performing their graded duties and responsibilities imposed by Vedic culture and its requirement. See, S. Dutt, *BMMI.,* p.39.

[71]Literally, a 'Sharesman'—one who receives a share of public resources. See, Trevor Ling, op. cit., pp.150-51.

[72]The word is derived from root—*Śram*—to exert, effort, labour or to perform austerity, See, Monier Williams, *A Sanskrit English Dictionary.* p.1096.

[73]The Jaina monk is usually designated as a *yati.* See, Sinclair Stevenson, *The Heart of Jainism,* p.233.

In this community of religious wanderers, the class known as the *Samaṇas* is given a superior status.[74] They are usually paired with *Brāhmaṇas* in Buddhist and Jaina literature denoting equality of status.[75] 'The two classes' as G.S.P. Misra observes 'actually represented two different trends and theories in the ascetic community, viz., Vedic and non-Vedic'.[76] The *Śramaṇas* represented a casteless and classless institution in opposition to the Brahmaṇical one,[77] where only a *dvija* after clearing of his obligations to society in the first three *āśramas* could become a *Parivrājaka*.[78]

Foundational Beliefs of Śramaṇism

Ascetic *Śramaṇism* posed a negative challenge by being at total variance with Brahmaṇic values. The Brahmaṇas living in secular society accepted the fulfilment of social and ritual obligations, emphasized happiness in this world as in the other and hoped to gain it from the Gods. Contrary to this the *Śramaṇas,* having abandoned secular society, entered a new society based on spiritual relations.[79] 'They rejected much of the traditional ritual, emphasized inward morality and accepted social obligations, not as something absolute but as

---

[74]S. Dutt (op. cit., p.49) refers to them as the 'elite in religious life'. See, 'Kassapa-Sīhanāda Sutta', *Digha Nikāya* (SBB.), I, p.232.

[75]The compound term also appears in the *Edicts of Aśoka* (RE., III, IV, VIII, XI; PE., II, VII) but in the reversed order. Megasthenes (J.W. McCrindle. *Ancient India as described by Megasthenes and Arrian*, Frag.XLI, p.97) refers to them as *Brachmanes and Sarmanes. Patañjali* while illustrating the rule of compound formation with names of things 'at perpetual enemity' *(Yeṣāñ ca virodhaḥ śāśvatikaḥ)* cites the same expression.

[76]G.S.P. Misra, op. cit., p.37.

[77]G.C. Pande, op. cit., p.327; S. Dutt, *EBM.,* p.31; See also G.S.P. Misra, 'Some reflections on early Jaina and Buddhist Monachism', *'Jijñāsā',* Vol.I, Nos.3-4, July-Oct.1974, pp.4-5. For a summary of the Śramaṇic challenge to brāhmaṇical orthodoxy see P.S. Jaini, 'Sramaṇas: Their Conflict with Brāhmaṇical Society', in Joseph W. Elder, ed., *Chapters in Indian Civilization,* Vol.I, pp.39-81.

[78]P.V. Kane, *History of Dharmaśāstra*, Vol.II, Pt.II, pp.942-46.

[79]G.C. Pande, loc. cit., p.332.

something which provided an occasion for the practice of certain voluntary accepted moral vows.'[80]

Looking upon suffering as a concomitant condition of life, they rejected the authority of the Vedas and did not believe in the existence of God as a creator or determiner of destiny. Their opposition to the idea of God arose from their belief in the centrality of the doctrine of *Karman*. In the *Śramaṇic* tradition the universe is determined by an impersonal natural law.[81] According to it, a being is himself responsible for his own deeds. Salvation, therefore, can be obtained by anybody through self-reliance. The goal of every person was to evolve a way to escape from the cycle of rebirth.

Common endorsement of asceticism in practice and sharing of a soteriological goal, brought the *Śramaṇas* together[82] The moral vows were accepted as binding with difference of emphasis and interpretation in the different sects.[83]

Sakyaputtiyā Samaṇas

The '*Sakyaputtiyā Samaṇas*' were the followers of the *Mahā Samaṇa*[84] (the great *Samaṇa*-Buddha) one amongst the numerous wandering sects of the age.[85] Many of such sects abounded with leaders professing various doctrines and, as it appears from the *Jachandavaggo,* were not unoften

[80]G.C. Pande, *Śramaṇa Tradition,* pp.49-50.

[81]Ibid., p.72.

[82]Ibid., p.37.

[83]The Jainas have their *pañca-mahāvratas,* the Buddhist in course of time developed the *pañca-silas* into ten *silas.* The Brahmaṇa mendicant was similarly required to abstain from causing injury to living beings, lying, misappropriation, incontinence and niggardliness. See, P.V. Kane. op. cit., Vol.II, Pt.II, pp.930ff.

[84]A honorific accorded to the Buddha at numerous places in the Pāli Canon, See, *Mahāvagga,* pp.26, 35, 42.

[85]The leaders of the other sects contemporary to the Buddha are named as: Pūraṇa Kassapa, Makkhali Gosāla, Pakudha Kaccāna, Nigaṇtha Nāṭaputta, Ajita Kesakambali and Sanjaya Belaṭṭhiputta. See, 'Sāmaññaphala Sutta'. *(Dīgha Nikāya,* I, pp.41-42): *Cullavagga,* p.199.

unpleasantly quarrelsome and contentious about them.[86] Each of these leading *Samaṇas* had his own followers who adhered to the *Dhamma* propounded by their leaders. The conventional descriptive compound for such a leader is *Saṅghī-ganīgaṇācariyo* which literally means the instructor *(ācariya)* of a *Saṅgha* or *gaṇa.*[87] In the Pali Canon, *'Bhikkhu Saṅgha'*[88] is the name for the *Sakyaputtiyā Samaṇas* who looked upon Buddha as the *Satthā* (leader) and were bound by common allegiance to his *Dhamma.* During the years between the initial formation of the *Saṅgha* by the Buddha and the advent of Aśoka some three hundred years later, the organization of monks *(Bhikkhu Saṅgha)* evolved from a free wandering sect of *Samaṇas* to a highly organized settled monastic order living in well established *vihāras* and governed by rules of *Vinaya.*

II
FROM EREMETICAL TO CENOBITICAL LIFE

The Eremetical Stage

Numerous passages of the Buddhist Canonical literature set forth the ideal life for a *Bhikkhu*—'to be free, unsocial and eremetical'.[89] The same ideal is recommended in the four

---

[86]*Khuddaka Nikāya,* I, pp.142-50. Their doctrines are set forth in the 'Brahmajāla Suttanta' of the *Dīgha Nikāya.*

[87]In the community of wanderers, the term *Saṅgha* or *gaṇa* meant just a sect. See, S. Dutt, *BMMI.,* p.50.

[88]The Buddha calls it *'Cātuddisa Saṅgha'*-'the *Saṅgha* of the four quarters', comprising all monks and nuns as adherents to the teachings of the Lord, including even those who would embrace the fold of the Buddhist Order in future. See, *Mahāvagga,* p.319; *Cullavagga,* p.259. As against this, the term *'Sammukha Saṅgha'* denotes the monks and nuns residing at a particular local *vihāra.*

[89]*Mahāvagga,* p.23. *(Mā ekena dve agamittha)*: Mahāparinibbāna Suttanta, *Dīgha Nikāya,* II, p.62-*Yāvakivañ ca bhikkhave bhikkhū āraññakesu senāsanesu sāpekhā bhavissanti. Vuddhi yeva bhikkhave bhikkhūnaṁ pāṭikaṅkhā no parihāni;* 'khaggavisāṇa Sutta', *Sutta Nipāta,* pp.274-80-*Eko care khaggavisāṇa-kappo,* vv.35-75.

Nissayas[90]—*Piṇḍiyālopa-bhojanaṁ* (mendicancy), *Paṁsukūlacīvaraṁ* (clothing in cast off rags), *Rukkhamūlasenāsanaṁ* (sitting and lying at the foot of a tree), and *Pūtimuttabhesajjaṁ* (using urine as medicine). The *Sāriputta Sutta*[91] of the *Sutta Nipāta* extols the ideal of a *Bhikkhu* as one 'who is loth of the world and affects an isolated seat or the root of a tree or a cemetery or who lives in the caves of the mountains'. In several hymns of the *Dhammapada* and the *Theragāthā* this exaltation of eremetical life is reiterated.

The observance of a lonely peripatetic life by retiring to the forest was an old practice.[92] Buddha adopted this practice and strongly recommended it to his followers as a necessary aid in the attainment of the spiritual goal. On occasions he himself retired to the seclusion of the forest cutting of all contact with others. The Vinaya texts inform us, that the members of the *Saṅgha* having no fixed habitat, took shelter 'now here, now there—in the woods, at the foot of trees, on hill sides, in grottoes, in mountain caves, cemeteries, in forest, in open plains and in heaps of straw'.[93] Evidently, there was no localized monastic settlement in the beginning.

The Vassā: The Āvāsas and the Ārāmas

The primitive principle of wandering and eremetical state of life was never formally given up by the *bhikkhus.* It remained, but only in the form of an ideal.[94] Complete fulfilment of

---

[90]*Mahāvagga,* p.55.

[91]*Sutta-Nipāta* (Sariputta suttaṁ, 193) *Bhikkhuno vijigucchato bhajato rittaṁāsanaṁ rukkhamūlaṁ susanaṁ vā pabbatānaṁ guhāsu vā.*

[92]*Jābāla Upaniṣad,* 6, 'the *Yati or Sannyāsin* should remain homeless in a deserted house or a temple of the gods, on a heap of grass, or an ant-heap, or among the roots of a tree, in a potter's shed, by a sacrificial fire, on an island in a river, in a cave in the mountain, a glen, or a hollow tree, by a waterfall or on the bare earth'. The *Uttarādhyayana Sūtra* (SBE., Vol.XLV, Pt.II. p.12) prescribes that 'alone, living on allowed food', the monk 'should wander about, bearing all troubles'.

[93]*Cullavagga,* p.239 *(Te ca bhikkhu tahaṃ tahaṃ viharanti-araññe, rukkhamūle, pabbate, kandarāyaṃ giriguhāyaṃ, susāne, vanapatthe, ajjhokāse, palālapuñje.*

[94]S. Dutt, *BFAC.,* p.67; G.S.P. Misra, op. cit., p.117.

itinerancy was prevented by the inclemencies of weather—the monsoonal rains of India, specially in the regions where these ascetic sects were active.[95] It was at an early date[96] that the Buddha introduced the system of observance of *vassā* at a fixed place, following the custom prevalent in other religious sects.[97] The Buddhists called it *vassā;* the Jainas *pajjusaṇa,*[98] the Brahmaṇcal *sannyāsins* were enjoined to be 'of fixed residence' *(dhruvaśila)* during that time.[99]

Unlike the Jaina and Brahmaṇical wanderers who had no regulations prescribing 'living together' during rain retreat, the Buddhists framed special regulations for the general custom which seems to have assumed with the lapse of time a sort of ceremonial significance.[100] This was the first step in the individuation of the *Bhikkhu Saṅgha,* differentiating it in character from other sects.[101] Buddhist *vassāvāsa* meant living in a congregation. Provision was made for a residence with its own boundary (*sīmā*). Gradually people came forward to

---

[95]G.C. Pande, *BDVI.*, p.151.

[96]G.S.P. Misra, op. cit., p.122. Contra., Gokuldas De *(Democracy in the early Buddhist Saṅgha,* p.89), states that it was introduced at a much later date, perhaps in the 17th or 19th year of Buddha's mission.

[97]S. Dutt, op. cit., p.67. It is quite uncertain whether initially the mendicants spent the *Vassā* only in the company of the members of their respective sects. In the Mahāparinibbāna Sutta (*Dīgha Nikāya*, II, p.79), the Buddha asks the *bhikkhus* to spend the rains with friends and companions—*yathāmittaṃ yathā sanditthaṃ yathāsambhattaṃ vassaṃ upetha*—while he himself goes to Beluva with Ananda to spent the *Vassā.*

[98]H. Jacobi, *Jaina Sutras*, (SBE.), I, pp.296-311.

[99]*Āruṇeyopaniṣad,* 3—*Varṣāsu dhruvaśilo aṣtou māsānekāki vatiścaret dvāveva vā caret,* T.R.C. Dikshit (Ed.), *The Samnyāsa Upanishads*, p.13; *Kaṭharudropaniṣad,* I (Commentary)—*Caturo māsān vārṣikān grāme vā nagare vāpi vaset* (Ibid., p.18); *Nāradaparivrājakopaniṣad*, 3—*Ekavāsa* avāso vā... *ekadṛṣṭir alolupah: eka eva carennityaṁ varṣāsyekatra saṁvaset'* (Ibid., p.68); *Gautama Dharmasutra,* III, 13; *Baudhāyana Dharmasutra* II, 6, II, 20.

[100]S. Dutt, *EBM.*, p.102.

[101]S.Dutt, *BMMI.*, p.53.

donate their own private parks or pleasure gardens for the use of the monks for dwelling purposes.[102]

The *āvāsas* and the *ārāmas*, in their earliest stage 'were in the nature of encampments', meant to be retained for the three months of the rainy but not for the dry season.[103] Only during the three-month period of the *vassā*, the *bhikkhus* had the right to a *senāsana* (accommodation) in an *āvāsa*.[104] With the passage of time such residences ceased to be regarded as a natural necessity and assumed a sacred and a religious character. This 'living together' developed into a collective life which found expression in practices of a congregational character, like the *pātimokkha* recital, the *pavāraṇā* and the *kaṭhina*. The *bhikkhus,* at this stage came to be distinguished from 'wanderers' and they themselves seem to have recognized the distinction.[105]

Within its boundaries an *āvāsa* or an *ārāma* had huts for the monks' dwelling, and *vihāra* was the name originally given to such a hutment,[106] although the term in the later times,

---

[102]Such gardens with rest houses for wandering mendicants of all sects were not uncommon and the Buddha apparently stayed in them before the Veluvana *Vihāra* was built. See, *Majjhima Nikāya*, I, p.256 *(Gosinga-sālatvanadāye): Dīgha Nikāya*, III, p.3 *(Ārāma of Bhaggava-gotta); Saṃyutta Nikāya*, IV, p.68 *(Añcana-vane Migadāye at Saketa)*; *Majjhima Nikāya,* I, p.146 *(Nigrodha ārama* at Kapilavatthu); II, pp.224, 225 *(Mora-nivāpe Paribbājakārāme); Dīgha Nikāya.* I, p.150 (Queen Mallika's *ārāma* at Savatthi).

[103]*Cullavagga,* p.269 *(Anujānāmi Bhikkhave vassānam temāsaṁ paṭibāhituṁ utukālaṁ panana paṭibāhitum' ti).*

[104]S. Dutt, *EBM.*, p.103.

[105] *Nāyya ete Bhikkhū, Paribbājakā' ti* (They are not *bhikkhus*, but Paribbājakas)—*(Cullavagga)*, p.220. See also the *Pātimokkha* rule. The *Pācittiya,* Pt.II, p.128—*Yo pana bhikkhu acelakassa vā paribbājakāya vā sahatthā khādaniyaṁ vā bhojaniyaṁ vā dadeyya pācittiyam.* (The *bhikkhu* who with his own hand gives food or edibles to an *acelaka* (naked ascetic) or to a *paribbājaka* (wanderer) is guilty of a *pācittiya* offence.)

[106]*Mahāvagga,* p.307—where the monks of a *Saṅghārāma,* having gone out in the rain and wetted their bodies, come back and enter each into his own *vihāra.* These might be similar to the first lodgings, sixty in number, built for the *bhikkhus,* in a day by a seṭṭhi of Rajagaha in the lifetime of Lord Buddha. See, *Cullavagga,* p.239.

almost always was used to designate the whole of a building where many *Bhikkhus* resided.[107] A *vihāra* might be occupied by a single monk or by a small group of monks and, in the latter case, the allotted portion for each monk was called a *pariveṇa.*[108] This fact is borne out by archaeological evidence also.[109]

S. Dutt, however, classifies the *āvāsas* and the *ārāmas* as 'two types of residence for the *bhikkhus,* the former in the countryside, built and organized by the monks themselves, and the latter situated in private enclosures in or near towns and maintained by the donor'.[110] I.B. Horner takes the term *ārāma,* not as a 'park' but as a 'monastery'.[111]

This was the beginning of cenobitical life among the Buddhist—the settling down to monastic life and organization. From the *Mahāvagga,* we learn that King Bimbisāra of Magadhạ offered his *Velūvana ārāma* (park) to the fraternity of *bhikkhus* with the Buddha at its head.[112] This was the first *vihāra* presented to the *Saṅgha* and its acceptance for the dwelling of monks marks a turning point in the history of early monasticism.

The Saṅghārāmas

The *āramās* when utilized as permanent domiciles were also named as *Saṅghārāmas.* The term *Saṅghārāma* later became synonymous with *vihāra* and signified a large monastery

---

[107] *Vinaya Texts* (SBE.), Pt.II, pp.386fn.

[108] *Mahāvagga,* p.234—where Suppiya entering a *Saṅghārāma* goes in search of monks 'from *vihāra* to *vihāra* and from *pariveṇa* to *pariveṇa*'—(*Viharena vihāraṁ pariveṇena pariveṇaṁ* upasaṁkamitvā *bhikkhu pucchati.)*

[109] Fergusson and Burgess, *The Cave Temples of India,* pp.xv-xvi. 'The oldest vihāras consist of one cell only; little hermitages in fact for the residence of a single ascetic.'

[110] S. Dutt, *BMMI.,* pp.54-5. The word *ārāma* in the sense of a park or garden occurs in the inscriptions from Mathura, Padana and Bhattriprolu. See, *Lüders list,* Nos.82, 973-74 and 1336.

[111] I.B. Horner, *The Book of the Discipline,* III. p.325fn.

[112] *Mahāvagga,* p.38.

occupied by a company of monks.[113] The Pāli legends name several *Saṅghārāmas,* making them contemporaneous with the lord and describe them as having been sanctified by his visits or temporary residence, viz.:

(a) *Veḷuvanārāma* at Rājagaha gifted to the *Saṅgha* by king Bimbisāra.[114]

(b) *Jīvakārāma* at Rājagaha donated by the physician Jīvaka, a lay devotee of the Buddha.

(c) *Ambapāli-vana* at Vesāli donated by Ambapāli, city-courtesan of Vesāli.

(d) *Kukkuṭārāma, Ghositārāma* and *Pāvārikāmbavana* at Kosambi.

(e) *Jetavanārāma* near Sāvatthi.

(f) *Badarikārāma* at some distance from Ghositārāma.

(g) *Nigrodhārāma* at Kapilavatthu.

Only three of these *ārāmas* have been traced by archaeologists, viz., (1) *Jīvakārāma*[115] (2) *Jetavanārāma,*[116] and (3) *Ghositārāma.*[117] The sites of the second and third *ārāma* were occupied by monks for many centuries and monasteries were built on them from age to age.[118]

Leṇas

In due course of time one notices a transition from the old type of settlement in an *āvāsa* or an *ārāma* to a *leṇa.*

---

[113]James Fergusson, *History of Indian and Eastern Architecture,* Vol.I, p.170; P.K. Acharya, *An Encyclopaedia of Hindu Architecture,* p.466: S. Beal, *BRWW.,* II, p.74 Hsüang-tsang uses the term *Saṅghārāma* and *Vihāra* interchangeably.

[114]In Pāli literature (*Mahāvagga,* p.144) it is referred to as *Veluvana-Kalandakanivāpa.* Fa-hien mentions it as *Venuvana-karaṇḍa.* See, J. Leggé. *Travels of Fa-hien,* p.84. For other sites see, D.N. Sen. 'Sites in Rajgir associated with Buddha and his disciples', *JBRS.,* Vol.I, 1956, pp.136ff: Adris Banerji, 'Buddha's Rajgir'. *Journal of Oriental Research* (Madras), Pts.I-IV, Vol.XXII, 1952-53, pp.21ff.

[115]*IAR.,* 1954-55, pp.16-17; 1958-59, p.13.

[116]*ASIAR.,* 1907-08 (Series No.8), p.120.

[117]G.R. Sharma, *Excavations at Kauśāmbi,* 1960; *IAR.,* 1955-56, pp.20-21.

[118]J. Legge, op. cit., pp.56-62; T. Watters, *On Yuan Chwang's Travels in India,* II, p.382; Ibid., II, p.369.

Etymologically *'leṇa'* means 'private abode' (from Sanskrit *layana,* derived from the verb *Li,* to hide).[119] This abode was meant for a limited and specific body of monks, specially for a single resident of the *Saṅgha.* A *leṇa* so to say was a monastery proper, different in layout and construction, 'not a shifting and seasonal settlement of monks'.[120]

The Pāli canon specifies five kinds of *leṇas (pañca-leṇāni)*[121] each according to its structural peculiarity, though no detailed description is given about them. Buddhaghosa, the commentator, explains the term *vihāra* as a dwelling house with a chamber in it, well-protected and containing private lodgings,[122] *aḍḍhayoga* as a *'supaṇṇavankaṁ gehaṁ;*[123] a *pāsāda* as a 'long-storied mansion', i.e. with an upper storey completely covering the lower; a *hammiya* as a *pāsāda* with an attic on top, a *guhā* as a 'hutment made of bricks or scooped out of rock or made of wood or laterite *(paṁsu)';*[124] Buddhaghosa's descriptive explanations are mostly conjectural (specially in respect of his explanation of *Aḍḍhayoga)* though perhaps they are backed by tradition.

The *vihāra* was one kind of *leṇa,* private dwelling house, the use and utility of which arc described in *Cullavagga.*[125]

---

[119]T.W. Rhys Davids and Stede, ed. (PTS.), *Pāli-English Dictionary*, p.586.

[120]S. Dutt, op. cit., p.93.

[121]*Cullavagga,* p.239; *Mahāvagga,* pp.55, 100, 196-97 *(Vihāra, Aḍḍhayoga, Pāsāda, Hammiya* and *Guhā*).

[122]*Vihāro ti antogabbho vā aññaṁ va sabbaparicchannaṁ gutta-senāsanaṁ.*

[123]The meaning of the phrase is rather obscure. It has rightly been said that the reading *'suvaṇṇavaṅgaṁ gehaṁ'* giving the meaning 'a gold coloured Bengal house' is a misreading for *'supaṇṇavaṅkaṁ gehaṁ'.* (See, *PTS., Dictionary,* S.V. *Aḍḍhayoga).* Miss Homer translates *'aḍḍhayoga'* as a 'curved house', *The Book of the Discipline,* V, p.205. See also G.S.P. Misra, op. cit., p.221.

[124]*Samantapāsādikā,* (PTS.), Vol.VI, p.1215 *('addhayogo' ti suvannavaṅga geham pāsado ti digha pāsado. hammiyam ti upariākāsatale patitthitakūtāgāro pāsado yeva, guhā ti itthakaguhā silāguha dāru guhā paṃsu guhā.*

[125]*Cullavagga,* p.240 *(Sitaṁ uṇhaṁ paṭihanti tato Vālamigāni ca Siriṅasape ca makase sisire cāpi vuṭṭhiyo, Tato vātā tapo ghoro sañjāto paṭihaññati lenatthaṁ ca sukhatthaṁ ca jhāyituṁ ca vippassituṁ Vihāradānaṁ saṁghassa aggaṁ budden vaṇṇitaṁ tasma hi paṇḍito poso sampassaṁ atthaṁ attano Vihāre kāraye ramme vāsayettha bahussute); The Questions of King Milinda,* Pt.II, pp.1-4.

This text refers to the construction of the first set of *Vihāras*, sixty in number, in the course of a day by a *Seṭṭhi* of Rājagaha[126] who dedicated the same for the use of members of the Order of the four corners (*Cātuddisa Bhikkhu Saṅgha*).[127] It was only when the *vihāra* was converted into a communal (*saṅghika*) establishment, did the term signify 'the whole of a building where many *bhikkhus* resided'.[128]

The name *pāsāda (prāsāda)* for a storeyed monastery was always in use. The Pāli legends mention one, owned by a wealthy lady called *Migāramāta* at Jetavana, being the Lord's sojourn during his visit to Kosāmbi. Whether it had ever been dedicated to the *Saṅgha* or was retained by the owner is uncertain. Excavations at Taxila have brought to light remains of storied monasteries. The name *pāsāda* is applied to Baladitya's temple-cum-monastery at Nālandā.[129]

As regards the *Aḍḍhayoga,* it appears to be a fairly big structure, bigger than a small *vihāra* although smaller than a *prāsāda* or a large *vihāra.*[130] *Hammiya*[131] consisted of a storeyed building with a hall below, surrounded by pillars only. The pillars supported a gabled roof. On this roof was a chamber which was the Buddha's private retiring room known as *gandhakuṭī.*[132] The whole structure took its name from this

---

[126]*Cullavagga,* p.239 *(Atthako Rajagahako Seṭṭhi ekāheneva aṭṭhivihare patiṭṭhāpesi).*

[127]Ibid., p.240 *Saṭṭhim vihāre āgatānāgatassa cātuddessasa saṃghassā patiṭṭhāpehiti.*

[128]H. Sarkar, *Studies in Early Buddhist Architecture,* p.9.

[129]It is mentioned by Hsüan-tsang. See, T. Watters, op. cit., II, pp.164-65.

[130]H. Sarkar, op. cit., p.9.

[131]H. Sarkar, (loc. cit.,) distinguishes *hammiya* from *pāsāda.* See also *Samantapāsādikā* (PTS.), VI, p.1215.

[132]The *gandhakuṭi,* as a dwelling of the Buddha is referred repeatedly throughout the Pāli commentarial literature and in a number of important Sanskrit *Avadānas* also. See, Henry Clarke Warren, *Buddhism in translations,* Vol.3, p.93, *Avadāna-śataka;* pp.1ff; T.W. Rhys Davids (trans.), *Buddhist Birth Stories,* p.130. The name *gandhakuṭi* (perfumed chamber) may have been given to the chamber from the fragrance *(gandha)* of flowers and incense offered by the laity.

sacred top chamber and was called *kuṭāgārasāla*[133] (the chamber topped mansion). Moreshwar Dikshit discovered in January 1942 an inscription on a votive stone of the facade of a cave at Kondāṇe in western India which records: 'This is the Hamma of (i.e. donated by) Paraka'.[134]

Guhā, as is clear from Buddhaghosa's account denoted, a small cell which could be made of bricks, stone, wood or leaves. Originally *guhā* might have been a natural habitat or a cave. This is clear from the *Mahāvagga*[135] which mentions the clearing out of a mountain-cave at Rājagṛha with a view to make it a dwelling place. Even *'Gṛdhrakūṭa'* appears to be a cave-resort. But dwelling in caves did not possibly assume any magnitude in the early phase, may be more because of the non-availability of suitable natural caverns in the early centuries of Buddhism.

Of the *pañca-leṇāni,* only two types survived in India—the *vihāra* and the *guhā*. The brick or stone, *vihāra* became the typical monastic building for the plains of the north while the orographic conditions of the south favoured the construction of the *guhās*. Thus the distinct geographical conditions operated in varying degree as a factor determining the nature of the monastic abodes.

Early Vihāras

The early *vihāras* represented one of the important forms of ancient Indian architecture. Though no *vihāra* belonging to such an early date has come down to us, we are able to form a

---

[133]A stele from Amaravati contains a fine representation of the *kūṭāgāraśalā* of Vaiśāli (a place often visited by Lord Buddha—*Dīgha Nikāya*, II, p.93). The vaulted roof of the structure bears an inscription which reads as follows: *'Vesāliya viharati Mahāvane Kuḍāgā(ra)—salaya'*. See, A. Ghosh and H. Sarkar, 'Beginnings of Sculptural art in South-East India: A stele from Amaravati', *AI.*, No.20, pp.168-79.

[134]S. Dutt, *BMMI.*, p.96.

[135]*Mahāvagga,* p.225. Fa-hien spent a night on mount *Gṛdhrakūṭa,* which he described as a cavern in the rocks. See, *J. Legge,* op. cit., pp.82-84.

picture of it with the help of later rock-cut *vihāras,* which seem to have been designed in imitation of their earlier counterparts in timber architecture.[136] The literary evidence is there to provide some information in this connection.

Beginnings

The *Cullavagga* tells us that in order to avoid accumulation of water, the *pariveṇa* or the courtyard of the *vihāra* should be floored with sand *(marumbaṁ upakirituṁ)* or paved with stone *(padarasilaṁ nikkhipituṁ).*[137] On the basis of this, it has been suggested that 'in the beginning, the ordinary *Vihāras* consisted of huts grouped around an open space' and that 'this supposition is testified by the Jetavana scene depicted on the Bhārhut railing.'[138] From this humble design must have evolved the later well arranged *vihāras,* the open space converted into a hall and the surrounding huts attached to it in the form of cells.

The entire monastic complex, if the Pāli texts can be relied upon as depicting the condition in Buddha's time, consisted of dwelling rooms, cells, gate-chambers, service-halls, halls with fire places, store-houses, closets, cloisters, rooms for walking exercises, wells, sheds for the wells, bathing places, bathrooms, tanks, pavilions.[139] The various units of a monastery seem to have been, for the most part, detached structures and thus the *Saṅghārāma* did not consist of one single and comprehensive building.[140]

---

[136]Prithvi Kumar Agarwal, 'Paschimi Bhārata kā Hīnayāna-Kāleen Leṇa Sthapatya', *Prajñā,* Vol.XI, Pt.II, 1965-66, p.xxxvii.

[137]*Cullavagga,* p.247.

[138]See, G.S.P. Misra, 'Monastic and Civil Architecture in the Age of the Vinaya', *East and West.* New Series, Vol.19, Nos.1-2, March-June 1969. pp.124-45.

[139]*Mahāvagga,* p.146; *Cullavagga,* p.253 *(Vihāra, pariveṇa, koṭṭhaka, upaṭṭhānaśālā, aggiśālā, kappiyakuṭi, vaccakuṭi, caṅkamana, cankamanaśāla, udapāna, udapānaśālā, jantāghara, jantāgharaśālā, pokkhariṇi maṇḍapa.*

[140]*Marshall and Foucher, The Monuments of Sānchi,* ed. by N.G. Majumdar, Vol.I, p.61.

Selection of the Site

Considerable attention was paid to the selection of the site which was 'not too far from the town and not too near, convenient for going and coming, easily accessible for all who wish to visit, by day not too crowded, by night not exposed to too much noise and alarm'.[141] The choice invariably fell on a site which fulfilled the two conditions required for an ideal monastic life, namely, proximity to a habitation where the monks could go on their begging rounds and at the same time seclusion, ensuring a proper atmosphere for meditation.

A few examples can be cited in favour of the above view, that almost all important Buddhist establishments were found slightly away from towns. The *'Jetavana Ārāma'* presented by the merchant Anāthapiṇḍika to the *Saṅgha* was situated on the outskirts of the capital city of Śrāvastī. The magnificent establishment of Sāñchi was outside the populous city of Vidiśā. The *Dharmacakra Vihāra* of Sārnāth was established four miles north of Vārāṇasi, the *Dharmarājika* monastery was near Takṣaśilā.

Most of the sites have a picturesque background. The caves of Maharashtra have an idyllic setting and are shut from the humdrum of the mundane life. Some of the sites were situated at the confluence of a river or streamlet such as Lumbini, Bodh Gaya, Bagh, Devnimori, sites of Andhra Pradesh in the lower valley of Krishna and Ratnagiri. The navigability of the rivers fostered trade which resulted in the rich mercantile lay community bestowing various endowments on the *Saṅgha.*

Structural Amenities

Vihāras had plastered walls, white-washed or coloured, were fitted with doors *(kavāta),* door-posts and lintel, with arrangements for bolts, lock and key; with windows made by

---

[141]*Cullavagga,* p.252; *Mahāvagga,* p.38.

railings,[142] network[143] or slips of wood,[144] window blinds and shutters; solid benches against the walls of a room or under the verandah[145] against the outside wall. To maintain the privacy of the monks due arrangements were made for 'inner chambers' which were in 'shapes like a palanquin, chambers in shape like a quart measure and chambers on an upper storey.'[146]

Thatched *vihāras* were covered with 'skins and plaster', enabling the inmates to live comfortably therein during the winter or summer.[147] The *Cullavagga* mentions 'five kinds of roofings *(pañcha-chhadanāni)*: a roofing of bricks *(iṭṭakachhadanaṁ)*, stucco *(sudhā)*, grass *(tiṇa)*, stone *(silā)* and leaves *(paṇṇa)*.[148] The whole compound of the *vihāra* was enclosed with ramparts of three kinds, viz., brick, stone and wooden walls,[149] which were surrounded by three kinds of hedges—of bamboo, thorns or a ditch.[150]

The earliest *vihāras,* some of which, no doubt, made of perishable materials like wood and bamboo, have either mostly perished or have been renovated to such an extent in later periods that it is now difficult to identify their original nucleus. None of the structural examples of the centuries immediately preceding and following the Christian era is completely intact. But one thing is certain, that the later

---

[142]*Cullavagga,* p.241 *(Vedikā-vātapānam nāma ketiya vedikā sadisam).*

[143]Ibid., p.241 *(Jāla-vātapānam nāma jālaka-baddham).*

[144]Ibid., p.241 (*Salāka-vātapānam nāma thambhakavātapānam*). Possibly this means with slips of wood arranged horizontally as in the Venetian blinds.

[145]Ibid., p.241.

[146]Ibid., p.245; *Samantapāsādikā* (PTS.), Vol.VI, p.1219—

(a) *Sivikā-gabbho ti caturassa-gabbho.*

(b) *Nāḷikā-gabbho ti vilthārato dviguṇa tiguṇāyāmo digha-gabbho.*

(c) *Hammiyo-gabbho ti ākāsa-tale kutāgāra gabbho muṇḍacchadana gabbho va.*

[147]*Cullavagga,* p.241.

[148]Ibid., p.248. See, I.B. Horner, *The Book of Discipline*, V, p.216.

[149]*Cullavagga,* p.247.

[150]Ibid., p.248.

vihāras were modified, enlarged and enriched with the ideological growth of the Order.

Early Guhās and their Evolution

The *guhās* have played an important role in the evolution of Buddhist monasteries in India. The excavation of caves was not an innovation of the Buddhists. The idea of rock-cut caves seems to have been derived from natural caverns used by hermits for solitary meditation since pre-Buddhist times.[151] Considering the religious tradition associated with caves, it is not unnatural that the Buddhist monks should have developed a category of monumental art of quite a different kind, namely that which served the needs of Buddhist monasticism. Rock-cut caves excavated by Aśoka and his grandson Dasaratha for the Ājivaka monks in the Barābar and Nagārjuni hills at Gaya mark the beginning of cave architecture in India.[152] But, surprisingly enough, there is no Aśokan rock-cut cave dedicated to the Buddhists. It is possible that the monks stayed in natural caves and *ārāmas* donated by the laity till 200 BC.

The exploration of the Bayan and Pangoraria complex[153] in district Sehore (Madhya Pradesh) has brought to light nearly forty five rock shelters and several *stūpa* complexes. One of the main rock shelters named Saru-Maru-ki-kothadi contains

---

[151]It seems that this predilection was probably due to the reason that the cave with its naked simplicity and solitude was conducive to meditation. The Buddha himself says in the 'Mahataṇhā saṅkhayasutta' that a virtuous monk dwells in a cave *(giriguhaṃ)—Majjhima Nikāya*, I, p.271. The Pāli Canon names several caves associated with Lord Buddha or other *parivrājakās*. See, *Dīgha Nikāya*, II, pp.91-92 *(Vebhāra passe Sattapaṇṇi-guhāyaṁ)*: Ibid., *(Sita-vane Sappa-Soṇḍika-pabbhāre)*; Ibid., p.97 *(Indasāla-guhāyaṃ)*; *Samyutta Nikāya*, IV, p.74 *(Pipphali-guhāyaṃ) Majjhima Nikāya*, II, p.211 *(Pilakkhaguhayaṃ)*.

[152]B.C. Law, 'Evolution of Cave Architecture in India and Ceylon', *Indological Studies*, Pt.II, 1952, p.100. *Contra.*, S.P. Gupta's statement *(The Roots of Indian Art*, pp.196-97) that the 'Barabar caves mark the culmination of a long process and not the debut in cave architecture'. He is of the opinion that the roots of Mauryan caves at Barābar can be traced to the natural caves of Ramgarh, Budhani, Son Bhandar, etc. (ibid., pp.198ff).

[153]*IAR.*, 1975-76, pp.28ff. See also, S.R. Goyal, op. cit., p.428.

two Aśokan inscriptions. One is a version of the *MRE I* while the other records the visit of Piyadasi as Maharaja Kumara to the site. Several *stūpas* have been unearthed near Budhani in the Talpura village. The entire site, the antiquity of which is traced to 3rd century BC is studded with *stūpas* and rubble revetments. This leaves no doubt that the nearby rock caves were utilized as monastic cells by the monks.

Rock-cut caves and brick constructions have been found near Pauni[154] (Vidarbha) which are ascribable to 3rd-2nd century BC. The Deotek inscription[155] is a definite evidence of the fact that Aśoka's propagation of the *Dhamma* did cover the region of Vidarbha.

How did this art begin? What made the cave particularly appropriate to the Indian religious mind and why is it that caves in any religious system produce the most perfect atmosphere for some meditative worshippers? Art scholars attribute various external influences in the development of rock-cut architecture in India,[156] though there is nothing improbable in the evolution of the excavated shrine *(caitya)* or monastic dwelling *(leṇa)* from its earlier prototype, the natural cavern. As G. Yazdani puts it, 'the idea of dwelling in caves, in the primitive period for personal safety and later, in a stage of intellectual and spiritual advancement, for contemplation and enlightenment, has been inherent in man in the East as well as in the West'.[157]

Why Caves?

Curiously enough, no writer has attempted to answer fully the question-Why Caves? The answer has a number of facets, each of which will be analysed in turn. The basic impetus behind the extensive use of caves lies in the fact that Indian religions have emphasized that within the personal self lies the

[154]S.B. Deo and J.P. Joshi, *Pauni Excavations,* p.7.
[155]V.V. Mirashi, *CII.,* Vol.V, pp.1-2.
[156]For Achaemenian influence, See A. Grunwedel, *Buddhist Art in India,* p.16.
[157]G. Yazdani, *History of the Deccan,* Vol.II, Pt.X, pp.719-20.

true self *(Ātman)* which is God (*Brahman*).[158] The true abode of the *Ātman* has been compared to a cave[159] which because of its darkness or semi darkness produces psychological effect on men seeking the Divine within.

R. Lannoy emphasizing the psychological aspect writes thus: 'The retreat to the primeval dark woods meant retreat to the hidden depths of the mind as well. These inner wanderings are projected by the creative imagination in analogous convolutions of line.... Such labyrinthine plasticity, which attains an unusual monumentality in the caves, is man's most natural artistic mode of expressing inner richness and a yearning for self-realization in a severely inhibited setting.'[160] He further observes, 'caves on the other hand, are scooped out by a downward plunge of the chisel from ceiling to the floor in the direction of gravity; the occupant empathizes with an *invisible* but sensed resistance, an unrelenting pressure in the rock enveloping him'. For Lannoy, to enter an Indian cave sanctuary is to experience a 'relaxation of physical tension in response to the implacable weight and density of the solid rock'.[161]

Besides the psychological and philosophical factors there were physical factors which led to rock-cut art being so long and elaborately developed specially on the flank of the western ghats. As S. Dutt puts it, 'the topography of the caves was mainly determined by the orography'.[162] The rocks of this

---

[158]Subtler than the subtle, greater than the great is the self that is set in the cave of the (heart) of the creature'—*Śvetāśvatara Upaniṣad* III.20; 'Realizing through self contemplation that primal God, difficult to be seen, deeply hidden, set in the cave (of the heart), dwelling in the deep, the wise man leaves behind both joy and sorrow'—*Kaṭha Upaniṣad*, 1, 2, 12.

[159]'Into blinding darkness enter those who worship ignorance and those who delight in knowledge enter into still greater darkness, as it were'—*Iśa Upaniṣad,* 9; 'Into blinding darkness, enter those who worship the Unmanifest and into still greater darkness, as it were, those who delight in the manifest'—Ibid., 12.

[160]R. Lannoy, *The Speaking Tree,* p.39.

[161]Ibid., p.44.

[162]S. Dutt, *BMMI.,* p.144.

region are chiefly a variety of trap in horizontal strata, suitable for architectural treatment and of excellent uniform texture.[163] The climatic factor cannot be ignored because no structural building could have served the monks better as a monastery, from the point of view of protection from heat and torrential rain, than a rock cut *vihāra*. The socio-economic factor also cannot be overlooked. As Vidya Dehejia puts it, 'perhaps social changes—a wealthy trader class, a general increase of wealth, and the rise of great families—explain this sudden artistic activity'.[164]

To these can be added the artistic factor. In most Indian rock-cut caves can be seen the work of a unique type of artistic imagination and aesthetic integration which combines the qualities of a sculptor and architect.[165] The *bhikkhus* seemed to have understood the spiritual dimension of aesthetics, 'that all that is holy and wholesome and is conducive to the attainment of supreme goal, is indeed beautiful'.[166]

Locale

The *Guhā* settlements extend from Karāḍ in the south to Ajantā and Pitalkhora in the north, with extensions to Saurashtra in the west. They are located in ravines between hill-ranges and were accessible from passes which were then known as routes of inland communication and trade.[167] The Sher and Tal ghāts connect Sopara with Nāsik and then inland; the Nanāghāt links Kalyān to Junnar and from there to Paithan; and the Bhor ghāt connects Kalyān to Kārle and then to Ter.[168] Such routes were traversed by the commercial class which

[163]A.V.T. Iyer, *Indian Architecture, Book* II, p.399; Owen C. Kail, *Buddhist Cave Temples of India,* p.3; Fergusson and Burgess, op. cit., p.167.

[164]Vidya Dehejia, *Early Buddhist Rock Temples,* p.146.

[165]See, Owen, C. Kail, loc. cit., pp.2-3.

[166]L.M. Joshi, *Studies in the Buddhistic Culture of India,* p.360.

[167]D.D. Kosambi, 'Dhenukakata', *JASB.,* Vol.30, 1955, pp.51-52: D.D. Kosambi, 'The Buddhist Caves of Western India', *TOI.* (Annual), 1961, p.79.

[168]Vidya Dehejia, loc. cit., p.30. See, K.de.B. Codrington, 'Ancient Sites near Ellora, Deccan' *IA.*, Vol.LIX, 1930, pp.10-13.

gave ample donations for the construction, maintenance and repairs of these rock-cut complexes.

Technique of Excavation

Cave hewing[169] was done in two stages, namely, scooping and dressing. In the first stage two processes were involved. The first was blocking, whereby large chunks of rocks were removed with the help of heavy chisels all along the required area of the cave. This was followed by rough chiselling.

After this the work of dressing was taken up. The work area was divided into small blocks and parallel or horizontal grooves were made. The next stage was that of grinding with a coarse stone, sand and water to make the surface smooth. This was followed by polishing with a rubbing stone of fine texture which left the surface shining.

One can follow the various stages of excavation from a careful study of the unfinished caves at various sites. Slowly working with the simplest of tools, principally chisel and hammer, a portion of the steep scarp of the hill was cleared until it was perpendicular. A level was thus obtained from which the workmen could begin their operations.[170] The outline of the intended facade was indicated upon this vertical surface. The work was commenced from top downwards. In this way it was unnecessary to erect any scaffolding.[171] 'After the ceiling and roof were completed, the workmen continued quarrying downward, removing the debris of rock through the open facade and disengaging the columns and the carved stūpa at the rear end of the edifice.'[172]

---

[169]S.P. Gupta, op. cit., p.206.

[170]At Bedsa, for example, a passage was first cut which was then expanded into a verandah with columns and only then could the excavation of the cave begin. See, Fergusson and Burgess, op. cit., p.225; Owen C. Kail. op. cit., pp.93ff.

[171]Cave 3 at Ajanta clearly reveals this process. Here the roof has been smoothed out and the pillars are blocked out but the floor was not reached at all. See, Fergusson and Burgess, loc. cit., p.336.

[172]Benjamin Rowland, *The Art and Architecture of India—Buddhist, Hindu, Jaina*, p.70.

The *caityas* on the Manmodi hill at Junnar suggest that rough cutting, sculpting and polishing were undertaken simultaneously.[173] The pillared verandahs of the Bhima Shanker and the Amba/Ambika caves are complete while the interiors remain unfinished due to a bad stratum of rock combined with leakage of water.[174] In the case of the Budh *leṇa caitya* the decorative carving of the facade is complete while the interior has been roughly blocked out and abandoned.[175]

It would be reasonable to assume that at any cave site, one or more of the *vihāras* was excavated before the *caitya.* At the three Manmodi hill sites at Junnar, the work on the *caityas* has been abandoned, while the *vihāras* appear complete.[176] All the *vihāras* at a site, however, were by no means cut before the *caitya,* several being added with the growth of the monk community.[177]

---

[173]Owen C. Kail, op. cit., p.102.

[174]Vidya Dehejia, op. cit., p.181.

[175]Ibid., pp.66, 88.

[176]Ibid., pp.180-81; Fergusson and Burgess, op. cit., pp.258-60.

[177]An example of such a later addition is the double storeyed *vihāra* at Karle which contains an inscription recording the gift of the cave in the reign of Pulumāvi, while we know that the *caitya* was completed much earlier. See, Vidya Dehejia, loc. cit., p.178.

CHAPTER 2

Buddhist Sects—Background and Post-Aśokan Developments

Saṅghabheda: It's Genesis

Life with its dynamism does not allow any institution—whether religious or secular—to remain static. It demands continuous adaptation and change. The Buddhist *Saṅgha* witnessed such a transformation as time went by. There arose sects and schools *(nikāya and ācaryavāda)* named after some prominent teachers, place or after the kind of doctrinal viewpoint professed.[1] Each with its increasingly distinctive emphasis on *Dhamma* existed side by side with others as members of the universal *Saṅgha*.[2]

The term *ācaryakula* and *nikāya* occur in literature[3] and inscriptions[4] to denote a school or sect. B.M. Barua and

---

[1]For example, the Dharmottarīya, Bhadrāyaṇīya, Dharmaguptika, Kāśyapīya, Andhakas, Uttarāpathakas, Avantakas, Vātsīputrīyas, Sarvāstivādins, Ḳukkulikas and the Lokottaravādins. See, E.J. Thomas, op. cit., pp.37-38; *Kathāvatthu,* (trans.), prefatory notes, p.xliv.

[2]The term 'sect' in the European sense cannot be equated with 'Nikāya', i.e. a body of believers in one or more doctrines not held by the majority, a body with its own endowments, its own churches or chapels and its own clergy ordained by itself. See, T.W. Rhys Davids, *ERE.*, Vol.V, S.V. 'Sects (Buddhist)'.

[3]The term *ācariyavāda* occurs in the Pali commentaries *(Kathāvatthu-Aṭṭhakathā,* Nāl.ed., pp.2ff; *Samantapāsādikā*, I, pp.223-34) and Ceylonese Chronicles (*Mahāvaṁsa*, V.2) for all the Buddhist schools other than Theravāda.

[4]J. Marshall, *Monuments of Sāñchī*, I, Nos.396, 509; *Lüders list,* Nos.340, 350 *(ācharyakula); EI.,* VII, Kārle Cave inscription No.19, pp.47ff; *Lüders list,* Nos.787, 1105, 1123, 1124, 1248 *(nikāya).*

G.N. Sinha observe, 'the expression *nikāya* excepting in the sense of a sect or school or denomination is not found in use among all Buddhists. This naturally leads to infer that the term *nikāya* in the technical sense of the Buddhist canon was current exclusively in a particular sect, namely, the Theravāda.'[5]

N.G. Majumdar[6] is of the opinion *ācharyakula* is a technical term which denotes a sect or a Buddhist school and as the expression *aññācaryavāda* in the *Mahavaṁsa*[7] stands in contrast to the Theravāda, it should be taken to denote a school other than Theravāda. This interpretation is accepted by J.N. Bannerjea.[8] It should be noted, however, that the expression *aññācaryavāda* has been used here as a term relative to the Theravāda. This is confirmed by the use of the term *ācaryavāda* even for the Mahāsāṅghika school.[9] *Ācaryakula, Ācharyavāda* and *vāda* are used as synonyms. The Theravāda is also designates as one of the 18 *vādas* or schools.[10] The term *aññācharyavāda,* thus, should not necessarily be taken to denote the Buddhist schools other than the Theravāda. It can, on the other hand, denote any school in contrast to the other. Ajay Mitra Shastri states that certain Chinese commentators used the term *'nikāyāntara'* for the Sthavira school in Sanskrit texts, a term which may be equated to *aññācharyakula* or *aññācharyavāda.*[11]

From Apprehensions to Open Dissensions

The feeling of the unity of the Order *(Samaggāparisā)* and the actual striving to promote or to restore this unity assert

---

[5]Barua and Sinha, *Barhut Inscriptions,* pp.28ff; See. Rhys Davids and Stede, *Pāli English Dictionary*, S.V. 'Nikāya'.

[6]See, J. Marshall, *Monuments of Sāñchī*, p.297.

[7]*Mahāvaṁsa,* v.2.

[8]J.N. Bannerjea, 'Schools of Buddhism in Early Indian Inscriptions', *IHQ.*, Vol.XXIV, No.4, 1948, p.255.

[9]*Mahāvaṁsa,* v.4.

[10]Ibid., v.10.

[11]Ajay Mitra Shastri, *An Outline of Early Buddhism*, p.70.

themselves in the sermons of Lord Buddha.[12] To encourage the *Saṅgha* to stand united, he held out the prospect of a happy and glorious life like that of God Brahmā to a monk in his after life, if any act of his serves to re-unite bodies of monks separated from one another, while he declared that the monk sowing dissension among his brethren was to be doomed to perdition for a *Kalpa*.[13] Time and again the Buddha inquired whether the monks were living together on friendly terms, were harmonious as milk and water blend, and regarded one another with the eye of affection.[14]

But inspite of all such attempts, there were instances when his teachings were misinterpreted.[15] Two such examples are recorded in the *Majjhima-Nikāya.* The first is the statement by a monk named Ariṭṭha that the pleasures of senses, according to the Buddha, are not 'stumbling blocks' *(antarāyikā dhammā)*.[16] The other was the case of the monk Sāti who insisted that in the Buddha's teaching, it is the 'consciousness' *(viññāṇa)* that transmigrates and not something else.[17]

While the Buddha was alive he was kept informed of such misconceptions and he immediately took steps to correct them. The Buddha often exhorted his disciples to learn and grasp the doctrine as he had put before them.[18] He was apprehensive that some monks master the *Dhamma* without testing it by intuitive wisdom. 'They master this Dhamma,' said the Buddha 'simply for the advantage of reproaching others and for the advantage of gossiping. ... These things

[12]Mahāparinibbāna Suttanta', *Digha Nikāya*, II, p.62; *Aṅguttara Nikāya*, III, pp.168-69.

[13]*Cullavagga,* pp.299, 307; *Aṅguttara Nikāya,* IV, p.15; *Kathāvatthu* (trans.), XIII.I.

[14]*Majjhima Nikāya,* I, p.256.

[15]This is clear from a conversation between Prasenjit of Kośala and Lord Buddha, where the latter, denying the statement of the former, pointed out that this was a misrepresentation of his contention. See, *Majjhima Nikāya,* II, pp.374-75.

[16]*Majjhima Nikāya,* I, p.174.

[17]Ibid., I, p.315.

[18]*Saṁyutta Nikāya,* II, p.222.

badly grasped by them conduce for a long time to their woe and sorrow.'[19]

He recommended the guidance of senior monks[20] in case there arose a dispute over the fruits *(magga)*, path *(paṭipadā)* or the congregation *(Saṅgha)*.[21] Regarding his method of teaching *Dhamma* according to classification, he pointed out to Ānanda that those of his followers who will not accede, approve or accept what has been well said, 'will live wrangling, quarrelsome, disputatious, wounding one another with the weapons of the tongue'.[22]

The remarks of elder monks like Śāriputra are equally suggestive in this connection. He speaks of monks occupied with 'evil unskilled wishes' and tries to establish them by means of disquisition on *Dhamma*.[23] The death of Nigaṇṭha Nāṭaputta and the consequent dissension in his order led the Buddha to warn Ānanda to see that no such developments took place in the Order.[24]

But differences with regard to some minor points of discipline appeared in the Buddha's life time as is evident from the Pāli canon.[25] The first dissension *(Saṅgharāji)*[26] occurred in a monastery at Kauśāmbi[27] where a monk through ignorance of the law committed a breach *(āpatti)* of discipline. The *bhikkhus* attached undue gravity to the offence and punished

---

[19]*Middle Length Sayings*, I, p.171.

[20]The Buddha had charged Ānanda, Sāriputta and Mogallāna with the duty of settling disputes whenever they took place among the monks. See, *Aṅguttara Nikāya*, II, p.254; *Majjhima Nikāya*, III, p.38.

[21]*Majjhima Nikāya*, III, pp.38ff.

[22]*Middle Length Sayings*, II, p.66.

[23]*Majjhima Nikāya*, I, pp.34ff.

[24]Ibid., III, p.38.

[25]One often hears of *Upananda (Mahāvagga*, pp.315-16), Channa *(Cullavagga*, p.412) and the *Chhabbaggiya (Mahāvagga*, pp.331-32) *bhikkhus* who were always on the lookout for an opportunity to transgress the Vinaya rules.

[26]*Cullavagga*, pp.305-06. Less than nine monks could bring about dissension *(Saṅgharāji)* which is clearly distinguished from schism (*Saṅghabheda*). See, *infra*.

[27]*Mahāvagga*, pp.368ff; *Majjhima Nikāya*, I, 'Kosambiya Sutta', pp.393-98.

him by *ukkepanā* (excommunication). The accused, on the other hand, attributed the offence to his ignorance of the law which did not deserve the severe penalty inflicted on him. The justice of the cause gained for him several adherents who resolved to have his punishment set aside. This caused a division not only among the *bhikkhus* but also among the lay devotees and ultimately led to the Buddha's mediation. This dissension did not last long owing to the presence of the Buddha who removed the doubts of both the parties by his lucid explanations but 'yet it argues the existence of germs of dissension which bore fruits of far reaching importance in later times.'[28] The first serious attempt at schism *(Saṅghabheda)*[29] was made by the Buddha's cousin, Devadatta[30] who, in his advocacy for more austere discipline, requested the teacher to introduce the following five rules in the *Saṅgha*[31]—The Brethren were to:

---

[28]N. Dutt, 'Evolution of the Schools of Buddhism', *JDL.*, Vol.3, 1920, p.263.

[29]A specific type of *vivāda* (dispute over *Dhamma* and *Vinaya—Cullavagga,* pp.170-72) accompanied by the conditions laid down in the *Vinaya Piṭaka* was designated as *Saṅghabheda.* Difference of interpretation on *Dhamma*, *Vinaya* and *Prātimokṣa* could bring about schism (ibid., p.306) if at least nine or more than nine qualified *bhikkhus* were involved in it. *Saṅghabheda* is described in the *Vinaya Texts* (SBE., Pt.III, p.271n) as follows: 'For not only is a formal putting forward and voting on the false doctrine essential to schism as distinct from mere disagreement, but the offending bhikkhu must be quite aware that the doctrine so put forth is wrong, or at least doubtful, and also that the schism resulting from his action will be or will probably be disastrous to the Dharma.' *Contra.,* S.N. Dube *(Cross Currents in Early Buddhism,* p.41) states that 'In fact, the mere entertainment of a dissident view, which, in its turn, arises due to various reasons such as difference of understanding or interpretation, was sufficient for a dispute to arise and thus give rise to a schism and doctrinal confrontation. Schism was perhaps rarely intended to be caused. It followed automatically if the confrontation was irreconcilable.'

[30]On the nature and significance of Devadatta's attempt, See, B.G. Gokhale, 'Devadatta and His Life', *JBBRAS.* (N.S.), Vol.XX, 1944, pp.61-64; See also, G.S.P. Misra, 'A Buddhist legend re-written: Devadatta and his character', *BV.*, Vol.XXVIII, Nos.1-4, 1968, pp.22-29.

[31]*Cullavagga,* p.298.

(a) live only in the forest;
(b) subsist solely on alms collected out-doors *(piṇḍāpatika);*
(c) dress themselves in rags picked up from dust-heaps *(pāṁsukūlika);*
(d) dwell always under a tree *(rukkhamūla)* and never under a roof;
(e) never eat fish or flesh.

The Buddha refused to make the observance of these rules obligatory upon all the *bhikkhus,* as in his view it would be more conducive to their welfare to make these rules optional.[32] Devadatta took this opportunity to create a division in the *Saṅgha* and with his five hundred followers broke with the Order.[33] It seems that this secession of Devadatta from the *Saṅgha* gave rise to a sect which existed up to the fourth century AD,[34] and a remnant of this sect was found in three *Saṅghārāmās* of Karṇasuvarṇa in the seventh century AD.[35]

Subhaddha's Remark: Convening the 1st Council

These dissenting tendencies became stronger after the demise of Lord Buddha as is clear from the significant remark made by Subhaddha: 'Enough, brethren! Weep not, neither lament. We are well rid of the Great Samana. We used to be annoyed by being told, "This beseems you, this beseems you not." But now we shall be able to do whatever we like, and what we do not like, that we shall not have to do.'[36] This remark of

---

[32]*Cullavagga,* pp.298-99. There were among the Buddha's direct disciples some *dhūtavādins* (practicers of *dhūtaṅgas*—rigorous practices). That this practice continued even in later times is clear from *Bedsā Buddhist Stūpa Inscription* (*Lüders list,* No.1110) which records the erection of a *thupa (stūpa)* of the hermit (*araṇaka*) the mendicant (*peḍapātika*) Gobhuti by his pupil.

[33]*Cullavagga,* p.300.

[34]J. Legge, op. cit., p.62.

[35]T. Watters, op. cit., II, p.191.

[36]*Cullavagga,* p.406. In the Southern tradition *(Mahāvaṁsa,* III.7) this subversive utterance of Subhaddha is said to have been the reason for convening the first Buddhist Council after the Buddha's demise.

Subhaddha, if not the motive, was at least a clear indication of the necessity of convening a Council.

A Council did take place at Rājagṛha soon after the *Mahāparinirvāṇa* of the Buddha. As S. Dutt puts it 'the practical need must have been felt by the monks, not long after they had settled in the āvāsas, of defining and stabilising the *Dhamma-Vinaya*'[37] which existed only in the collective memory of monks and laymen. This could be done by joint recital[38] of the recollections of the 'Specialists' who were custodians of different sections of the *Dhamma-Vinaya*. It is true that certain V*inaya* rules and some Suttas were collected at the first Council held at Rājagṛha but a definitive and universal canon of *Dhamma-Vinaya* was not presented.[39]

Regarding the nature of the first council G.S.P. Misra adduces many arguments to observe that it should fundamentally be considered a *Vinaya* Council.[40] That factional elements were present in the Order is clear from the fact that Mahākassapa failed to secure Gavaṁpati and Purāṇa's approval of the texts settled by his Council. As N. Dutt[41] writes, 'In the proceedings of the first council, it will be observed that Mahākassapa was keen on securing the approval of all the senior monks, particularly of Gavaṁpati

---

[37]S. Dutt, *BFAC.*, p.97.

[38]Recital of sacred texts had been an old practice of *bhikkhus*. See, *Mahāvagga*, p.215; *Dialogues of the Buddha*, Pt.III (SBB.), pp.203-04.

[39]G.C. Pande, *BDVI.*, p.159; A.K. Warder, op. cit., p.206; *Contra.*, S. Dutt (op. cit., p.100) who remarks. 'In the Pali canon is recorded an interesting tradition in the form of two appendices to the *Vinaya Piṭaka* section *(Cullavagga, Khandhakas* XI and XII) to the effect that the canon received in this way, by united congregational recital, a stamp of authoritative definiteness and the texts recited were therefore the only definitive canon of Buddhism.'

[40]G.S.P. Misra, *The Age of Vinaya,* p.11. Even the concluding portion of the Pali canon *(Cullavagga,* p.414) refers to the occasion as *Vinaya-Saṅgiti* (chanting of *Vinaya).* The *Mahāvaṁsa* (trans., III.18) 'perhaps by an oversight of scribes' as Mrs. Rhys Davids puts it (A Manual of Buddhism, p.264, fn.1) calls the first, *paṭhama-dhamma-sangiti.*

[41]N. *Dutt, EMB.*, II, pp.10-11; For Gavampati's disapproval of the Vinaya settled by the Council, See, W. Rockhill, *The Life of the Buddha,* pp.149-50.

and Purāṇa of the texts settled by his council as *Buddha-vacana,* Gavaṁpati remained neutral, i.e. he did not whole-heartedly accept the proceedings of the council as final while Purāṇa expressed his inability to accept the same as the words of the Teacher. He further insisted on the incorporation into the Vinaya of eight rules relating to food.'[42]

Mahāsaṅghika Sthavira Schism: A Review

There is no homogenous tradition with regard to the great schism separating the Sthavira and Mahāsaṅghika *nikāyas* of early Buddhism. The *Cullavagga* of the Pāli Vinaya refers to the convening of the second Buddhist council at Vaiśāli, a hundred years after the *parinirvāṇa* of the Buddha to discuss the ten undesirable practices *(daśa-vastūni)* of the Vajjian monks.[43] The Ceylonese sources add that the council was held in the reign of Kālāśoka and that after their condemnation at the Vaiśāli council, the schismatics held another and called it 'Great Assembly' or *'Mahāsaṅgiti'* and established the Mahāsāṅghika sect.[44]

Another tradition is represented by the treatises of *Vasumitra, Vinītadeva* and *Bhavya. Vasumitra* who wrote a treatise on the sects *(Samayabhedoparacanacakra)* tells us that in AB 100 a council was held in the time of Aśoka to discuss the five propositions of Mahādeva which consequently divided the church by giving birth to the Mahāsāṅghika sect.[45]

---

[42]These rules were incorporated into the Vinaya of the Mahiśāsakas and Purāṇa was recognized as one of the foremost leaders, next only to Kauṇḍinya. See, N. Dutt, op. cit., Vol.II, p.11. See also, J. Przyluski, *Le Concile de Rājagṛha,* pp.144-48.

[43]*Cullavagga,* Chap.XII; The *Vinayakṣudrakavastu* of the Sarvāstivāda *Vinaya* refers to the council, placing it 110 years after the demise of the Buddha.

[44]*Mahāvaṁsa,* Chap.IV.

[45]A Bareau, *Les Sectes boudhhiques* (translation of the text by Jiryo Masuda, 'Origin and Doctrines of Early Indian Buddhist Schools', *Asia Major*, 2, 1925, p.14; Ibid., Trois traités sur les sectes bouddhiques attribués a Vasumitra, Bhavya et Vinitadeva, *Journal Asiatique*, Tome CCXLII, 1954 (Ie partie), p.235 quoted G.S.P. Misra, op. cit., p.15.

Vinītadeva (Samayabhedoparacanacakra-nikāyabhedo-padarsana saṁgraha) follows Vasumitra.[46] The *Nikāya-bhedavibhaṅgavyākhyāna* affirming the Saṃmitiya tradition states that the division was fostered by the activities of a monk named Bhadra who possessed magical powers and advocated the five theses.[47]

The *Abhidharma-mahāvibhāṣā-śāstra*,[48] a Sarvāstivādin work, relates that the schism was created by Mahādeva, who propounded the five heretical theses. The Mahāsāṅghikas accepted his views and the Sarvāstivādins (not the Sthaviras, as in the other sources) did not.

The *San Louen hiuan yi* of Ki-tsang[49] a Mahāyāna commentary on Vasumitra's *Samayabhedoparacanacakra,* based on the earlier work of Parmārtha, which has survived only in fragments describes the schism between the Mahā-sāṅghikas and the Sthaviras as a result of the activities of a certain Mahādeva, who in addition to advocating the heretical five points, tried to incorporate Mahāyāna Sutras into the Tripiṭaka.

Basing their analysis on the evidence of the *Śariputrapari-pṛcchā-sūtra*, an Abhidhamma work of the Mahāsāṅghikas and a comparative study of Mahāsāṅghika Prātimokṣa rules with other Prātimokṣa recensions, Janice Nattier and Charles Prebish[50] have given a new dimension to the Mahāsāṅghika Sthavira schism.

The Theravādin and the Mahāsāṅghika sources cite the *Vinaya* as the source of the schism, while the Sarvāstivadin

---

[46]Ibid., Tome CCXLIV, 1956 (IIe Partie), p.192. N. Dutt, *EMB.*, II, p.41.

[47]A Bareau, 'Trois traités sur les sectes bouddhiques', pp.172-91. For a discussion of the Saṃmitiya origin of this tradition, See, Bareau, *Les Sectes bouddhiques*, p.17; A.K. Warder, op. cit., p.215.

[48]*'Taisho,* 1545; See, T. Watters, op. cit., I, pp.267-68.

[49]This is translated by Paul Demiéville, 'L' Origine des sectes bouddhiques d'après Paramārtha', *Mêlanges chinois et bouddhiques*, I (1931-32), p.20. See, N. Dutt, *BSI.*, p.23.

[50]Janice J. Nattier and Charles S. Prebish, 'Mahāsāṃghika Origins: The Beginnings of Buddhist Sectarianism', *HOR.*, Vol.16, No.3, Feb.1977, pp.237-72.

works attribute the schism to matters of doctrine.[51] In the opinion of G.C. Pande, the schism began openly with points of discipline, but soon the doctrinal differences which are discernible in a germinal form in the *nikāyas,* flowered forth.[52] One has therefore to agree with Charles Prebish that 'the sectarian movement in the second century following Buddha's parinirvāṇa was a product of both doctrinal and disciplinary issues'.[53]

Laxity in the observance of ten rules can easily be examined by comparing the accounts as presented in the Pāli *Vinaya* and the Mahāsāṅghika *Vinaya*. The first point in the Pāli list refers to the practice of preserving salt in a horn *(siṅgiloṇakappa)*. This practice is contrary to *Pācittiya* 38 which prohibits the storage of food.[54] It corresponds to Mahāsāṅghika *Pācattika* rule 37 which reads, 'In eating (food) that has been laid aside (as a store), there is a pācattika.'[55]

---

[51]There is discrepancy with regard to the details between different traditions. In the Tibetan tradition (Rockhill, op. cit., pp.171-72) only the last four practices agree with those preserved in the southern tradition. Yuan Chwang (T. Watters, op. cit., II, pp.76-77) mentions the ten points but, differing from the Pāli tradition, states that the Vajjian monks renounced all their deviations from the orthodox rules of discipline and followed those that were approved by the second council. Elsewhere (ibid., pp.268-69) he traces the origin of the Mahāsāṅghika school to the five points enunciated by Mahādeva.

[52]G.C. Pande, *Studies,* pp.558-59.

[53]Charles Prebish, *BMD.,* p.27. An interesting point regarding the second council is that the Vinayic division was accompanied with a more or less clear geographical demarcation between the two parties. The Vaiśālians were Easterners while their antagonists were Westerners. Mrs. Rhys Davids suggests that 'the real point at issue was the rights of the individual, as well as those of the provincial communities as against the prescriptions of a centralized hierarchy'. This view is supported by N. Dutt *(EMB.,* II, pp.43-44,) who remarks that the Vajjians imbued with a thorough democratic spirit would have been unlikely to submit to the exclusive powers and privileges which the Arhants claimed for themselves. As G.S.P. Misra has pointed out it is surprising that the very *bhikkhus* of Vaiśāli, Vajjiputakas are represented in the *Cullavagga* (p.300) as having adhered to the five rigorous propositions of Devadatta, see, G.S.P. Misra, op. cit., p.18.

[54]*Vinaya Texts* (SBE.), Vol.XIII, Pt.I, p.40.

[55]Charles Prebish, op. cit., p.80.

The second point in the Pāli list refers to taking food when the shadow is beyond two fingers wide *(dvaṅgulakappa)*. This is against *Pācittiya* offence 37 which forbids taking of food whether hard or soft, at the wrong time.[56] The Mahāsāṅghika rule *(Pācattika* 36) states, 'In eating at the wrong time, there is a pācattika.'[57]

The third point in the Pāli list refers to the practice of taking meals and then going to another village and taking a second meal there on the same day *(gāmantarakappa)*. This is opposed to *Pācittiya* rule 35 which forbids over eating, i.e. after finishing a meal to partake of more food that is not left over.[58] The Mahāsāṅghika rule *(Pācattika* 33) reads, 'Whatever monk who has eaten what is offered and risen from his seat, should chew or consume hard food or soft food that has not been left over, that is a pācattika.'[59]

The fourth point involves holding several *uposathas* within the same *simā (āvāsakappa)*. This practice contravenes the *Mahāvagga* rules of residence in a parish *(sima)*.[60]

The fifth point in the Pāli list forbids monks of obtaining sanction for an act after it is done *(anumatikappa)*.[61] The sixth point involves carrying out an act improperly, citing habitual practice as an authority *(āciṇṇakappa)*.[62] We do not have Mahāsāṅghika rules on the condemnation of these points as no Sanskrit counterpart for the *Skandhaka* portion of the *Vinaya* seems to be extant.[63]

---

[56] *Vinaya Texts* (SBE.),Vol.XIII, Pt.I, p.40.

[57] Charles Prebish, op. cit., p.80.

[58] *Vinaya Texts* (SBE.), Vol.XIII, Pt.I, p.39.

[59] Charles Prebish, loc. cit., p.80.

[60] *Vinaya Texts* (SBE.), Vol.XIII, Pt.I, p.251; See, also Vol.XX, Pt.III, p.386.

[61] Ibid., Vol.XX, pt.III, p.386; Vol.XVII, Pt.II, p.266.

[62] Ibid.

[63] There is a summary of the *Bhikṣu-Prakirṇaka* (which is the Mahāsāṅghika-Lokottaravādin counterpart of the *vastus* comprising the Skandhaka of the various other *Vinayas)* but it affords no help. See, Gustav Roth, ed., *Bhikṣuṇi-Vinaya,* pp.327-34.

The seventh in the Pāli list refers to drinking buttermilk after meals *(amathitakappa)*. This practice is in contravention to *Pācittiya* rule 35 which prohibits overeating.[64] It corresponds to the Mahāsāṅghika rule, *Pācittiya* offence 33.[65]

The eighth point in the Pāli list refers to drinking unfermented wine *(Jalogipānakappo)*. This rule *(Pācittiya* 51) makes it an offence for monks to have intoxicating drinks.[66] The Mahāsāṅghika rule *(Pācattika* 76) states, 'in drinking intoxicating beverages, spirits and liquors, there is a *pācattika'*.[67]

The ninth point in the Pāli list refers to using a rug without a border *(adasakaṃ nisīdanam)*. This is contrary to *Pācittiya* rule 89 which prohibits the use of borderless sheets. It cites the dimensions for new rugs, noting that the border should measure one Sugata-span.[68] The Mahāsāṅghika rule *(Pācattika* 86) states, 'This is the measure here: in length, two spans of the Sugata-span, in width, one and one half, the border a span.'[69]

The tenth point in the Pāli list refers to accepting gold and silver *(jatarūparajatam)*. This makes it an offence *(Nissaggiya-Pācittiya* 18) for monks to receive gold or silver, or for having another act as his agent or to have such money deposited for him.[70] The Mahāsāṅghika rule *(Niḥsargika-Pācattika* 18) states, 'whatever monk should have (another) acquire it (for him), even so much as to say: "Deposit it here" or should consent to having it deposited, that is a niḥsargika pacattika'.[71]

Thus the points listed in the Pāli account of the council held at Vaiśāli as presented in the 12th Chapter of the

[64] *Vinaya Texts* (SBE.), Vol.XX, Pt.III, p.386.
[65] Charles Prebish, op. cit., p.80.
[66] *Vinaya Texts* (SBE.), Vol. XIII, Pt.I, p.44.
[67] Charles Prebish, loc. cit., p.90.
[68] *Vinaya Texts* (SBE.), Vol.XIII. Pt.I, p.54.
[69] Charles Prebish, loc. cit., p.90.
[70] *Vinaya Texts* (SBE.), Vol.XIII, Pt.I, p.26.
[71] Charles Prebish, loc. cit., p.70.

Cullavagga appear to be nearly in agreement with the Mahāsāṅghika statements.[72] One has, therefore, to agree with André Bareau when he notes, 'the nine practices of the monks of Vaiśāli could not have been one of the causes of the schism which separated the Mahāsāṅghikas from the Sthaviras as the Sinhalese chronicles maintain and, in their course, certain historians of Buddhism'.[73] Moreover, the Mahāsāṅghikas cannot be identified with the Vajjiputtaka *bhikṣus* of Vaiśāli.[74] Even Gustav Roth remarks on the issue of the schism, 'and why are the Mahāsāṅghikas not mentioned in the report of this council when they already existed at the time'.[75] He dates the schism later than the *Dipavaṁsa.*[76] It is thus clear that the Mahāsāṅghika Sthavira schism does not seem to have appeared for the first time in connection with the second council as pictured by the Pāli tradition.

The *Śāriputraparipṛcchāsūtra,*[77] a Mahāsāṅghika text resolves the cause of the schism. It relates an incident about an elderly monk who re-arranged and expanded the *Vinaya* said to have been codified by Kasyapa at the first council of Rājagṛha. This annoyed the other monks who asked the king to intervene. The king brought the two parties together and suggested a vote with black and white tablets (*śālākā*), black

---

[72]For divergence of interpretation on the ten points among the different schools, See, N. Dutt, *EMB.*, II, pp.35-40; Louis de La Vallée Poussin, *The Buddhist Councils,* pp.41-57.

[73]André Bareau, *Les Premiers Conciles bouddhiques,* p.78. He maintains that the council was convened solely on the issue of the tenth point, that of accepting gold and silver, and that the other nine points represent later Sthavira accretions. Even the Mahāsāṅghika *Vinaya (Nanjio,* No.1110, Chap.33) is aware only of the tenth point.

[74]M. Hofinger (*Étude sûr le concile de Vaiśāli,* p.179), emphasizes that the monks at Vaisāli cannot be regarded as the founders of the Mahāsāṅghikas, because the unruly monks at Vaiśāli are dealt with in the Mahāsāṅghika *Vinaya* report in the same way as in all other sources with contempt, by rejecting their unruly behaviour. See, A.K. Warder, op. cit., pp.213-14.

[75]Gustav Roth, ed., op. cit., p.x.

[76]Ibid., p.viii.

[77]The same passage has been translated from Chinese into French in Lamotte's, *Histoire du bouddhisme Indien,* p.189. He refers to *Taishō* 1465, p.900b.

in favour of the traditional *Vinaya* and white for those who preferred the re-arranged *Vinaya*.

The majority of the monks voted with black tablets in favour of the traditional *Vinaya,* the minority for the new. The king considered the doctrines of both the parties as representing the word of the Buddha. The monks who were in majority and studied the traditional *Vinaya* were called Mahāsāṅghikas (*Mo-ho-seng-k'i*) while those who studied the new *Vinaya,* though in a minority, were all Sthaviras (*Chango tso,* senior members). They were thus named *T'a-pi-lo* (*Sthaviras*).

This above passage is in full accord with Fa-hien's remark at the end of his Mahāsāṅghika *Vinaya* translation. While referring to the schools and their differences he says, 'King Aśoka asks himself how to decide between right and wrong in these matters'. He puts this question before the *Saṅgha*—'How to reach a fair judgement according to the law of the Buddha'. All tell him that according to the law they must follow the majority. The king replied, 'If that is so, one should proceed to vote by tablets (*śālākā*) in order to know where the majority is'. After the vote had taken place, there were those in great number who had picked up the tablets of the 'original assembly'. And as this assembly was in the majority, it called itself Mahāsāṅghika, i.e. 'The great Assembly'.[78] It is thus

[78]*Taisho,* XXII, p.548b. Samuel Beal *(Travels of Fah-hian and Sung-Yun,* p.144, fn.3 contd.) relying on the Tibetan accounts gives a similar rendering when he states that 'there arose a considerable difference between the rendering recommended by some of the chief Sthaviras or heads of convents, and the body of priests, who belonged to the less considerable establishments. They appealed to Aśoka, who ordered a general vote to be taken by ballot, each priest voting for the party representing the ancient or traditional rendering, or the modern conventual use. The majority was in favour of the ancient opinions, and this party was called the Mahāsāṅghika (the great body of priests), the others were called the Sthaviras or Mahāsthaviras, because they followed the opinions of certain great establishments. The Mahāsāṅghikas were called the followers of Kāsyapa, because they adhered to the rendering of the law supposed to have been authorized by him, at the first great convocation at Rajgriha, over which he presided.' *Contra.,* The *Dipavaṁsa* (v.32-38) written as it is with a sectarian bias, attributes the alterations in the *Vinaya* to the Mahāsāṅghikas.

clear that from the Mahāsāṅghika viewpoint, corroborated by Fa-hien's statement and the Tibetan accounts, that the real issue leading to the schism was expansion of *Vinaya.* The Mahāsāṅghikas are referred to as those who studied the 'Ancient Vinaya' and this is corroborated by the conclusions of Bareau,[79]*Pachow,*[80] *Hofinger,*[81] Frauwallner[82] and Roth[83] that the Mahāsāṅghika *Vinaya* represents the most ancient of all the *Vinaya* traditions.

A comparative assessment of the *Prātimokṣa-sūtra* shows how the Sthaviras and other sectarian groups began to expand their respective texts. This can be substantiated by referring to the table concerning the number of rules in the different *Prātimokṣa* texts.[84] A comparison of the Pāli *Patimokkha* with the Mahāsāṅghika *Prātimokṣa* text makes it clear that the number of rules in the Sanskrit text is less than that of the Pāli version. There are 218 rules in the former as against the 227 rules in the Pāli version. This difference is chiefly in the section of *Śaikṣa dharma,* the Pāli has 75 rules and the Mahāsāṅghika only 66 or 67.[85] 'If we believe the usual process of historical development, it appears that the Mahāsāṅghika text seems even older in existence than that of the present Pali version.'[86] The added restrictions introduced

[79]A Bareau, 'La Construction et le culte des stupa d'après les Vinayapitaka', *Bulletin de l'Ecole Francaise d'Extrême Orient,* 50, No.2, 1962, 273.

[80]W. Pachow, *A Comparative Study of the Prātimokṣa,* p.42.

[81]M. Hofinger, op. cit., p.237.

[82] E. Frauwallner, *The Earliest Vinaya and the beginnings of Buddhist literature,* p.61.

[83]G. Roth, op. cit., p.vii.

[84]W. Pachow, loc. cit., p.11.

[85]The *Śaikṣa dharma* section shows great diversity in various schools both in number and content. Dr. Pachow (op. cit., p.49) notes that some of the *Śaikṣa* material is extremely old. The Dharmaguptakas can be cited here who have 26 rules in this section for appropriate conduct at a *stūpa* (ibid., pp.51-52). For other examples, See Prebish, 'The Prātimokṣa puzzle: Fact versus fantasy', *JAOS.,* Vol.94, No.2, 1974, pp.174-76.

[86]W. Pachow and Ramakanta Mishra, 'The Prātimokṣa-sūtra of the Mahāsāṅghikas', *JGJRI.,* Vols.11-12, 1953-54, p.246. The Chinese translation of the Mahāsāṅghika *Prātimokṣa-sūtra* agrees with the Sanskrit version of the Mahāsāṅghika school in number (except one rule), in substance, and in arrangement, with regard to the serial order (ibid., p.249).

from time to time suggest advancements in the *Vinaya* itself. 'It is probable that the Mahāsāṅghikas were convinced at an early stage that they must possess the original version of the Vinaya. They did not want to be looked at as heretics or holders of lax principles as the report on the council of Vaisāli in the Chinese version of the Mahāsāṅghika *Vinaya* clearly shows.[87]

Thus the issue of *Vinaya* expansion as stated in the *Śāriputraparipṛcchā-sūtra* is amply substantiated by the Mahāsāṅghika *Prātimokṣa-sūtra* presenting the shortest list of offences.

Now as to the question why the future Sthaviras chose to enlarge the *Vinaya,* Prebish remarks: 'It is not unlikely that the council of Vaiśāli, in representing the first real threat of division in the quasi-unified Buddhist *Sangha,* made all Buddhists aware of the problem of concord now that the Buddha was long dead. In seeking to ensure the continued unity that all Buddhists must have desired, they simply began to expand the disciplinary code in the seemingly appropriate direction. Just as the respect for orthodoxy inhibited the participants at the alleged first council of Rājagṛha from excluding the "lesser and the minor points" which the Buddha had noted to be expendable (and since Buddha gave no indication of what the specific points were, the monks would have had to risk orthodoxy by guessing, however, intelligently they performed their task), the same respect for orthodoxy inhibited the future Mahāsāṃghikas from tolerating this new endeavour, however well intentioned it was.'[88]

Now coming to the five points of Mahadeva, we find that the Sarvāstivādin and the Saṃmitiya sources[89] make it the real issue of Mahāsāṅghika-Sthavira schism. Contrary to this

---

[87]This report has been translated from Chinese into French in M. Hofinger's *Étude les sûr concile de Vaiśālī*, pp.146-48 referring to *Taisho* 1426, K.33, p.493a21-493C.11.

[88]Janice J. Nattier and Charles Prebish, 'Mahāsāṃghika Origins: The Beginnings of Buddhist Sectarianism', *HOR.*, Vol.16, No.3, Feb. 1977, p.270.

[89]See, *Supra.*

Nattier and Prebish have sought to establish for the first time, the fact that Mahadeva's five points receive a strong affirmation from the southern school of the Mahāsāṅghikas, which brought about an intra-Mahāsāṅghika schism.[90] An analysis of these points show that the first four deal with the nature and attainments of the *Arhat* while the last emphasizes the utterance of the word 'sorrow' and its relation to the Path.[91]

The five points, if taken at their face value, suggest one important aspect, namely, demotion of the *Arhat* from the perfect state,[92] implying thereby that the status of *Arhat* was easily attainable. But such laxity in doctrinal matters can be over-ruled if a higher goal was being substituted and advocated by those that felt that *Arhatship* was not the culmination of perfection.[93] This brings us to the real issue—

[90]J. Nattier and C. Prebish, op. cit., pp.257ff.

[91]These five points can be identified with a set of propositions noted in the *Kathāvatthu.* The *Arhats:*

(a) are subject to temptation (11.1).
(b) may have residue of ignorance (11.2).
(c) may have doubts regarding certain matters (11.3).
(d) gain knowledge through other's help (11.4).
(e) the path is attained by an exclamation as 'aho' (11.3-6; IX.9; XI.4, 6).

For a critical appraisal of the five propositions as represented by various traditions, see, J. Nattier and C. Prebish, loc. cit., pp.251-57; N. Dutt, *BSI.,* pp.22-29.

[92]In early Buddhism, the term *Arhat* assumed a technical significance as denoting only the fully and finally emancipated saints. The idea of perfection which is set up for emulation by the disciples in the 'Old Wisdom School' was that of an *Arhat.* See, E. Conze, *Buddhism, Its Essence and Development,* p.93. Numerous passages in the Canonical texts refer to the spiritual state and claim that the *Arhat* is one who is free from attachment, hatred and delusion, relieved of the burden of *Khandhas,* accomplished in all that is to be accomplished and devoid of any future existence. See, *Aṅguttara Nikāya,* I, p.133; *Majjhima Nikāya,* I, pp.7, 94; *Dīgha Nikāya,* III, pp.65, 76; *Saṁyutta Nikāya,* I, p.70; IV, pp.142-43, 258. He possesses *Kaṣayajñāna* (the knowledge that he has no more *Klēsas)* and *anutpādajñāna* (the knowledge that he will have no more rebirth). See, N. Dutt, BSI., pp.24, 82.

[93]One begs to differ here with the argument (written as it is from a Theravādin point of view) put forth by S.N. Dube (op. cit., p.110) that, 'It may be observed that the Theravāda tendency contributed by way of a reaction in a significant measure towards the growth of heretical and unwholesome notions about Arahant and Arhantship.' The concept of *Lokottara* Buddha and the *Bodhisattvas,* it may be noted, could not have developed without antecedents. It is highly probable that by pointing out the imperfections of *Arhathood,* the Mahāsāṅghikas were trying to differentiate the Buddha from the *Arhats,* thereby raising Buddha's status from an enlightened to a transcendental being.

was Mahādeva trying to replace the old ideal of *Arhatship* with that of the *Bodhisattva,* leading to the attainment of *Buddhahood*? There are two evidences to support the above view. First, Mahadeva is referred to as a *Bodhisattva* in *Fen-pie-kong-yo-louen,* a half-Mahāsāṅghika, half-Mahāyānist commentary on the Chinese Ekottarāgama.[94] Second, the Mahāsāṅghikas are well known for their concept of the *Lokottara* (transcendent) Buddha and the *Bodhisattvas.*[95]

It will be observed that all the Mahāsāṅghikas[96] did not subscribe to identical doctrines and so some of them were distinguished from the rest by the term 'ekacce mahāsāṅghika' which occurs frequently in the *Kathāvatthu commentary.* The Śaila (southern) schools held the view that the *Bodhisattvas* are average beings and are not exempt from being born in the

---

[94]See, Etienne Lamotte, 'Buddhist Controversy over the Five Propositions.' *IHQ.,* Vol.32, 1956, p.156.

[95]Statements like, 'The Buddhas are all supramundane *(Lokottara)',* 'There are no sāsrava dharmas or defiled elements in all the Tathāgathas', 'The Buddha can expound all the doctrines with a single utterance', 'The divine power of the Tathāgata is limitless', 'The Buddha has neither sleep nor dream', 'The Blessed One understands all things *(dharmas)* with a moment's mind' *(Ekakṣaṇacitta)* are attributed to the Mahāsāṅghika, the Ekavyavāhārikas, the Lokottaravādins and the Kaukkuṭikas in the treatise of *Vasumitra* (Masuda, *op. cit.,* pp.18-20). *Bhavya* (A. Bareau, 'Trois traités sur les sectes bouddhiques', Pt.II, p.173) attributes some of these views to the Ekavyāvahārikas while *Vinitadeva* (ibid., p.193) ascribes them to the Lokottaravādins.

Regarding the *Bodhisattvas* also it is said that they do not pass through the usual embryonic stages in the mother's womb, that they all assume the form of elephants upon entering their mother's womb, that they are not born in the usual fashion, but emerge from the right side of their mothers and that no *Bodhisattva* entertains any thought of lust *(Kāmasaṁjña),* anger *(vyāpādasaṁjñā)* or harm to others *(vihiṁsāsaṁjñā).* See, Masuda, loc. cit.. p.21; L. De La Vallée Poussin, *ERE.,* IV, S.V., 'Bodhisattva', p.741; N. Dutt, op. cit., pp.76-77. The *Lokottara* conception of the Buddha and the *Bodhisattvas* is presented in the *Mahāvastu* (I, pp.112-51), the *Vinaya* of the Lokottaravādins.

[96]N. *Dutt (BSI.,* pp.64-68) labels the Mahāsāṅghikas as 'Northern' or 'Earlier' and 'Southern' or 'Later'. The former included the sects of the Lokottaravādins, the Ekavyavāharikas Kaukkuṭikas, Bahuśrutiyas and Prajñaptivādins. The latter included the Caitikas, the Pūrvaśailas (or Uttaraśailas), the Aparaśailas, the Rājagiriyas and the Siddhārthikas. See, S. Dutt, *BFAC.,* pp.134-35.

lower states of existence *(durgati)*[97] and offerings made to a *Caitya* are not necessarily of great merit.[98]

The Mahāsāṅghikas and their sub-sects differed even on the status of an *Arhat*. The Northern group including the Ekavyāvaharikas, the Lokottaravādins and the Kaukkuṭikas, though admitting the four failings of the *Arhat*,[99] did not subscribe to the view that *Arhats* can retrogress but rather pointed out that a *Srotāpanna* has a chance to regress while an *Arhat* has not.[100] The *Kathāvatthu*[101] ascribes a contrary view to the Mahāsāṅghikas and some sects of the orthodox groups like the Sarvāstivādins and the Saṃmitiyas, that an *Arhat* is liable to fall from his perfect state but not a *Srotāpanna*.

The Mahāsāṅghikas of the *Kaṭhāvatthu* must be the Śaila schools who, subscribing to the failings of the *Arhat* as pointed out by Mahādeva's first four propositions, claimed that an *Arhat* is liable to fall from the perfect state. The fifth point of Mahādeva is concerned with the issue of entry and realization of the Path with a verbal utterance associated with the exclamation of *'dukkha'*. Buddhaghosa attributes to the Pubbaseliyas and others a view that one who has entered into first *jhāna*, at the moment of attaining the first or stream winner's way, utters the truth: 'Sorrow'.[102] Similarly to the Andhakas is attributed the view that from the words 'this is *dukkha*' insight into the nature of *dukkha* is received.[103]

---

[97]Vasumitra (Masuda, op. cit., p.38; A. Bareau, *'Trois traités sur les sectes bouddhiques,* Pt.II, pp.196.) ascribes this view to the Caityaśailas, the Aparaśailas and the Uttaraśailas. The *Kathāvatthu* (XXIII.4) associates the Andhakas with the view that the Bodhisattvas take birth in the bad states of existence *(durgati)* out of their own free will. See also, *Kathāvatthu Aṭṭhakatha,* p.197.

[98]N. Dutt, op. cit., p.115.

[99]J. Masuda, loc. cit., p.24; A. Bareau, *'Trois trailés sur les sectes bouddhiques,* Pt.II, pp.172ff.

[100]J. Masuda, loc. cit., p.26.

[101]*Kathāvatthu*, 1.2.

[102]*Kathāvatthu Aṭṭhakathā,* pp.55-56.

[103]Ibid., p.130.

The doctrinal thesis of the Mahāsāṅghikas which seems to be related to the fifth point of Mahādeva, based on André Bareau's[104] translations, are the following: (1) 'To say suffering can help'; (2) 'Suffering leads to the way'; (3) 'to say, "O suffering!" causes one to know suffering'; (4) 'there is vocal utterance by one who has entered into possession of the way'; (5) 'there is vocal utterance in Samadhi'. None of these statements are ascribed to the northern Mahāsāṅghika sub-sects, like the Lokottaravādins', Kaukkuṭikas or the Ekavyāvahārikas. They are attributed to the Mahāsāṅghikas as a whole in four cases, where the term is used as a general title, most of them belong to the southern group of the Mahāsāṅghikas. Thus it becomes clear that the fifth point of Mahādeva, like the first four, harmonizes much more with the doctrinal positions of the Southern Mahāsāṅghika sub-sects than with those of the northern ones.

All four of the earliest sect-lists mention a division within the Mahāsāṅghika sect which occurred sometime after the initial Mahāsāṅghika-Sthavira schism.[105] In the *Śāriputra-paripṛccā-sūtra,* the name of Mahādeva is referred in connection with the later schism which occurred amongst the Mahāsāṅghikas.[106] This evidence gains support from

---

[104]According to the listing given in Bareau's *(Les Sectes bouddhiques)* the doctrinal points are as follows:

(1) Thesis 32 of the Mahāsāṅghikas;

(2) Thesis 31 of the Mahāsāṅghikas;

(3) Thesis 43 of the Andhakas;

(4) Theses 27 and 30 of the Mahāsāṅghikas and thesis 7 of the Purvaśailas;

(5) Theses 27 and 30 of the Mahāsāṅghikas, as well as thesis 2 of the Bahuśrutiyas, 3 of the Cetiyas, 7 of the Aparaśailas and thesis 5 of the Haimavatas.

[105]The newly formed sub-group is called Cetiya in *Dipavaṁsa* (cited in A. Bareau, *Les Sectes bouddhiques,* p.16): Caitra in *'Śāriputraparipṛcchā-sūtra'* (ibid., p.17); Caitika in Bhavya's Saṃmitiya tradition (List 3) and *Vasumitra's Samayabhedoparacanacakra* (ibid., pp.17, 18).

[106]*Taisho,* 1465, p.900C, 6-12.

Bareau's'[107] statement that the oldest versions of Vasumitra's treatise do not name Mahādeva in connection with the first schism, but only in discussing the later schism of Caityaśaila. A duplication of Mahadeva's name occurs in the translation of Hiuen-tsang[108] who associates him with both schisms and in the work of *Bhavya*[109] where the first schism is said to be the result of the activities of a monk named Bhadra who preached the five doctrines. The second schism is caused by Mahadeva who again propounded the five theses and found the Caitya sect.

It seems that the name of Mahādeva and with him the five points were only later read back into the original schism by subsequent sources. As a result the later texts attribute the original schism of the Mahāsāṅghikas from the Sthaviras to the activities of Mahadeva when in fact he was involved only with the second. There are also strong doctrinal indications that the five points of Mahadeva originally were accepted only by the Southern/Caityaśaila schools and only later were considered to be doctrines of the northern Mahāsāṅghikas as well.[110]

Orthodoxy vs *Heresies: An Age of Critical Transition*

Sectarian divisions in the Buddhist *Saṅgha* did not stop short after the initial schism which occurred early or late in the fourth century BC. The following century witnessed the emergence of further sub-sects[111] within the *Saṅgha* which put forth doctrines which varied in meaning, significance and implications: It was an age when the forces of '*Orthodoxy*' were pitted against the rising tide of so called '*heresies*'. The term '*Orthodox*' *is* coined specifically for that section of

[107] A. Bareau, *Les Premiers Conciles bouddhiques,* p.98.

[108] *Taisho,* 2031, pp.15b, 1-4.

[109] A. Bareau, *'Trois traités sur les sectes boudhiques',* pp.172, 176.

[110] J. Nattier and C. Prebish, op. cit., pp.261, 264.

[111] See, *infra.*

monks who appropriated the title 'Theravādins'[112] in order to establish their claim as the spiritual descendants of the elders *(Therās)* and as the preservers of the purity of Buddhist tradition.[113] The *Dipavaṁsa*[114] compares the Theravāda with the great banyan tree while the term *'kaṇṭaka'* (thorns) is used for schools other than itself.

An attempt was made by the Theravādins in this age to make the *Sāsana* a fixed and immutable system and any dogma or doctrine which was found inconsistent with their

---

[112]The Ceylonese chronicles, *Mahāvaṁsa,* (V.1-2), and *Dipavaṁsa,* (V.16) inform us that the *Saṅgha* was called Theravāda before its division, because its tradition was first set up by Mahakassapa and other *mahātheras* when they recited the Buddha's teachings in the first council of Rajagṛha. *Contra.,* the Northern tradition as recorded by *Bhavya* (W.W. Rockhill, op. cit., p.184) defines the Sthaviravādins as 'those who teach that the Sthaviras belong to the body of the elect *'(Ariyas)'.* Bu-Ston (E. Obermiller, trans., *History of Buddhism,* p.100) says Sthaviras bore this name since they maintained to belong to spiritual descent of the Sthavira saints'. This term is not met with in the *Vinaya* accounts of the first and second Council. It is referred in the 'Ariyapariyesanasutta' of the *Majjhima Nikāya* but not in the sense of *Saṅgha.* The *Papañcasudanī* (II, p.171) defines the term Theravāda as *'Thirabhāvavādam'* implying a doctrine which is lasting and firm. It is, therefore, highly probable that this term might have been picked up from the *Nikāyas* and applied to the *Saṅgha* and later to their school as the Ceylonese chronicles testify.

[113]Preservation of the purity of Buddhist tradition in the *'Theravādin'* sense meant merely the literal interpretation or rather the insistence on the 'letter of the law'. Such a statement can be credited to the Mahāsāṅghikas also:

(a) who resisted the attempt of elderly monks bent on augmenting the *Vinaya.* See, *supra.*

(b) The testimony of Hiuen-Tsang, (T. Watters, op. cit., I, p.227; II, pp.136, 198, 248) who states that there existed groups of Mahāyānist monks who were of the Sthavira school, implying thereby that they were meticulous in the observance of *Vinaya* rules.

(c) By trying to read the *paramārtha* (real meaning) as distinguished from *Laukikārtha* (apparent meaning) of the scriptures, they preserved and enhanced the spirit of the *Dhamma.*

[114]*Dipavaṁsa,* v.52.

doctrinal stand was dubbed a 'heresy'.[115] This is clear from the account of third council as preserved in the Ceylonese chronicles and the *Aṭṭhakathas*.[116] The absence of its reference in Sanskrit Buddhist literature, Chinese as well as Tibetan sources suggests that it was purely sectarian in nature.[117]

The Ceylonese account runs as follows: Owing to the prosperity of the Order under Aśoka who was ruling at Pātaliputra, heretics had come to live with the monks at Aśokārāma. They held unorthodox views in matters of both doctrine as well as discipline. The result was that the most important *Uposatha* ceremony could not be held for seven years. The legend further relates how Aśoka deputed one of his ministers to persuade the monks at Aśokārāma to hold the *Uposatha*. On the monks' refusal to comply with the king's wishes, the minister beheaded them.

Aśoka was stunned at this news and approached Moggaliputta Tissa, the most learned monk of the time for solace. The latter consoled him on the ground that he had harboured no deliberate intention to have the monks beheaded. At his advice Aśoka tried to purge the *Saṅgha* of unorthodox monks. He arranged to get them examined batch by batch, inquiring from them as to what the teaching of the Buddha is. Excepting those monks who replied that the Buddha is a *Vibhajyavādī*, a fact corroborated by Tissa, all the others were expelled from the monastery.

---

[115]Mrs. Rhys Davids *(A Manual of Buddhism,* p.323), comes too near the truth when she states: 'For too long have the sympathies of writers on Buddhism (and readers of them) been all on the side of this specious partisanship, regarding all so-called "sects" other than the Therāvāda as mere heretical mushroom growths. The hour is now at hand for better vision and for discerning that it is in this Patna Analyst majority, exercising most mischievous mutilation on its best elements, that we ought to see the cancerous growth of changed and decadent values'.

[116]*Mahāvaṁsa,* v.228-81; *Samantapāsādikā*, I, pp.53f; *Kathāvatthu Aṭṭhakathā* (Nal. ed.), pp.7-10.

[117]G.C. Pande, *BDVI.,* p.195; N. Dutt, *EMB.*, II, p.265: D.R. Bhandarkar, *Aśoka,* p.85, H. Kern (op. cit., p.110) terms it as a party meeting of the Theravādas or Vibhajyavādins.

Tissa chose a thousand monks, learned, possessing the higher knowledge, knowing the three *Piṭakas,* versed in analysis, to form the council of the true doctrine. In the meeting of the council he compiled the *Kathāvatthu* for the refutation of heretical doctrines. This *Dhamma*-council held under the protection of King Aśoka in his seventeenth regnal year was completed by a thousand monks in nine months and was closed with a great *Pavāraṇā* ceremony.

The whole account is so much coloured with dogmatical and sectarian feelings that it requires a thorough reappraisal. The principal point is concerned with the *'heretics'* who held different views *(diṭṭhis).* N. Dutt takes them to be none others than the Mahāsāṅghikas and their offshoots.[118] As already pointed earlier, the Mahāsāṅghikas sticking to the 'Ancient Vinaya' may have differed on certain disciplinary rules added to the *Vinaya* by the Sthaviras.[119]

The non-observance of the *Uposatha* and the *Pavāraṇā* for seven years at Aśokārāma can be explained by the fact that *bhikkhus* of various sects initially did not reside in different *avāsās.* They could not as is understandable enough agree to perform the collective ceremonies in the same *āvāsa* because of their differences regarding the performance of *Vinaya* rules. According to the *Pātimokkha* code of every sect, all the members present, and the absentees by proxy, must declare that they had not, during the preceding fortnight, committed any breach of the rules embodied in the *Vinaya* code accepted by them.[120]

There was no supreme authority to say which rules were orthodox (in the sense of original) and which were not, with every group claiming to be the possessor of the original rules. The testimony of the *Nikāya-Saṅgraha,* a late Sinhalese work, also corroborates N. Dutt's view. It states that the monks who

---

[118]N. Dutt, *EMB.*, II, p.269.

[119]See, *supra.*

[120]W. Pachow, op. cit., pp.69-73.

were compelled to leave the *Saṅgha* of the *Theriya Nikāya* (Theravādins) became members of the non-Theravāda sects, particularly the Mahāsāṅghikas.[121] The Mahāsāṅghikas were by this time a powerful body with a large following. They probably left Magadha to make their seat in Andhra country.[122]

A.C. Banerjee on the other hand states that 'the monks other than the Theravādins had to leave Magadha, the principal seat of the Theravādins and went to Kashmir-Gandhara. They occupied a prominent place there and later on came to be known as Sarvāstivādins.'[123]

It is not altogether improbable that the Sarvāstivāda[124] seceded from the Sthaviravāda during the reign of Aśoka. The expulsion of monks for holding false views can be understood for this doctrine which implied a form of eternalism and which forms the first topic for debate in the *Kathāvatthu.*[125] As A.K. Warder puts it, 'We can merely point out that this was the period of the elaboration of the *Abhidhamma* as a comprehensive statement of the nature of the universe, of what exists as well as the causal processes which are the essence of Buddhist doctrine. Consequently a somewhat metaphysical disagreement could loom large in debates among Buddhist communities at the time. The schools were now going beyond the doctrines as stated by the Buddha and raising points not clearly covered, even by implications, in his dialogues and discourses.'[126]

The second point which needs elucidation is regarding king Aśoka who is represented in the Ceylonese chronicles as

---

[121]Quoted, N. Dutt, op. cit., II, p.268.

[122]Ibid., II, p.269.

[123]A.C. Banerjee, *Sarvāstivāda literature,* p.6.

[124]The peculiar doctrine of this school which gave it its name is that all dharmas exist in past, present and future. See, *Abhidharmakośa* (ed., Rahula Sankrityayana, Chap.V, 25). "*Tadastiv ādāt tesam (dharmānam) traikalye astitvam vadati.*"

[125]*Kathāvatthu* (trans.), XXI.I; See, Mrs. Rhys Davids, op. cit., p.319.

[126]A.K. Warder, op. cit., p.275.

an active and earnest adherent and patron of that school. D.R. Bhandarkar[127] has pointed out that Aśoka's intervention and subsequent purging of the *Saṅgha* is amply corroborated by certain edicts. His directives to *Mahāmātras* as contained in the Sāñchī.[128] Sārnāth[129] and Kauśāmbi[130] pillar inscriptions to quash all rifts in the *Saṅgha,* his recommendations in the Calcutta Bairāṭ edict[131] of certain texts for special study of monks, the declaration that the *Saṅgha* was made one[132] and that he wanted concord in the Buddhist church clearly show his concern and active interference in matters of the Buddhist *Saṅgha.*

In Aśoka's schism edicts there is no reference to the council.[133] 'This ex-silentio evidence' observes S. Dutt, 'is more weighty than the motived assertions of the monk makers of the Aśokan legends. That all those who did not subscribe to *Vibhajjavāda,* the orthodox method, employed by monks for explication of the doctrines of the scripture—should be unfrocked—an order so flagrantly partisan would be least likely to issue from the promulgator of the non-doctrinal non-monkish Dhamma of the edicts.'[134]

H. Bechart,[135] who approached the schism edicts from the point of view of *Vinaya* terminology, has shown that the king,

---

[127]D.R. Bhandarkar, op. cit., p.83.

[128]Hultzsch, *CII.*, I, pp.160f. *(Ye saṁghaṁ bhākhati bhikkhu vā bhikkhuni vā odātāni dusāni sanaṁdhāpayitu anāvāsasi vāsāpetaviye).*

[129]Ibid., pp.16lff.

[130]Ibid., p.159.

[131]Ibid., pp.172ff.

[132]The phrase *'Saṅghe samage kaṭe'* (the *Saṅgha* is made whole and entire) occurs in the Sāñchī and Kauśāmbi pillar inscriptions.

[133]G.C. Pande *(BDVI.,* p.197) however, maintains that a council of Buddhist *bhikkhus* was held in the time of Aśoka is hinted at in the Bhābru edict. To this council, he argues, might have come many *bhikkhus* who did not belong to his empire, and here lies the reason why Aśoka, addressing the council refers to himself as '*Lājā Magadhe*', i.e. king of Magadha.

[134]S. Dutt, *BFAC.,* p.157.

[135] H. Bechert, Aśokas 'Schismenedikt' und der Begriff Saṅghabheda, *WZKSO.,* Vol.V, 1961, pp.18-52, quoted Gustav Roth, op. cit., Intd., p.IX.

in these inscriptions expresses his concern about the completeness of the local *Saṅghas* for the sake of their ability to function properly and to perform a formal act of *Vinaya,* especially that of the observance *(Uposatha).* Therefore: *Saṅghe samagge kaṭe.* It is to be pointed out that a particular *Saṅgha* can only enact proceedings of the *Vinaya* in a complete chapter. The three inscriptions do not indicate that King Aśoka tried to reach decisions in favour of certain dogmatic view-points. As a Buddhist ruler, he only insisted that law and order should be observed in the *Saṅgha* according to its established disciplinary rules.

As S. Dutt[136] puts it, 'the Saṅgha-bhedaka edict was in discharge of his constitutional duty[137] as a ruler to prevent disruption of a recognized 'association'—the Saṅgha of Buddhist monks.' The *Saṅgha* as coming under the jurisdiction of the *Dhamma-Mahāmātra* is mentioned in the Delhi Topra Pillar Edict VII.[138] Aśoka's promulgation of the schism edicts was strictly in accordance with the old *Vinaya* rule that 'a schism monger, if he has not been ordained, should not be ordained, if ordained, is to be expelled'.[139]

The last point is regarding the compilation[140] of the *Kathāvatthu,* one of the seven books of the *Abhidhamma*

---

[136]S. Dutt, *BMMI.,* p.114.

[137]The *Vinaya* of the Buddhist monks had also a constitutional aspect called '*Samaya*' or 'conventional law'. The *Smṛti* writers enjoin upon the king to protect the *Samaya* of sects, guilds, classes, corporations, armies, association, etc. See, *Nārada Smṛti,* X.1-2, The *Bhikkhu Saṅgha* of the Buddhists is expressly mentioned as a type of corporation the 'conventional law' of which is within a king's proper function to maintain. See, Medhātithi's comment on *Manu.* VIII.219 —*Ekadharmānugatānāṁ nānādesavāsināṁ nānājātiyānāmapi samuhah: yatha bhikṣuṇāṁ saṁgho, vaṇijām saṁghascaturvidyānaṁ saṁgha iti'.*

[138]R.B. Pandey, *Historical and literary inscriptions,* p.36; Hultzsch, *CII.,* I, pp.130ff.

[139]*Mahāvagga* (pp.60, 67, 69)—*Saṅghabhedako bhikkhave anupasaṁpano na upasaṁpādetabbo upasaṁpanno nāsetabbo ti.* See, *Theragathā* verse 973: *odātakaṃ arahati kāsāvam kiṃ karissati*; Ibid., verse 975: *Titthiyānaṃ dhajaṃ, kechi dhāressanty avadātakaṃ.*

[140]S.N. Dube, 'The date of Kathāvatthu', *East and West,* Vol.22, Nos.1-2, March-June 1972, pp.79-86.

collection by Moggaliputta Tissa. The main purpose of the text seems to have been the regulation of those doctrines and dogmas which had developed with regard to the Buddha and the Buddhist way and which were inconsistent with Theravāda. S. Dutt remarks, 'A polemical work of this character, the object of which was the regulation of heresies, would scarcely have been conceived or commenced unless (1) heterodoxies had gathered strength (2) there was danger of the true Theravāda being swamped by them and (3) there was an urge to preserve and stabilize its orthodox standpoint in the religion.'[141]

All the evidence adduced, if not wholly satisfactory, is sufficient to prove, not that the pretension of the *Vibhajjavādins* to claim themselves as the real and original orthodox sect was unfounded, but that it was disputable and that, consequently, it was in the interest of the sect to back their claim by refuting the doctrines of the other sects and pronouncing them as *'heretical'*.

The Traditional Eighteen

There are two independent traditions about the secession of sects (*Nikāyas*), one preserved in the Ceylonese chronicles and the *Kathāvathu Aṭṭhakathā* and the other in the treatises of *Vasumitra, Bhavya* and *Vinītadeva.* According to the *Mahāvaṁsa*[142] the divisions were as follows:

From the Mahāsāṅghikas arose the Gokulikas and the Ekabbohārikas; the former of these two gave rise to the Paññattivādins[143] and Bāhulikas or the Bahussutikas out of whom sprang the Cetiyavādins, apparently all these schools coming into being in the second century after the *parinirvāṇa.* In the same century there arose in the Theravāda the school of

---

[141]S. Dutt, *BFAC.,* p.217.

[142]*Mahāvaṁsa,* v.5ff.

[143]E.J. Thomas (op. cit., p.289, fn.2), referring to the Prajñaptivādins states that 'it is a complete anachronism to place its origin as early as the 2nd century after Buddha's death'.

the Mahiṁsāskas and the Vajjiputtakas, the latter giving rise to four branches, Dhammuttariyas, Bhadrayānikas, Channāgarikas and Sammitiyas.

From the Mahiṁsāskas there arose the Sabbatthivādins and the Dhammaguttikas. The former school gave birth to the Kassapikas and these in turn gave rise to the Sankantikas, from whom divided off the Suttavādins. The *Mahāvaṁsa*[144] tells us that besides these schools there were six later ones that arose in India and two in Ceylon: the Hemavatas, Rajagiriyas, Siddhatthakas, Pubbaseliyas, Aparaseliyas and the Vajiriyas.[145] These six separated in Jambudīpa, the Dhammarucī and the Sāgaliyā separated in Ceylon.

Contradictory statements occur in the *Kathāvatthu* regarding the Vajjiputtakas. The Vajjiputtakas are acknowledged as the arch-disturbers of *Saṅgha* concord, a century after the founder's death.[146] Mrs. Rhys Davids is of the view that they amalgamated, after that, with the stronger growth of dissentients called Mahāsāṅghikas. In continuation to this it is further remarked, 'In the second century only two schools seceded from the Theravāda (a) The Mahiśasakas and (b) the Vajjiputtakas.'[147] But while illustrating the secessions according to the commentary on the *Kathāvatthu,* she makes the Vajjiputtakas the first secession with the Mahāsāṅghikas leading nowhere.[148] Even when judged from the introduction to the second debate, they are still considered a distinct group, siding with the Mahāsāṅghikas and two other schools in holding a certain view.[149]

The Sarvāstivādin tradition as preserved in the *Samayabhedoparacanacakra* of Vasumitra[150] states that the Mahā-

---

[144]*Mahāvaṁsa,* v.12-13.

[145]See, *Kathāvatthu-Aṭṭhakathā,* p.7.

[146]*Kathāvatthu* (trans.), Commentator's Introduction, p.3.

[147]Ibid.

[148]Ibid., Facing page xxix.

[149]Ibid., 1.2. Here the term is Vajjiputtiyas.

[150]J. Masuda, op. cit., pp.15-17; See, E.J. Thomas, op. cit., Appendix II. pp.290-91; *Kathāvatthu* (trans.), p.xxxvi.

sāṅghikas were divided into Ekavyavahārikas, the Lokottarvādins and Kukkuṭikas. Later on the Bahuśrutiyas issued out of the Mahāsāṅghikas and, still later, the Prajñaptivādins out of the latter. Towards the close of the second century arose the schools of Caitikas, Aparaśaila and Uttaraśaila.

Sthaviravāda divided itself into Sarvāstivāda or Hetuvāda and Mulasthaviravāda which changed its name into the Haimavata school. Subsequently, the Vatsīputriyas arose from Sarvāstivāda and themselves gave rise to the Dharmottariyas, the Bhadrayāniyas, the Sammatīyas and the Channagarika or Ṣaṇṇagarika.

Immediately afterwards the Mahiśāsakas arose from the Sarvāstivādins,[151] then the Dharmaguptas out of the Mahiśāsakas, and at the end of the third century, the Kaśyapiyas or the Suvarṣakas out of the Sarvāstivādins. Finally, at the beginning of the fourth century, the Sautrāntikas or the Sankrāntivādins arose out of the Sarvāstivādins. With this account agrees fairly well that of *Bhavya,*[152] preserved in a Tibetan version. The Kukkulikas disappear from the Mahāsāṅghika list, and the Channāgarikas from that of the Sthaviravāda, but in the latter the Mahiśāsakas reappear and the Hetuvidyas and the Vibhajyavadins appear as distinct, thus bringing up the number to the orthodox eighteen. Though there is substantial agreement of *Bhavya* with *Vasumitra,* he is less concerned to locate the secessions in successive centuries. He simply starts with one great schism in 'Dharmāśokas' reign, 160 years after the *parinibbāna,* and states that after that, all the remaining sixteen secessions took place gradually.

The *Mahāvyutpatti* lists arrange the school in four groups: The Sarvāstivādas, the Sammatīyas, the Mahāsāṅghikas and

[151]in the *Kathāvatthu Aṭṭhakathā* (pp.5, 6) the order is reversed. This contradiction is explained by the fact that there were two Mahiśāsaka schools, an earlier one agreeing more with the Theravādins and a later one agreeing more with the Sarvāstivādins. See, N. Dutt, *EMB.*, II, pp.111-12.

[152]W.W. Rockhill, op. cit., pp.181f. For secessions according to Bhavya. See chart in *Kathāvatthu* (trans.), p.xxxvi.

the Sthaviras. From the first emerged the Mūlasarvāstivādas, Kāśyapiyas, Mahiśāsakas, Dharmaguptas, Bahuśrutiyas, Tāmraśāṭiyas, Vibhajyavādins. The second broke up into Kaurukullakas, Āvantakas and Vātsīputriyas. The third was split into Pūrvaśailas, Aparaśailas, Haimavatas, Lokottaravādins and Prajñaptivādins. The fourth gave rise to the Mahāvihāravāsins, Jetavanīyas, Abhayagirivāsins.[153] This list appears to be of a later date. We do not find any reference of the Ekavyavahārika, Gokulika, Dharmottariya and Bhadrayānika. Probably they were extinct by this time. The Jetavaniyas can be identified with Sāgalika[154] of the *Mahāvaṁsa* and the Abhayagirivasins with the Dhammarucikas.[155] The Jetavanīyas came into existence as late as the reign of Mahāsena (5th century AD).

Tāranātha however reconciles many differences by identifying the Kāśyapiyas with Suvarṣakas, the Saṅkrāntivādin with Uttarīya and Tamraśāṭiya, the Caityaka with Pūrvaśaila and Lokottaravāda with Kaukkuṭika. He takes Ekavyavahārika as a general name for the Mahāsāṅghikas and the Kaurukullaka, Vatsiputriya, Dharmottariya, Bhadrayāniya and Channagarika as doctrinally very similar.[156]

Literary evidence is partially substantiated by the eyewitness accounts of Chinese pilgrims who visited India. Fahien surprisingly takes no notice of the sectarian development of Buddlhsm. Hsüang-tsang however, took special note of the three major sects, viz., the Sammitiya, the Sarvāstivāda and the Mahāsāṅghika. He states that the monks at Uddiyana were familiar with the Sarvāstivādins, Dharmaguptas, Mahiśasakas, Kaśyapias and the Mahāsāṅghikas.[157] The term Lokottara-

[153]See, E.J. Thomas, op. cit., p.38. This list is in complete agreement with Vinitadeva's list. See, N. Dutt, *BSI.*, p.49.

[154]See, Walpola Rahula, *History of Buddhism in Ceylon,* pp.195, 303; W. Adikaram, *Early History of Buddhism in Ceylon.* pp.80, 90ff.

[155]Ibid., p.303; Ibid., pp.90ff.

[156]Tāranātha, *History of Buddhism in India,* p.341 See, N. Dutt, *EMB.*, II, p. 49.

[157]S. Beal, *BRWW.*, Vol.II, p.167.

vādins occurs in his description of Bamiyan[158] while the general term Mahāsāṅghikas are referred in connection with Kashmir.[159] Hsüang-tsang found the monks of the Sammitiya school residing in Śravasti, Kapilavastu, Benaras, Vaiśāli and parts of western India.[160] He also takes note of the convent called Purvasila and the Avarasila in the city of Dhanakataka (identified with Amaravati).[161]

I-tsing admits four principal groups: (a) Mahāsāṅghika (with seven subdivisions), (b) Sthavira (with three sub-divisions), (c) Sarvāstivāda (with Mūlasarvāstivāda, Dharmagupta, Mahiśāsaka and Kāśyapiya as sub-division, and (d) Saṃmitiya (with four sub-divisions). Here too, eighteen is given as the sum-total of the schools.[162] He speaks of the geographical distribution of Buddhist sects towards the end of the seventh century AD in a very general manner. At that time the Sarvāstivādins prevailed in Magadha, the Saṃmitiyas in northwest India, the Sarvāstivādins in the north and the Sthaviras in the south. In the east the four great groups (Sthaviras, Saṃmitiya, Sarvāstivāda and the Mahāsāṅghikas) existed as mixed with each other.[163]

Early sects and the rise of Mahāyāna

The bifurcation of Buddhism into Hīnayāna and Mahāyāna dates later than the division of the Sthaviras and the Mahāsāṅghikas into different sub sects and schools. The original insight of the Master was subsequently elaborated by his disciples in various schools, each claiming to base their system on the actual teachings of the Buddha. Sharing the basic truth, they presented their doctrines with different emphasis and

[158]Ibid., Vol.I, p.114.
[159]Ibid., Vol.II, p.199.
[160]Ibid., Vol.III, pp.259, 269, 291, 308; Vol.IV, p.458.
[161]Ibid., pp.423-24.
[162]J. Takakusu, op. cit., pp.xxiii-xxiv.
[163]Ibid., pp.8-9.

from different standpoints paving the way for the emergence of Mahāyāna.[164]

Recognizing Buddha's perfection, the Theravādins admitted and stressed his humanity. For them he was a man possessed of a physical body (*Rūpakāya*).[165] There is just one unconditioned state (*asaṃskṛta dharma*), *nirvāṇa*. All other things in the world *of Saṃsāra* are conditioned *(Saṃskṛta).*[166] The past and the future *dharmas* do not exist. They recognized only one *bodhisattva*—Gautama Buddha[167]—and considered all *arhats* to be perfect.[168]

Next came the Sarvāstivādins who derived their name from the Sanskrit phase '*Sarvam asti*'. The 75 *dharmas,* recognized as ultimate by their school, had a permanent existence throughout the three periods of time. They held that the past is made manifest in the present and the future is latent in the present through the transmission of *dharmas.*[169] As regards the nature of Buddha, they affirmed his form body (*Rūpakāya*) but at the same time the Sarvāstivādin *ācāryas* gave a metaphysical twist to the concept of Buddhahood, one which was carried to its radical conclusion by the Mahāyānists.[170]

The Sarvāstivādins emphasized the practice of the six *pāramitās* or perfections—*dāna, śila, kṣānti, virya, samādhi and prajñā.*[171] This doctrine of the *pāramitās* became one of

---

[164]The Mahāyāna grew out of the Original Buddhism and it traced its final authority to Buddha himself. See, *ERE.,* Vol.VIII, p.33. For tradition of a second *Dharmacakrapravartana* at Gṛdhrakūṭa mount. See, S. Beal, BRWW., pp.371-72; *Saddharmapuṇḍarīka* (BST.), p.50.

[165]N. Dutt, *EMB.*, II, p.204.

[166]G.C. Pande, *BDVI.*, p.253.

[167]N. Dutt, op. cit., II, p.84.

[168]A.K. Warder, op. cit., pp.295, 356; S.N. Dube, *Cross Currents in Early Buddhism,* p.91.

[169]G.C. Pande, loc. cit., p.279: J. Takakusu, *Essentials of Buddhist Philosophy,* pp.63, 122; A.K. Warder, op. cit., p.274.

[170]G.C. Pande, loc. cit., p.344.

[171]*Lalitavistara* (BST.), p.247.

the primary tenets of the Mahāyānists.[172] Regarding the *Arhat*, the Sarvāstivādins affirmed like the Mahāsāṅghikas that they could regress and were bound to their past *karmas*[173] This was not the case with the *srota-āpannaka* (stream winner) who could not fall back.

The Sarvāstivādins had to withstand the criticism raised by other sects who denounced their eternalism and pointed out that they failed to make room for change or becoming. All those who dissented from the Sarvāstivādins emphasized the meaningfulness of subjectivity and the organic unity of personality. The Vātsīputrīyas, the Sāmmitiyas and the Sautrantikas maintained the actuality of becoming, change and maintained the meaningfulness of the sense of self. In contrast with the Sarvāstivādins they interpreted becoming as the arising and perishing of events essentially related in and through a common ground which persisted while the particular events arose and perished. As the Sāmmitiyas put it: 'Momentary extinction is not (a total) an extinction. It is a proceeding from moment to moment.'[174]

The *Pudgalavādins* asserted that there is something permanent in the cycle of rebirths, namely the 'person' (*puggala*). The person is neither identical with the 5 *skandhas* nor different from them. The *skandhas*, constituting the phenomenal person, are mere designations, not real substances.[175] The *pudgalavādins*, denying that either *dharmas* (elements) or persons are real things, affirmed that both exist as designations, that is, as objects of commonsense knowledge and statements. It was also the position that Mahāyānists later took.

Like the Theravādins, the Sautrāntikas held that the conditioned *dharmas* exist only as long as they are effective

---

[172]*Infra*.

[173]G.C. Pande, op. cit., pp.280, 282; N. Dutt, *BSI.*, p.153.

[174]V. Raman, 'Sāmmitiya Nikaya Śastra', *Visvabharati Annals,* Vol.V, 1953, p.187.

[175]G.C. Pande, loc. cit., p.298; N. Dutt, *BSI.*, pp.183, 185; E.J. Thomas, op. cit., p.39; A.K. Warder, op. cit., pp.241-42.

but behind the chain of *dharmas* they assumed a substratum (*āśraya*)—a consciousness acting as a continuum (*santāna, santati*). This consciousness formed a rail for the five groups. According to the Sautrāntikas these five groups continue to exist after death in subtle form and move over along the rail of consciousness to the next birth. By developing the idea of a static consciousness the Sautrāntikas supplied the central concept for the monistic idealism of the Yogācāra system.[176]

The Mahāsāṅghikas, speculating on the nature of Buddha, held him to be supramundane and possessing all perfections. This speculation set the stage for the later development of the Mahāyāna expressed first in the *Prajñāpāramitā sūtras.*[177] The special doctrine of the Bahuśrutiyas was that Buddha had a 'transcendent' teaching which directly led one to freedom from defilements. They held that Buddha's teachings relating to *anātman, anityatā, dukkha, nirvāṇa* and *śūnya* were *lokottara* while his other teachings were *laukika.*[178]

The characteristic doctrine of the prajñaptivādins was the distinction of real (*tattva*) phenomena or entities referred to in the Buddha's teaching from mere concepts (*prajñapti*). Thus the 12 spheres (*āyatana*), i.e. 6 senses and their 6 corresponding objects are not 'real' but 'conceptual', similarly the 18 'elements' (*dhatus*). On the other hand the 5 groups (*skandhas*) are real, so is misery.[179] It is in the Ekavyavahārikas that one finds the full developed doctrine of the non-substantiality of elements. They maintained that all things, mundane as well as transmundane, the self as well as the elements are only derived names and devoid of substantiality.[180]

---

[176]See, E. Conze, *Buddhist Thought in India,* pp.132-34; David J. Kalupahana, *Buddhist Philosophy, A Historical Analysis,* p.142; A.K. Warder, op. cit., p.422.

[177]The Mahāsāṅghikas, Ekavyavahārikas, Lokottaravādins and the Vetullyakas elevated the status of the *bodhisattva* also. See, *infra.*

[178]The first three (non-soul, impermanence, misery) are common to Buddhism along with *nirvaṇa* as a way out of them. The inclusion of the last (emptiness) implies a special stress by the Bahuśrutiyas presumably anticipating the Mahāyāna. See, G.C. Pande, *BDVI.,* p.291; N. Dutt, *BSI.,* p.117.

[179]See, E.J. Thomas, op. cit., p.289; G.C. Pande, loc. cit., p.292.

[180]See, J. Takakusu, op. cit., pp.122-23; G.C. Pande, loc. cit., p.290.

The Lokottaravādins maintained that only transcendent phenomena were real; worldly phenomena being mere concepts resulted from error (delusion).[181]

The best known doctrine of the lokottaravādins was the distinction between the conventional selfhood of the Buddha and the transcendental essence of Buddhahood.[182] The Kaukkuṭikas maintained that only *Abhidhamma* (enquiry into the ultimate nature of everything) is the true, essential teaching of the Buddha, while both the *Vinaya* and *Sūtra* are expedients.[183]

Thus it is among the Mahāsāṅghikas that one finds the emphasis on the distirction between the conventional and the transcendental as well as the emphasis on the transcendental as the real, the substantial, the eternal.

With regard to the ultimate nature of the individual, the Mahāsāṅghikas held the view that *vijñāna* or *citta*, the selfconscious principle is in its very nature pure. It becomes impure by the advent of impurities *(kilesas)* and *āgantuka-rajas* (adventitious defilements).[184] In this view of the ultimate nature of the self they were virtually one with the Sāmmitiyas and the Sautrāntikas.[185]

Making the *Arhat* liable to regressions the Mahāsāṅghikas offered a new ideal—that of the *bodhisattva*—whose path and goal were systematized by the Mahāyāna. In the Theravādin doctrine there was only one *bodhisattva*—Siddhārtha Gautama. The Mahāsāṅghikas however pointed out that the final goal was open to all—monk and laity alike. The stages of a *bodhisattva's* path, though only outlined in the *Mahāvastu* and not fully coinciding with the ten Mahāyānic stages, do represent a fundamental point from where the Mahāyāna

---

[181]See, J. Takakusu, op. cit., p.122; G.C. Pande, op. cit., p.290.

[182]E.J. Thomas, op. cit., pp.173-74.

[183]See G.C. Pande, loc. cit., p.291; N. Dutt, *BSI.*, p.69; A.K. Warder, op. cit., p.242, fn.1.

[184]N. Dutt, op. cit., p.91.

[185]This view of the Mahāsāṅghikas may be considered the precursor of the idealistic philosophy of Yogācāra, in which the *ālayavijñāna* is the storehouse of pure consciousness which becomes impure only when it is polluted by worldly objects. See, *supra*.

developed its mature *bodhisattva* doctrine emphasizing that all creatures may strive for and attain the complete perfect enlightenment.

Thus the various sects and subsects working together by common criticism at different centres provided much of the soil from which the Mahāyāna emerged.

The Mahāyānic Phase

The period between 100 BC to AD 100 witnessed a significant movement within Buddhism that called itself the Mahāyāna, the 'Great Vehicle',[186] in contrast to the *Hīnayāna,* the 'inferior vehicle'. The ideas and doctrines supplied by various Buddhist sects became typical of the great course.[187] The Mahāyānic innovation was to proclaim that the *bodhisattva*-path is open to monk and laity alike, to chalk out a way for aspiring *bodhisattvas* to follow and to create a new pantheon and cult of superhuman *bodhisattvas* and cosmic Buddhas who respond to the pleas and supplications of devotees.[188]

Regarding the geographic context in which Mahāyāna emerged, it can be safely asserted that it arose in areas where the Mahāsāṅghikas were strong.[189] The *Aṣṭasāhasrikā prajñāpāramitā* informs us that the *prajñāpāramitā* would originate in the south (*Dakṣiṇāpatha*), pass to eastern countries (*Vartanyām*) and prosper in the north.[190] G.C. Pande[191] opines that Mahāyāna arose among the Purvaśailas and the Vetullyaka branches of the Andhra Mahāsāṅghikas in the 1st century BC. Most of the Mahāyāna masters also belonged to the south. From Andhra, Mahāyāna travelled to Magadha

---

[186]'The key to understanding Mahāyāna,' states Charles Prebish (*Buddhism, a Modern Perspective,* p.72) 'is finding that particular emphasis which is given in the teaching, for it is this which may make it peculiarly Mahāyāna.'

[187]*Supra.*

[188]*Infra.*

[189]N. Dutt, op. cit., pp.256-58.

[190]*Aṣṭasāhasrikā Prajñāpāramitā* (trans.), pp.79-80.

[191]G.C. Pande, op. cit., p.321.

which was an ancient centre of the Mahāsāṅghikas.[192] From Magadha it traversed the ancient trade route towards north. Uddiyana and Bamiyan in the north were well known centres of Lokottaravādins.[193]

The New Mahāyānic Ideal

Change took place in the notion of the ideal man in Mahāyāna Buddhism. In deprecation of the old *Arhat* ideal, a new ideal—that of the *bodhisattva*—was put forth by the Mahāsāṅghikas, the Lokottaravādins, and the Vetulyakas.[194] The Sarvāstivādins also upheld the existence of numerous Buddhas and *bodhisattvas*. For the strictly orthodox Theravādins there were no *bodhisattvas* as a class of beings as envisaged in the developed Mahāyāna school.[195]

No longer was this term reserved for the past lives of the Buddha Śakyamuni. It referred to a way of life, a career that was open to all his followers. Hardayal makes an important observation concerning the origin of the *bodhisattva* doctrine. 'The doctrine was promulgated by some Buddhist leaders as a protest against this lack of true spiritual fervour and altruism among the monks of that period—the bodhisattva ideal was taught in order to counteract this tendency to a cloistered placid, inert monastic life.' [196]

The *bodhisattva* ideal was neither 'promulgated' nor 'taught'. It can be understood as a natural development within Buddhism. Every religion has its practical and social side without which it will lose its reason of existence. The Mahāyānist monks, while attempting to unfold the religio-philosophical teachings of the Buddha, gave creater attention to the life of the laity.

This entailed the conception of the *bodhisattva*—the ideal man who could sacrifice his interests or atone for the evil

[192]N. Dutt, op. cit., p.61.
[193]Ibid., p.62.
[194]*Supra.*
[195]S.N. Dube, op. cit., p.162.
[196]Hardayal, *The Bodhisattiva Doctrine,* p.3.

deeds of others by his good deeds and thereby promote universal goodness. This also led to the mitigation of the rigour of the earlier notion of the doctrine of *karman,* which was completely individualistic and the conception of the transfer of merit *(pariṇāmanā)* was evolved. But the point is what actuated the ideal man *(bodhisattva)* whether a monk or a layman to such an altruistic service? Social sympathy and altruistic service, an innovation of the Mahāyānist monks through the *bodhisattva* ideal, was itself an *upāya-kauśalya,* a means towards salvation of all *(sarva-mukti).*

The laity was asked to accrue merit *(puṇya)* through faith, devotion and worship ensuring happiness on earth and in heavens while the *bodhisattva* trudged along on the path to final achievement of *bodhi.*

The *bodhisattva's* superiority to the *arhat* is clear from the fact that the former chose to remain in *saṃsāra* for the sake of helping all sentient beings achieve enlightenment. This attitude was directed by compassion *(karuṇā),* the wish without self-interest, to make others happy. He sacrificed his bodily, material and *karmic* possessions if by so doing he could bring a being closer to liberation.[197] Glimpses of Mahāyānic doctrine of universal compassion are conveyed through literature of the various sects.[198] The *bodhisattva* took the vow that 'I shall not enter into final *Nirvāṇa* before all beings have been liberated.'[199] The idea of a *bodhisattva's* renunciation of personal *nirvāṇa* is stated clearly in the

---

[197]*Bodhicaryāvatāra* (BST.), Chap.III, vv.6-23; *Śikṣāsamuccaya* (ed.), Karika 4, p.xl.

[198]*The Jātakamālā* (BST., pp.1-6) relates in the Vijāghrijātaka how the *bodhisattva* sees a hungry tigress about to devour its young and sacrifices himself to be her nourishment; The *Divyāvadāna* (BST., pp.307-13) relates the story of a lady who offered her flesh to a poor woman about to devour her newly born child; The *Avadānaśataka* (BST., pp.84-85) relates the story of King Śibi who through extreme compassion attained perfect enlightenment.

[199]A similar vow occurs in *The Large Sutra on Perfect Wisdom* (trans., E. Conze, p.168)—'for the sake of the weal of every single being will I roast in the hells for aeons countless as the sands of the Ganges, until that being has been established in the Buddha cognition.' See, also, D.T. Suzuki, *Studies in the Laṅkāvatara Sutra,* pp.205, 220.

Bodhisattvabhūmi[200] and *bodhi* is set up as the new ideal in the *Saddharma-puṇḍarīka.*[201] The *Prajñāpāramitā* texts stress that the *bodhisattva* has to control his compassion by wisdom *(prajñā).*[202] Compassion regulates his relationship with beings, wisdom that with the Absolute.

The foregoing analysis clearly shows that the *bodhisattva's* supreme aim was happiness and welfare of all sentient beings thereby leading them to supreme enlightenment. The impact of such a viable aim is visible on the laity who made meritorious gifts to the *Saṅgha*—(a) 'For the continuance in welfare and happiness of mother, father and all people and living things,'[203] (b) 'Attainment of supreme enlightenment by her father, mother and by the whole sentient world.'[204]

The Bodhisattva Path

The journey of spiritual progress begins with arousing the thought for supreme perfect enlightenment *(bodhicittotpāda)* and practising the six (later ten) perfections *(pāramitās)* synchronizing with the ten stages *(bhūmis)* until the goal was reached. Faith worship, prayer, confession of sins and other practices of piety and devotion lead to *cittotpāda.*[205] Faith was an integral part of the religion since its inception.[206] Along

---

[200] *Bodhisattvabhūmi* (ed.), Bk.1, Chap.III *(Svaparārthapaṭala).*

[201] *Saddharma Puṇḍarīka* (SBE.), pp.29, 97.

[202] *The Large Sutra on Perfect Wisdom,* pp.77-79.

[203] The verse *'matāpituna Piyasavasatāna hita Sugasṭhataya…'; 'Savalokahitasukhave'* occurs in many donatory inscriptions. See, Jas Burgess and Indraji, ICTWI., Ins. No.20 (Kārle), Ins. No.3 (Ajantā), No.4 (Junnar), painted inscription, No.15 (Ajantā); *Lüders list,* Nos.5, 43, 952, 1046, 1148, 1207.

[204] Jas Burgess and Indraji, loc. cit., Ins. Nos.7, 8, 10 (Mhār and Kuḍa), Nos.5, 7, 9 (Ajantā), painted inscription, Nos.25, 30 (Ajantā). The salvation of the world must be our thought when making votive offerings and at other times is also stressed in the *Śikṣāsamuccaya* (ed.), pp.348-50.

[205] *Bodhicaryāvatāra* (BST.), Chap.II.

[206] *The Tri-ratna* formula is one such example. The faith of the laity in the three jewels which produces rebirth in heavenly mansions is related through the stories of the *Vimānavatthu* (SBB., pp.31, 34). Similarly the Sarvāstivādin text *Lalitavistara* (BST., p.65) states, 'To all who believe in me I do good. Like friends are they to me who seek refuge in me. And many a friend the Tathāgata has. And to those friends the Tathāgata only speaks the truth, not falsehood … To believe Ananda should be thy endeavour. This I commend unto you.'

with the Buddha, the *Dharma* and the *Saṅgha* which constituted the Buddhist trinity, the Mahāyānists added the group *of bodhisattvas* as an object of faith and refuge.[207] It was believed that faith produces *karmic* merit (*puṇya*) and is also the means to invoke the compassion and help of the Buddhas and *bodhisattvas.*[208] According to the Mahāyānic ideology of faith even ungrateful and unjust persons become bestowers of good if they are dedicated to the Buddha's spiritual person.[209]

Devotion and worship was another medium for the acquisition of merit.[210] This could be done by erecting *stūpas,* worshipping relics, making images, offering incense and flowers.[211] The Mahāyānists simplified this further by adding that the mere utterance of the Lord's name[212] or the preservation, recitation and honouring of the *sūtras* led to the increase of one's merit .[213]

Regarding the 10 stages of the *bodhisaittva's* career, the Mahāsāṅghikas worked out a primitive and rather unsystematic scheme in the *Mahāvastu.* Taking the Buddha Śakyamuni

---

[207]*Bodhicaryāvatāra* (BST.), Chap.II, v.26, 49.

[208]*Infra.*

[209]'... and even an ungrateful and unjust person dedicated to his (Buddha's) virtuous person, becomes the bestower of good.' See, Burgess and Indraji, ICTWI., Ghatotkacha inscription, p.80.

[210]*Mahāvastu*, Vol.II, pp.328f; Śāntideva in his *Śikṣāsamuccaya* (ed., pp.297ff) quotes *sūtra* passages which regard ritual practice as instrumental to better rebirth; See, *Bodhicaryāvatāra* (BST.), Chap.II, vv.1-27.

[211]'... Even the gift of a flower is the cause of fruit called heaven and final beatitude.' See, Burgess and Indraji, ICTWI., Ins. No.6 (Ajantā), p.78.

[212]Buddhahood was assured to those who worshipped the relics of the Buddha or erected thereon *stūpas* of any material, be it of jewel or sand, or made images of Buddha with any metal or even clay, or drew sketches of the figure of Buddha on paper, wall, etc., or even offered flowers or played musical instruments or sang songs in adoration of Buddha's images or just uttered the words 'Homage be to Buddha' even with a distracted mind. See, *Saddharmapuṇḍarīka* (SBE.), pp.50-52.

[213]*The Large Sutra on Perfect Wisdom* (pp.256-57);*The Diamond Sutra* (pp.50, 67) states that if the devotee recites one stanza of four lines and demonstrates and illuminates it to others, then he would be on the strength of that beget immeasurable and incalculable merit.

as a type the ten *bhumis* are explained.[214] The description of the ten *bhumis* in a more developed form appears in the *Prajñāpāramitas*.[215] The fullest Mahāyāna statement of the *bodhisattva's* stages occurs in the *Daśabhūmika sūtra* (which allots one *pāramitā* for each stage)[216] the *Bodhisattvabhūmi* and the *Madhyamakavatāra*.[217]

An analysis of the *bodhisattva's* path shows that an attempt was made to make the *Saṅgha* all inclusive.[218] Glimpses of the subconscious psychology of the monks is revealed through the injunction which made merit of a charitable deed *(dāna)* dependent on the spiritual status of the recipient.[219] It is therefore not surprising that the usual

---

[214]The stages are—(l) *Durārohā* (hard to reach), (2) *Baddhamānā* (bound) (3) *Pushpamaṇḍita* (adorned with flowers), (4) *Rucirā* (beautiful). (5) *Cittavistarā* (of varied experience), (6) *Rūpavati* (of fair form), (7) *Durjayā* (Hard to conquer), (8) *Janmanideśa* (discussion of birth), (9) *Yauvarajya* (viceroyship), (10) *Abhisheka* (consecration as king). See, *Mahāvastu.* I, pp.53-124; G.C. Pande, *BDVI.*, p.359.

[215]*The Large Sutra on Perfect Wisdom,* pp.163ff.

[216]To the earlier six *pāramitās (dāna, śila, kṣānti virya, dhyāna* and *prajñā)* were added four more *(upāya kausalya. praṇidhāna, bala, jñāna).* These ten are specified in the *Mahavyutpatti.* See, G.C. Pande, loc. cit., p.263.

[217]The ten stages are—(1) *Pramudita* (joyous,), (2) *Vimalā* (pure), (3) *Prabhā-kari* (luminous), (4) *Arcishmati* (brilliant), (5) *Sudurjaya* (hard to conquer), (6) *Abhimukhi* (facing), (7) *Dūrangamā* (going far), (8) *Acalā* (unmovable), (9) *Sādhumati* (the stage of the good) (10) *Dharmameghā* (cloud of *dharmas).* See, *Bodhisattvabhūmi*, Bk.III, Chap.III *(Bhumi-paṭala).* See, G.C. Pande, loc. cit., pp.361-63; E. Conze, *Buddhist Thought in India.* pp.234-37, Hardayal, op. cit., pp.284-92: E.J. Thomas. op. cit., pp.206-10.

[218]'The early Mahāyānists,' states Hardayal (loc. cit., p.170) 'were perhaps proud of having combined the social virtues of a righteous layman with the ascetic ideals of a meditative monk in this formula of the pāramitās.'

[219]The words of the Buddha as quoted in the *Vimānavatthu* (SBB., p.1) are worth consideration. 'Not merely by efficacy of the gift does giving become especially productive of reward, but rather through efficacy of the thought and efficacy of the field of those to whom the alms are given. Therefore even so little as a handful of rice flour ... bestowed with pure heart upon a person who is worthy of receiving a gift of devotion, becomes a thing which will bring an especially great reward, of great splendour and of great pervasiveness.' The *Śikṣāsamuccaya* (trans., p.89) states that it is more meritorious to give to a monk than to a pious layman or an ordinary person. See, *Bodhicaryāvatāra* (BST.), Chap.V, v.83.

donative phrase found in *caityas* and *vihāras* is *'deya dharmoyam'* (meritorious gifts) which comprised gifts ranging from ghee lamps,[220] railings, arches,[221] images,[222] cisterns[223] to *stūpas*,[224] *caityas*,[225] *guhas*[226] and money for repairs.[227]

Buddhological Speculation

The earliest conception of the nature of the Buddha seems to have been that of a historical person but the gradual glorification and deification led to speculation about the metaphysical nature of his personality. The Theravādins and the Sarvāstivādins conceived the Buddha as a human being who was subject to mortal frailties and who attained perfection and became omniscient at Bodhgaya. This human aspect is confirmed by epigraphs[228] and sculptural representations. The Barhut railings amply illustrate the descent, renunciation, enlightenment and the first discourse of the Buddha.[229] An inscription from Sārnāth belonging to the third regnal year of Kaniṣka, describes Varāṇasi as a place sanctified by the movements of the Blessed one (*Vārānasiye bhagavato*

[220]'*Tailasya stokam yacayitva pradipam prajvālya bhagavatah cankrame dattah'—Divyāvadāna,* (BST.), p.56; *Lüders list,* No.950.

[221]*Lüders list,* Nos.125, 1207.

[222]*Lüders list,* Nos.43, 144, 146, 148, 149, 911, 952, 989, 990; Burgess and Indraji, ICTWI., painted ins., No.24 (Ajantā), p.86; No.30, p.88.

[223]Burgess and Indraji, ICTWI., Mhar Ins. p. 2; Ins. No.3 (Kuḍa) p.5; Ins. No.26 (Kuḍa), p.19; Ins. No.2 (Bhājā), p.24; Ins. No.1 (Junnar), p.41; Ins. No.5 (Junnar), p.43, Ins. Nos.23, 27, 28 (Junnar), pp.51, 52, 53.

[224]*Lüders list,* No.1110.

[225]Burgess and Indraji, ICTWI., Ins. No.15 (Kuḍa), p.14; Ins. No.4 (Junnar), p.42.

[226]*Lüders list,* No.959; Burgess and Indraji, ICTWA., Ins. No.I (Kārle), p.28, Ins. No.2 (Ajantā), p.68; Ins, Nos.16, 19, 20, 24. 27, 28 (Kuḍa), pp.14, 15. 16. 18, 19.

[227]Burgess and Indraji, ICTWI., Grant of a village, Ins. No.14 (Kārle), p.34.

[228]The Rummindei pillar inscription (*CII.*, I., p.164) confirms the fact that Buddha was born in Lumbini.

[229]Barua and Sinha, *Barhut Inscriptions,* pp.52, 54, 57; The Ayaka pillar inscription C3, B4 and B5 *(EI.,* XX, pp.16ff) from Nāgārjunikoṇḍa describe the Buddha as receiving enlightenment under the bodhi tree.

chankame).[230] In a Nāgārjunikoṇḍa inscription he is referred to as one 'who has set in motion the wheel of the law' (*Dhama-chakra-pavatakasa*).[231]

Human epithets abound in the epigraphs.[232] The Nāgārjunikoṇḍa inscriptions call him *'Sava-satānukaṁpakasa'* (compassionate to all sentient beings), *'jita-rāga-doṣa-moha-vipamutasa'* (freed from lust, hatred and delusion which was conquered by him), *'Mahāgaṇi-vasabha (gaṁ) dhahadhisa'* (the bull and the musk elephant, i.e. the best among the great religious leaders),[233] *'Saṁma-saṁbudhasa'* (the perfectly enlightened one).

Some additional epithets found in a Nāgārjunikoṇḍa inscription[234] refer to him as—

(a) *Ikhāku-rāja-pavara-risi-sata-pabhava-vamsa-saṁbhavasa* (the Buddha was born of the race, sprung from hundreds of sages and excellent beings of Ikṣvaku's lineage).

(b) *Deva-manusa-sava-sata-hita-sukha-magadesikasa* (a teacher of the path leading to the good and happiness of all gods and men).[235]

(c) *Jita-kāma-kodha-bhaya-harisa-tarisa-moha-dosasa* (one who conquered lust, anger, fear, joy, thirst, delusion and hatred).

(d) *Aṭhaṅga-maga-dhama-chaka-pavatakasa* (one who taught the eight fold path leading to the cessation from miseries and one who turned the wheel of the law).

But attempts were made by some of the followers of the Buddha, chiefly the Mahāsāṅghikas and their offshoots, to

---

[230] *EI.*, VIII, pp.173-79.

[231] Second Apsidal Temple Inscription F. (*EI.*, XX, p.22)

[232] Ayaka Pillar Inscription C3 (*EI.*, XX, pp.16ff). See, D.C. Sircar, *Select Inscriptions*, pp.219-20.

[233] Buddha is termed as *Naravasabha (naravṛiśabha)*, i.e. the chief of men, the best. See, Jas Burgess, *Notes on Amaravati Stupa*, p.53.

[234] Second Apsidal Temple Inscription F. (*EI.*, XX, p.22).

[235] Inscription No.3 (Ajantā) terms him as *Lokaguru* (the teacher of the world). See, Burgess and Indraji, ICTWI., p.72.

ascribe supra mundane existence to him.[236] His appearance in the mortal world, they asserted, was only fictitious in order to follow the ways of the world (*Lokānuvartana*).[237] They attributed perfections and omniscience to him from his so-called birth in the womb of Queen Maya.

The *Kathāvatthu* puts forth the doctrine of the Vetulyakas, which was rejected by the Theravādins, that the Buddha did not live in the world of men, neither should he be located anywhere and it was his created form that delivered the religious discourses.[238]

The attribution of occult powers (*pātihāriyas*) to Buddha is indicated by the Barhut sculptures.[239] The Barhut inscriptions describe the *bodhisattva* (then in the Tushita heaven) as being entreated by the gods of the Kāmāvachara and Rūpāvachara devalokas to be born as a man.[240] The influence of the Brahmanic pantheon is clear on Buddhism since this was an age of Brahmanical revival.

In the Mathura pedestal inscription of the 14th year of the Kushāna era (AD 92), the Buddha is styled as a god in whom the donor had his faith (*svamatasya devasya*).[241] In a few Nāgārjunikoṇḍa inscriptions the Buddha is honoured by the lord of Gods (*devarāja-sakatasa*).[242] He is noted as *'Bhagavato Buddhasya Devatidevasya'* in the Kura stone inscription of the time of Toramāna (AD 500-515)[243] Though

---

[236] *Mahāvastu*, I, pp.125, 132-33, 167-70.

[237] N. Dutt, *BSI.*, p.72.

[238] *Kathāvatthu* (trans.), XVIII.1-2; XXI.6.

[239] Barua and Sinha, op. cit., pp.61, 66f.

[240] Ibid., pp.44ff; See, T.V.G. Shastri, 'Cultural Heritage of Nāgājunikoṇḍa', *JOIB.*, Vol.XI, No.1, Sept.1961, p.8, Pl.V, Fig.6.

[241] Ayaka Pillar Inscription C3 (*EI.*, XX, pp.15f), B4 (ibid., p.18), B5 (ibid., p.20).

[242] *EI.*, XIX, pp.290f. The Second Apsidal Inscription F at Nāgārjunikoṇḍa (*EI.*, XX, p.22) describes Buddha as '*Dapita-māra-vala-dapa-māna-pasamana-karasa*' (one who curbed the pride and arrogance of Māra) and *Dosa-vala-mahavalasa* (one who is very powerful because of possessing the ten powers).

[243] *EI.*, I, pp.239f; D.C. Sircar, *Select Inscriptions*, pp.422f.

the Buddha had condemned the practice of interpreting bodily signs, portents and dreams, yet 32 major and 80 minor marks were attributed to his person by his disciples.[244]

The Trikaya Doctrine

The docetism of the Mahāsāṅghikas and partially the impact of the *bodhisattva* ideal and of the new ontological conception of the Mahāyāna gave rise to the *trikāya* doctrine which is typical of the range and subtlety of Mahāyāna thought. As noted earlier the Theravādins conceived Buddha's *rūpakāya* as that of a human being and his *dharma-kāya* as the collection of his *Dhamma,* i.e. doctrines and disciplinary rules collectively.[245] But there are passages in the Pāli canon[246] which were interpreted differently by other sects.

In contradistinction to the *rūpa-kāya,* the Mahāyānists speak of a Buddha's *dharma-kāya.*[247] This body which is also

---

[244]*Mahāvastu,* I, pp.180ff; II, pp.40f; *Abhisamayālaṅkara* (ed. E. Conze), pp.98-102. The *Buddhacarita* (E.H. Johnston, pp.88, 142) also refers to the marks of a superman. The 2nd Apsidal Temple inscription F at Nāgārjunikoṇḍa (*EI.*, XX, p.22) describes the Buddha as *'Chaka-lakhana-sukumāra-sujata-charaṇasa'* (one possessing the mark of the wheel with 1,000 spokes, the rim and nave on the soles of his feet); See, E.H. Johnston, 'Ratnagotravibhāga Mahāyānottaratantra śāstra' *JBRS.,* Vol.36, Nos.1-2, March-June, 1950, pp.94-95; V.S. Agrawala's article 'The 32 Marks of the Buddha Body', *JOIB.*, Vol.I, No.1, Sept.1951, pp.20-22) is based on the above text; Edward Conze. 'The Buddha's Lakṣaṇas in the Prajñāpāramitā', *JOIB.*, Vol.14, Nos.3-4, March-June, 1965, pp.225-29; N.H. Samtani ('A fresh light on the interpretation of the 32 Mahāpurusha lakshaṇas of the Buddha, *Bharati,* Vol.6, Pt.I, 1962-63, pp.1-20) has presented a comparative study of the lakṣaṇas on the basis of *Arthaviniścayasutra, Dīgha Nikāya, Abhidharmadīpa vṛtti* and *Abhisamayālankārāloka.*

[245]N. Dutt *Aspects of Mahayana Buddhism in its Relation to Hinayana*, p.102.

[246]For example, *Saṁyutta Nikāya*, II, p.341. To the monk Vakkali, who on his death bed had desired to see the Buddha in person the Buddha said, 'He who sees the Dhamma sees Me. He who sees Me sees the Dhamma'.

[247]*The Diamond Sutra,* p.63—'Those who by my form *(rūpa)* did see me, And those who followed me by voice; Wrong the efforts they engaged in, Me those people will not see.

From the *dharma* should one see the Buddhas, For, the *dharma*-bodies are the guides (the Buddhas), Yet *dharma's* true nature should not be discerned, Nor can it, either, be discerned.'

called *sad-dharma kāya, bodhi-kāya, buddha-kāya, prajñā-kāya svābhāvika-kāya* (essential body) is invisible and universal. It is the essence of all worldly beings variously called *dharmatā, dharmadhātu, tathatā, bhūtatathatā, śūnyata* and *ālayavijñāna.* It is also the inward nature of the Buddha styled as *buddhatā, buddhasvabhāva* and *tathāgata-garbha.*[248]

According to the Madhyamikas, the *dharma-kāya* of the Buddhists consists chiefly of *prajñā.* In other words, his personality is ultimately identical with the cognition of reality, the void which lies underneath every phenomenal thing.[249] The transcendental nature of the *Rūpakāya* was established by the Yogācārins. They were aided in this by the ten stages of the *bodhisattva's* career. At the eighth stage, *Acalā,* the *bodhisattva* is supposed to renounce individual *nirvāṇa* and simultaneously attain a transcendental body by means of which he continues to appear in the various realms of phenomenal existence to lead all sentient beings to enlightenment. This doctrine is clearly enunciated in the *Laṅkāvatāra Sūtra.*[250]

The Yogācārins further subdivided the, *rūpakāya* into a gross and a subtle form. The basis of this distinction is the idea that a Buddha or a *bodhisattva* appears to different beings in different ways according to their degree of spiritual refinement. The *sambhoga-kāya* (Body of enjoyment) is the *dharma-kāya* as perceived in the celestial realms by the bodhisattvas coursing in any one of the ten *bhumis.* This body is radiant and glorious and bears thirty two special marks and eighty minor signs. It is the result of the merit, which a Buddha has acquired by his good deeds during many aeons.[251]

---

[248]See, Takakusu, *Essentials of Buddhist Philosophy*, p.43; A.B. Keith, *Buddhist Philosophy in India and Ceylon,* pp.268-69.

[249]A.B. Keith, loc. cit., p.267.

[250]D.T. Suzuki, op. cit., pp.225f.

[251]E.J. Thomas, op. cit., p.242: E. Conze. *Buddhist Thought in India,* pp.233-34; A.B. Keith, loc. cit., pp.269-70.

The *nirmāṇa-kaya* is the same reality as perceived on earth by *Śravakas, Pratyekabuddhas* and ordinary folks. To this category belong all those Buddhas who like the historical Śākyamuni, appear in the world in physical shape. They are called *nirmāṇa* (manifest beings) because of their gross nature. The function of the Earthy Buddhas is to expound the *dharma* in the world.[252]

The Mahāyānic Pantheon

With the evolution of the *tri-kāya* doctrine it was held that the historical Śakyamuni was an apparition of the *dharma-kāya* and that there were apparition bodies in all times and places. Later Mahāyānic cosmology posited the universe as consisting of thousands of worlds 'as numerous as the sands of Ganges'. It was assumed that some of these were Buddha-lands in each of which a Tathāgata lives and teaches the *dharma.*

The Mahāyānic pantheon with its transcendent Buddhas and *bodhisattvas* was essentially the product of monkish mind. The radical expansion of world view with a corresponding change in the values was another of those moves to popularise Buddhism, to win the laity to its fold. Salvation was open to all through the grace of the transcendental Buddhas but grace and faith were not sufficient enough. One had to take recourse to the visionary mode of consciousness. The vision of the Buddha in meditation would lead to an individual 'becoming Buddha'. Exemption from sins and rebirth in 'Pure lands' was promised to the devotee.

The Transcendent Buddhas were assigned three functions namely—expounding the truth to the *bodhisattvas* and disciples, controlling the various paradises in which believers wished to be reborn and acting as spiritual fathers of Earthly Buddhas whom they, out of compassion for all beings, projected into the world by their meditation. Among the Transcendent Buddhas, Amitābha, Akṣobhya, Vairochana,

[252]E.J. Thomas, op. cit., p.243; A.B. Keith, op. cit., pp.271-72.

Amoghasiddhi and Ratnasambhava are foremost. While Maitreya, Mañjuśrī, Avalokiteśvara, Samantabhadra and Mahāsthāmaprāpta are prominent in the list of transcendent *bodhisattvas*.[253] These non historical beings eventually assumed so much importance that their representations were found along with the Buddha or standing alone in a shrine or monastery.[254]

Amitābha

Of these the cult of Amitābha[255] (of immeasurable radiance) and also called Amitāyus (of immeasurable life span) goes back to AD 100. He is described as the lord of the Sukhāvati,[256] the most blissful of all paradises which he had obtained as a consequence of his forty eight resolutions *(mahapraṇidhana)* made long ago. *The Longer Sukhāvati Vyūha* states that those who have done good deeds, who direct their thoughts to enlightenment and meditate (either continuously or by means of a single thought only) on Amitābha and his Buddhaland in the hour of death reach the Sukhāvati heaven.[257] Birth in Sukhāvati is believed to be the last birth. *The Smaller Sukhā-*

---

[253]'The cumulative evidence of art, history and literature leads one to believe' states B. Bhattacharyya (*The Indian Buddhist Iconography*, p.41) 'that the pantheon of the northern Buddhists was not widely known before the 7th century AD, nor was the underlying philosophy, which may warrant the formation of a pantheon well developed before that time, although the origin of it is definitely earlier.' Further, it is in the *Guhya Samāja* that the idea of a pantheon rationally classified, is properly and systematically crystallized (ibid., p.32).

[254]Sculptural representations of Buddhas and *bodhisattvas* (as such or as guardians bearing *chauris* along with their attendants) abound in the caves of Ajantā, Aurangabad, Bāgh and Ellorā. The fully developed pantheon of the *bodhisattvas,* their *śaktis* and other cognate male and female divinities are represented in Caves XI and XII at Ellorā.

[255]G.P. Malalasekera, 'Amita', *Encyclopaedia of Budddhism,* Vol.1, Fas.3, 434a-63b.

[256]*Saddharma Puṇḍarīka* (BST.), pp.119, 256-57.

[257]*The Larger Sukhāvati-Sūtra* (SBE.), p.45.

vati Vyūha stresses the hearing of the name of Amitābha. Without its continued repetition there will be no salvation.[258]

The Amitāyurdhyāna Sūtra contains a series of sixteen meditations whose aim is to form a perception of the western quarter (Sukhāvati). Meditation upon this vision results in the realization of Sukhāvati at death.[259] On the evidence of these sutras, it is clear that faith alone did not suffice for rebirth. It was just an adjunct to meditation.

Maitreya

All Hīnayānic sects acknowledged Maitreya[260] as the future Buddha. His future coming is prophesized in the *Dīgha-Nikāya*[261] and in the *Mahāvastu.*[262] His name appears in the *Saddharma-Puṇḍarīka Sutra* also.[263] By Hiuen-tsang's time he had become an object of reverence and adoration.[264]

Mañjuśrī

Mañjuśrī (of sweet beauty or gentle glory) is regarded as 'primus inter pares' among the oligarchy of *bodhisattvas* in Early Mahāyāna.[265] The Mahāyāna school regarded him as the apotheosis of perfect wisdom. His most common titles

---

[258]*The Smaller Sukhāvati Sūtra* (SBE.), p.99.

[259]*The Amitāyurdhyāna Sūtra* (SBE.), pp.169ff.

[260]R.S. Gupte, *Iconography of the Hindus, Buddhists and Jains,* pp.110-12.

[261]*Digha Nikāya*, III, p.60.

[262]*Mahāvastu,* III, p.230.

[263]*Saddharkma-Puṇḍarīka* (BST.), pp.3, 4, 11, 19, etc.

[264]Yuan Chwang (T. Watters, op. cit., I, p.239) refers to wooden image of Tzu-Shih-P'usa (Maitreya *bodhisattva)* at Dārel possessed of miraculous powers. He also saw images of the same at Varāṇasī (ibid., II, p.59) and at Gaya (ibid., II, p.116). A broken image of Mañjuśri ascribed to 5th century AD was found in the excavations at Sārnāth. See, *ASIAR.,* 1904-05, p.82.

[265]Hardayal, op. cit., pp.45-46.

are Mahāmati[266] and Kumāra-rāja.[267] In the *Lotus Sutra* he remembers deeds of previous Buddhas which were unknown even to Maitreya.[268] In the *Vimalakīrti Nirdeśa Sūtra,*[269] he alone of all disciples has wisdom to face the householder Vimalakīrti. In the *Gaṇḍavyūha* he advises Sudhana in his search for enlightenment.[270] Fa-hien refers to the worship of Mañjuśrī along with Avalokiteśvara and Prajñāpāramitā by students of Mahāyāna.[271]

Avalokiteśvara

Another transcendent *bodhisattva* enjoying particular popularity as a helper to salvation is Avalokiteśvara[272] whose outstanding characteristic is the virtue of compassion. He is also referred to as *Padmapāṇi* (He who holds the lotus) or *Lokeśvara* (Lord of the world). He is introduced and eulogized in the *Saddharma Puṇḍarīka Sūtra.*[273] His first significant role is in the *Sukhāvati-vyūha Sūtra* where he and Mahasthamprāpta are Amitābha Buddha's chief attendants.

It is said that anyone who utters the words 'Oṃ maṇipadme hūṃ' would be saved from all calamities of shipwreck, fire, moral impurity, flood, robbers, enemies, etc., as this

---

[266]He is considered patron *bodhisattva* of scholars. He appears in Buddhist art after AD 400 with a flaming sword in his right hand and the book of transcendent wisdom on his left side suggestive of the destruction of ignorance and the awakening of knowledge. See, R.S. Gupte, op. cit., p.114. See also, *ASIAR.,* 1904-05, PI.XXVIII, Fig.C.

[267]The complimentary epithet *'Kumāra'* is applied to him signifying 'ever youthful' and perhaps as 'prince of Buddha's realm'. See, Hardayal, op. cit., pp.46-47.

[268]*Saddharma puṇḍarīka* (SBE.), p.23.

[269]*Vimalakīrti Nirdeśa Sūtra* (trans.), pp.49-61.

[270]Quoted, A.K. Warder, op. cit., p.425.

[271]J. Legge, op. cit., p.46. See, also, T. Watters, op. cit. I, pp.302-04.

[272]On the interpretation of the term *'Avalokit'*. See, E.J. Thomas, op. cit., p.189, fn. 1; J. Legge, loc. cit., p.46, fn.5; Hardayal, op. cit., pp.47-48.

[273]*Saddharma-puṇḍarīka* (SBE.), pp.4, 406ff.

bodhisattva would take the forms of the beings he is to save and deliver them from all troubles.[274]

That Avalokiteśvara had become an object of adoration[275] is testified by Hsüang-tsang who refers to the image of the *bodhisattva* Avalokiteśvara (*Kuan-tzu-tsai P'usa*) in a Buddhist temple in the vicinity of a city called 'Mangkil'[276] in Magadha,[277] Malakuṭa,[278] Maharastra[279] and Nālandā.[280] In the Tantric period he came to be represented in art with a crown (with a small picture of the transcendent Buddha Amitābha), halo and a garland of shinning flowers.

Mutual Relations

Mutual relations among sects and schools of the Buddhist Order when seen in a historical perspective, present many interesting features. Epigraphs, religious literature and the testimony of the Chinese travellers reveal their apparent amity

---

[274]*Kāraṇḍavyūha (Mahāyāna sūtra saṅgraha,* BST.), pt.I, pp.286, 289; The learned pilgrim Fa-hien thought of *Kwan-shi-yin* (Avalokiteśvara) when the ship faced a tempest. See, J. Legge, op. cit., pp.112-13; On the back wall of the verandah of Cave 7 at Aurangabad is a huge figure of *bodhisattva* Padmapāṇi in *abhaya* mudra, flanked by four rectangular panels on each side. These represent the eight fears, viz., fire, enemy's sword, chains, shipwreck, attack by a lion, snake, maddened elephant and death as symbolized by a demonness from which Padamapāṇi is supposed to rescue his devotee. See. Amita Ray, 'Sculptures in Aurangabad', *Marg*, Vol.XVI, No.3, June 1963, p.44. Fig.D, 45. This scene occurs in a painting at Ajantā in Caves 2 and 4.

[275]Avalokiteśvara was worshipped by Harṣa before becoming the ruler. See, T. Watters, op. cit., I, p.343. An image with broken arms had been unearthed in the excavations at Sārnāth. This is proved by the small figure of the dhyāni Buddha Amitābha in his head dress. On the base of the statue is an inscription in Gupta characters of the 5th century. See, *ASIAR.*, 1904-05, p.81, Pl.XXVIII, Fig.5. Another image in octo-alloy ascribed to the 8th-9th century AD has been discovered at Bandarbazar, Sylhet. See, N.K. Bhattasali. *Iconography of Buddhist and Brahmanical Sculptures in the Dacca Museum,* p. 25.

[276]T. Watters, op. cit., I, pp.238, 279.

[277]Ibid., II, pp.105, 175-76.

[278]Ibid., II, p.229.

[279]Ibid., II, p.239.

[280]Ibid., II, p.170.

and inherent animosities. The continuity and longevity of these various sects and schools was primarily due to the person of the Buddha and the concept of the ideal *Saṅgha* as established by him.[281]

The age of Aśoka witnessed several brachiations in the *Saṅgha* and it is clear from the schism pillar edicts that Aśoka wanted to stamp out these dissenting tendencies. An imprecatory inscription of the 1st century BC found at Sāñchī states: 'He who dismantles or causes to be dismantled an arch or a rail of the Kākanāda (old name of Sāñchī), or causes it to be transferred to another "ācariyakula", shall have the same fate as one who murders his mother, father or arhat, one who

---

[281]The full term in the Pali Canon *(Mahāvagga,* p.319; *Cullavagga,* p.259) is *'Āgatanāgata-catuddisa-bhikkhu-saṅgha' (Saṅgha* of the four quarters including all who had become and were to become *bhikkhus* in future). This phrase was first suggested by Buddha to the *setthi* of Rajagṛha who got 60 *vihāras* constructed and wished to donate the same to the *Saṅgha.* Buddha being a practical realist laid down the formula so that in future ownership of a *vihāra* was not vested in a particular body of monks due to their permanent residence but was sharable by all, both now and in the future. The phrase implied an ideal confederation beyond restriction of time and space, ever since its inception. [See, G.S.P. Misra, 'Some reflections on Early Jaina and Buddhist Monachism,' *Jijñāsā,* Vol.I, Nos.3-4, July-Oct.1974, p.8, fn.12; *Contra.,* S. Dutt, *EBM.,* (p.85) maintains that 'as time passed on, the original *Saṅgha* underwent divisions and subdivisions but it began at the same time to be idealized']. Ajay Mitra Shastri (op. cit., pp.147-49) has ably controverted S. Dutt's interpretation of the term *'Catuddisa Saṅgha'.* He maintains that the expression occurring in epigraphs actually represented the donor's mental disposition (ibid., pp.149-50). S.N. Dube (op. cit., Chap.VII) takes into account the Theravādin stand as presented in the *Kathāvatthu,* which he states was diametrically opposed to the ideality of the *Saṅgha* and it upheld the idea of the *Saṅgha* merely as a body of individuals. It is not understandable how the author whose work 'seeks to elucidate the controversies presented in the Kathāvatthu in the light of the historical development of Buddhist thought and its wider milieu' accepts the Theravādin stand as the Buddhist stand ...

... The actuality of the Buddhist *Saṅgha* (as *Sammukhibhuta Saṅgha)* operating within a fixed boundary, does not preclude its ideality (the *Catuddisa Saṅgha*—Universal in character), a fact which was understood even by the lay donor while giving gifts to the *Saṅgha.* Hence the occurrence of the term *Catuddisa bhikkhu Saṅgha* appearing in inscriptions at Kāṇherī, Kārle and Nāsik, when the practice of making donations in favour of particular sects had also come into vogue. See, *Lüders list,* Nos.1024, 1099, 1127, 1128, 1133, 1137, 1140 and 1146.

sheds blood and one who causes schism in the Order.'[282] This epigraph points to the apprehensions of the Theravādins caused by the establishment of an alien sect at Sāñchī.[283] The method by which the Sarvāstivādins tried to establish their supremacy at Sārnāth shows the sectarian animosities that governed the relations between different schools. Their first inscription[284] was found on the Aśokan *harmika* which was later on removed to enclose a brick *stupa,* in the southern chapel of the main shrine. It was found on the eastern side of the railing. The second inscription[285] is on the northern side of the base of the railing while a third inscription[286] is found on the top of a staircase on the eastern side of the *Dhammarājikā stūpa.*

---

[282] J. Marshall, *Monuments of Sāñchi,* I, Nos.389, 396, 409; *Lüders, list,* No.340.

[283] In the Sāñchi records, two donors, viz., Buddharakshita and Avisinā *(Lüders list,* No.352, 319) are styled as *Sutātika* and *Sutātikini.* Barua and Sinha (*Bharhut Inscriptions*, p.15) point to the possibility of the donor being an adherent of the Suttavāda or Sautrāntika school. J.N. Bannerjea ('Schools of Buddhism in Early Indian Inscriptions', *IHQ.*, Vol.XXIV, No.4, 1948, pp.255-56) takes the term in the sense of a sect. If the term is taken for a sect, it is possible that the alien sect which established itself at Sāñchī was no other than the *Sautrāntikas* from whom the Theravādins suspected dismantling of their establishment. Another sect which flourished at Sāñchi in the 2nd-1st century BC were the *Haimavatas.* The inscription on the steatite relic casket No. 1 in the *stūpa* No.III at Sānchi mentions *Sapurisa Kassapagota,* who is extolled as '*Sava Hemāvatāchariya*' (*Lüders list*, Nos.158, 654, 655). W. Geiger (*The Mahāvaṁsa*, Intro., p.xix) takes *'Sava Hemāvatāchariya'* as confirming the Ceylonese tradition, according to which Kassapagota was one of the five missionaries sent by the 3rd Council to the Himalayan region. N.G. Majumdar, renders it as a 'teacher of the whole community of the Haimavatas'. This is supported by a relic casket inscription found at *stūpa* No. II at Sonari. It describes Gotiputa, the heir of Dudubhisara as a Hemavata or a member of the community of the Haimavatas (*Lüders list*, No.156).

[284] *'Achariya nam sarvvastivadinam parigahetavam'*. (Homage of the elders of the Sarvāstivādin sect)—See, *ASIAR.,* 1904-05, p.68, Pl.XXXII, Fig.IX.

[285] *'Acharyanam sarvvastivadinam parigarhe'*. (Homage of the elders of the Sarvāstivādin sect)—ibid., 1906-07, pp.96-97, Pl.XXX, Fig.IV.

[286] *'Achar (ar) yanam sarvvastivadinam parigrahe'*. (Homage of the elders of the Sarvāstivādin sect). Ibid., 1907-08, p.73, Pl.XXI. Dr. Vogel assigns this inscription to the 2nd century AD.

In case of the first two records, the commencing words are inscribed after defacing an earlier record, while the latter part *parigrahe* and *parigahetavam* were allowed to exist. We have in the same epigraphs characters of different centuries. The characters on the eastern side of the railing are slightly earlier than those on the southern side, while the first record is in Prakrit, the second is in Sanskrit. The Sarvāstivādin sect seemed to have occupied the holy site and for some reason they defaced the earlier record substituting their name.[287] An inscription of the early Gupta period, engraved on the Aśokan pillar at Sārnāth in the Brahmi characters reads:

Acha (a) [ri] yyanam parigrahe Vastiputrikanam

(Homage of the elders of the *Vatsiputriya* (*Sammitiya*) sect.[288]

It seems that the Sarvāstivādins and the Sammitiyas were settled at Sārnāth and were struggling for predominance and in the end the latter succeeded in pushing out the former. This is clear from Yuan Chwang's account that the monastery at Sārnāth was the stronghold of the Sammitiyas in the 7th century AD.[289]

Being well versed in the doctrines of the rival sect was also not uncommon in the early centuries of the Christian era. The Mathura Lion Capital Inscription, Group III (N) refers to Buddhila, hailing from Nagara (near Jallalabad in the easternmost region of Afghanistan) as a Sarvāstivādin *ācharya,* who was well versed in the doctrines of the Māhāsāṅghikas also.[290] The motive which might have inspired such learning

---

[287]It is probable that the alien sect was that of the *Theravādins* whose inscription in pure Pāli of the Kushāna period is found there. It enumerates the four truths which formed the crux of Buddha's first sermon at Isipatana (Sārnāth). See, *EI.*, IX, pp.291ff.

[288]*EI.,* VIII, p.172, No.1; *Lüders list,* No.923.

[289]T. Watters, op. cit., II, p.217.

[290]*EI,* IX, pp.141f; *CII.*, 11, pp.48f; D.C. Sircar, *Select Inscriptions*, I, pp.116-19.

was simply counteracting the truth expounded by the rival sect and thereby gaining supremacy.

Mathura was the home of the Sarvāstivādins,[291] Mahāsāṅghikas[292] and the Sammitiyas[293] in the Kushāna period.[294] Mutual co-existence of numerous sects such as the Bhadrayaniyas[295] and the Cetikas[296] at Ṅāsik caves, the Dharmottariyas[297] and Cetiyavāda[298] at Junnar and the Mahāsāṅghikas[299] and the Kaśyapiyas[300] at Karle during the reign of the Sātvāhanas is confirmed by epigraphs. Similarly, inscriptions of 2nd-3rd century AD from Nāgārjunikoṇḍa and Amarāvati refer to the existence of the Theravādins[301] or

---

[291]The Mathura Lion Capital Inscription A. II *(EI., IX.* p.141; D.C. Sircar, *Select Inscriptions,* I., pp.114-19) of the time of Mahāṣatrapa Rājula records the deposition of some relics in a *stūpa* and the dedication of the *stūpa* and the *vihāra* for the acceptance of the Sārvāstivādins.

Another fragmentary inscription from Mathura belonging to the Kushāna period records the installation of a *bodhisattva* image for the Sarvāstivādins—See, Ph. Vogel, *A Catalogue of the Archaeological Museum of Mathura,* No.A.66, p.63; *Lüders list,* No.1394).

[292]A Mathura inscription of the time of Vasudeva. yr. 64 or 67 (*EI.*, XXX, pp.183-84) refers to the installation of an image of Śākyamuni for the acceptance of the Mahāsāṅghika teachers. Another epigraph from Mathura belonging to the year 91 *(EI.,* XIX, p.68) records the erection of an object at the Chutaka-Vihāra (mango-grove monastery) for the increase of the religious merit and strength of the Mahāsāṅghikas.

[293]A Mathura inscription of the Kushāna period (*EI.*, XIX, p.67) records the installation of a *bodhisattva* image by a monk along with his mother and father and his teacher Dharmaka in the Sri-vihāra for the acceptance of the Sammitiyas.

[294]B.N. Puri, 'The Sarvāstivādins and the Mahāsāṅghikas in the Kusāna Period,' *QJMS.,* Vol.XXXII, No.1, July 1941, pp.38-45.

[295]*EI.,* VIII, pp.60, 65ff, No.3; *Lüders list,* Nos.1123-24.

[296]Ibid, p.77; *Lüders list,* No.1130.

[297]Burgess and Indraji, *ICTWI,* p.42, No.3; *Lüders list,* No.1152.

[298]Ibid., p.51; *Lüders list,* No.1171.

[299]*EI.,* VII, p.64ff; *Lüders list,* No.1105.

[300]D.C. Sircar, *Select Inscriptions,* I, p.203.

[301]The Nāgārjunikoṇḍa second apsidal temple inscription F (*EI.*, XX, pp.lff) refers to Nāgārjunikoṇḍa as a stronghold of the Theravādin fraternities of Ceylon (*Theriyānāṁ Taṁbapaṁṇakānāṃ*).

Vibhajyavadins,[302] Purvaśailas,[303] the Aparaśailas,[304] the Bahuśrutiyas,[305] the Rajagirinivasikas,[306] or Rajaśailas,[307] the Siddhattikas,[308] the Chaityakas,[309] and the Mahaśāsakas.[310]

But mutual co-existence could not rule out ideological differences which are manifested in monastic architecture as at Nāgārjunikoṇḍa.[311] The ruins of a monastery and a *mahācaitya* (Site 1) belonging to the Aparamahavanaśailiyas shows that they did not accept image worship while the same sect occupying site 9 revealed a *mahācaitya,* two *caityagṛhas* and three winged monastery evidently pointing to the acceptance of image worship.

The Monastery of Mahiśāsakas (Sites 7-8) had two large *stūpas* but no *caityagṛha.* The Mahavihāravāsins gradually assimilated the idea of constructing votive *stūpas* and also possibly of Buddha-worship. The Monastery of the Bahuśrutiyas (Site 5) has laid bare *caityagṛhas* for enshrining *stūpas* but not Buddhas. It is only at a later date that an oblong shrine contains a pillar portraying a seated Buddha.

---

[302]An inscription from Nāgārjunikoṇḍa records the installation of the footprint slab of the *Bhagavat* (Buddha) in the monastery of the āchāryas who are styled Theriyas (Theravādins), Vibhajyavādins and Mahāvihāravāsins. See, *EI.*, XXXIII, pp.247ff; *MASI.,* No.71, pp.36-37.

[303]The Nāgārjunikoṇḍa second apsidal temple inscription F (*EI.*, XX, p.23) refers to Puvasela as a place name.

[304]The Aparaśaila is mentioned as Aparamahavina-Śeliya in Nāgār-junikoṇḍa Ayaka pillar inscription C1 (*EI.*, XX, p.17), C2 (ibid., p.19), and in the Amarāvati inscriptions. See, J. Burgess, *Buddhist Stupas of Amaravati and Jagayyapeta,* p.105, No.49.

[305]The Nāgārjunikoṇḍa detached pillar inscription G (*EI.*, XX, pp.23-24; Ibid., XXI, p.62) records the establishment of a monastery of the Bahusuttiya teachers by the mother of the King Siri-Ehuvula Chātamūla.

[306]J. Burgess, loc. cit., p.53; *Lüders list,* No.1250.

[307]Ibid., p.104; *Lüders list*, No.1280.

[308]J. Burgess, *Notes on Amaravati Stupa,* p.19.

[309]Ibid., p.27; *Lüders list,* No.1248.

[310]The Nāgārjunikoṇḍa detached pillar inscription H records the erection of a pillar and the gift of a monastery for the acceptance of the Mahiśāsaka teachers. See, *EI.,* XX, p.24.

[311]H. Sarkar, 'Some aspects of the Buddhist Monuments at Nāgār-junikoṇḍa'. *AI.*, No.16, 1960, pp.68ff.

Changes in the doctrines and religious life shedding light on sectarian differences can be gleaned from the Mahāyāna *sūtras* which were composed from 100 BC until AD 400. In their earliest phase the *sūtras* do not disparage the Hīnayāna but try to establish their standpoint.[312] From the systematization and elaboration of the teachings of the *sūtras* arose the philosophical Mahāyāna schools. The later Mahāyānic *sūtras* and *śāstras,* while presenting the new Buddhist doctrines, also make an attempt to reject the Hīnayānic ones.[313] In this period, *Sthaviravāda* on the one hand, the Sarvāstivāda with their allied schools as well as that of the Mahāsāṅghikas even on the other were included in the scope of Hīnayāna while the Madhyamika school of Nāgārjuna, Yogācāra school of Maitreya, Asaṅga, Vasubandhu and Asvaghoṣa II did alone come under the scope of Mahāyāna.[314]

Nāgārjuna in his *Prajñāpāramitā Śāstra* tries to disparage the Śrāvakayāna and the Pratyekabuddhayāna thus affording glimpses of sectarian rivalry which continued to prevail between Hīnayāna and Mahāyāna.[315] The *Abhisamayalaṃkāra* states that 'the mind (of the Bodhisattva) striving after enlightenment is the mind directed towards the attainment of

---

[312]*The Large Sutra on Perfect Wisdom* (p.186) states—'The Bodhisattvayāna is the Mahāyāna.' *The Saddharamapuṇḍarīka Sūtra* (SBE., p.129) says—'In like manner Kasyapa, is there but one vehicle, viz., Mahāyāna: there is no second vehicle, no third.' *The Aṣṭasāhasrikā-Prajñā-pāramitā* (pp.88, 108, 145) states that the Srāvakas and the Pratyekabuddhas (i.e., the Hīnayānists) are of lesser intelligence than the Bodhisattvas. The *Mahāyānaviṁsakā of* Nāgārjuna (ed., trans., V *Bhattacharya*, p.12) declares that without embarking on the great vehicle (Mahāyāna) the ocean of Saṃsara cannot be crossed.

[313]It seems that the composition of the Śāstras was a direct answer to the challenge of the Sthaviravādins who called the Mahāsāṅghikas—'*Adharmavādin*' (holder of the heretical doctrine) and '*Pāpa bhikṣu*' (sinful monk). See, R. Kimura, 'A Historical study of the terms Mahāyāna and Hinayāna and the origin of Mahāyāna Buddhism', *JDL.*, Vol.XII, 1925, p.116, fn.1.

[314]See, R. Kimura, loc. cit, p.158.

[315]The big contains the small, while the small cannot contain the big'—T.1509, Vol.25, pp.416a, 86a. 'The knowledge of the Bodhisattvayāna is said to excel that of the Śrāvakas and the Pratyêkabuddhas'—Ibid., 266b-c, 267c.

omniscience; it is the incomparable mind which has nothing in common with that of the Śrāvakas and the Pratyêka-buddhas'.[316]

Among the Mahāyāna Ācāryas, those of the Yogācāra school emphatically asserted to prove that the Mahāyāna Buddhism is Buddha's true doctrine. 'That what controls our foes, the passions, what from rebirth and misery delivers is (our) revelation, since it rules and saveth, all other creeds do not possess it, this double benefit (of Mahāyāna).'[317] Maitreya-nātha and Asaṅga pronounced Hīnayāna as a 'narrow doctrine, narrow in its aim and narrow in its method and equipment'.[318]

With the emergence of Buddhist logic[319] in the beginning of 6th AD began an era of philosophical controversies and intellectual debates among the various schools of Buddhism.[320] Criticism of each other's views was also not uncommon. Diṅnāga is said to have criticised Vasubandhu's views and Diṅnāga's pupil Iśvarasena was criticised by Dharmakirti.[321] The followers of Vijñānavāda who came after Vasubandhu and lived before Hsüan-tsang's visit to India disagreed amongst themselves.[322] Chandrakirti and Śāntideva

---

[316]*Analysis of the Abhisamayālaṃkara*, ed., E. Obermiller, Fas.1, p.101.

[317]*Madhyānta Vibaṅga*, trans., Th. Stcherbatsky, p.20.

[318]*Mahāyāna Sūtralaṅkara* (BST.), pp.5f.

[319]Diṅnāga is regarded as the 'father of Indian logic', rather of Buddhist Logic. See, Th. Stcherbatsky, *Buddhist Logic*, I, pp.31f. On account of his love for discussion, he was during his life time, called the 'Bull in discussion' (*Tarka-puṅgava*). See, S.C. Vidyabhusana, *History of Medieval School of Indian Logic*, p.81.

[320]Logic was studied 'in order to vanquish one's adversary in controversy' and thereby to increase the monetary resources of the Order. See, *Bu-ston, History of Buddhism*, p.44; E. Conze, *Buddhism, its Essence and Development*, pp.164-65. The Madhyamika school as a result of controversies was divided into two groups, the *Svātantrika* and the *Prāsangika*. The former headed by Bhavaviveka emphasized logical reasoning and independent arguments while the latter headed by Buddhapālita which was purely dialectical, and applied the method of reductio ad absurdum. See, L.M. Joshi, op. cit., p.172.

[321]Th. Stcherbatsky, loc. cit., I, pp.34-35; S.C. Vidyabhusana, loc. cit., p.106.

[322]Narendradeva, *Bauddha Dharma Darśana*, pp.422f.

directed their criticism against *the Abhidhamma* categories and the law of causation.

When the *Saddharma* was questioned or the omniscience of Buddha challenged, the Buddhist philosophers, in order to defend their fundamental, transcendental and mystical position reduced the truth to a series of rational propositions and logical conventions.[323] It was merely a manifestation of 'skill in means' and its methods as E. Conze observes 'implied a radical departure from the spirit of ahiṁsā and tolerance which was so characteristic of Buddhism in its heyday'.[324]

Coming to the testimony of Chinese pilgrims we find that Hiuen Tsang (AD 629-45) refers to monasteries which were catholic enough to study the doctrine and discipline of different Buddhist sects. The Mahāyānists in a monastery of Uḍḍiyāna taught and studied five redactions of the *Vinaya,* namely, those of the Dharmaguptas, Mahiśāsakas, Kāśyapiyas, Sarvāstivādins and of the Mahāsāṅghikas.[325] Monks in some of the monasteries at Jalandara[326] and Mathura[327] studied both Hīnayāna and Mahāyāna. Similarly many monasteries of Ayodhya,[328] Vriji Country,[329] Kannauj,[330] Pundravardhana,[331] Ujjeni,[332] Maharaṣṭra[333] and Parvata[334] were occupied by monks of both Hīnayāna and Mahāyāna schools. The 'Mahāyānists of the Sthavira School' are referred to at Buddha Gaya, Kalinga, Bharoch and Surat.[335] The term refers to monks who were perfect in *Vinaya* observances.

---

[323]L.M. Joshi, op. cit., pp.193-94.

[324]E. Conze, *Buddhist Thought in India,* p.265.

[325]T. Watters, op. cit., I, p.226.

[326]Ibid., I, p.296.

[327]Ibid., I, p.301.

[328]Ibid., I, p.355.

[329]Ibid., II, p.81.

[330]Ibid., II, p.136.

[331]Ibid., II, p.184.

[332]Ibid., II, pp.250, 231.

[333]Ibid., II, p.239.

[334]Ibid., II, p.255.

[335]Ibid., II, pp.136, 198, 241, 248.

Equally revealing is Hiuen-Tsang's observation that 'Buddhism now is pure or diluted according to the spiritual insight and mental capacity of its adherents. The tenets of the schools keep these isolated and controversy runs high; heresies on special doctrines lead many ways to the same end. Each of the eighteen schools claims to have intellectual superiority and the tenets (or practices) of the great and small systems (lit-vehicles) differ widely ... and many are the noisy discussions. Wherever there is a community of brethren it makes (its own) rules of gradation.'[336]

The Hīnayāna monks of Orissa are seen ridiculing Emperor Harṣa for the latter's patronage of Nālandā *vihāra*, the chief centre of Mahāyāna. According to them the monks of Nālandā University were *'heretics'*, their doctrine was a system of *'sky flower'* which 'was not delivered by Buddha'. On being requested by Harṣa, the chancellor of Nālandā sent Sāgaramati, Prajñāraśmi, Siṃharaśmi and Hiuen-tsang to refute the views of the Orissan monks.[337] Elsewhere Harṣa is seen complaining about one Devasena, 'the chief Sthavira of the priests' who, by advancing 'his strange opinions, ever opposed the great vehicle'.[338]

It seems that adherence to a sect had become a matter of intellectual preference by I-tsing's time (AD 671-95). It was creditable for a monk to be versed in the scriptures of all schools. At Nālandā monks received sacred as well as secular

---

[336]Ibid., I, p.162; *Śāntideva* also lends a glimpse into the old controversy between Hīnayāna and Mahāyāna. See, *Bodhicaryāvatāra* (trans.), Chap.IX, vv.42-50.

[337]S. Beal, *Life*, pp.159ff. It is related that one of the most famous teachers of the Sammitiya school, Prajñāgupta by name, had composed 'a polemical treatise in 700 ślokas against the principles of Vijñānavāda'. Hsüang-Tsang is represented as challenging it with a work in 1,600 ślokas, entitled 'the destruction of heresy'. Ibid., p.165. Posting of heretical documents was common in Nālandā. The *Life* (ibid., p.161) refers to the tearing of one such document by the servant of Hiuen-Tsang on the orders of his master.

[338]Ibid., pp.175-76.

knowledge.[339] Monks of Hīnayāna as well as Mahāyāna school were taught Māṭrçetas two hymns as soon as he could recite the five and ten precepts (*śila*). And as I-tsing puts it 'the priests learn besides all the Vinaya works and investigate the sūtras and sastras as well. They oppose the heretics as they would drive beast (deer) in the middle of a plain and explain away disputations as boiling water melts frost.'[340]

He refers to the adoption of the same *Vinaya* and the same prohibitions of the five *skandhas* (groups of offences) and also the practice of four noble truths by the Hīnayānists and the Mahāyānists.[341] His statements seem to imply that one and the same school adheres to the Hīnayāna in one place and to the Mahāyāna in another; a school does not exclusively belong to the one or the other. What constitutes the difference between the two is, according to him, the worship of a *bodhisattva* and the reading of a Mahāyāna *sūtra,* which are peculiar to the Mahāyānists. He refers to Madhyamika and Yogācāra schools as Mahāyāna.[342]

---

[339]Such learning was common to monks of the Hīnayāna and Mahāyāna schools. See, Chap.IV.

[340]J. Takakusu, op. cit., p.181.

[341]Ibid., p.14.

[342]Ibid. pp.14-15.

CHAPTER 3

Life in the Monasteries

The long and continuous history of the Buddhist *Saṅgha* was marked by many transformations. An attempt is made here to delineate the life of the inmates which was reoriented in certain spheres in response to the waves of social and cultural change.

Admission

The *Pabajjā* and *Upasampadā* ordinations were essential for every individual who desired the membership of the Buddhist *Saṅgha.* The meaning of *Pabajjā,*[1] viz., the initial conversion and entry into the *Saṅgha* is retained in later literature and inscriptions. The minimum age required for the novitiate ordination was reduced to seven years.[2] A monk who attained the *Pabajjā* was called a *Samaṇera* (Sk. *Śrāmaṇera).*[3]

---

[1]*Pabajjā* (Sk. *Pravrajyā)* denoted the 'outgoing' rather the going forth from a prior state—from home into homelessness *(agārsmā anagāriam pabajjati)* or from a monastic sect holding another faith.

[2]*The Questions of King Milinda* (SBE.), pt.I, p.20. The *Mahāvagga* (p.82) prescribed fifteen years as the ordination age for a novice but seemed to have made a concession to children under fifteen who could scare a crow.

[3]The term *Sāmaṇera* occurs in the Sāñchī Buddhist *Stūpa* I. Inscription *(Lüders list,* Nos.184, 283) and a few Andhau inscriptions. In some inscriptions one also comes across such terms as *pavajitā* (Besnagar Buddhist Rail Inscription, ibid., No.674), *Pavaita* (Kuḍa Buddhist Cave Inscriptions, ibid., No.1040), *Pāvayitika* (ibid., No.1041) and *pavajitikayā* (Jas Burgess, *The Buddhist Stupas of Amaravati and Jaggayyapeṭa* pp.78, 90) which could have meant, one who was ordained *(pravrajita)* but had not received the higher ordination *(upasampadā).* See also, *Lüders list,* Nos.1006, 1099, 1128, 1130 and 1139.

Collectively they were termed as *Samuddesas (Śramaṇoddeśas)*,[4] i.e. aspirants for the state of monkhood[5] and with a view to prepare themselves for that stage, were required to observe the ten *śikṣāpadas*.[6] The *Mahāvastu*[7] elucidates the rules concerning the ordination of novices *(Śrāmaṇera)* while recounting Rāhula's admission to the Order. The most interesting fact which it reveals is that while uttering the *triśaraṇa* formula the novice included his name[8] in it, after which he took the vow of the ten moral precepts.

With the growth of monastic life, even the *Pabajjā* ceremony now became an elaborate procedure. I-tsing informs us that one desirous of joining the *Saṅgha* had to first select a teacher[9] to whom he would express his wish. The

---

[4]The term *Samaṇudêśa* in the sense of a novice occurs in the Bhaṭṭiprolu Buddhist Casket Inscription (*Lüders list*, No.1339). The term *Śramaṇodeśah* and *Śramaṇodeśikā* occur in the *Divyāvadāna* (BST.), pp.94, 99.

[5]H. Kern, op. cit., p.78.

[6]The ten precepts *(Mahāvagga,* p.87) for a moral life are to abstain from—

(a) Taking life (*pāṇātipātā veramaṇī*).
(b) Taking what is not given (*adinnādānā veramaṇī*).
(c) Sexual misconduct (*abrahmacariyā veramaṇī*).
(d) Lying (*musāvādā veramaṇī*).
(e) Drinking liquor *(Surāmeraya majjapamādaṭṭhānā veramaṇī).*
(f) Eating after noon (*vikālabiojana veramaṇī*).
(g) Dancing, singing, music and seeing stage plays *naccagītavādit-avisūkadassanā veramaṇī*).
(h) Adorning oneself with garlands, perfumes and ointments *(mālagandhavilepanadhāraṇamaṇḍana-vibhūsanaṭṭhānā veramaṇī).*
(i) Using high and large beds (*uccāsayana mahāsayanā veramaṇī*).
(j) Receiving gold and silver (*jātarūparajatapaṭiggahaṇā veramaṇī*).

It is a point to note that *Saṅgha* life could not be conterminous with the system of *Vinaya* which enjoined the ten *Śikṣāpadas* and two of them became debatable issues at the second council (see, *supra,* Chap.II). For example the acceptance of gold and silver on the part of the *bhikkhu* was abstained but from the communal viewpoint it was utilized since it was essential for their maintenance.

[7]*Mahāvastu*, III, p.256.

[8]Ibid., p.256-57.

[9]See, *The Questions of King Milinda,* Pt.II, p.96.

teacher would accept him as a candidate and leave him at leisure for ten days or a month after which he would impart to him the five *Śikṣapadas*. Thereafter he would arrange a *paṭa* (simple cloak), a *saṅkakshikā, a nivāsana,* a bowl and a filter and would address himself to the *Saṅgha* and relate the candidate's desire. When the *Saṅgha* permitted the candidate, the teacher would ask the *Ācārya* to conduct the ceremony. The candidate had to get his head and beard shaved and after taking a bath, would receive the priestly dress and bowl. This ceremony would make him a *pravrajita* (homeless priest).

Next, in the presence of the *Upādhyāya,* the *Ācārya* would impart to him the ten *śikṣāpadas*. After the instructionṣ in these precepts he was called a *Śrāmaṇera.*[10] He had to observe the twelve particulars[11] setforth in the *Vinaya* texts, though a

---

[10]I-tsing interprets *Śrāmaṇera* as 'one who seeks for rest', meaning 'one who wishes to enter Nirvāna, the complete rest'. See, J. Takakusu, op. cit., p.96.

[11]The twelve particulars mentioned by I-tsing (J. Takakusu, loc. cit., p.97) are as follows:

(a) One must distinguish (between legal and illegal robes (*Nissaggiyā* 1-10).
(b) One must not sleep without garments.
(c) One must not touch fire (probably *Pācittiyā* 56).
(d) One must not eat too much food (*Pācittiyā* 34, 35, 36).
(e) One must not injure any living things (*Pācittiyā* 61).
(f) One must not throw filth upon the green grass (*Pācittiyā* 11 and 20).
(g) One must not recklessly climb up a high tree (unless in emergency).
(h) One must not touch jewels (*Pācittiyā* 84; *Nissagiya* 18 and 19).
(i) One must not eat food left after a meal (*Pācittiyā* 38).
(j) One must not dig the ground (*Pācittiyā* 9).
(k) One must not refuse offered food.
(l) One must not injure growing sprouts.

Curiously enough, I-tsing's point (a) finds confirmation in the *Vinaya* of the Mūlasarvāstivādins, Mahāsaṅghikas, Sarvāstivādins and the Theravādins. Point (c) corresponds to *Pācittiya* 52 of the Mūlasarvāstivāddins and Sarvāstivādins, 41 of the Mahāsāṅghikas and 56 of the Theravādins. Point (d) corresponds to *Pācittiya* 34 of the Mulasarvāstivādins and Sarvāstivādins, 33 of Mahāsaṅghikas and 35 of Theravādins. *Pācittiya* 35 of the Mulasarvāstivādins and Sarvāstivādins corresponds to 34 of the Mahāsaṅghikas and 36 of Theravādins. *Pācittiya* 36 of Mulasarvāstivādins and Sarvāstivādins corresponds with 40 of Mahāsaṅghikas and 32 of Theravādins...

transgression of these rules, in their case, did not involve guilt.

The *Upasampadā,* on the other hand, made the *Śāmaṇera* a regular member of the Order—a *bhikkhu.* The age bar of twenty years continued even in later times.[12] The ceremony, attitude, method and rites of asking instruction and announcing one's intention were the same for those who proceeded to receive full ordination.

The six requisites[13] were arranged by the teacher. Participation of nine other *bhikkhus* besides the candidate's teacher was essential.[14] This was followed by salutation (thrice) or touching the feet of every priest by the candidate.

... Point (e) corresponds to *Pācittiya* 61 in all the four versions and reads as follows—'Whatever monk should intentionally deprive an animal of life, that is a pācattika.'

Point (f) mentioned as *Pācittiya* 11 and 20 corresponds to *Śaikṣa* 107 of the Mulasarvāstivādins, 110 of the Sarvāstivādins, 65 of the Mahāsaṅghikas and 74 of the Theravādins.

Point (g) corresponds with 108 *Śaikṣa* rule of the Mulasarvāstivādins and 113 of the Sarvāstivādins.

Point (h) corresponds with rule 59 of Mulasarvāstivādins, 49 of Mahasaṅghikas, 58 of Sarvāstivādins and 84 of Theravādins.

Point (i) mentioned as *Pācittiya* 38 is close to rule 34 of Mulasarvāstivādins and Sarvāstivādins, 33 of Mahāsaṅghikas and 35 of Theravādins.

Point (j) corresponds to *Pācittiya* 73 of Mulasarvāstivādins, Mahāsaṅghikas, Sarvāstivādins and 10 of Theravādins.

Point (l) corresponds to *Pācittiya* 11 which is common to all versions.

Point (b) and, (k) are not traceable in the *Vinaya*—see, W. Pachow, *A Comparative Study of the Prātitmokṣa*; Charles Prebish, *BMD.*, Appendix Concordance table.

[12]Nāgasena was admitted to full membership in the higher grade of the Order at the age of twenty. See, *The Questions of King Milinda*, Pt.I, p.22. See, also J. Takakusu, op. cit., p.99.

[13]The *saṅghāti* (double cloak), the *uttarāsaṅga* (upper garment), the *antarvāsa* (inner garment), *pātra* (bowl), *nishīdana* (water strainer). See, J. Takakusu, op. cit., p.54. The Pali texts omitting *nishidana* mention the girdle, the razor and the needle constituting the eight requisites of the *bhikkhu.*

[14]Ordination was conferred by an assembly of at least ten *bhikkhus.* See, *Mahāvagga,* p.56; *Gilgit Manuscripts* (ed.), N. Dutt, Vol.III. Pt.II, p.205.

He was instructed to seek to learn the *mahāsīlas*. The *Upādhyāya* then invested him before the assembly with the garments and the bowl. The candidate carried the bowl successively before every priest who proclaimed it 'a good bowl'.

It was only after this that the bowl was to be accepted by the candidate according to the law. The *Karmācārya* then imparted the great precepts *(mahāṣīla)* by reading or muttering before him. After duly receiving the precepts, the candidate was called an *upasampanna,*[15] i.e. one who had received the *upasampadā* ordination.

The ceremony was followed by immediately measuring the shadow of the sun in order to determine the time of ordination and even the name of the season was noted down. It was recorded that the ordination had taken place before the meal or after it[16] since seniority in the Order commenced from the time of ordination.[17]

I-tsing[18] notes that the priests in the Nālandā monastery often received the *upasampadā* ordination in the early morning, on the first day of the 'long season' (17th of the 6th moon), when the day dawned. Thus they claimed seniority among those who were ordained in the same summer. They were therefore not required to make gifts to others after ordination except to their teachers. It was after this that the candidate was taught the character of offences as embodied in the *prātimokṣa* and the manner of reciting the precepts. It cannot be denied that later Mahāyānistic literature, with its emphasis on the cultivation of attitude of mind rather than rules and regulations, suggested that entry in the *Saṅgha* meant entry into the discipline of the *bodhisattvas* by taking

---

[15]I-tsing (J. Takakusu, op. cit., pp.99-100) interprets *upasampanna* as *upa* (near) and *sampanna* (full or complete), signifying *Nirvāṇa*. In receiving the complete precepts a person is nearer to *Nirvāṇa*.

[16]Ibid., pp.100-01.

[17]This was a practice of long standing mentioned even in the *Milinda-pañho*. See, *The Questions of King Milinda*, Pt.I, p.38.

[18]J. Takakusu, loc. cit., p.103.

the vow of discipline in the presence of one who himself is under this discipline.[19]

Discipline here implied following the proper course of conduct. As the 'Ratnamegha sutra'[20] puts it, 'it is not by the restraint of the monk's code alone that I can gain enlightenment. How then? I must learn in all the Sūtrāntas the various rules and precepts of conduct enjoined in each by the Tathāgata for the bodhisattva.'

Bars to Admission

The honour and respect, esteem and devotion that the *Saṅgha* received from the society, depended to a great extent on the admission of the right type of persons as desired by public opinion.[21] Entry into the *Saṅgha* was, as a rule, open to all without any distinction of rank or caste. But practical necessity caused the imposition of certain restrictions on admission into the Order.[22]

The circumstances disqualifying persons from admission and ordination, which are minutely expounded in the *Mahāvagga*,[23] continue even in later times. Bars to admission in the *Saṅgha* had to be imposed as is clear from Nāgasena's[24] reply in which he states that not all join the Order with the

[19]A change in the *triśarana* formula is noted in the *Śikṣāsamuccaya,* (ed., p.170), and the *Bodhicaryāvatāra* (BST.), Chap.II, vv.26, 49.

[20]*Śikṣāsamuccaya* (trans.), p.19.

[21]Buddha had a great respect for social customs and traditions and, on that account he was always ready to modify and formulate his rulings in accordance with them, if possible. He wanted a healthy relation between society and his Order. See, G.S.P. Misra, *The Age of Vinaya,* p.116.

[22]The Jainas have also a similar list debarring people from entering the *Saṅgha.* See, Haripada Chakraborti, op. cit., p.362: S.B. Deo. op. cit., p.140.

[23]The admittance of those afflicted with diseases like leprosy, boils, dry leprosy, consumption and fits was forbidden—*Mahāvagga,* p.76. In the interest of the state, the admission of men in royal service, declared thieves, jail breaker, proclaimed robber, scourged offender, branded thief, debtor and slave was checked, evidently in view of the liabilities they bore to the state and society—ibid., pp.78-80. Sons whose parents had not given their consent were similarly excluded. Children, too, were considered unfit for admission into the Order—ibid., p.87.

[24]*The Question of King Milinda*, II, pp.176-77.

object of renunciation but some leave the world in terror, at the tyranny of kings, to be safe from being robbed, some harassed by debt and some perhaps to gain a livelihood. Therefore, admitting candidates with such questionable motivations was contrary to the *bhikkhu* ethic of discipline.

Nāgasena[25] specifically states that the following cannot attain insight into the truth—a matricide, a patricide, an *arhat* killer, a schism creator, one who sheds Buddha's blood, an eunuch, a hermaphrodite, a child under seven years of age and others.

The *Vinaya* of the Mulasarvāstivādins[26] mentions a similar list. It disqualifies a heretic, a matricide, a patricide, an *arhat* killer, a person who, out of evil intention, attempted to spill the blood of the Tathagata, anyone who had committed the four *pārājikas*, a *bhikkhu* who had been removed from the *Saṅgha,* for not acknowledging the offence committed by him.

The aforesaid bars to admission clearly point out the fact that the sacredness and the inviolability of moral, political, social and economic obligations were properly emphasized and recognized by the *Saṅgha* in order, not to entail in any way state annoyance and disgrace to itself.[27]

Grading of Monks in the Saṅgha

The most intrinsic feature of the early Buddhist *Saṅgha* was the absence of a hierarchy of positions. But with the growth of corporate life, one notices that the organizational structure of the *Saṅgha* which was anti-hierarchical in the beginning, now specified status positions with seniority and associated competencies.[28]

---

[25]For a corresponding list. See, *Mahāvagga,* pp.91-93.

[26]*Gilgit Manuscripts*, Vol.III, Pt.IV, pp.52-65, 67-68; See also, *Samantapāsādikā* (Nal. ed.), Vol.II, p. 447; *Divyāvadāna* (BST.), p.160.

[27]G.C. Pande, *BDVI.*, p.140. See also, John C. Holt, *Discipline,* pp.119ff.

[28]The basis of seniority in the *Saṅgha* was dependent on the number of summer retreats observed by the *bhikkhu,* the season in which he had been ordained, the number of days left in the season, priority going to that person whose ordination had taken place before meal on that day and the length of the sun's shadow at that time. If all being equal, seniority was to be determined by the earliest arrival. See, J. Takakusu, op. cit., p.102.

We find the *Mahāvastu*[29] referring to three grades, viz., the *Sthavira* (the *thêras)*, the *madhyama* (those of middle status) and *navaka* (newly ordained *bhikkhu).* The Mathura Buddhist Inscriptions[30] refer to dedication of a gift by the *Saṅgha-sthavira* (elder of the congregation). The term *sthavira* here need not be taken simply in the sense of a venerable member but as a senior officiating as head of the *Saṅgha.* This receives ample corroboration from the *Abhisamācārikā*,[31] a text of the Lokottaravāda school. Here the *Saṅghasthavira* is entrusted with the duty of conducting the *uposatha* ceremony, of appointing able members of the assembly to conduct multifarious duties such as taking votes, recitation of the *prātimokṣa* and delivering discourses.

Further there is reference to the *Dvitīyasthavira*[32] (the second *thêra*) whose main function was to act on behalf of the *Saṅghasthavira* when the latter was unable to perform his duties owing to personal difficulties.

I-tsing minutely describes the grades of Buddhist monks. The first stage[33] was that of the candidate *(upāsaka)* expressing his desire to be a seeker and who thereafter becomes a *pravrajita.* The next higher rank was that of the *cha-gā-ra* (i.e. *Dahara*) which is translated as 'small teacher', a designation given after the *upasampadā* ceremony.[34] The term *dahara bhikkhu* (young monk) occurs also in the Amarāvatī Buddhist Sculpture Inscription.[35]

The third stage,[36] according to I-tsing, was that of the *Sthavira,* a position granted to a member who had passed ten

---

[29]*Mahāvastu,* III, p.47. This gradation may well agree with I-tsing's (J. Takakusu, op. cit., pp.56-57) classification of monks as superiors, mediocres and inferiors.

[30]*Lüders list,* Nos.129, 130, 131.

[31]*Abhisamācārikā*, pp.1f.

[32]Ibid., pp.5f.

[33]J. Takakusu, loc. cit., p.96.

[34]Ibid., p.104. This translation is incorrect. The term *dahara* in the sense of a young monk occurs often in the Pāli canon. See, *Saṁyutta Nikāya*, I, p.67: *Majjhima Nikāya,* II, p.249, *Sutta Nipāta* (Muni Sutta), v.218.

[35]*Lüders list,* No.1295; Jas Burgess, op. cit., p.93.

[36]J. Takakusu, loc. cit., p.104.

summer retreats. Such a person could become an *upādhyāya.* I-tsing refers to another term, viz., the *bahuśruta*[37]—one learned both in the sacred and secular literature and famed as virtuous. This appears to be an epithet rather than a rank.

I-tsing,[38] while describing the worship of the *caitya* and the ceremony of chanting at the Tamralipti monastery, states that the head priest bowed to the lion seat and then the seat of the saints, followed by the second and the third priests respectively.

Privileges

Seniority in the Order entailed a number of privileges.[39] The privileges enjoyed by monks as *Upādhyāya* and *Ācāryas* are detailed elsewhere.[40] Even the residential quarters of the monks designed with functional utility betray certain striking features in this direction. The famous *Vihāra* No. 19 at Bhājā, with Indra and Surya in attendance, is an elegant separate residence, perhaps for a chief monk.[41] The Bahuśrutiya monastery (site 5) at Nāgārjunikoṇḍa had three special chambers besides the twenty eight cells and a Buddha shrine.

---

[37]Ibid.

[38]Ibid., pp.153-54.

[39]The Vinayavastu of the Mulasarvāstivādins *(Gilgit Manuscripts*, Vol.III, Pt.3, pp.124-25) specifies the Lord's injunction regarding the first seat, first food, etc., to the monk who had the longest ordination. The calculation of seniority was to be made by *varṣa* (rainy season) passed by the monk. The *Cullavagga* (p.257) also lays down that paying reverence, rising up in reverence, salutation, proper respect and apportionment of the best seat, water and food should be according to seniority. But as Rhys Davids and Oldenberg, (*Vinaya Texts,* SBE., XX, Pt.III, p.195, fn.2) observe, 'the prohibition to reserve exclusively according to seniority the use of property belonging to the whole *Saṅgha* was held to imply that the temporary use of it was to go according to seniority.'

[40]Infra, Chap.IV.

[41]Michael W. Meister, 'Sub-urban planning and rock cut architecture in India', *Madhu* (*Recent Researches in Indian Archaeology and Art History*), p.157. An inscribed potsherd from Salihundam, datable 2nd century AD bears the term *'(A?) riya parivene'* which when read in its full context probably suggests the donation made to a distinguished *bhikkhu* residing in a cell or private chamber. See, R. Subrahmanyam, *Salihundam—A Buddhist site in Andhra Pradesh*, p.86.

These chambers might have been meant for the *Ācarya vinaya-dhara,* etc., who might have preferred to have separate cells of their own. Site 26 also possessed two such special chambers.[42]

Fa-hien[43] refers to the monks of Khotan who took their meals seated in a regular order. Hiuen-tsang's[44] comment that 'where the spiritual attainments are high, the distinctions conferred are extraordinary', merits attention. In his own words, 'the brother who expounds orally one treatise (or class of scripture) in the Buddhist canon, whether Vinaya, Abhidharma or Sutra, is exempted from serving under the prior; he who expounds two is invested with the outfit of a superior; he who expounds three has brethren deputed to assist him; he who expounds four has lay servants assigned to him; he who expounds five rides an elephant; he who expounds six rides an elephant and has a surrounding retinue.'[45]

During I-tsing's time, the best room in the monastery, together with a servant were provided to a very learned monk and also to him who thoroughly studied one of the three collections.[46] Such a person was free from routine work assigned to monastics, when he delivered lectures.[47]

Riding in a sedan chair was a privilege enjoyed by a learned monk when he went out.[48] The venerable monk was assigned a lay servant[49] who often performed odd tasks such as carrying a chair and utensils when he attended a reception,[50]

---

[42]H. Sarkar, op. cit., p.93.

[43]J. Legge, op. cit., p.18.

[44]T. Watters, op. cit., I, p.162.

[45]Ibid.

[46]J. Takakusu, op. cit., p.64. I-tsing (ibid., p.86) definitely makes a distinction between very learned priests and merely elder priests (*sthaviras*). He says, 'before the varsha (rainy season) rooms are assigned to each member; to the elders (i.e., *sthaviras)* better rooms are given and thus gradually to the lowest'.

[47]Ibid., p.64.

[48]Ibid., pp.30, 64.

[49]Hiuen-tsang was assigned such a 'pure man'. See, S. Beal, *Life*, p.161. Fahien too (J. Legee, loc. cit., p.18, fn.1) refers to a 'pure man' attending at a meal.

[50]J. Takakusu, loc. cit., p.36.

carrying the remnant of the food eaten by him,[51] carrying incense and flowers in a chanting ceremony.[52] To top it all, as I-tsing reveals that a priest who had a page could let the latter wash him.[53] The seniors ate their meals on chairs while the junior members used blocks of wood.[54] With respect to the distribution of articles, if they were not sufficient for all the monks of the monastery, only the elders took it.[55]

Though all such privileges were granted to elder and accomplished monks yet the very fact that they were taken advantage of reveals that the monks were not immune to the prevailing social mores.

MONASTIC OBSERVANCES

Vassāvāsa (Sk. varṣāvasa)

The custom of rain retreat *(vassāvāsa)* had been in observance by generations of religious wanderers—the brāhmaṇical *sannyāsins*, the *Yatis* of the *Niganṭḥa* sect as well as by the Buddhists.[56] It originated presumably as an enforced necessity, for the tropical rains of India made wandering about a physical impossibility. Shelter and retreat, for a fixed period in a year, gradually acquired a certain sanctity and ceremonial character.[57] *Vassā* continued to be observed even after *bhikṣus* had taken up a fixed residences.[58]

The Buddhist *vassā* had two periods, an earlier, commencing from the day after the full moon of *āṣāḍha* and a

---

[51]Ibid., p.47.

[52]Ibid., p.154.

[53]Ibid., p.92.

[54]Ibid., p.22.

[55]Ibid., p.191.

[56]S Dutt, BFAC., pp.66-67; C. Prebish, *BMD.*, p.4.

[57]S. Dutt, *EBM.*, p.102; C. Prebish, loc. cit., p.4.

[58]*The Questions of King Milinda*, I, p.23. See, also *Divyāvadāna*, (BST.), pp.11, 58, 257, 430, 442; *Avadānaśataka*, (BST.), p.84. The *Abhisamācārikā* (pp.44f) enumerates rules for *bhikṣus* observing rain retreat.

later, a month after that date.[59] As I-tsing[60] states: 'the first summer-retreat is on the first day of the dark half of the fifth moon and the second summer-retreat is on the first day of the dark half of the sixth moon; only on these two days should the summer-retreat be entered upon'.

Whether the *Vassāvāsa* as Gokuldas De[61] asserts was instituted out of consideration for the laity and its welfare or not, it is all too clear that during these three months, the *Saṅgha* was completely dependent upon the gifts of the laity of the particular place as confirmed by inscriptional evidence.

Several Nasik inscriptions, which aim at recording donations for the maintenance of the monks observing rain retreat in certain caves, refer to the *vassākāla.* For instance, inscription No. 20 records the gift of a cave and one hundred *Kārshāpaṇas* as robe money (*chivarikaṁ*) for the monks dwelling in the caves during the rainy season.[62] Certain Kāṇherī cave inscriptions recording donations to meet the expense of robes for the monks, mention *vassākāla* as *utukāla* (*ṛtu kāla*).[63]

Fa-hien[64] himself observed the summer-retreat at various places during his sojourn. Hiuen-tsang[65] simply refers to this custom as prevailing in the *Saṅgha* as late as the seventh century. I-tsing provides details of the practice. All the five assemblies[66] (*pariṣads*) had to observe the *vassā.* If anyone wanted to absent himself from the retreat, he had to obtain the permission of the assembly, the maximum time allowed was forty nights.[67] One could go off without taking leave of

---

[59]T. Watters, op. cit., I, p.144; II, p.138.

[60]J. Takakusu, op. cit., p.85.

[61]Gokuldas De, op. cit., p.90.

[62]*ASWI.,* Vol.IV, p.115.

[63]Ibid., Vol.V, Nos.15, 18, 21, 28.

[64]J. Legge, op. cit., pp.22, 29, 53.

[65]T. Watters, op. cit., I, pp.102, 124, 144; II, p.138.

[66]They were, the *bhikṣus, bhikṣunis, Śrāmaṇeras, Śrāmaṇeris, Śikṣmanas.* See, J. Takakusu, loc. cit., p.86.

[67]Ibid., p.85. See, *Mahāvagga,* pp.146f.

absence in case of sickness or emergency.[68] In case of necessity permission on behalf of the other monk could be given to a member of the lower rank.[69]

It seems that the rank of a *bhikṣu* was degraded if he did not observe *vassā* which makes I-tsing[70] remark, 'but there is no reason why they should be degraded from their original position in the Order to a lower place.... The rank of the bhikṣu ought to be determined by the date of the ordination.'

Uposatha

The *Uposatha*[71] ceremony which was introduced by Buddha in his *Saṅgha* at the instance of Bimbisāra, the king of Magadha evolved successively, as times went by. Tbe Buddhist monks were enjoined to observe the *Uposatha* ceremony by the recital of the *Sikhāpadas* or the rules of discipline prescribed by the Buddha.[72] The recital of the *Pātimokkha* with the confession of breaches committed, was adopted by the *Saṅgha* at a comparatively late stage of its growth.[73] The recital was an occasion whereby the collective Order could affirm its adherence to discipline.

---

[68]J. Takakusu, op. cit., p.86.

[69]Ibid

[70]Ibid., p.21.

[71]It was a pre-Buddhist ceremony coming down from Vedic times laid down for both recluses and laymen for the purification of both body and mind. See, *Śatpatha Brāhmaṇa*, Pt.I, p.5, G.S.P. Misra, op. cit., p.119; Gokuldas De, op. cit., p.59; S. Dutt, *BMMI.*, p.73. The other sects observed it by imparting injunctions in their respective *Dhamma* to the laymen on the 8th, 14th and the 15th day of a fortnight. See, *Mahāvagga,* p.105. The lay observance of the *Uposatha* consisted in the acceptance of eight precepts of morality (*Aṭṭhaṅgika sīla*) and its aim and purpose was stated to be 'purification of a soiled mind by a proper process'—see, *The Book of Gradual Saying*, I, p.187.

[72]*Mahāvagga,* p.106.

[73]G.C. Pande, *BDVI.,* p.144; G.S.P. Misra, op. cit., p.120; S. Dutt, *EBM.,* pp.81, 84.

The 8th day function was subsequently dispensed with, as is confirmed by the expression *'dhuvāye cha anuposathāye'* used in the fifth pillar edict of Aśoka.[74] The Sārnāth schism pillar edict also testifies to the 8th day continuing to be the non-*Uposatha* day.[75]

The Lokottaravāda text, *Abhisamācārikā*[76] provides sufficient information regarding the *Uposatha* ceremony being conducted by the *Saṅghasthavira* and in his absence by the *Dvitiyasthavira.* The preliminary task which devolved on the *Saṅghasthavira* was to determine whether the *Uposatha* was *Cāturdaśika, Pancadaśika* or *Sandhiposadha.* Seats were arranged accordingly. He appointed able members to conduct multifarious duties such as taking votes, recitation of *Prātimokṣa* and delivering discourses to the laity.

The later history of the *Uposatha* custom is interesting, when it emerged as a colourful festival with the ceremony of image worship dominating the scene. Hiuen-tsang[77] refers to the 'three longs' and 'six fast days' of every month, when monks took materials of worship and paid homage to the images[78] of their respective saints. 'The Abhidharma Brethren offer worship to Sāriputra, the Samādhists to Mudgalaputra, the *Sūtraists* to Pūrnamaitriyāniputra, the *Vinayists* to Upāli,

---

[74]A.C. Sen, *Aśoka's Edicts,* p.155; H. Chakraborti, *Early Brahmi Records in India,* p.90.

[75]Ibid., p.131.

[76]*Abhisamācārikā,* pp.1-4.

[77]T. Watters, op. cit., I, p.302. Fa-hien (J. Legge, op. cit., pp.45-46) makes the festival of patron worship occur once a year after retreat, each set having its own day. He states that it was the people who provided the illuminations and flowers for the topes while the monks preached.

[78]Fa-hien (J. Legge, loc. cit., pp.44-46) in his general survey of 'Mid-India' including the Mathura district, tells us that at the Buddhist *vihāras* there were topes to Śāriputra, Maudgalyāyana, Ānanda and to the *Sūtras*, the *Vinaya* and the *Abhidharma.* To some of these topes services were offered, but he describes the *Śrāmaṇeras* as making offerings to Rāhula and not to his tope and he describes the Mahāyānists as offering worship to 'Prajñāparamitā, Mañjuśrī and Kuan-shi-yin'.

the *bhikshunis* to Ānanda and *Srāmaṇeras* to Rāhula: and the Mahayanists to the various P'usas'.[79]

I-tsing[80] refers to the *upavasatha* day as a day of religious observance and celebration for the laity as well as the monks. The laity observed the eight *śilas* during the four fast days[81] and invited the monks for meals. Meal taking was preceded by image worship. The host offered lights, flowers and incense. Music accompanied by songs was played after which meals were served.[82] It seems that the monks regaled on the repast served to them for as I-tsing observes, 'the ceremony of the Upavasatha-day is observed on a scale so grand that all the trays and plates are full of the cakes and rice remaining over; and melted butter and cream can be partaken of to any extent'.[83]

It cannot be denied that monkish (hence considered ideal) character had departed from the norms so much that it baited the gullible laity to believe (and hence to practice) that if the intention of giving food be generous, the reward obtained for the good work will be correspondingly abundant.

Thus, *Uposatha* which signified the gradual cleansing of the mind 'still sullied by imperfection' ceased to conform in practice to the ancient canonical rules.

*Pavāraṇā (*Sk. *Pravāraṇā)*

The other major communal ceremony was the *Pavāraṇa*

---

[79]T. Watters, op. cit., I, p.302. Hiuen-tsang is perhaps wrong in representing the Abhidharmists as worshipping Sāriputra, the Samadhists as worshipping Purṇa-Maitriyaniputra. Śāriputra was distinguished among Buddha's disciples for his *prajñā*. Abhidharma came into existence after his death. Mahamaudgalyāyana was adept in superhuman powers but not in samadhi. Maitrayaniputra is praised as a good expounder of the Master's teachings but he is not especially associated with the sūtras.

[80]J. Takakusu, op. cit., pp.36ff.

[81]Ibid., p.188. The four fasting days were, (a) in the dark half of the moon, the 8th and 14th or the 10th and 15th, (b) in the bright half of the moon, the 8th and 15th.

[82]Ibid., p.42.

[83]Ibid., p.40.

which was held at the end of the rainy season.[84] This was in the form of a confessional assembly where the monks themselves requested the assembly to point out the offences that they might have unknowingly committed but however came into the notice of the *Saṅgha*. Unlike the *Pātimokkha* ritual, a violation of the rules is not voluntarily given by the *bhikkhu* under scrutiny.[85] Although both rituals were designed to maintain *parisuddhi*, the *Pāṭimokkha* was clearly a liturgical rite while the *Pavāraṇā* occasion served as a type of court of law.[85A] During I-tsing's[86] time the custom prevailed in its usual form. The only noticeable feature was that the laity participated in the pre-*Pavāraṇā* festivity.

On the *pre-Pavāraṇā* day (the last day of the retreat) the assembly invited a priest to recite a Buddhist *sūtra* before the monks and lay devotees. The next morning was spent going round towns and villages to worship *caityas*.[87] They returned

---

[84]The *Pavāraṇā* and *Kaṭhina*, rites continued to be held at the end of the *vassā* even after the monks had abandoned the eremitical life for a cenobitical one. See, *Divyāvadāna* (BST.), pp.58, 59.

[85]I.B. Horner (*Book of the Discipline*, Pt.4, p.xvii) comparing the two rituals has observed that 'the recital of the Pātimokkha was to "remove" offences, by confessing them, during the nine dry months of the year; the Invitation (Pavāraṇā) was to remove any offences that the monk had committed during the three wet months (vassa), and would help them to aim at grasping discipline.'

[85A]John C. Holt, op. cit., pp.131-32.

[86]*Pravāraṇā* is translated as '(Doing) as one wishes': it also means 'satisfying' and it again conveys the sense of 'pointing out another's offence according to his wish'. See J. Takakusu, op. cit., pp.89-90.

[87]Fa-hien (J. Legge, op. cit., pp.44-46) refers to community of monks worshipping topes of Śāriputra, Mahā-maudgalyāyana, Ānanda, topes in honour of *Abhidharma, Vinaya*, Sūtra, and worship of Rāhula by *Śrāmaṇeras*. He mentions students of Mahāyāna presenting offerings to the Prajñā-pāramitā, to Mañjuśri and to Kwan-she-yin. This patron worship occurred once a year after the rainy retreat. It was the laity which brought flowers and incense and heard the law. Hiuen-tsang (T. Watters, op. cit., II, p.138) seems to be referring to the *Pavāraṇā* festivity when he remarks, 'every year, when the bhikshus break up the rain-retreat, clergy and laity come from all quarters in myriads and for seven days and nights bearing fragrant flowers and making music they wander through the wood and perform acts of worship'.

to the monastery in the forenoon. The atmosphere was festive with lights and offerings of incense and flowers. The laity brought storied carriages, images in sedan chairs, accompanied by drums, banners and canopies. This as I-tsing remarks is called Sa-ma-kin-li which is translated as 'concord' or 'thronging together'.

Thereafter the monks received the *Pavāraṇā* ceremony, i.e. if the offence was pointed out by another, it was followed by confession and atonement on the part of the guilty *bhikkhu*.[88] The idea behind the ritual was to evaluate each other's conduct according to the rules of discipline.[89] This became an institutionalized procedure for bringing shortcomings into the open.[90] Once the individual corrective procedures were adopted, the *Saṅgha* as a whole was considered to be collectively pure with regard to rules. This confirmed the spiritual status of the monks and served as a preliminary event for the *Kaṭhina* ritual where the laity expressed its admiration for the community by bestowing gifts on it.[90A]

Kaṭhina

The *Kaṭhina*[91] ceremony followed the *Pavāraṇā* closely. The original custom was the making and distribution of robes presented by the laity to the *Saṅgha*.[92] Unanimous consent of

[88] J. Takakusu, op. cit., p.87.

[89] It was' as G.S.P. Misra (op. cit., p.123) observes 'an external means applied for the purification of the monks.'

[90] It seems that the Buddha himself recognized the therapeutic value of catharsis when he stated: 'The rains fall heavily on that which is covered; not upon that which is revealed. Reveal, therefore, what thou hast concealed, and the rain shall touch thee not'—(*Vinaya Texts*, SBE., Vol.XX, p.305).

[90A] John C. Holt, op. cit., p.134

[91] The word *Kaṭhina* (Lit. hard) denotes cotton cloth. See, Edgerton, *Buddhist Hybrid Sanskrit Dictionary*, S.V. Kaṭhina.

[92] I-tsing (J. Takakusu, loc. cit., p.85) as late as the 7th century AD admits, 'the 16th day of the 8th moon is the day on which the Kaṭhina robes are spread out (as a present to the Saṅgha) which is an ancient custom'.

the members was sought, followed by a formal announcement entrusting a worthy *bhikkhu* to receive the *Kaṭhina* cloth from the laity on behalf of the resident monks.

After the robe-material had been approved as *Kaṭhina* cloth by the *Saṅgha* and a monk had been approved as *Kaṭhina* spreader by the *Saṅgha,* this robe material was handed over to this monk by the *Saṅgha* and this material was spread by the *Kaṭhina*-spreader.[93] According to the Pali and the Sarvāstivādin tradition the stitching of robes was to take place within one day, followed by washing, dyeing and drying it in the sun, whereas the Mūlasarvāstivādin tradition prescribes that the ceremonial actions are to be held in three days.[94]

Fa-hien[95] while describing the post-*vassā* ceremonies, states, 'One month after the annual retreat, the families eager for merit, advise each other to present offerings and refreshments to the monks. A meeting is held by the monks, in which dharma is preached to the people. After the sermon, they offer to Sāriputra's stūpa all kinds of flowers, incenses and burn the lamps throughout the night. They hire actors to play one episode in the life of Sāriputra in which he was a great brāhmaṇa and begged lord Buddha to ordain him as a monk. The same performance is done for the life of Mahāmaudgala-putra and Mahākāsyapa.' 'When the monks receive their monastic year, the elders, the laity, the brāhmaṇas etc. bring all kinds of requisites for the monks and offer them to the *Saṅgha.* The monks also after having received the offered

[93]Kun Chang, *A comparative Study of the Kaṭhinavastu,* pp.28-30. According to the Lokottaravāda text *Abhisamācārikā* (p.92) the *Kaṭhina* is to be bound on two pins on a wall of the monastery. The procedure and rules that govern the proper enactment of the *Kaṭhina* rite are discussed at length by Heinz Bechart, 'Some remarks on the Kaṭhina rite,' *JBRS.,* 54 (1968), pp.319-29.

[94]See, Heinz Bechart, loc. cit., pp.322-24.

[95]See, Bhikkhu Thich Min Chan, 'Monastic life in India in the 5th century as seen by Fa-Hsien,' *JBRS.,* Vol.XLVII, Jan.-Dec.1961, Pts.I-IV, pp.67-68; J. Legge, op. cit., pp.45-47.

requisites, distribute them among themselves. Since the Buddha's passing away, these rules of conduct for the noble Order and these traditions in accordance with the law have been handed down without interruption.'

By I-tsing's time it seems that a formal ceremony was held in which the five venerable persons (one from each of the *Pariṣads)* asked the heads of the Assembly (i.e. *Sthaviras)* whether the gifts could be made to the members of *Saṅgha.* This was followed by the presentation not only of customary robe cloth but other necessities such as knives, needles, awls, etc., which were distributed by the *Saṅgha.*[96]

Thus the *Kaṭhina* rite provided an occasion whereby the laity admiring the spiritual purity of the *Saṅgha,* considered it fit to bestow gifts upon them. As Alec Robertson[97] has pointed out: 'One great advantage of the Kaṭhina ceremony is that it brings together the bhikkhus and the lay-devotees. The bhikkhus receive from the laity the requisites of the monk life which are necessary for the physical well-being, and at the same time, promote their spiritual progress on the path to deliverance. The bhikkhus reciprocate the liberality of the laity by providing the latter with spiritual nutriment for their well being here and hereafter. This mutual interdependence of the Saṅgha and the laity is essential for the strength, the unity, the solidarity and the longevity of the Buddha-sāsana.'

Food and Drinks

The mode of begging food *(piṇḍapāta)* was maintained by the monks along with accepting invitations from the laity[98] and

---

[96]J. Takakusu, op. cit., pp.87-88.

[97]Alec Robertson, *The Triple Gem and the Uposatha.* p.116. A similar view is expressed by John Holt (op. cit., p.15).

[98]This could be in the form of *Saṅghabhattaṁ, Uddesabhattaṁ, Nimantana, Pakkhikaṁ, Uposatikaṁ* or *Paṭipadikam* as referred in the *Cullavagga* (p.272). I-tsing (J. Takakusu, loc. cit., pp.35-44) refers to elaborate meals served to the *Saṅgha* on the *Upavasatha* days.

preparation of meals in the refectory.[99] It is interesting to note that inspite of the ideal, 'hath he but eaten mouthfuls four or five, let him drink water: here is sure enough refreshment for a bhikkhu filled with zeal',[100] monks developed culinary tastes and were provided with sumptuous meals.[101]

Food was classified, according to the nature and quality, into two categories, viz., soft food *(bhojanīya)*, and hard food *(khādanīya)*.[102] The five *bhojanīyas*[103] were *odana*[104] (rice),

---

[99]Fa-hien (J. Legge op. cit.,) refers to monks at Khotan (p.16) and Saṅkasya (p.52) receiving food from a common store, being called for meals by the sound of the bell (pp.17-18), being served by monastic servants. The *Abhisamācārikā* (pp.13f) refers to regulations which are to be observed at *bhaktāgra* (refectory).

[100]*Psalms of the brethren* (PTS.), v.983. The *Nikāyas* are replete with injunctions for moderate eating. As the Buddha puts it, 'a monk takes food with reflection and judgement, not for sport, not for indulgence, not for personal charm, not for beautifying, but just enough for support, for the upkeep of body, for its resting unharmed, for helping the living of the God-life'—*Book of the Gradual Sayings*, II, p.149. The *Milindapañho (The Questions of King Milinda*, II, p.340) also states that the right outcome of eating is the maintenance of life for the pursuit of holiness. The *Mahavastu* (III, p.387) specifies that 'though his stomach be empty he should eat sparingly, have little desire and be not greedy'. The *Visuddhimagga (Path of purification*, I, p.33) has a similar explanation when it states that a *bhikkhu* 'makes use of the alms food for the purpose of the endurance, for the purpose of the continuance, of the body'. The 'Ratnamegha sutra' *(Śikṣāmuccaya* (trans.), pp.127, 129) says, 'he eats in order not to become too emaciated and not too stout. And why is that? Too emaciated, he fails in health; too stout, he is confirmed in sloth. Therefore in partaking of the food he must have health in view'. This is similar to what is expressed in the Hindu Dharmasutras *(Vasistha Dharmasutra*, SBE., Vol.XXIX, X.22) regarding the ascetic: 'Let him not be dejected when he obtains nothing, nor glad when he receives something. Let him only seek as much as will sustain life, without caring for household property.'

[101]Cakes and fruits, gruel of dried rice, bean soup with hot butter sauce as flavouring, ghee and sugar were served on *Upavasatha* day. See, J. Takakusu, op. cit., p.40.

[102]*Mahāvastu*, I, p.32; II, p.375. *Pañcabhojanīyam* and *pañcakhādanīyam* are often mentioned in the *Vinaya.*

[103]See, *Pācittiya,* pp.98, 117, 119, 121, 129, 240, 243, 311, 413, etc.: *Samantapāsādikā* (Nal. ed.), Vol.II, pp.842-44.

[104]*Odāna* implied seven kinds of cooked grains, viz., sāli (rice), vīhi (a kind of rice), *yava* (barley), *godhūma* (wheat), *kaṅgu* (millet white, red and black), *varaka* (a kind of millet probably *bājrā), kudrūsaka* (a kind of rice). See, *Samantapāsādikā* (Nal. ed.), Vol.II, pp.842-43.

sattu (baked grain flour whether barley, wheat or gram), *kummāsa* (pulse and rice mixed), *maccha* (fish) and *maṃsa* (meat). I-tsing gives a somewhat different list which includes, rice, a boiled mixture of barley and peas, baked cornflour, meat and cakes.[105]

Yāgu[106] (rice gruel) seems to have been a favourite breakfast since the Buddha's time. It was taken after morning wash.[107] The *Mahāvastu*[108] contains casual references to eight or nine varieties of rice-preparations which suggests the popularity of rice as the main food. Rice *(sāli)* from which the black grains have been picked out, was served with curries and gravies of various sorts.[109]

The *pañcakhādanīyam* were roots, stalks, leaves, flowers and fruits.[110] Milk and milk products such as curd *(dadhi),*

---

[105]J. Takakusu, op. cit., p.43.

[106]It was highly praised by the Buddha as a source of life, joy and strength. See, *Mahavagga,* pp.237-38.

[107]Ibid., pp.44, 218.

[108]*Mahāvastu,* Vol.III, p.14. Hiuen-tsang (T. Watters, op. cit., II, p.86) refers to a kind of rice with large grain of extraordinary savour and fragrance called by the people 'the rice for grandees'. I-tsing (J. Takakusu, op. cit., pp.43-44) remarks, 'in the north, wheat flour is abundant, in the western district, baked flour (rice or barley) is used above all; in Magadha (central India) wheat flour is scarce, but rice is plentiful and the southern frontier, the eastern borderland have similar products to those of Magadha'.

[109]*The Questions of King Milinda*, Pt.I, p.26; *Mahāvastu*, Vol.II, p.112; *Abhisamācārikā,* p.16.

[110]J. Takakusu, loc. cit., p.43. Twelve varieties of *khādanīyas* as mentioned in the *Aṭṭṭhakathas* (see, *Samantapāsādikā* (Nal. ed.), Vol.II, p.853). These are:

Mūla khādanīya (food from root).

Kanda khādanīya (tuberous root-food).

Mulāla khādanīya (root food like lotus-root).

Matthaka khādanīya (food from the top of the tree, such as *tūḷa, Nārikela, khajjūra, kadalī*, etc.)

Khandha khādanīya (stem food, e.g. sugar cane).

Taca khādanīya (food from bark).

Patta khādanīya (food prepared out of leaves).

Puppha khādanīya (flower-food).

Phala khādanīya (fruit-food).

Piṭṭha khādanīya (a pastry prepared from flour).

Niyyāsa khādanīya (food from exudation of plants).

sour milk (*takka*), butter (*navanīta*), ghee (*sappi*) were allowed.[111] Among sweetmeats (*modaka*), *ukkārika*[112] is mentioned, which is to be understood as a 'sort of sweet meat made with milk, treacle and ghee'.[113] Another class of confectionary was *khajjaka*[114] including those made with sesame (*tilakṛta*).[115]

Monks were allowed eight kinds of drinks[116] which were classified as *yāmakālika*[117] (taken in the afternoon or night). During Fa-hien's[118] time, food eaten at any other part of the day (except between sunrise and noon) was forbidden but a stranger monk on his arrival could be offered liquid food as refreshment.

Hiuen-tsang[119] also refers to grape syrup and sugar cane drink being taken by Buddhist monks and brahmins. During I-tsing's[120] time also, a visitor monk could be offered ghee, honey, sugar or any other eatables and drink[121] as desired.

---

[111]*Mahāvagga*, p.258. Rice, butter and milk was supplied to the inmates of the Nālandā monastery. See, S. Beal, *Life*, pp.112-13.

[112]*Mahāvastu*, II, p.183; III, p.153, fn.3.

[113]V.S. Agrawala, *India as Known to Pāṇini*, p.109.

[114]*Mahāvastu*, III, p.145.

[115]Ibid., p.124.

[116]*Mahāvagga*, p.260. These were madhu, *muddikā* (grape), *sālūka* (water-lily root), *coca* (wild banana with seeds), *moca* (banana without seeds), *amba*, *jambu* (rose apple) and *phārusaka* (phālasā).

[117]*Samantapāsādikā*, Vol.II, pp.860-61.

[118]J. Legge, op. cit., p.44.

[119]T. Watters. op. cit., I, p.178.

[120]J. Takakusu, op. cit., p.125. It is noteworthy that the well known rule as to not eating solid food after sun-turn at noon was not applicable to visitor monks.

[121]I-tsing gives a slightly different list of drinks in the *Ekasata Karman*, Bk.V, p.57 (*Nanjio's Catalogue*, No.1131). It is as follows—

(a) *Cocapāna* (sour like plums).

(b) *Mocapāna* (banana or plantain).

(c) *Ku-la-ka-pāna* (kolaka, 'black pepper'? The fruit is like sour date).

(d) *Udumbarapāna* (its fruit is like li = plum).

(e) *Asvatthapāna* (syrup prepared from fruit of bodhi tree).

(f) *Parūsakapāna* (a kind of wild grape vine).

(g) *Mridhvikāpāna* (syrup prepared from grapes).

(h) *Khorgūrapāna* (it is like a small date in its shape). The *ambapāna, madhupāna, jambupāna* and *sālukapāna* have no corresponding names in I-tsing's list. See, J. Takakusu, loc. cit., pp.220-22.

It seems that *ḍāka*[122] (vegetables, green and cooked) and fruits[123] were also taken by the monks. I-tsing[124] as late as the 7th century AD mentions five fruits namely *harītaka, vibhītaka, āmalaka, marica, pippali* which agree perfectly with those given in the *Mahāvagga.*[125]

Fish and flesh could be taken by monks provided it was not seen, heard or suspected to have been prepared solely to gratify their hunger.[126] This might have caused unfavourable comments from followers of other religions and hence a new effort to prohibit meat-eating was started among the Mahāyāna advocates.[127] The *Hastikakshya*, the *Mahāmegha*, the *Nirvāṇa,* the *Angulimalika* and the *Laṅkāvatāra Sūtra*[128] reprehend and forbid meat eating. The evil effects of meat eating are recounted in the *Laṅkāvatāra Sūtra.*[129] The proper food enjoined for a *bodhisattva* is 'rice, barley, wheat, all kinds of beans, clarified butter, oil, honey, molasses and sugar prepared in various ways'.[130]

But it seems that inspite of such efforts on the part of some Mahāyānists, there were certain sects which continued to partake such food unmindful of moral qualms for as I-tsing reports that 'pure meat could be eaten without incurring guilt'

[122]*Mahāvagga,* p.262; *Samantapāsādikā,* Vol.II, pp.856f.

[123]Ibid., p.263; Ibid., Vol.II, p.857.

[124]*Ekasatakarman,* Bk.V, p.69 (*Nanjio's Catalogue*, No.1131). See, J. Takakusu, op. cit., p.222.

[125]*Mahāvagga,* p.220.

[126]*Cullavagga,* pp.298-99, See, Chandra Shekhar Prasad. 'Meat-Eating and the rule of Tikoṭiparisuddha', in *Studies in Pali and Buddhism* (ed. A.K. Narain), pp.289-95.

[127]T. Watters, op. cit., II, p.173.

[128]D.T. Suzuki, op. cit., p.368.

[129]Ibid., pp.369-71. See, P.C. Divanji, 'Lankavatara Sutra on non-vegetarian diet', *ABORI.,* Vol.XX, Pts.3-4, 1940, pp.320f.

[130]D.T. Suzuki, loc. cit., p.371. Contra, *Śikṣāsamuccaya* (trans., p.133) states 'but if one who will not eat what is not permitted, or a bodhisattva, be ill, with such a disease as is a danger to life or a hindrance to good, then without remorse and without hesitation he may put the idea of a remedy upon these things (ghee, oil, choice roots, raw sugar and fruit) and eat them'.

and further adds that 'if the spirit of this rule be disregarded, it will involve some offence though small'.[131]

Wine was not allowed to the monks,[132] though *jālogi*[133] (unfermented toddy or the like which has not reached the stage of becoming an intoxicating liquor) was among the ten points which the Vajji monks pleaded as 'proper' for the monks. Sweet wine was not allowed but if it turned sour it could be used as vinegar.[134]

Dress

With the rise of monastic living, monks were allowed to accept gifts of robes from lay donors and there began the annual distribution of material (*kaṭhina*) for robes at the end of the rainy season. A *bhikkhu* normally possessed three robes (*ticīvara*):[135] (a) *antarvāsaka*, (b) *saṅghāti* and (c) *uttarā-saṅga*.

The *antarvāsaka* was an under garment which was wrapped round the loins and reached below the knee, being fastened round by a girdle. The *saṅghāti* was the waist cloth wrapped round the waist and back and secured with a girdle.[136] The *uttarāsaṅga* was the upper robe which was wrapped round the legs from the loins to the ankles and the end was then drawn, at the back, from the right hip, over the left shoulder, and either allowed to fall down in front or drawn back again over the right shoulder and allowed to fall down on the back.[137]

---

[131]J. Takakusu, op. cit., p.58.

[132]*Mahāvagga*, p.87. *Pācittiya*, No.51.

[133]*Cullavagga*, p.423.

[134]J. Takakusu, loc. cit., p.192.

[135]*Mahāvagga*, p.305. The *Bodhicaryāvatāra* (BST.), Chap.V, v.85 refes to the *bodhisattva* who ought to sacrifice all except the three robes (*tri-chīvaram*).

[136]*Antaravāsaka* and *saṅghati* were tied round the waist by girdles called *kāyabandhana* and *gaṇṭhikapāsaka*. See, *Cullavagga*, p.226: *Samantapāsādikā* (Nal. ed.), II, pp.286-87.

[137]*Vinaya Texts* (SBE.), Vol.XVII, p.212, fn.2.

Hiuen-tsang, besides referring to the three robes, mentions *Sêng-kio-ki* and *Ni-p'o-sa-na.*[138] 'The *Sêng-kio-ki* goes over the left shoulder covers the armpits, joined on the right and opening on the left side and in length reaching below to the waist.'[139] The *Sêng-kio-ki* is identified with Pāli *Samkachchika* (Sk. *Sañkakshikā).* Rhys Davids translates the Pāli word as 'vest'.[140]

The *Ni-p'o-sa-na* or *nivāsana* was a skirt, an under robe on lower garment, gathered into plaits and secured by one of these. This was according to regulation, four 'ells' long by one and a half in width, and it reached from the waist to about three finger breadths above the ankle. [141]

I-tsing[142] mentions besides the *ti-cīvara* (three robes), the *nivāsana* (the undergarment), the *prati nivāsana* (a second *nivāsana), saṅkakshikā* (a side covering cloth), *prati Saṅkakshikā* (a second *saṅkakshikā*).

From Hiuen-tsang and I-tsing's descriptions one can infer that the full costume of the monk, besides the three robes, consisted of the *saṅkakshikā* and the *nivāsana.* But a careful study of the Pāli canon enables one to solve the dilemma. The *antarvāsaka* was synonymous with the *nivāsana,* call it inner garment, undergarment, lower garment. The *saṅkakshikā* was a vest or a bodice. I-tsing[143] informs us that only the *saṅkakshikā* and the *nivāsana* are usually worn in one's room. The other garments were worn when one went out to worship the image.

The *saṅghāti* and the *uttarāsaṅga* were both upper robes, the former worn in summers and the latter worn in winter.[144]

---

[138]T. Watters, op. cit., I, p.149.

[139]Ibid., p.150.

[140]*Vinaya Texts* (SBE.), Vol.XX, p.351; *Cullavagga*, p.342. In the case of nuns, it was a form of bodice. See, *Pācittiya,* p.480; *Samantapāsādikā* (Nal. ed.), Vol.II, p.991.

[141]T. Watters, loc. cit., I, pp.150-51. The *Mahāvagga* (p.58) mentions the *nivāsana* and the *parinivāsana* as undergarment and second undergarment.

[142]J. Takakusu, op. cit., pp.54-55.

[143]Ibid., p.75.

[144]C.S. Upasak, A *Dictionary of Early Buddhist Monastic Terms*, pp.40, 212.

Instead of the usual term *pātracīvaramādāya* occurring in early Buddhist literature, one finds that *saṅghāti* is mentioned besides *pātracīvara.*[145]

Robes could be made of cotton, wool, silk, coarse cloth, hempen cloth[146] depending upon the fabric's seasonal suitability and the wish of the donor. By I-tsing's time the material often donated to the monks was silk (fine or rough) and linen.[147] This cloth had to be dyed[148] and to be worn in patches.[149] A robe of a single piece of cloth was forbidden as it was thought to make a monk appear similar to layfolk.

Regarding the mode of wearing garments Hiuen-tsang[150] informs us that 'the schools adhere to different styles having broad or narrow fringes and small or large folds', the size and colour of the plaits (of a nivāsana) varying in different schools.

I-tsing[151] says that the Āryamūlasarvāstivāda-nikāya cuts the skirt of the lower garment straight, while the other three schools cut it of irregular shape. In a layman's house, the skirt was to cover from navel to four finger width above one's ankle-bones. But it was permissible to have the lower half of one's shanks bare in a monastery.[152]

Enumerating the thirteen necessaries, I-tsing[153] mentions

---

[145]'*Saṅghāti pātra cīvara dhārena marge sthitam*'—see, *Lalitavistara* (BST.), p.138; *Abhisamācārikā*, pp.40, 153.

[146]*Mahāvagga*, pp.298f.

[147]J. Takakusu, op. cit., p.75.

[148]The garments of a homeless priest must be dyed to *kan-da* (i.e., yellow colour). The dye may be prepared from *Ti-huang* (*Rehmannia glutinosa*), yellow powder, or a thorny nieh-tree (*pterocarpus indicus*). These dyes, however, are to be mixed with the colours made of red stone-powder. One should see that the colour is not too deep or too light. See, J. Takakusu, loc. cit., p.77. See also, *Mahāvagga,* pp.302-03.

[149]*Mahāvagga,* p.306. Robes made entirely from untorn pieces were forbidden. Whosoever wore them, was guilty of *dukkaṭa* offence. See, ibid., p.313.

[150]T. Watters, op. cit., I, p.150. The Sthaviravādins wore the *nivāsana* in such a way as to conceal the three circles (viz., the navel and the two knees) and to cover the body all around, secured with a girdle. See, *Mahāvagga,* p.58.

[151]J. Takakusu, loc. cit., pp.7, 76.

[152]Ibid., p.76.

[153]Ibid., p.55. See *Mahāvagga,* pp.296, 308-09, 311-12.

the *kāya-proñchana* (a towel for wiping the body), *mukha-proñchana* (a towel for wiping the face), *kesapratigraha* (a piece of cloth used for receiving hair when one shaves), *kandupraticchandana* (a piece of cloth for covering itches) and *bheshajaparishkāracīvara,* (a cloth kept for defraying the cost of medicine in case of necessity).

Material Possessions

Buddhist literature often refers to the *bhikkhu* as *akiñcana*[154] (possessing nothing at all) and terms the state of renunciation as *ākiñcañña*[155] (the state of complete non-possession). The ideal of non-possession demanded that they be frugal and keep their requisites to the bare minimum. Recounting the blessings and advantages of the homeless state of monkhood, the *Mahāvastu*[156] states, 'even a kingdom means nothing to a monk who fares all alone. He goes from village to village and traverses kingdoms and towns and still nobody hinders him. There may be robbers on the way he takes, but he, with his sole possessions of bowl and robe, has nothing to fear, and ever moves in security and safety. He has nothing to lose even when the whole city is burning aflame. There is no need for him to hoard in granaries, pots and baskets, for, begging being his only source of provisions.' But the true state of affairs never remained the same.

The material possessions of the *bhikkhu* can be broadly divided into two categories—(a) personal or individual (b) communal or *saṅghika.* The first consisted of the six requisites and thirteen necessaries enumerated by I-tsing.[157] The six requisites[158] were (a) *saṅghāti*, (b) *uttarāsaṅga*, (c) *antarvāsa*, (d) *pātra*, (e) *nishīdana*, (f) *pariśrāvana*.

---

[154]*Dhammapada,* vv.88, 421; *Milindapañho* (ed. R.D. Vadekar), p.216.

[155]*Therīgāthā,* v.343; *Sutta-nipāta* (Magha Sutta), vv.88, 100.

[156]*Mahāvastu,* III, p.454.

[157]J. Takakusu, op. cit., pp.54-55.

[158]The Pāli texts mention eight requisites, viz., three robes, bowl, razor, needle, girdle, water strainer.

The thirteen necessaries were—(a) *saṅghatī*, (b) *uttarā-saṅga*, (c) *antarvāsa*, (d) *nisīdana*, (e) *nivāsana*, (f) *prati-nivāsana*, (g) *saṅkakshika*, (h) *prati-saṅkakshika*, (i) *kāya-proñchana*, (j) *mukha proñchana*, (k) *kandupratikkhandana*, (l) *kesapratigraha*, (m) *bheshajaparishkāracīvara*.

Looking to the needs of the community, there was a greater need to acquire property. Gradually the communal property increased to such an extent that it was difficult to distinguish the individual from the communal property.[159] This is clear from two of I-tsing's statements which say: 'If the original intention of the benefactor was unreservedly charitable, then the benefits of the gift can be considered as conferred upon all, though presented to the church only'[160] and secondly 'it is unseemly for a monastery to have huge wealth, granaries full of rotten corn, many servants, male and female, money and treasures hoarded in the treasury, without using any of these things, while all the members are suffering from poverty.'[161]

It is all too clear from these statements that it was becoming on the part of the monks to accept charities in the name of the *Saṅgha* but it cannot be denied that the recipients of the gifts became in fact the partakers of the gifts.

It is true that the Pāli canon details the material possessions allowed to the monks or to the *Saṅgha* from time to time by the Buddha but the extent to which a monk could own property can be gleaned from I-tsing's narration of the rules regarding the distribution of property of a deceased *bhikkhu*.[162] This

---

[159]*See, Pācittiya* 82, pp.208-09.

[160]J. Takakusu, op. cit., p.193.

[161]Ibid., p.194.

[162]Ibid., pp.190-93. This list agrees with the one given in the *Mūlasarvāstivāda vinaya vastu* (*Gilgit Manuscripts*, Vol.III, Pt.II, pp.141-44). *Contra.*, in the *Dīgha Nikāya* (I, pp.5-6) the recluse is said to abstain from accepting uncooked grain, raw meat, sheep or goats, fowls or swine, elephants, cattle, horses or mares, cultivated fields or wastes and from buying and selling. See, also *Mahavagga*, p.319.

property consisted of: lands,[163] houses, shops, bed gear, woollen seats, iron and copper implements (which included copper bowls, iron bowls, needles, door keys, gimlets, razors, knives, iron ladles, braziers, axes, chisels, etc., together with their bags), earthen utensils,[164] wooden and bamboo implements, leather bedding, shaving things, male and female servants,[165] liquor,[166] food, corn, shoes, robes, long rods, metal staff, quadrupeds, elephants, horses, mules, asses, bulls, sheep,[167] helmets, coats of arms,[168] miscellaneous weapons, nets, paints, wine, medical substances, precious stones and

---

[163]It is true that the *Mahāvagga* (p.263) refers to the *Saṅgha* being in possession of fields and lending out grain seeds to householders, a practice which became so developed by the 7th centur AD that I-tsing refers to cultivation of fields by the *Saṅgha.* See, J. Takakusu, op. cit., pp.61, 62, 65, 193.

[164]Excavations at Salihundam (R. Subrahmanyam, op. cit., have revealed various potsherds (datable 1st to 3rd century AD) inscribed with the word *pāti* and its variants *(pati, pathi)* obviously denoting the *patta, pāti, pāti* (bowl, vessel or dish) of the Buddhist *bhikkhu,* along with the name of the donee. These are as follows—

(a) budispati (ibid., p.49).

(b) [sa] pati (ibid., p.50).

(c) rahilasa pa (ibid.).

(d) [da] gasa [pa] ti (ibid., p.51).

(e) bodhi kasa pati (ibid.).

Similarly excavations at Vaiśāli have unearthed 2 mud *stūpas* which yielded several copper utensils, one of which contained relics, besides an earthen bowl and dish. Debala Mitra (*Buddhist Monuments*, p.75) suggests 'it was both a *śārīrika* and *pāribhogika stūpa* of a Buddhist teacher'.

[165]These were employed chiefly to till the lands in possession of the *Saṅgha* (J. Takakusu, loc. cit., p.61) or to serve a monk (T. Watters, *op. cit.*, I, p.62) or perform menial tasks (J. Takakusu, loc. cit., p.154, fn.3(b).

[166]This appears in contradiction to one of the *śikṣāpadas* enjoined on the monk (*Mahāvagga*, p.87) and a monk contravening the rule is said to commit a *Pācittiya* (p.151).

[167]These might have been utilized for tilling the land (J. Takakusu. loc. cit., p.61) or as beast of burden or simply to ride (T. Watters, loc. cit., I, p.162).

[168]It is surprising to find helmets and coats of mail listed among the possessions of a monk. *Contra.*, *Pācittiya* 48-50 (pp.144-49).

gems,[169] wooden chairs,[170] books, gold, silver,[171] wrought or unwrought goods, shells, coins, deeds and contracts and the six requisites.

Management of the Vihāras

In order to conduct the multifarious business of the community life and to procure and distribute properly the material possessions permitted to the members, it was indispensable to appoint office-bearers. Further expansion of the staff arose according to the need of the time and nature of the work that lay before the *Saṅgha.* Seniority, character and learning were the requisite qualifications for such posts.[172] Many of the official posts mentioned in the Pāli canon find interesting corroboration in some inscriptions and later literature. In some cases two offices have been combined in one person. With the growth of monasteries, many new official posts were created.

---

[169]*Contra., Pācittiya* 84 (pp.214f). *Stūpa* 18 at Srāvasti revealed a relic chamber containing an earthen bowl with semi-precious stones and large pearls. See, Debala Mitra, op. cit., p.78.

[170]Some inscriptions refer, among articles donated for the use of monks, to items of furniture, such as seats (*Satta-Lüders list,* Nos. 985, 988), straight backed chairs *Piṭhas*—ibid., No.998) and stools to sit on *(Āsana-peṭhikas.* ibid., No.998.

[171]D.D. Kosambi ('Dhenukakaṭa', *JASB.*, Vol.30, Pt.II, 1955, p.52) notes that 'the cells were clearly provided with substantial wooden doors whose purpose was not privacy but the protection of valuables. Such doors (replaced in modern times) may still be seen at the Gaṇesh leṇa Junnar. Occasionally, a large hole cut through the partition into an adjoining room shows that one of the pair was used as a treasury and access to it was shut off except through the neighbouring cell, which would always be occupied'.

[172]The *Abhisamācārikā* (p.49) specifies the five qualities to be possessed by a *bhikkhu* appointed as an officer. They are: freedom from lust, hatred, delusion, fear and ability to distinguish between what is proper and improper. This agrees completely with the qualities mentioned in the Pāli canon. See, *Mahāvagga,* p.300; *Cullavagga,* p.273.

A. Officers connected with commissariat

(1) *Bhattudeśaka*[173]—Apportioner of cooked food.
(2) *Yāgubhājaka*[174]—Distributor of *Yāgu*, a kind of rice pulp.
(3) *Phalabhājaka*[175]—Distributor of fruits.
(4) *Khajjaka bhājaka*[176]—Distributor of eatables (other than the meal).
(5) *Bhaṇḍāgārika*[177]—Overseer of stores.

B. Officers connected with lodgings, robes and other requisites

(1) *Śayanāsana prajñāpaka*[178]—Distributor of lodgings.[179] His business was to arrange seats and allot them to the *bhikkhus*. The seats were arranged three times a year—on the day of the commencement of the earlier *vassā* , on the day of the commencement of the later *vassā,* and on the day after the *Pavāraṇā.*[180]
(2) *Senāsanagāhapaka*[181]—Monk entrusted with the duty of accepting *vihāras, pariveṇas* on behalf of the *Saṅgha.* Some scholars[182] take the above two terms as

---

[173]*Cullavagga,* p.273. This term occurs in the Bharhut Buddhist Pillar Inscription. See, *Lüders list,* No.812.

[174]*Cullavagga,* p.273. It is surprising that S. Dutt (EBM., p.154) and following him D.K. Barua (*Viharas in Ancient India,* p.40) mention *cīvabhājaka* as distributor of congey. The term does not find mention in the source quoted and to the best of my knowledge in the entire *Vinaya Piṭaka.*

[175]*Cullavagga*, p.273.

[176]Ibid.

[177]Ibid., *Mahāvagga,* p.301. Buddharakṣhita is termed as *Bhaṇḍaksha* to the community of monks in the Mathura Buddhist inscription on the base of a pillar. See, *Lüders list,* No.133, Appendix.

[178]*Cullavagga,* p.273; *Abhisamācarikā*, p.49.

[179]G.C. Pande, *BDVI.*, p.154.

[180]S. Dutt, op. cit., p.155.

[181]*Cullavagga,* p.262; G.C. Pande, loc. cit., p.154. Rhys Davids (*Vinaya Texts,* SBE., XX, p.8) translates it as regulator of lodging places.

[182]Patrick Olivelle, *The Origin and Early Development of Buddhist Monachism*, p.62.

synonymns. C.S. Upasak on the one hand defines *Senāsanapaññāpaka* as one 'in charge of arrangements of seats, etc., particularly for the guests. He is like a receptionist, and so he is expected to look after the convenience of the guest monk.'[183] On the other hand he defines *senāsanagāhapaka* as one 'in charge of allotting the lodgings (seats, *seyya)* in a *vihāra* for the monks during the first *vassāvāsa (purimika)* or the second *(Pacchimikā)* or just after the *pavāraṇā (antarāmuttako).*[184]

(3) *Ārāmikas*[185]—Besides looking after the *ārāma* he could accept the robe fund on behalf of the *Saṅgha* from the donor.[186] In the absence of any *bhikkhu* or *sāmaṇera,* he was incharge of sleeping places and its material possessions if the other *bhikkhus* went out of the *vihāra.*[187]

(4) *Cīvarapatiggahāpaka*[188]—He was appointed to receive the robes or robe cloth which was offered by lay people to the *bhikkhus* generally at the end of the *vassāvāsa.*

(5) *Cīvara-nidahaka*[189]—Monk in charge of received robes.

(6) *Cīvara bhājaka*[190]—Distributor of robes. He may be the same as *Kaṭhina vatthāraka.* The difference in names may be due to different local traditions.

(7) *Sāṭiya-gāhapaka*[191]—Distributor of outer cloaks,[192] rain cloaks[193] or undergarments.[194]

---

[183]C.S. Upasak, *Dictionary of Early Buddhist Monastic Terms*, p.242.

[184]Ibid., pp.242-43, See, C. Prebish, *BMD.*, pp.8-9.

[185]*Mahāvagga*, p.226, See, *Divyavadāna* (BST.), pp.26, 96, 97; *Abhisamācārikā*, p.146.

[186]*Vinaya Texts* (SBE.), Vol.XIII, p.24 (*Nissagiya Pācittiya*).

[187]Ibid., Vol.XX, p.282.

[188]*Mahāvagga*, p.300; *Cullavagga*, p.273.

[189]*Mahāvagga*, p.300.

[190]Ibid., p.301; *Cullavagga*, p.273.

[191]*Cullavagga*, p.274.

[192]I.B. Horner, *Book of Discipline*, V, p.248.

[193]H. Kern, op. cit., p.83.

[194]S. Dutt, *EBM.*, p.155.

(8) *Paṭṭagāhapaka*[195]—Monk who accepts the bowls offered to the *Saṅgha* by the laity.

(9) *Appamattaka-vissajjaka*[196]—Disposer of trifles like needles, scissors, sandals, girdles, butter, honey, etc., among members of the *Saṅgha* according to their need.

Superintendents

(1) *Nava-kammika*[197]—Overseer of *vihāras*. New *vihāras* in course of erection were kept under the supervision of the *bhikkhu* overseer, because he was expected to know the type of residence required.

(2) *Ārāmika-pesaka*[198]—Superintendent of the *ārāmikas*.

(3) *Sāmaṇera-pesaka*[199]—Superintendent of the novices. Probably he looked after the discipline of the novices who had not yet obtained *upasampadā*.

---

[195]*Cullavagga*, p.274.

[196]Ibid.

[197]This officer which is mentioned in the *Cullavagga* (pp.254, 269-70) is referred to in the Sônāri Stupa I Rail Inscription *(Lüders list,* No.154); Barhut Buddhist Pillar Inscription (ibid., No.773); Taxila Copper Plate Inscription of Patika, year 78 (*CII.*, Vol.II, Pt.I, p.29); Manikiala Inscription, year 18 (ibid., pp.149-50); Kāṇhêrī Buddhist Cave Inscription (*Lüders list*, No.987); Amarāvatī Buddhist Sculpture Inscription (ibid., No.1250).

In the Māṇikiala Inscription, the term viharakara [vha] eṇa occurs as synonymous with *navakammika*. Another synonym of *Navakammika* is *uparakhita* which occurs along with it in the Kāṇhêrī Inscription (ibid., No. 987). I-tsing (J. Takakusu, op. cit., p.83) also refers to the *bhikṣu* superintending the monastery which is to be built.

This technical post was enjoyed by the *bhikkhunis* also. As Rhys Davids and Oldenberg (*Vinaya Texts*, SBE., Pt.II, p.189, fn.5) write 'If the buildings were for the bhikkhus, then a bhikkhu, if for the bhikkhunīs, then a *bhikkhuni* was appointed to superintend the work in order to ensure the buildings being in accordance with the rules of the Order as to size, form and object of the various apartments.'

Details of her duty are incidentally mentioned in the *Bhikkhunī Vibhaṅga, Pārājika* I (p.283). The *Vinaya* evidence is corroborated by inscriptional evidence. Dadhanadarī is mentioned as a female *navakarmika* in an Amarāvati Inscription. See, *EI.,* XV, p.270.

[198]*Cullavagga*, p.274.

[199]Ibid., pp.274-75. In a personal letter, K.R. Norman writes, 'it does not seem unreasonable to assume that there should be someone in the vihāra who had responsibility for the sāmaṇeras as whole when they were not actually with their acariyas or upādhyāyas'.

Other office-bearers

(1) *Āsanapaññāpaka*[200]—Arranger of seats at the meetings of monks.
(2) *Salākāgāhāpaka*[201]—Receiver of sticks.

H.Kern[202] refers to certain officers which are not mentioned in theVinaya Piṭaka. They are as follows:

(a) *Pānīya-vārika* [203]—Officer in charge of drinking water.
(b) *Bhājana vārika*[204]—Officer in charce of vessels.
(c) *Upadhivāra*[205]—Probably an intendant or steward.
(d) *Pariṣaṇḍa vārika*[206]—The guardian of the grove around the monastery.

---

[200]*Cullavagga*, p.428. According to Durga Bhagvat (*Early Buddhist Jurisprudence*, p.153) the āsana-*prajñāpaka* had merely to see that all were provided with the requisites (chiefly mats or rugs to sit on) in the hall or grove where they met. Rhys Davids and Oldenberg (*Vinaya Texts,* Vol.XX, p.408, fn.1) do not consider it as an office of authority. It seems probable that after the growth of *Saṅgha* life, monks met in the *upasthāna-śālā* where preliminary requisites for the meeting were arranged by monastic servants.

[201]*Abhisamācārikā,* pp.6-7; See, *Cullavagga,* pp.164, 182, 184.

[201]H. Kern, op. cit., p.83.

[203]*The Abhisamācārikā* (pp.148, 150) refers to the *pānīyavārika* as incharge of the water shed *(Pānīya-maṇḍapa)* in the *vihāra.*

[204]The Mathura Buddhist Inscription on the base of a pillar refers to the gift of a monk Buddhisrêshṭha, the keeper of vessels *(bhajanaka)* to the community of four quarters. See, *Lüders list,* No.62b (1371), Appendix.

[205]In a personal communication K.R. Norman writes, 'upadhi (in the form uvahi) occurs in Prakrit in the sense of a monk's equipment and so the translation "the one in charge of the equipment or material possessions (of the vihāra) seems likely. He was clearly an important person, since he is among the four Divy 542.21) or seven (Divy 543.17) persons whose commands are akopyā. From Avadānaśataka (11.87.2) it is seen that he struck the gong (for meals or for some other activity?) and he also made the announcements from (lunar dates—adya pakṣasya dasamityevamadi yathā upadhivārika ārocayanti (Mulasarvāstivādin Vinaya 111, 98.8-9)".'

[206]K.R. Norman writes in his letter 'the word pariṣaṇḍa seems to mean "steps" the translation, the one in charge of the "steps" seems reasonable'. Thus the *pariṣaṇda vārika* was incharge of the flight of steps (to a building, no doubt a *stūpa*). See, F. Edgerton, *Buddhist Hybrid Sanskrit Dictionary*, S.V. Pariṣaṇḍa.

(e) *Muṇḍa senāsana varika*[207]—The person taking care of lodgings temporarily not in use.

Besides the above there was the—

(f) *Mahāgandhakuṭivārika*[208]—He was in charge of the sanctuary. He had to keep it clean and make arrangements for the daily worship.
(g) *Dipavārika*[209]—Officer appointed for keeping lamps. It was his responsibility to supply all necessary things such as oil and wicks and to light the lamps at regular times.

The *Vinayavastu* of the Mūlasarvāstivādins supplies names of few other officers such as:

(1) *Vaiyāvṛtyakara*[210]—Secretary of the *Saṅgha.*
(2) *Prahāṇapratijāgraka*[211]—Monk duly appointed by the *Saṅgha* as caretaker of the meditating monks. His duty was to keep the meditation chambers clean. He was to strike the gong at the right time. He had to go to the chamber before others and return only after they had left.
(3) *Kriyākara*[212]—He was a supervising monk whose function was to prepare a list of members who would

---

[207]On this K.R. Norman has written, 'there is a prakrit word muṇḍi "veil" and so muṇḍa-senāsana-vārika could mean "the one who looks after the veiled (i.e. curtained) beds or curtains and beds'.

[208]The Kāṇhêrī Buddhist Cave Inscription *(Lüders list,* No.989) refers to this officer.

[209]*Abhisamācārika,* pp.203-07.

[210]*Gilgit Manuscripts*, Vol.III, Pt.IV, p.48 (Pravrajya-vastu); The *Śikṣāsamuccaya* (ed., pp.55-58) details his duties. He had to look to the comfort of the monks residing in the forest, who lived on alms, who were meditative and preachers of law. He was also incharge of the accounts.

[211]*Gilgit Manuscripts*, Vol.III, Pt.IV, pp.77-80 (Poṣadhavastu); The Mathura Buddhist Inscription (*Lüders list,* No.126) refers to the dedication of the base of a pillar (*kuṁbhaka*) by the monks Surīya and Buddha-rakshita, the *prahaṇīkas*, for the gift of health to all *prahaṇikas*.

[212]Ibid., p.133. It seems plausible that the *kriyākara* combined in his person the duties of the *śayanāsana-prajñāpaka* and *śalākāgāhāpaka*.

spend the *varṣa* in a particular *āvāsa* and to allot the *āvāsas* by the distribution of sticks (*salāka*) if there be more than one in any locality, to a *Saṅghasthavira*, who is to take charge of the *āvāsa*.

The technical terms: Saṅghasthavira, Mahāvihārasvamin and Vihārasvamin

(1) *Saṅghasthavira*[213]—This was the most responsible post in the spiritual hierarchy. The *bhikkhu* appointed for this post functioned as the head of the entire unit[214] and was sort of director, chief priest or head abbot.[215] He is to be clearly distinguished from the *thera* who was simply an elder mentioned often in literature and inscriptions. The *Saṅghasthavira* enjoyed a position of pre-eminence, as is evident from the *Divyavadāna*[216] which mentions him as one among the seven whose orders could not be violated. The *Abhisamācārikā*[217] informs us that the *Saṅghasthavira* was incharge of conducting the entire *Uposatha* ceremony.

In the seventh century Yaśa was the *Saṅghasthavira* in a monastery at Kashmir.[218] Rāhulamitra enjoyed this position in the Tamralipti monastery.[219] in the Taladha monastery near

[213]The Mathura Buddhist Image Inscriptions *(Lüders list*, Nos.129, 130, 131) refer to the *Saṅghasthavira* as elder of the congregation.

[214]Prajñāvarman, a native of Korea who visited Nālandā says, 'the oldest man of the monastery is regarded as the director. It is the rule to hand over the keys of the doors to the director when the doors are put under lock and key'. See, S. Dutt, *BMMI.*, p.313 (Appendix).

[215]S. Dutt, loc. cit., p.313; L.M. Joshi, op. cit., p.75. The use of the term 'kulapati' instead of *Saṅghasthavira* by L.M. Joshi is ambiguous for the former term has secular overtones and does not explicitly mean the head of a monastic order.

[216]*Divyāvadāna* (BST.), p.464. An inscribed potsherd from Salihundam (R. Subrahmanyam, op. cit., p.88) reads as follows—'Akarana panati catasihan sihasana parigahaka na (bha?). Perhaps it refers to the acceptance of the chief seat by the *Saṅghasthavira* Catasimha by name.

[217]See, *Supra*.

[218]S. Beal, *Life*, p.69.

[219]J. Takakusu, op. cit., pp.63-64.

Nālanda Jñānachandra was the *Saṅghasthavira*[220] while this chair was graced by Śīlabhadra[221] at Nālandā and probably by Ratnasiṁha[222] during I-tsing's time.

(2) *Mahāvihārasvāmin* and *Vihārasvāmin*—The above two terms have been totally misinterpreted by scholars like J.F. Fleet[223] and Ajay Mitra Shastri.[224] The term in its female form *(Vihārasvaminī)* occurs for the first time in the Sui Vihāra Inscription of the 11th regnal year of Kaniṣka which Sten Konow[225] translates as 'mistress of the vihāra' and again in the Mathura Stone Image Inscription of the Gupta year 135 (AD 454-55) which is rendered wrongly as 'the wife of a viharasvāmin' by J.F. Fleet.[226] Ajay Mitra Shastri, unable to subscribe to the opinion of Fleet according to which *vihārasvāminī* would cease to be a technical religious title, emphasizes the important role played by women in the history of Buddhism and remarks '... it is not impossible that this high office may have been held by them'.[227]

From a careful analysis of the inscriptions in which the term appears and the respective contexts in which it is used it becomes clear that the term is used in the sense of the master

---

220Ibid., p.184. He could be the same person referred by Hiuen-tsang (T. Watters, op. cit., II, p.169) as a man of exceptional virtue and learning at Nālandā.

221T. Watters, loc. cit., II, pp.109, 165; S. Beal, op. cit., pp.106, 158.

222J. Takakusu, loc. cit., p.184.

223'*Mahāvihārasvāmin,* literally 'a great master (Superintendent) of a *vihāra* is evidently a technical religious title of office, denoting the officer who came, in the management of a *vihāra,* next above the *vihārasvāmin* (see, *CII.*, III, p.273, fn.3). *Vihārasvāmin,* lit. 'master of a *vihāra*', is a technical religious title of office, applied to certain functionaries who came next in rank below the *Mahāvihārasvāmin* (ibid., p.279, fn.5).

224'Like the Pāmukhā of the Bhaṭṭiprolu Inscriptions, the *mahavihārasvāmin* also was probably the chief officer-in-charge of the management of a given *vihāra* and *vihārasvāmin* next below him' (see, Ajay Mitra Shastri, op. cit., p.132).

225Sten Konow, *CII.*, II, Pt.I, p.141.

226*Vihārasvāminī,* lit. 'mistress (Lady-Superintendent) of a *vihāra*' seems not to be a technical religious title denoting an office held by a female, but to mean simply, 'the wife of a *vihārasvamin*' (see, *CII.*, III, p.263, fn.3).

227Ajay Mitra Shastri, loc. cit., p.132.

(founder) of the *vihāra* who happened to be a devout lay devotee.

(A) The Sui Vihāra Inscription[228] of the 11th regnal year of Kaniṣka refers to *Vihārasvaminī* Balanaṁdi, a *kuṭimbini* (house lady) who being an *upāsikā* (lay devotee) donated the staff and the enclosure along with her mother.

(B) The Tor Ḍherai inscribed potsherds[229] (ascribed roughly to AD 200) read as follows: 'Of the Shāhi Yola Mira, the master of the vihāra (vihārasvāmin), this water hall (is) the religious gift, in his own Yola-Mira-Shāhi-Vihāra, to the Order of the four quarters, in the acceptance of the Sarvāstivādin teachers. And from this right donation may there be in future a share for (his) mother and father, in future a share for all beings and long life for the master of the law.'

(C) The Mathura Stone Image inscription[230] of the Gupta year 135 (AD 454-55) reads as follows: '... this is the appropriate religious gift of the *vihārasvāmini* Devata. Whatever religious merit (there is) in this (act),—Let it be for the acquisition of supreme knowledge by (her) parents and by all sentient beings.

(Line 3) Good fortune; the condition of being a model (worthy of imitation), abounding in virtuous qualities; fame; the destruction of the enemies (of religion); riches abounding in prosperity, births that result in happiness; (and) finally, an auspicious nirvāṇa;—(all these) are not permanent (?); having once fixed the thoughts upon the happiness of making gifts ...'

(D) The object of the Sāñchī Stone Pillar lnscription[231] ascribed roughly to 5th century AD is to record the gift of a pillar by *Vihārasvāmin* Rudra, the son of Gôsūrasiṁha-bala.

---

[228]*CII.*, II, Pt.I, p.141.
[229]Ibid., II, Pt.I, p.176.
[230]Ibid., III, pp.263-64.
[231]Ibid., pp.279-80.

(E) The Kasia Stone Image Inscription[232] (end of the 5th AD) states, 'This is the appropriate religious gift (*deya-dharma*) of the *Mahavihārasvāmin* Haribala. And this image has been fashioned by Dinê-māśvara.'

(F) The Kura Buddhist Stone-Slab Inscription[233] (AD 500-15) of the time of rājātirāja mahārāja Tôramāṇa Shāhi Jauvla reads as follows: 'Erection of a *vihāra* for the congregation of the monks *(bhikshu Saṅgha)* of bhagavat Buddha by the lord of the *vihāra (vihārasvāmin)* Roṭa-Siddhavṛiddhi, the son of Roṭṭa-Jayavrddhi, the lord of many *vihāras (anêkavihāra Svāmin),* whose name was honoured by the lord *(pati)* of Naśchira, for the benefit of the relatives of the donor and the queens, princes and princesses of Mahārāja Toramāṇa Shāha Jaūvla for the acceptance of the teachers *(āchāryas),* the Mahisāsakas.'

(G) This inscription[234] occurs on the pedestal of a huge Buddha image in the shrine inside Cave IV and Ajanta. The first sentence states that the object on which the inscription is incised (i.e. the Buddha image) was the *deya-dharma* or gift of a person named Mathura who was the son of Abhayanandin and Skandavasu and belonged to the *kārvaṭiyā gôtra.* Mathura is described as the *vihārasvāmin* or the owner of the monastery. The second sentence states that the merit accruing to the pious act of Mathura was meant for the attainment of the supreme knowledge by all beings including his parents, his father's mother, step mother or aunt, the prominent friends of his family and his own self.

These inscriptions point to certain specific features:

(1) Four of the seven inscriptions (viz., B, C, E & G) refer to the gift as *dêya-dharma* (appropriate religious gift) a term occurring often in epigraphs recording donations of lay followers;

---

[232]Ibid., p.273.

[233]*Lüders list*, No.5; D.C. Sircar, *Select Inscriptios,* p.423.

[234]*EI.*, Vol.XXXIII, pp.261-62.

(2) Inscription (A) and (B) respectively, refer to the house wife and a person belonging to the Shāhi family as donators of gifts;

(3) Inscription (C) records the donor's wish, for benefits worldly and other worldly;

(4) In inscription (D & G) the pedigree is traced, a feature more noticeable in epigraphs of lay-devotees;

(5) Inscription (F) makes it extremely clear that the practice of donating *vihāras* to the *Bhikkhu Saṅgha* (and thus earning the title of *vihārasvāmin* and *anekavihāra-svāmin)* continued in many families from father to son;

(6) Inscriptions (B, C, F and G) refer to parents, relatives and all sentient creatures to whom merit should accrue through the gift.

All these facts bring home the point that *mahavihāra-svāmin* or *vihārasvāmin* (or *svāminī)* was not a technical religious office held by a *bhikkhu* (or *bhikkhuni)* but rather an epithet earned by the lay devotee for donating the *vihāra* or *vihāras* to the *Bhikkhu Saṅgha.*

The epigraphical information regarding the term receives curious confirmation from literary sources such as the *Divyāvadāna*[235] and the *Abhisamācārikā*[236] where the term *vihārasvāmin* is used as a synonym for *upāsaka* and *dānapati* (giver of gift).

The most conclusive evidence is provided by I-tsing[237] in his memoirs of Chinese travellers in India, where he states that

---

[235]*Divyāvadāna* (BST.), p.303—*Kiṁ manyadhve bhikṣavoyāni tāni pañca bhikṣuśatāni, etānyeva tāni pañca karśaka śatāni. Yo' asau vihārasvāmi, sa evāsau gṛhapatirasyaite kārṣakāḥ. Yadebhīravihāra-svāmisantakaṁ sraddhādeyaṁ paribhujya na pathitaṁ na svādhyāyitaṁ nāpi manasikāro vihitaḥ, kiṁ tu saṅgaṇikābhiratai kausiddyenābhināmitaṁ, tena karmaṇā pañca janmaśatani tasya vihārasvaminah karṣakāḥ saṁvṛttāḥ.* See, *Avadānaśataka* (BST.), p.126.

[236]*Abhisamācārikā*, pp.127-28—*Atha khalu vaktavyaṁ-sālohite, kiṁ āṇapesi kiṁ karomi eśo bhikṣuḥ upāsakāṁ va dānapatīnāṁ va vihārasvāminīṁ vā śabdāyituṁakāmo bhavati nāpi kṣamati aṁvetiṁ vā atteti vā bhadde [ti va] Atha khalu upāsaka-ketti vā dānapatitti vā vihārasvāminitti va sabdāyayitavyaṁ.*

[237]*Nanjio's Catalogue*, No.1491, Vol.I.

'one who builds a monastery is called the "owner of the monastery", i.e. viharasvamin'. This is further supplemented by Prajñāvarman's[238] (a Korean monk) statement that the founder of a *saṅghārāma* is known as *vihārasvāmin.*

Other Officials

(1) *Karmadāna*[239]—The secular affairs of the monastery were entrusted to this monk. He regulated time by striking the gong (bell), indicating the commencement of any ceremony or service.[240] He arranged the order of precedence at a congregational feast and supervised the preparation of food.[241] In short, he preserved the regularity and order in the establishment.

(2) Officer-in-charge of screening examination—The designation of this officer is given as 'men-chi' in Chinese which is translated as janitor or porter but he must have been a responsible officer of considerable learning with sufficient ability to pronounce on the merits of candidates for admission.[242]

(3) *Vihāra-pālas*—The keeper, the warden of the gate and he who announces the affairs of the *Saṅgha.*[243] Prajñāvarmana Korean monk refers to *vihārapāla* as a person in charge of announcing time and reporting it to the inmates.[244]

---

[238]S. Dutt, *BMMI.,* p.313 Appendix.

[239]I-tsing's (J. Takakusu, op. cit., p.148) fanciful derivation of the term *karmadāna* is as follows—

'Karma being action, *dāna,* giving', i.e. 'one who gives others various actions'.

[240]Ibid., pp.145, 146, 147.

[241]Prajñāvarman, a Korean monk refers to *karmadāna* as a subdirector, but also says that the person in charge of kitchens is also known as *karmadāna.* See, S. Dutt, *BMMI.,* p.313, Appendix.

[242]Ibid., p.332.

[243]J. Takakusu, loc. cit., p.148, fn.1.

[244]S. Dutt, loc. cit., p.313, Appendix.

Bauddha Goṣṭhī

In some of the Sāñchi votive inscriptions[245] of the 2nd and 1st BC there is mention of '*Bodhagothiya Dhamavadhana*' and '*Barulamisana gothiyadama vedisato*'. According to Buhler,[246] a *goṣṭhi* is a committee of the trustees in charge of a temple or charitable foundation. It seems, therefore, that the village of Dharmavardhana possessed, perhaps a *vihāra* which was externally managed by such a committee. The Bhaṭṭiprolu inscription of the 3rd century BC speaks of '*Arahadinānaṁ goṭhiya*' (a *goṣṭhī* of the *arhats*).[247] This shows that there were two committees for the management of *vihāra*; one formed by lay devotees and responsible for the external management and the other formed exclusively by monks responsible for its internal and ecclesiastical management.[248]

The seals and sealings unearthed at Nālandā (Monastery No.9) throw light on the administration of the *mahāvihāra*. The subordinate colleges were simply called *vihāras* with their governing body described as *Saṅghas* such as—(a) *Śri Nālandā Mūla navakammavarika-bhikshūṇām* and (b) *Śri-Nāladā-chivara—kosṭhi-k-āyāt -ā[rya] bhikshu-Saṅghasya*. The term *Saṅgha* here is to be taken in the sense of units of administration in charge of the different interests of academic and collective life at the University.[249]

Functioning of the Saṅgha: Ecclesiastical Rules

The Buddhist *Saṅgha* appears from the very beginning to have been an organization governed by rules and regulations

---

245 J. Marshall, *Monuments of Sāñchī*, pp.298, 309, 317. Inscription Nos.96-8, 178; *Lüders list*, Nos.234, 273, 351.

246 *EI.*, II, p.92.

247 Ibid., II, p.229; *Lüders list*, No.1338.

248 Ajay Mitra Shastri, op. cit., p.321.

249 R.K. Mookerji, 'The University of Nalanda', *JBRS.*, Vol.XXX, Pt.II, June 1944, p.144.

which were intended to make the members properly regulate their course of action and make satisfactory progress in their spiritual journey. Much scholarly work has appeared on the various *Prātimokṣa* versions of the *Vinaya.*[250] I-tsing's reference to the offences of the first and second group (i.e. the *pārājika* and *saṅghādiśeṣa* offences)[251] make it clear that the rules were practical and operative during his time.

Saṅghakamma

All transactions pertaining to the community life were performed by joint acts called *Saṅghakamma.*[252] With the increase in the membership of *Saṅgha,* it was difficult to assemble all, for a *Saṅghakamma.* Therefore a select group out of the *Saṅgha* was taken to represent the entire body.

---

[250]See, Anukul Chandra Banerjee, ed., *Pratimokṣa-Sūtram* (Mulasarvāstivāda); N. Dutt, ed., *The Gilgit Manuscripts,* Vol.III, Pts.1-4 (Vinayavastu); S. Bagchi, ed., *Mulasarvāstivāda Vinayavastu,* BST., No.16; Raniero Gnoli, ed., *The Gilgit Ms. of the Sayanāsanavastu and the Adhikaraṇa vastu.* Being the 15th and 16th section of the Vinaya of the Mulasarvastivādin; Ernst Waldschmidt, *Bruchstücke des Bhikṣuṇi Prātimokṣa der Sarvāstivadins:* Valentina Rosen, *Der Vinayavibhaṅga Zum Bhikṣu-pratimokṣa Der Sarvāstivādins;* W. Pachow, *A Comparative Study of the Prātimokṣa;* Gustav Roth, *Bhikṣuṇi Vinaya;* Anantalal Thakur, ed., *Prātimokṣa-Sutram,* Tibetan Sk. works series No.16; Charles Prebish, *BMD.,* J.F. Dickson, ed., and trans., 'The Pātimokkha being the Buddhist office of the confession of priests', *JRAS.,* (NS), VIII (1876), pp.62-130; Louis Finot, (ed.), 'Le Prātimokṣasutra des Sarvāstivādins'. Texte Sanskrit par L. Finot, avec la version chinoise de Kumārajīva traduité en francais par Edouard Huber. *Journal Asiatique,* Série XI, 11 (Novembre-Décembre, 1913), pp.465-557; Satis Chandra Vidyabhusana, (ed. and trans.), 'So-sor-thar-pa; or a code of Buddhist Monastic laws: Being the Tibetan version of the Prātimokṣa of the Mulasarvāstivāda school', *JASB.,* (NS), IX, 3-4 (1915), pp.29-139; N. Dutt. 'Gilgit Ms. of the Vinaya Piṭaka', *IHQ.,* XIV, 2 (June 1938), pp.408-24; W. Pachow and Ramakanta Mishra, eds., 'The Prātimokṣa Sūtra of the Mahāsaṃghikas', *JGJRI.,* X, 1-4 (Nov.-Feb.-May-Aug.1952-53), Appendix. pp.1-48; A.C. Banerjee, 'Prātimokṣa-Sūtra', *IHQ.*, XXIX, 2, 3, 4, 1953; Lokesh Chandra, ed., 'Unpublished Gilgit Fragment of the Prātimokṣa-Sūtra', *Wiener Zeitschrift für die Kunde Südund Ostasiens,* IV (1960), pp.1-13.

[251]J. Takakusu, op. cit., pp.88-89.

[252]Buddha's last injunction to Ānanda ('Mahaparinibbana Suttanta', *Dīgha Nikāya,* II, p.80) itself speaks against the idea of individual leadership or personal guidance in the future policy of the *Saṅgha.*

A *Saṅgha* of twenty and upward was competent to perform all acts.[253] It is undoubtedly true that the assembly was the chief executive body. All affairs pertaining to the community life, disciplinary breaches and business of the *Saṅgha* life were managed by it. But by the 2nd-3rd century AD one finds that the *Saṅghasthavira* officiates as the head of the *Saṅgha*.[254] It was he who appointed able members of the assembly to conduct various duties such as taking votes, recitation of *prātimokṣa* and delivering of discourse at the *uposatha* ceremony.[255]

The functions performed by the assembly are referred at length by I-tsing.[256] These were—ordination of a *bhikṣu,* the holding of the *uposatha*, proper recitation and observation of the *Prātimokṣa* rules, assent to gifts distributed during the *pravāraṇā* celebration, summoning and examination of the guilty *bhikṣu*, yearly assignment of rooms, arrangement of the affairs of the deceased monk, distribution of his property, management of economic life such as clothing, meals, articles of worship, construction, cultivation and preservation of monastic fields and gardens.

I-tsing's[257] observation about the assembly's role in the Tamralipti monastery is more specific. He states that whenever anything was given to the priests by other persons, they made use of it through the assent of the assembly, that no principal office was appointed in that monastery; that when any business happened, it was settled by the assembly; and that if any priest decided anything by himself alone, or treated the priests favourably or unfavourably at his own pleasure, without regarding the will of the assembly, he was expelled (from the monastery), being called a *kulapati* (i.e. one who behaved like a householder).

---

[253] *Mahāvagga,* p.355.

[254] *Supra.*

[255] *Abhisamācārikā*, pp.2-3.

[256] J. Takakusu, op. cit., pp.63, 64, 87-88, 96ff, 190, 193.

[257] Ibid., p.62.

The opinion of the majority was also given due weightage as is clear from Prajñāvarman's description of what he observed at Nālandā. 'If something happened in the monastery, all the monks of the monastery got together to discuss the matter. The monks, one by one, with folded hands reported the matter. If one of the monks objected, nothing could be done. If anyone did anything without the consent of all the monks of the monastery, he would be forced to leave the establishment. If there were difference of opinion, they would try to convince the other group with reasons. No force was used to convince.'[258]

Disciplinary measures[259] were laid down for the breach of rules. The means of coercion at the disposal of the *Saṅgha* was not harsh, but quite sufficient. The severest punishment was expulsion from the community.[260] I-tsing states that the offender of the *Saṅghadiśeṣa* rules should after a penance, be reinstated in a community of the *bhikṣus* forming a body of twenty, but if the offence be small one, it should be confessed and atoned before those who are not one's equals.

Various modes to settle disputes[261] were adopted. We have a vague reference in the *Śikṣāsamuccaya*[262] to the *Yebhuyyasikā*[263] form which was adopted only when the matter at issue was of a grave nature. The decision was arrived at by the vote of the majority. Voting was done by *śalākās* (marked pieces of wood), which were distributed and subsequently counted to ascertain the majority opinion.

---

[258]S . Dutt, *BMMI.*, p.313, (Appendix).

[259]For details, see, G.S.P. Misra, op. cit., pp.132-34; S. Dutt, *EBM.*, pp.129-36.

[260]I-tsing (J. Takakusu, op. cit., p.65) states that violation of laws and failure in religious performances meant expulsion.

[261]G.S.P. Misra, loc. cit., pp.134-36; S. Dutt, loc. cit., p.140-42.

[262]*Śikṣāsamuccaya* (trans.), p.57. 'but if a deficit should arise in the oecumenical Order, and if the receipts of the local Order should amount to a surplus, then our serving monk, after gaining a unanimous vote of the monks of his Order, may do the business of the oecumenical Order by drawing on the receipts of the local Order'.

[263]*Cullavagga*, p.164.

Monastic Etiquette

Every religious institution enforces certain rules of decorum[264] on the part of those who belong to it or are under training. The *Sekhiya* dharma section of the *Prātimokṣa* contains rules of conduct, the violation of which did not involve any punishment but definitely lowered the *bhikṣu* in the estimation of society and his fellow brothers. The *Visuddhimagga*[265] defines *Ācāra* in the following terms: 'A bhikkhu is respectful, deferential, possessed of conscience and shame, wears his inner robe properly, wears his upper robe properly, his manner inspires confidence, whether in moving forward or backwards, looking ahead or aside, bending or stretching, his eyes are downcast, he has (a good) deportment, he guards the doors of his sense faculties, knows the right measure in eating, is devoted to wakefulness, possesses mindfulness and awareness, wants little, is contented, is strenuous, is a careful observer of good behaviour, and treats the teachers with great respect. This is called (proper) conduct.'

Proper etiquette was to be observed in and outside the monastic precincts. The mode of addressing senior *bhikṣus* as *thera (sthavira), āyuṣmān, ārya* and *bhadanta (bhante)* bespeaks of reverence on the part of the juniors. These appellations occur profusely in the entire Buddhist literature and inscriptions.[266] Juniors could be addressed by personal name or by clan-name.[267]

---

[264]A *bhikkhu* was required and expected by the Buddha to dwell restrained in conduct in accordance with the *Pātimokkha* rules of restraint, endowed with good manners and customs, perceiving slightest fear in the slightest thing to which exception might be taken and learning and practising precepts of conduct after formally accepting them for fulfilment. See, *Book of the Gradual Sayings*, I, p.199.

[265]*The Path of Purification*, Pt.I, p.19.

[266]Terms like *bhādata (bhayaṁta, bhayata), thêra, mahathêra, aya (ayira, āyyaka)* occur profusely in inscriptions from Sāñchī, Barhut, Bodhgayā, Kānhêrī, Kuḍa, Bhājā Kārle, Nāsik, Junnar and Amarāvatī. See, *Lüders list,* Nos.281, 338, 451, 530, 713, 762, 763, 766, 768, 773, 789, 792, 797, 800, 842, 850, 856, 858, 886, 939-42, 987, 989, 993, 998, 1001, 1002, 1006, 1007, 1012, 1020, 1041, 1060, 1080-83, 1089, 1094, 1095, 1107, 1128, 1171, 1223, 1233, 1237, 1240, 1246, 1250, 1263, 1272, 1280, 1286, 1289, 1295.

[267]*Abhisamācārikā*, p.127.

The juniors were enjoined to show respect and salute the seniors with the word *'vande'* (I salute) and the senior in accepting the salutation uttered *'ārogya'* (health) holding his hands right in front.[268] I-tsing mentions certain rules of etiquette which can be enumerated as follows:

(a) Covering the mouth with the left hand, if one comes near a senior while chewing tooth-wood.[269]

(b) Receiving or offering salutation was prohibited in case of impurity contracted through eating and drinking or having been to the lavatory. Only by joining the hands one could pay honour.[270]

(c) While showing reverence[271] or making an announcement a proper deportment was asked for.[272] As I-tsing[273] puts it, 'One must first adjust the priestly cloak, and gather it up over the left shoulder, pressing the garment (with the right hand) to one's left side, so that it may fit tightly the body. Now stretching down one's left hand, one should take hold of the left part of the undergarment, while the right hand must follow the grasped part of the skirt and fold (or double) the garment with the lowest part of the skirt so that it well covers the knees; in so doing one should not allow any part of one's body to be seen. Let the back part of the skirt quickly touch the body. Holding up the upper and under-garment one should not allow them to touch the ground.

Both heels must be placed together, thc neck and back on a level; with the ten fingers flat on the ground one should now

---

[268]J. Takakusu, op. cit., p.115. As Hiuen-tsang (T. Watters. op. cit., I. p.173) states—'Buddhist monks receiving the courtesies of respect only bestow a good wish.'

[269]J. Takakusu, loc. cit., p.33. See, *Śikṣāsamuccaya* (trans.), p.125.

[270]J. Takakusu, loc. cit., pp.90-91.

[271]Hiuen-tsang (T. Watters, loc. cit., I, p.173) enumerates nine ways of showing respect.

[272]As Hiuen-tsang (ibid.,) observes, 'all who are delivering messages or receiving orders tuck up their clothes and kneel down'.

[273]J. Takakusu, loc. cit., p.122.

bow his head. There should be no covering lower down than the knees. Then one should stretch forth one's folded hands and again touch the ground with one's head. Thus should one carefully salute three times. But in an ordinary salutation only once will suffice—and with the garments adjusted one should sit down in a corner of the room, or stand awhile. In the latter case, the honoured one will offer a seat. When one is being censured for some fault, one may stand all the time without fail.'

Special rules of conduct were enjoined on students.[274] The basic etiquette required in approaching a teacher was proper adjustment of robes (keeping the right shoulder bare), bare feet, keeping to his right followed by salutation and health enquiries.[275] The Lokottaravāda text *Abhisamācārikā*[276] delineates minute rules for the *Saddhivihārika* while entering the *Upādhyāya's* chamber. This consisted of knocking at his door, placing the right foot first, proper salutation leading to health enquiry.

Certain rules of demeanour were observed by *nevāsikas* (resident monks) towards *Āgantukas* (visiting monks). Commenting on the monks of Udyana, Fa-hien[277] states that when stranger *bhikṣus* arrive in their *vihāras,* their wants are supplied for three days after which they are told to find a resting place for themselves. Such monks were received well. They were offered water to wash their feet, oil to anoint and liquid food. Sleeping quarters together with its appurtenances were provided to them according to their rank.[278]

The *Abhisamācārikā*[279] details the regulations of formal dignity and respect to be observed by the *Āgantukas* who were provided with food and accommodation by the *nevāsikas.*

---

[274]See, *infra.*

[275]See, *The Questions of King Milinda*, I, pp.23, 24, 27; *The Diamond Sutra,* p.22; J. Takakusu, op. cit., pp.21-22.

[276]*Abhisamācārikā,* p.36.

[277]J. Legge, op. cit., p.29.

[278]Ibid., p.44. Hiuen-tsang (S. Beal, *Life*, pp.37, 103, 106) himself received proper welcome in various monasteries during his sojourn.

During I-tsing's time a stranger monk on arrival at a monastery was treated as a guest for five days and given the best of food so that he might recover from his fatigue, after which he was treated as a common monastic if he was not learned. If he was and bore a good character, he was assigned his proper rank and treatment with his name 'written down on the register of the names of the resident priests'.[280]

All visitors were cordially welcomed by the word *svāgata* and by the word *susvāgata* if they were strangers.[281] The ceremony of receiving them varied according to their position as teachers, students, strangers or friends.[282] On the arrival of the guest, his bowl and water jar were taken and hung on the peg by the host and he was asked to take rest. 'If the host be junior to the visitor, he, in honour of his superior, holds the calves of the visitor's legs, then strokes all parts of his body; and if the host be the senior, he strokes his back, but not so far down as his waist and his feet, in order to soothe him. But if they be both equal in age, then no difference is made.'[283]

The newcomer after having recovered from his fatigue, was to have a wash, before approaching his senior. After having exchanged greetings and compliments of friendship and civility, the junior withdrew to one side and sat down with respect. He could then be offered eatables and drink according to his desire.[284]

It seems that perfection of reverence led many sects such as the Dharmaguptakas[285] to frame rules of conduct before an object of worship. Such objects were paid reverential

[279]*Abhisamācārikā*, pp.117-25.

[280]J. Takakusu, op. cit., p.64.

[281]Ibid., p.124.

[282]Ibid., p.125.

[283]Ibid., p.124.

[284]Ibid., p.125.

[285]The *Śaikṣa* rules of the Dharmaguptakas (Nos.60-85) incorporate rules which speak of proper deference to the *stūpa* as an object of worship. See, W. Pachow, op. cit., pp.51-52.

services—by circumambulation either once or thrice.[286] I-tsing[287] refers to the rule of turning to the right in worship, meaning walking towards one's own right, i.e. turning one's left hand towards an object. But I-tsing's explanation seems to be against the general rule. *Pradakṣiṇā*[288] (to go round so as to keep the right side turned to a person, a mode of reverential salutation) means turning one's right hand towards an object whether *stūpa* or Buddha image. While going round the *stūpa* or approaching the temple *(gandha kuṭī)* the monk was required to take off his shoes and uncover his right shoulder.[289]

Certain rules regulated the daily conduct of the *bhikṣus* such as, while approaching the laity for alms, his mode of eating, placing and washing of bowl, preaching, appearance and personal hygiene. The *Milindapañho,*[290] *Mahāvastu*[291] *Abhisamācārikā*[292] and the *Śikṣāsamuccaya*[293] emphasize the subdued demeanour[294] which had to be adopted by the *bhikṣu* going for his daily round of alms.

Regulations demanded that he should stand for alms at each house in regular order *(sāvadāna)*[295] at a place where he could be easily seen, in silence and point to his alms bowl.[296] When visiting the houses of the laity he was not to annoy them

[286]T. Walters, op. cit., I, p.173.

[287]J . Takakusu, op. cit., p.142.

[288]See, Rhys Davids and Stede, *Pali English Dictionary,* S.V. Padakkhiṇa.

[289]J . Takakusu, loc. cit., pp.22, 70.

[290]*The Questions of King Milinda*, Pt.II, pp.34, 339, 346.

[291]*Mahāvastu*, III, pp.386, 419-20.

[292]*Abhisamācārikā,* pp.105, 197-99.

[293]*Śikṣāsamuccaya,* pp.127ff.

[294]'With senses carefully guarded, the eye not being raised from the ground, and looking ahead no more than a yoke's length; with mind noble and disciplined, that forgets not the doctrine it has learnt, with nature not bent on desire you should go a begging'—*Sikṣāsamuccaya* (trans.), p.127.

[295]*The Questions of King Milinda*, II, pp.339, 346: *Avadānaśataka* (BST.), p.4; *Śikṣāsamuccaya* (ed.), p.128.

[296]'The Āryan deigns not to make his need known. The Āryans stand and show their alms bowls. Such is the way the Āryans beg'—see, *Mahāvastu*, III, p.420.

by persistent requests or by pointing out what he wanted or by wrong demeanour or by chattering. He was not supposed to scorn a gift whatever it was, nor slight the giver. He was not to make a distinction between good and poor (inferior) food,[297] was not to notice the flavour, the donor or the way it was given.

He was not to utter expressions of gratitude or blessing on receiving alms and was to keep the same frame of mind even when he was not offered anything.[298] The Mahāyānic disposition becomes crystal clear when a *bhikṣu* shares his alms food with other creatures. 'Whatsoever company of birds or beasts may wish for food, let them accept the gifts and enjoy it.'[299]

Proper restraint and deportment was essential if *bhikṣus* were invited for meals in the laity's house.[300] Moderation, grace and propriety marked their mode of eating.[301] Food was to be taken with proportionate curry, without pressing down from the top. It was to be made up into round morsels of moderate size. The mouth was not to be opened till the morsel was brought close. Tossing the food into the mouth and nibbling were to be avoided.

Food was to be taken without stuffing the cheeks, shaking the hands, scattering the lumps, putting out the tongue, smacking the lips, making sound, licking the fingers, hands, lips and the bowl.

Certain sects like the Mahāsaṅghikas[302] and the Mula-sarvāstivadins[303] enjoined the proper washing, drying and placing of bowls and other utensils.

---

[297]'Whatever drops in the bowl, be it poor or nice, good or bad, that he should eat without annoyance, with simplicity of heart'—see *Śikṣāsamuccaya* (trans.), p.130.

[298]*Mahāvastu*, III, p.386.

[289]*Śikṣāsamuccaya* (trans.), p.128.

[300]See. Charles Prebish, op. cit., pp.96, 97, 98, 99, 100 (*Śaikṣa* rules); W. Pachow, op. cit., pp.16-19. The *Abhisamācārikā* (p.128f) deals with rules to be observed in approaching Kṣhatriyas, Brahmaṇas, Gṛhapatis and ascetics.

[301]*Śikṣāsamuccaya* (trans.), p.125.

[302]*Abhisamācārikā*, pp.101-04, 171-72.

[303]See, Charles Prebish, op. cit., pp.103, 105 (*Śaikṣa* rules).

Dhamma was also to be preached in accordance with certain rules.[304] It was not to be taught to a person with a staff, parasol, knife or weapon in his hand, with a crown, garland, veil or cap on his head, or with his shoes on. Similarly the doctrine was not to be preached to one mounted on an elephant, horse, palanquin or a vehicle. The *utsaktika, vyastikā* and *paryastika* postures were to be avoided.

Seated on a low seat he was not to teach the *Dhamma* to a person on a high seat; while standing, he was not to preach to a person sitting, while sitting, he was not to preach to a person lying. While walking behind he was not to preach the doctrine to a person walking in front of him and walking by the side of the path he was not to preach the doctrine to a person walking on the path.

These rules were intended evidently not only to keep up the dignity of the preacher but also to avoid the awkwardness of the situation and ineffectiveness of the preaching itself. Reasonable exception (of sickness) was taken into view. The Lokottaravāda text, *Abhisamācārikā*[305] lays down rules for wearing and using two sets of robes, viz., *Grāmapraveśanaka* and *Vihāracaraṇaka.* I-tsing[306] elaborates upon them, taking into view whether the monk is in the *vihāra,* before the image of the Buddha, is entering the laity's house, taking meals or executing private business.

All sects observed rules of personal hygiene and sanitation[307] with a view to observe propriety, prevent destruction of plant life and pollution of water.

These rules of restraint (if exercised) present the monks as gracious, firm, reverent, modest, cautious and calm. For truly

---

[304]W. Pachow, op. cit., pp.20-21 (Appendix IV, *Śaikṣa* rules); See, *Bodhicaryāvatāra* (BST.), Chap.V, vv.88, 89.

[305]*Abhisamācārikā,* pp.179-80.

[306] J. Takakusu, op. cit., p.73.

[307]See, W. Pachow, loc. cit., pp.21-22 (Appendix IV. *Śaikṣa* rules); Charles Prebish, op. cit., pp.102, 104, 107 *(Śaikṣa* rules); *Bodhicaryāvatāra* (BST.), Chap.V, v.91; The *Abhisamācārikā* (pp.217-28) enumerates rules regarding coughing, sneezing, itching of one's body, yawning and *vātakarma.*

it has been said, 'restrained everywhere, the monk from ill obtains release'.

Monastic Routine

The daily schedule of monks seems to have varied little since it transpired (with some exceptions) within the physical limits of the monastic compound. Texts like the *Milindapañho*, *Abhisamācārikā* and *Visudhimagga* provide sufficient information, which when corroborated with the eye witness account of Chinese pilgrims, aids in ascertaining the routine activities of the monks.

A large part of their daily life was regulated according to time. This was done by means of sun-dials called *velāchakras* (time wheels).[308] Besides, clepsydrae were also installed in the larger monasteries.[309] The monks arose early and performed their morning chores[310] which comprised personal cleanliness, seeing, to the personal requirements of elders (teachers) such as supplying tooth-wood, water, basin and towel, worshipping the *stūpa* (or image), learning the scriptures, cleaning the *vihāra* and going on their begging round.

---

[308]J. Takakusu, op. cit., p.143.

[309]The regulation of the clepsydrae was different in monasteries of Mahābodhi and Kuśinagara and at Nalāndā. The day at Nalāndā was of eight hours, each of which was indicated by four immersions of the smaller bowl in the large vessel of water. Each such immersion was indicated by one stroke of a drum, while the completion of one hour as defined above was announced by four strokes of a drum, two blasts of a conch-shell and an additional beat of the drum. The second hour ended at noon when eating was not allowed. The afternoon, like the forenoon, comprised two hours. The expiry of the first hour at night was announced by the beat of the drum by the *karmadāna*. Sunrise and sunset were announced by the beat of the drum at the outside gate of the monastery by 'the servants and porters' stationed there. See, ibid., p.145.

[310]*The Questions of King Milinda*, Pt.I, pp.22, 25, Pt.II, pp.185, 280-81; *Path of Purification*, I, p.102; *Abhisamācārikā*, pp.34, 36, 38; J. Takakusu. loc. cit., pp.116, 120.

The forenoon activities included bathing,[311] taking a walk[312] and ritual worship. As I-tsing[313] informs us, 'in Indian monasteries, when the monastics are going to bathe the image in the forenoon, the priest in charge *(karmadāna)* strikes a *ghanta* (gong) for an announcement'. An image is placed in a basin of the same material while a band of girls play music there. The image having been anointed with scent, perfumed water is poured over it.

Meals were to be taken at mid-day.[314] After getting rid of drowsiness due to the meal, monks sat down in a secluded place to meditate.[315] The late afternoon and evening twilight was spent in worship of images, *caityas* and *stūpas.*[316] The monks were to come out and walk three times round a *stūpa,* offering incense and flowers. They knelt down, while one of them chanted hymns. This was followed by *sūtra* recitation. The performance of these rites was observed by I-tsing[317] at Tamralipti.

---

[311]Just as there was a time for meals, there was also one for baths. As I-tsing (J. Takakusu, op. cit., p.108) says, 'there are more than ten great pools near Nālandā monastery and there every morning a *ghaṇṭi* (gong) is sounded to remind the priests of the bathing hour. Everyone brings a bathing sheet with him. Sometimes hundred, sometimes a thousand priests (a gross exaggeration) leave the monastery together and proceed in all directions towards these pools, where all of them take a bath.' The *Vinaya* rules were followed on the subject. There were also arrangements for baths in the monastery, if one did not like to go to the pond'. Further (ibid., pp.109-10) 'bathing should always take place when one is hungry. Two kinds of benefits are derived by having meals after bathing.'

[312]I-tsing (ibid., p.114) informs us that walking hours are in the forenoon (before 11 O'clock) and late in the afternoon.

[313]Ibid., pp.147-48; See, *Bodhicaryāvatāra* (BST.), Chap.II, v.11.

[314]It is curious that the rule as to not eating food after sunturn at noon is not expressly stated in *Pātimokkha* or indeed anywhere in the *Vinaya.* But it is often implied. See, for e.g. the 37th *Pācittiya* rule; *Mahāvagga,* pp.232, 264.

[315]*Path of Purification*, I, p.102. This was practised by the founder himself as Fa-hien (J. Legee, op. cit., p.85) refers to the Pippala cave where the lord was accustomed to sit in meditation after mid-day meal.

[316]T. Watters, op. cit., I, pp.302-03; J. Takakusu, loc. cit., p.152. Bana Bhaṭṭa (*Harṣacarita*, pp.137-38) has also portrayed the *bhikṣus* as performing *caitya vandanā* at evening twilight: '*Kamanḍalu jalaśucisayacaraṇeṣu caitya-praṇatipareṣu paraśariṣu*'.

In the Nālandā monastery, where it was difficult to assemble its numerous monks in one place for congregational worship, individual worship was allowed as convenient to each member.[318] This was followed by religious sermons and open discussions.

The first and the third watch of the night were spent in learning, prayers and meditation while the second was utilized for sleep.[319] This regular routine had its own variations. The resident monks had to perform various other activities such as preparing, washing and dyeing robes, safeguarding the furniture and repairing and renovating the *vihāra.*[320]

The Ascetic Life

There were always in the *Saṅgha, āraṇya bhikṣus,* partisans of an austere mode of life who had much in common with the *Pratyekabuddhas.* The *Milindapañho* provides glimpses of the two fold character of monastic living by citing a verse occurring in the *Saṁyutta Nikāya*[321] and the *Theragātha.*[322] It runs as follows:

> 'Seek lodgings distant from the haunts of men,
> Live there in freedom from the bonds of sin,
> But he who finds no peace in solitude
> May with the Order dwell, guarded in heart'.[323]

The eremitical ideal is upheld in the *Milindapañho*[324] though monastic life is taken as a fact.

---

[317]J. Takakusu, op. cit., pp.152-54.

[318]Ibid.

[319]Ibid., p.146.

[320]*Abhisamācārikā,* pp.63-67.

[321]*Saṁyutta Nikāya*, I, p.154.

[322]*Theragātha* (PTS.), v.142.

[323]*The Questions of King Milinda*, II, p.343.

[324]*'Yathā mahārāja dipiko araññe tiṇagahanaṁ vā vanagahanaṁ va missāya nilīyitavā mige gaṁhāti evamevakho mahārāja yoginā yogāvacarena vivekaṁ sevitabham araññaṁ rukkhamūlaṁ pabbataṁ kandaraṁ giriguhaṁ susanaṁ vanapathaṁ abhokāsaṁ palālapuñjaṁ appasaddaṁ atpīnadhosaṁ vijanavātaṁ manussarāhaseyyakam patisallānasārūppaṁ vivekaṁ sevamano hi mahārāja, hoti yogi yogāvacharo na cirasseva chalabhiññasu cha vasībhāvaṁ pāpuṇāti*— see, *Milindapañho* (ed. R.D. Vadekar), p.363. Certain ascetic practices are also hinted at in the *Milindapañho.* See, *The Questions of King Milinda,* Pt.I, pp.9, 231.

In the *Milindapañho*,[325] Nagasena enumerates twenty eight merits *(dhutaṅga guṇas)* accruing from ascetic observances. The existence of the *dhutaṅgas* shows that in theory as well as to some extent in practice, the ascetic ideal was maintained even within the monastic setting.

The Sāñchī Buddhist Stūpa I Inscriptions[326] refer to the term *tāpasiyas*. This term may probably refer to those Buddhists who laid much emphasis on the performance of austerities.[327] The *dhutaṅgas* and their excellence find their full exposition in the *Visuddhimagga,* which states that one may be very severe *(ukkaṭṭha),* moderately severe *(majjhima)* or moderate *(mudaka)* in practising them.[328]

Traditionally the *dhutaṅgas* are listed as thirteen in number.[329]

(a) Wearing robes made of rags collected from dust heaps—*Paṃsukūlika.*
(b) Possessing only three robes at a time—*Tecīvarika.*
(c) Living only on food obtained by begging—*Piṇḍapātika.*
(d) Begging from door to door—*Sapadāna-cārika.*
(e) Eating only once a day at one sitting—*Ekāsanikaṅgam.*
(f) Begging with a bowl—*Pattapiṇḍika.*
(g) Refusing food in excess of regulations—*Khalupacchā-bhattika.*
(h) Forest dwelling—*Āraññaka.*
(i) Residing at the foot of a tree—*Rukkhamūlika.*

---

[325]*The Questions of King Milinda*, II, pp.251-52. The practices are intended to achieve the aims and objects namely—little desire, contentment, few wants, strenuous life, easy maintenance, penetrating knowledge and complete destruction of yearning *(tṛṣṇa)*—see, *Vimuktimarga Dhutaguṇa—Nirdeśā* (ed. and trans. P.V. Bhapat), p.3.

[326]*Lüders list*, Nos.219, 220, 228, 256, 307, 409, 560.

[327]A.M. Shastri, op. cit., p.105. *The Saṁyutta Nikāya* (II, p.132) refers to Mahakassapa and his followers as keepers of *dhutaṅgas.* See, also *Aṅguttara Nikāya*, I, p.23; III, p.58. *Contra.*, N. Dutt, *EMB.*, I, pp.207-08.

[328]*The Path of Purification*, I, pp.59-83.

[329]Ibid., pp.60-79; *Samantapāsādikā* (Nal. ed.), I, p.217; II, p.902; J. Takakusu, op. cit., p.56, fn.3. In the Dharmasangraha *(Mahayana Sūtra Saṅgraha,* BST., Pt.I, p.333) and *The Large Sutra on Perfect Wisdom* (pp.338, 391, 435) only 12 are listed.

(j) Living in the open air—*Abbhokāsika*.
(k) Living in a cemetery—*Sosānika*.
(l) Sleeping at night wherever he may be—*Yathāsanthatika*.
(m) Sleeping in a sitting posture—*Nesajjika*.

Mahāyānic literature[330] pictures the ascetic with his meagre belongings which receives confirmation from inscriptions[331] which refer to the term *araññaka* and *peṁḍapātika (piṇḍapātika)*.

Hiuen-tsang[332] testifies to the practice of asceticism and refers to a spot near Rājagṛha where a *bhikṣu* practising *samādhi* committed suicide, attaining arhatship in the act.[333] I-tsing[334] says, 'such a bhikṣu would not accept any invitation and does not care for the gifts of any precious things such as gold, any more than for mucus or saliva, but lives retired in a lonely forest'.

Such a man yearns for solitude and speaks with Śāntideva[335]—'when may I walk with indifference, never looking behind, staying in an empty temple in a thicket of trees, or in caves? When shall I dwell without a resting place, following my own inclinations, in broad natural places without attachments? When shall I dwell without fear, without protecting the body; the measure of my property, a clay bowl; my robe worthless to thieves? It follows that solitudes are pleasing, kindly, the dawn of all that is auspicious, the tranquilizers of all disturbance. Let me always frequent them.'

The Order of the Bhikkhuṇīs

In the Pali canon the *Bhikkhuṇī Saṅgha* is recorded to have been instituted reluctantly by the Buddha at the request of his aunt and foster mother, Mahāprajāpati Gotami and upon the

---

[330] *Saddharma Pundarika* (SBE.), p.132, *Mahāvastu,* III, pp.61, 252-53, 453-54.

[331] *Lüders list*, No.1110 (Bedsā inscription), ibid., No.1272 (Amarāvatī Inscription).

[332] T. Watters, op. cit., II, p. 191.

[333] Ibid., p.155. See also, J. Takakusu, op. cit., p.198.

[334] J. Takakusu, loc. cit., pp.50, 194.

[335] *Bodhicaryāvatāra* (trans.), pp.196, 197.

intercession of Ānanda.[336] During the time of Aśoka, the *Saṅgha* is known to have *bhikkuṇis* as its regular members.[337] In the Suṅga-Sātavāhana period the number of women joining the *Saṅgha* increased considerably, as is evident from a number of votive inscriptions at Bharhut, Sāñchī, Bodhgayā and Mathura.[338]

Ordination and Discipline

It seems that the rules of ordination as prescribed in the Pāli canon continued even in later times. The *Bhikkhuṇīs* were required to wait for a period of two years during which they were subjected to six interdictions[339] besides submitting to eight restrictions *(Garudhammas)*.[340] They were ordained first by a chapter of nuns, than by a chapter of monks before whom they presented themselves accompanied by their female preceptor.[341] Eligibility for the membership of the *Saṅgha* rested on answering satisfactorily the twenty-four *antarayika dhammas*.[342]

The nuns had to observe the ecclesiastical rules as enjoined by their code,[343] which imposed a burden of eighty-four more rules on them. Meena Talim while analysing these rules has compared them with those of the monks. 'Looking to this large difference in number,' she remarks, 'one is inclined to think that favouritism was shown to monks, but considering

---

336 *Cullavagga,* pp.373-74: Gustav Roth, op. cit., pp.14f. Buddha is said to have commented that the entry of women in the *Saṅgha* would shorten the life of the Order.

337 Aśoka refers to nuns along with monks in the Bairat Rock Inscription. See, E. Hultzsch, *CII.,* I, pp.173-74.

338 See, *Lüders list* (*EI.*, X).

339 *The Pācitttya,* pp.436-37. She had to take a vow to abstain from killing living creatures, stealing, unchastity, lying, drinking intoxicating beverages and eating at the forbidden time.

340 *Cullavagga,* pp.374-75: Gustav Roth, loc. cit., pp.17-18.

341 I.B. Horner, *The Book of Discipline,* V, p.376.

342 *Cullavagga,* p.391.

343 *The Bhikṣuṇī-Vinaya* of the Mahaāsāṅghika-Lokottaravādins is the only complete disciplinary code for Buddhist nuns in its Indian version, with the exception of that in the Pāli Vinaya.

the nature of the rules, the gap of difference is almost nullified and made insignificant. Most of these rules are either corollary to one another or explanatory or a mere classification of the point. The scrutiny of these rules (which are exclusively meant for nuns) will reveal that nothing is so severe or unjustified as considered. There appears no motive to degrade woman by way of introducing these extra 84 rules, as critics hold.'[344]

Status in the Saṅgha—Early Phase[345]

Though as a collective expression the Buddhist *Saṅgha* is denominated as *Ubhato-Saṅgha* (the two sided Order) of *bhikkhus* and *bhikkhuṇīs* still the latter was not coordinate with, but was rather subordinate to the former.[346] Hermann Oldenberg has derisively labelled the Order of the nuns as a 'reluctantly tolerated element in the Church'.[347]

That they were 'submissively subjected' to a harsher discipline than monks is clear from the eight *garudhammas* which form the kernel of the *Bhikkhuṇī-Vinaya*.[348] They were technically subordinate to the monks. They were not allowed to go out of an *āvāsa* alone.[349] Only a *bhikkhu* duly selected

[344]Meena V. Talim, 'Buddhist nuns and disciplinary rules', *JUB.* (NS), Vol.34, Pt.II, No.4, Sept.1965, p.136.

[345]For a general reading, See, I.B. Horner, *Women Under Primitive Buddhism;* Nancy Falk, 'An Image of Women in Old Buddhist literature: The Daughters of Mara,' Women and Religion, pp.105-12.

[346]It may be noted that this attitude was not peculiar only to the Buddhist but was shared even by the Jaina and Brāhmaṇical systems as well which makes S.B. Deo (op. cit., p.467) remark, 'it should be noted that the nuns as a whole were always treated on an inferior basis in relatiop to the monks'. See, S.R. Goyal, op. cit., pp.294ff.

[347]H. Oldenberg, *Buddha, His Life, His Doctrine, His Order,* p.166.

[348]Ibid., p.381; G.S.P. Misra, op. cit., p.132. Gustav Roth (op. cit., p.xxxi, Intd.) observes, 'these rules rather betray the tendency to deter women from joining the Order'.

[349]M.M. Singh, *Life in North-Eastern India in Pre-Mauryan Times*, p.180. I-tsing (J. Takakusu, op. cit., p.63) while reporting about the Tamralipti monastery says that the nuns walked together in a company of two, if it was away from a monastery but when they had to go to a layman's house for some essential work, they went in the company of four.

by the *Saṅgha* could exhort them. The *bhikkhu Saṅgha* could exercise every power of interdicting the *Uposatha* or *Pavāraṇā* of the *bhikkhuṇī Saṅgha* but the latter had no such right over the former.[350] Atonements for transgressions and the settlement of differences of all kinds, were subject to control and partly to confirmations by the *bhikkhu Saṅgha.*[351] *Bhikkhuṇīs* while going to the *bhikkhus* had to announce their purpose to the assembly.[352]

Though inscriptional evidence[353] provides a glimpse into the literary achievements of certain *bhikkhuṇīs,* the overall picture as obtained from literary texts appears partisan against them. It must be understood that the Buddhist want of sympathy with women was not a unique phenomenon but rather one that was typical of the prevailing ascetic ethos.[354]

True that Buddha did not doubt their potentialities but his statements on their nature,[355] ambivalent as they are, indicate that he classed them apart from men. Buddha who discoursed so much on social equality could not propose sexual equality. His allusions to the weakness of female nature were probably intended simply as a device to warn monks against any unseemly involvement with women.

Women were exposed to unrestrained criticism and unlimited scorn by monks also. The *Aṭṭhasālini*[356] states, 'of

---

[350]*Cullavagga,* pp.396-97.

[351]Durga Bhagavat, op. cit., p.162.

[352]J. Takakusu, op. cit., p.63.

[353]See, Chap.IV.

[354]'Woman', observes A. Foucher, 'was the eternal enemy of all religious Orders'. See, A. Foucher, *The Life of the Buddha* (trans.), p.110.

[355]The *Nikāyas* are replete with examples of feminine iniquity. While recounting the five powers in women, Buddha states that they can be counteracted by one single power of male authority (*Book of the Kindred Sayings,* IV, pp.165-66). On being questioned by Ananda, Buddha replies: 'Womenfolk are uncontrolled, Ānanda. Womenfolk are greedy, Ānanda, Womenfolk are weak in wisdom, Ānanda. That is the reason, that is the cause why womenfolk do not sit in a court of justice, do not embark on business, do not reach the essence of the deed'—ibid., II, pp.92-93.

[356]*Aṭṭhasālini* (PTS.), II, p.421.

the two, the masculine sex is superior, the feminine is inferior'. The *Milindapañho*[357] lists woman, among the nine kinds of people, who reveal the secret through intimacy.

The Mahāyānic Phase

The status of the nuns was definitely effected by the general status of womankind as it prevailed in ancient Indian society. An attitude of contempt and aversion for her is reiterated in some of the Mahāyānic texts. The *Mahāvastu* has a word of caution, 'Woman high or low, like flames of fire in a wood, come forth to seduce the sages'.[358] 'Have nothing to do with them. They are like snakes, like poisonous leaves, like charcoal pits'.[359] She is scoffed at, for her 'two inches wit'.[360]

The *Saundarānanda Kavya*[361] takes woman to be the origin of all sins and dangers. Śāntideva goes to the extremes, when he remarks with his usual acuity that 'a woman is the destruction of destructions in the world and the next; hence one must ever avoid women if he desires happiness for himself'.[362] Her position is lowered all the more when she is classed with a person suffering from physical handicap, a slave, a dog, a swine, an ass, a camel and a venomous snake.[363]

---

[357] *The Questions of king Milinda*, I, p.141.

[358] '*Mahāvastu*, III, p.385. Compare, *Ācārāṅge-sūtra* (SBE., XXII, pp.48, 81) and *Sutrakṛtāṅga* (SBE., XLV, pp.274-75). For Mahāyāna Buddhism. See Diana Y. Paul, Women in Buddhism: images of the Feminine in Mahāyāna Tradition and The Buddhist Feminist ideal: Queen Srimala and the Tathagatagarbha.

[359] *Mahāvastu*, III, p.144.

[360] Ibid., p.391. For a similar view, see, *Book of the Kindred Sayings*, I, p.161.

[361] 'For women lead to disaster in the end, like creepers which are poisonous when touched, like caves still full of snakes after being swept, like naked sword-blades held (in the hand)'—The *Saundarānanda,* (trans.), E.H. Johnston, pp.44-47.

[362] *Śikṣāsamuccaya* (trans.), p.77; See also. *Bodhicaryāvatāra* (BST.), Chap.V, v.7.

[363] *Śikṣāsamuccaya* (trans.), pp.73-74

Inspite of her (so called) weaknesses, few Mahāyānic texts[364] have highlighted the idealism and devotion of certain ladies. The *Saddharma Puṇḍarīka*[365] speaks of 'sons and daughters of good families' as striving in the bodhisattva vehicle for the goal but discloses in Sariputra's words that a woman cannot occupy the five ranks,[366] viz., (1) the rank of Brahma, (2) the rank of Indra, (3) the rank of a chief guardian of the four quarters, (4) the rank of a Cakṛavartin, (5) the rank of a *bodhisattva* incapable of sliding back.

Further it is said that a women could be reborn as a man in the Sukhāvati land provided that after hearing the *sūtra* she had grasped its meaning.[367] But the *sūtra* was to be entrusted to her with certain reservations.[368] The *Mahāvastu* [369] states that a *bodhisattva* is not born as a woman, while the *Bodhisattvabhūmi* explain that a *bodhisattva* may be born as a woman during the first *asaṅkhyeya* of his career but not during the second and third *asaṅkhyeyas.*[370]

It may be inferred from the above passages that a woman was considered eligible only for the first step of the 'thought of enlightenment'[371] but had to be reborn as a man in order to ascend to the higher stages of a *bodhisattva's* career.[372] It is,

---

[364]*Avadānaśataka* (BST.), 8th Varga; *Divyāvadāna* (BST.), Chap.27 (Kuṇāla-vadānaṁ); *Jātaka-Māla* (ed.), H. Kern, pp.51ff.

[365]*Saddharma Puṇḍarīka* (SBE.), p.386.

[366]Ibid., p.252.

[367]Ibid., p.389.

[368]The four requisites were—(1) She shall stand under the superintendence of the Lord Buddhas; (2) she shall have planted good roots; (3) she shall keep steadily to the mass of disciplinary regulations; (4) she shall, in order to save creatures, have the thoughts fixed on supreme and perfect enlightenment. See, ibid., p.432.

[369]*Mahāvastu*, I, p.81.

[370]Quoted, Hardayal, op. cit., p.224.

[371]As Śāntideva (*Śikṣāsamuccava* trans., pp.12, 101) puts it, 'this discipline is attained even in the case of women, when their sinful inclinations are not violent and their minds have a longing for enlightenment'.

[372]Hardayal, loc. cit., p.224. Even the Digambaras hold nuns to be ineligible for liberation, unless they are reborn as men. See, S.B. Deo. op. cit., p.497.

therefore, not surprising to read Śāntidevas fervent prayer—'whoever are women in the world, may they achieve manhood'.[373]

Seen in a proper historical perspective it becomes clear that except for few references to nuns and their establishments from the inscriptions at Mathura, Kāṇerī, Kuḍa, Junnar and Amarāvatī, the number of nuns went on decreasing. The Chinese pilgrims[374] give a passing reference to them. I-tsing's observation reveals their actual position in the seventh century AD. 'The benefit and supply to the female members of the Order are very small, and monasteries of many a place have no special supply of food for them. This being the case, there will be no way of living if they do not work for their maintenance; and if they do so, they often act against the *Vinaya* teaching and disobey the noble will of the Buddha. How should they decide for themselves as to taking one course and rejecting the other? When once one's body is at ease, one's religion prospers.'[375]

I-tsing provides a typically monkish answer to the above situation when he says 'The five garments, a pot and bowl are enough for the nuns to subsist upon; and a small apartment is sufficient to maintain their lives. Personal possessions can be diminished and the troubles of the lay devotees can thus be avoided; they can be pure like a precious stone lying in the mud or a lotus-flower in water, and thus their life, though called a low one, is, in reality, a life of wisdom that is equal to that of an exalted person'.[376] From the foregoing discussion it becomes crystal clear that virulent diatribes were written intentionally against women, in an attempt to highlight the reclusive (hence celibate) ideal and to caution the unwary passion prone monk.

---

[373]*Bodhicaryāvatāra* (BST.), Chap. X, v.30. See also *Sukhavati Vyūha* (SBE.), Pt.II, p.19.

[374]J . Legge, op. cit., p. 45; T. Watters. op. cit., I, p.302.

[375]J. Takakusu, op. cit., p.80.

[376]Ibid., pp.80-81.

After Death Ceremonies

None of the texts mention the funeral rites of the monks anywhere in detail. Fa-hien[377] has provided us with some information. This refers to the cremation ceremony of an arhat in Ceylon. 'Four or five *li* east of the vihara there was reared a great pile of firewood, which might be more than thirty cubits square, and the same in height. Near the top were laid sandal, aloe and other kinds of fragrant wood. On the four sides (of the pile) they made steps by which to ascend it. With clean whitehair cloth, almost like silk, they wrapped (the body) round and round. They made a large carriage frame in form like our funeral car, but without the dragons and fishes. At the time of the cremation, the king and the people, in multitudes from all quarters, collected together, and presented offerings of flowers and incense. When this was finished, the car was lifted on the pile, all over which oil of sweet basil was poured, and then a light was applied. While the fire was blazing, every one, with reverent heart, pulled off his upper garment, and threw it, with his feather-fan and umbrella, from a distance into the midst of the flames, to assist the burning. When the cremation was over, they collected and preserved the bones, and proceeded to erect a tope.'

I-tsing[378] adds a few more details regarding the death rituals. The dead body was carried on a bier to the cremation ground where it was burnt on the same day. The assembled monks sat on one side, 'either on grass bound together, or on elevations of earth, or on bricks or stones' while the body was burning. A short sūtra on impermanence ('Anitya-Sūtra') was recited followd by meditation on the impermanency of all conditions.

On their return journey, they bathed together, in their clothes in the pond outside the monastery. If there was no

---

[377]J. Legge, op. cit., p.108. Hiuen-tsang (T. Watters, op. cit., I, p.175) informs us that the Buddhist brethren were forbidden to wail aloud.

[378]J. Takakusu, op. cit., pp.81-82.

pond, they went to a well and washed themselves, putting on dry clothes. This was followed by cleaning the floor of their respective apartments with powdered cow-dung. I-tsing states that 'they sometimes build a thing like a stūpa for the dead, to contain his sarira (or relics). It is called a 'Kula', which is like a small stūpa, but without the cupola on it'.

Archaeological evidence has confirmed Fa-hien's and I-tsing's testimony regarding the enshrinement of the relics of the deceased monk in a *Stūpa*. Cunningham found within a relic-chamber of *stūpa* 2 at Sāñchi, a relic box of sandstone with its eastern face inscribed with '*Savina vināyakāna araṁ kāsapa-gotaṁ upādaya araṁ cha vāchhi—suvijayitaṁ vināyaka*', '(relics) of all teachers including ara (arhat) Kāsapagota (Kāśyapa gotra) and are vāchhi (vātsi)-Suvijayita, the teacher'. Inside the box were found four small relic caskets of mottled steatite inscribed with the names of ten saints whose burnt bones were enshrined within. The saints were Kāsapagota, the teacher of all the Hemavatas, Majhima, Hāritiputa, Vācchiya—Suvi-jayata, Kosikaputa, Gotiputa and Mogaliputa. Other relics of distinguished monks were enshrined in the *stūpas* at Sonari and Andher. *Stūpa* three contained the relics of Sāriputra and Maudgalyāyana, the two foremost disciples of Buddha.[379]

Similarly *stūpas* as memorials for distinguished monks were found in Cells E1, E2 at Dharmarājikā,[380] Cell F12 at Kālawān[381] and Cell 9 at Mohṛā Morādu[382] at Taxila. The

---

[379]Debala Mitra, *Sāñchi*, pp.65-66; *Lüders list*, Nos.152(1), 153(2) Satdhāra Stūpa II inscriptions on steatite box; Nos.156(1), 157(2), 158(3), 159(4), 160(5)—Sonāri Stūpa II Inscription on crystal box; Nos.654, 655, 656, 657, 658, 660, 661, 662, 663, 664, 665, 666, 667, 668—Sāñchi Stūpa II Relic Box Inscriptions; No.680—Andher Stūpa II Earthen Jar Inscription; No.681—Andher Stūpa II on steatite box; No.682—Andher Stupa II on steatite vase; No.683—Andher Stūpa III Inscription outside steatite casket; No.684—Andher Stūpa III Inscription inside steatite casket.

[380]J. Marshall, *Taxila*, I, p.246.

[381]Ibid., p.335.

[382]Ibid., p.361.

Buddhist caves at Nenavali and Thanela (Kolaba district) have a *stūpa*-gallery which consists of a large low-roofed cell with eight *stūpas* carved from the same rock. The *stūpas* range from 3½ to 4½ ft. in height. They are regular *stūpas* with the rail pattern and have stone shafts and square abacus. 'They are not devotional stūpas but are funerary mounds, the relics and jewels of a Buddhist saint being enshrined in a hollow receptacle in the square abacus'.[383]

Ornate *Stūpas* 2, 3 and 6 at Nāgārjunikoṇḍa[384] revealed relics like bone, coral, pearls, gold leaf, flowers presumably associated with important persons. Similarly *Stūpa* 7 and 8 revealed a stone casket containing a pottery made casket which in its turn contained a copper and silver casket, the last containing a gold reliquary into the form of a *stūpa.* This contained a bone relic, gold lotus, jasmine flowers and decayed pearl and coral beads.[385]

The most interesting examples are *Stūpas* 4 and 5.[386] The former contained the remains of 12 monks and the ashes of a distinguished teacher. It seems that when a monk died the body was cremated and the ashes were placed in the water pot the mouth of which was closed by the inverted food bowl. *Stūpa* 4 revealed 12 water pots covered with inverted food bowls, standing in an upright position, together with 6 large begging bowls. The latter are of red pottery and double the size of the food bowls and were placed on the floor of the cell near the other vessels.

There was one pot globular in form and 9 inches in height found in a chamber. Its mouth was covered by a red earthernware saucer on top of which was placed an inverted food bowl. The pot was filled with earth and contained a small silver

---

[383]Owen C. Kail, 'The Buddhist caves at Sudhagarh', *JASB.* (NS), Vols.41-42, 1966-67, p.185. See also *Lüders list*, No.993—Kāṇhêrī Buddhist Stūpa Inscription, 1110—Bedsā Stūpa Inscription 1080-83—Bhājā Stūpa Inscription.

[384]*MASI.*, No.54, pp.19, 21.

[385]Ibid., p.22.

[386]Ibid., p.20.

casket shaped like a *stūpa*. Inside this was a tiny gold reliquary in the form of a miniature *stūpa* three quarters of an inch in diameter containing few gold leaf flowers, crystal pendant, decayed pearl and coral beads.

Thus the *stūpa* seems to have been built to enshrine the relics of a prominent teacher and his twelve principal disciples. *Stūpa* 5 was also erected to contain the remains of monks belonging to Monastery III. The water pots and bowls were all of the usual pattern and no gold or silver reliquaries were found. It appears to be an ordinary monastic *stūpa* containing the ashes of six monks only. These monastic *stūpas* had *āyaka* platforms supporting pillars and were of plain brick and plaster.[387]

[387]Ibid., p.21.

CHAPTER 4

Monasteries as Centres of Learning

Buddhist Philosophy of Education

Contribution of Buddhism to the philosophy of education is noteworthy. In the Buddhist context education is always understood in the terms of overcoming *avijjā*[1] and attainment of *jñāna* or *prajñā*. But *avijjā* (*avidyā*) is not mere lack of information. It is an expression of the fundamental human condition resulting in bondage.[2]. Awakening or freedom *(vimutti)* can be obtained by destroying this ignorance. From *avidyā* arise the *saṁskāras* and the consequent flood of misery. With the destruction of *avidyā* all its products and consequences also disappear.[3]

Another term which is extensively used as a synonym of *jñāna* in early Buddhism is *prajñā*. Both are derived from the root *jña*, 'to know'. The prefix *pra* indicates 'forward' 'forth', 'fore' and is a dynamic particle.[4] It was Rhys Davids who first drew a distinction between the two concepts by defining *jñāna*

---

[1]'Not understanding all ill, friend, not understanding about the arising of ill, the ceasing of ill, the way leading to the ceasing of ill—this, friend, is called ignorance'—*Book of the Kindred Sayings*, IV, p.173.

[2]'Ignorance is the origin, is the birth, is the source of the karma formations'—*Middle Length Sayings*, I, p.90.

[3]*BCAP.*, p.186: *Tatra avidyānirodhāt saṃskārā nirudhyante.* See also, *Middle Length Sayings*, I, p.354: 'By the fading away of ignorance, by the uprising of knowledge, by the stopping of craving, there is thus no recurrence of again becoming in the future.'

[4]T.W. Rhys Davids and Stede, *Pāli English Dictionary*, p.287.

as just knowledge 'in either a next to hand or a lofty sense'[5] while *prajñā*, not being merely an intellectual exercise of thought represents 'coming to know' and 'coming to be'.[6]

In the 'Mahāvedalla Sutta', *prajñā* is considered the knowledge to be practised *(bhāvetabbā)*.[7] The *Aṭṭhasālinī* designates *jñāna* as product or result and *prajñā* as the way to gain a product.[8] *Prajñā* has two meanings—to make known or to indicate *(paññāpana)* and to know the object *(pakārena jānāti)* from the viewpoint of impermanency, suffering and non-ego.[9]

As regards *jñāna*, the *Visuddhimagga*[10] states that *jñāna* means insight knowledge *(vipassanāñāṇa)*. It is said that in him who estimates and judges the states of matter and of non-matter there arises *jñāna* of unfaltering speed, sharp, exceedingly clear like a lightning flash. The *Aṭṭhasālinī*[11] presents a slightly different definition. *Paññā* has illumination (*obhasāna*) and understanding (*pajānana*) as its characteristic (*lakkhaṇa*). The following passage from the text makes it clear. 'Hence, the Elder has said: Just as when a man, your majesty, introduces an oil lamp into a daṛk house, the lamp so introduced disperses the darkness, produces light, sheds lustre, makes objects visible, so your majesty, *paññā* as it arises dispels the darkness of ignorance, produces the light of understanding (*vijjā*), sheds the lustre of *ñāṇa*, makes plain the Ariyan facts. Thus, your majesty, *paññā* has illuminating as its

---

[5]C.A.F. Rhys Davids, *The Birth of Indian Psychology and its Development in Buddhism*, p.263.

[6]Ibid., pp.267-68.

[7]*Majjhima Nikāya*, I, p.361.

[8]*The Expositor* (*Aṭṭhasālinī*), PTS., I, pp.83-84.

[9]Ibid., p.161. For the understanding of the concept of *prajñā*, See, Gopinath Kaviraj, 'The Doctrine of Pratibhā in Indian Philosophy', *ABORI.*, Vol.V, 1924, pp.122-26.

[10]*The Path of Purification*, II, p.741.

[11]*The Expositor*, I, p.161.

characteristic.'[12] Further—'It knows; thus, brother, it is in consequence called *prajñā*. And what does it know? This if ill, and so on. Thus it should be expanded. And thus knowing should be regarded as the characteristic of *paññā*.'[13] This explains the three aspects of *prajñā,* namely, it illuminates, it disperses darkness and it sheds the lustre of *jñāna* or produces the light of understanding.

The concept of *prajñā* and *jñāna* received further elaboration in the *Abhidharmakośa*.[14] In Sanskrit Buddhist literature[15] the different stages of *prajñā* are found represented by corresponding supernatural eyes, viz., the bodily eye, the heavenly eye, the eye of knowledge, the eye of law and the eye of Buddha. There is much confusion regarding the exact significance of the above terms in Buddhist literature, for in course of time and for various reasons imports have gradually changed.[16]

Prajñā as a means *(hetubhūta),* viz., the realization of the noble eight fold path, leads to *prajñā* which may be considered as the end *(phalabhūta)*, viz., *Nirvāṇa*. The former is the result of continued practice of the preliminary *prajñā* consisting in *śruta, cinta* and *bhavana*.[17]

Mahāyāna Buddhism highlighted the goal of the *bodhisattva* (a Buddha-to-be), i.e. someone content with nothing less than all knowledge attained through the

---

[12]Ibid., pp.161-62. See also *The Questions of King Milinda*, I, p.61: where Nāgasena states that 'enlightenment is the mark of wisdom. When wisdom springs up in heart, it dispels the darkness of ignorance, it causes the radiance of knowledge to arise, it makes the light of intelligence to shine forth and it makes the noble truths plain.'

[13]*The Expositor*, I, p.162.

[14]See, *Abhidharmakośa* and *Bhāṣya* of Acarya Vasubandhu (ed., Dwarikadas Shastri), chaps., Pudgalanirdeśah and Jñānanirdeśah.

[15]*Mahāvastu*, I, pp.125-28: *The Diamond Sūtra* (trans.), p.59.

[16]Gopinath Kaviraj, 'The Doctrine of Pratibhā in Indian Philosophy', *ABORI.*, Vol.V, 1924, p.124.

[17]*BCAP.*, pp.169-70; J. Takakusu, op. cit., p.162.

perfection of wisdom for the sake of all living beings. It was emphasized that a *bodhisattva* who courses in perfect wisdom, produces an even state of mind towards all beings. As a result he acquires insight into the sameness of all *dharmas* and learns to establish all beings in this insight.[18]

The *Bodhicaryāvatāra*[19] defines *prajñā* as the application of mind to the knowledge of truth, to the knowledge of what is. Its aim is to destroy the false views concerning the self and things; it is the awareness of true nature of things. The perfection of wisdom consists in the realization of emptiness *(śunyatā)* of the self and the things. It is the destroyer of suffering *(duḥkha śamanī);*[20] he who wants spiritual perfection must realise this great truth of *śūnyatā* and obtain omniscience.

An analysis of the Buddhist scriptures lays bare the educational principles observed by the members of the Order. The chapter entitled 'Jñānanirdeśaḥ' of the *Abhidharma-kośa*[21] dealing with *prajñā* from the standpoint of practice, distinguishes forms of *prajña* chiefly *śrutamayī*, *cintamayī*, and *bhāvanāmayi*. *Śrutamayī prajñā* is produced by hearing the truth as expounded in the *Sūtras*. *Cintamayī prajñā* is produced by reflection on the truth. *Bhāvanāmayi prajñā* is based on contemplation.[22]

It would not be far fetched to say that the Buddha himself had anticipated the apperceptive method of education according to which the student should take nothing on authority but should reflect himself in order to know the truth.

---

[18]*The Large Sūtra on Perfect Wisdom*, p.83.

[19]*Bodhicaryāvatāra* (trans.), pp.211f.

[20]See, *Bhagvad Gītā*, IV.33-34.

[21]*Abhidharmakośa* and *Bhāṣya* of Acarya Vasubandhu with Sphutārthā commentary of Ācārya Yosomitra (ed.), Swami Dwarikadas Shastri, Pt.IV, 7th Kosasthāna-Jñānanirdeśa.

[22]Contemplation is declared to be the only means for gaining *prajñā,* i.e. knowledge of things as they are in themselves as distinguished from what they appear to us. See, *BCAP.*, p.168.

Buddha's discourse to the Kalamas[23]asking them, after expounding his own doctrine, not to accept it—'because it is well reported, or has the sanction of tradition, or was so held in the past, or is given from the scripture, or seems logical or methodological or for the sake of tolerance or suitability or because it is propounded by a Samaṇa', but only after they have realised its merits by themselves *(attanā vā jāneyyātha)* suggests the primacy of self knowledge, individual realization and personal conviction in Buddhism.

Buddhist learning implied spiritual experience and insight and the focus of diverse subjects of the monastic curriculum was upon the overcoming of *avijjā* rather than accumulation of information. But as a matter of historical necessity, with the rise of Mahāyāna and the priority given to the laity, one finds that monasteries became not only centres of popular education and learning but even had secular subjects on their curriculum. Despite this fact, Buddhist monasteries continued to provide the highest stimulation to independent thinking, reflective meditation and spontaneous action.

Institutionalization of Buddhist Monastic Education

The Buddhist *Saṅgha* started as a union of the teacher (the Buddha) and his pupils with the ordination of Aññata-koṇḍañña and his four companions at Isipattana.[24] As noted earlier the *Pabbajjā* and *Upasampadā* ordinations were necessary for every individual to be incorporated in the

---

[23]*Aṅguttara Nikāya*, I, pp.174ff. Contrary to this Brāhmaṇism stressed the authority of tradition and of scripture. Saṅkara states: 'In matters to be known from scripture, mere reasoning is not to be relied on... As the thoughts of men are altogether unfettered, reasoning which disregards holy texts and rests on individual opinion only, has no proper foundation...we observe that even men of the most undoubted intellectual eminence such as Kapila, Kanāda and other founders of philosophical schools have contradicted one another. See, *Vedānta Sūtras* with the commentary by Saṅkarācārya (trans., George Thibaut), *SBE.*, Vol.XXXIV, Pt.I, pp.314-15.

[24]*Mahāvagga*, p.15.

Saṅgha as a *Śrāmaṇera* and a *bhikkhu* respectively. It was part of the monastic regimen to go through a period of training called *nissaya*[25] under an *Upājjhāya* and *Ācariya*. One attached to the former was called *Saddhivihārika* while the other was called *antevāsika*.[26]

Teachers are considered indispensable to the acquisition of knowledge[27] and this equally applied to the *Upādhyāya* and the *Ācārya* who, besides their seniority, were men of exceptional learning and competence.[28] Scholars hold different opinions about the actual relative positions and functions of the *Ācārya* and the *Upādhyāya*. The Pāli-English dictionary defines the term *Ācārya*[29] as a teacher almost synonymous with *Upādhyhāya* and the word *Upādhyāya (upat+adhi+ti)*, literally 'one who is gone close up to' is explained as 'a spiritual teacher or preceptor'.[30]

According to Buddhaghosa, the *Ācariya* (Sk. *Ācārya*, teacher) was one who would establish his pupil on teachable matters of Buddha's doctrines, while the *Upajjhāya* (Sk. *Upādhyāya)* was one who would examine the faults and

---

[25]The *nissaya* rule as advocated in the *Mahavagga* (p.83) seems to have undergone some change as time passed by. In the 7th century AD I-tsing (J. Takakusu, op. cit., p.119) states that after five years from the time that the pupil masters the *Vinaya,* he was allowed to live apart from his teacher but he was to put himself under the care of some teacher wherever he went until ten years had elapsed after he understood the *Vinaya.* If a monk did not understand the *Vinaya.* he was to be under another's care during the whole of his life time.

[26]*Mahāvagga,* pp.43, 67. *The Pāli English Dictionary* (PTS.), defines *antevāsika* (p.48) as one who lives with his teacher and *Saddhivihārika* (p.675) as co-resident, a fellow *bhikkhu.*

[27]The Exalted one said—'By him who knows not, who sees not decay and death as it really is, a teacher should be sought for knowledge about decay and death as it really is; by him also who knows not, who sees not as it really, is, the uprising and the ceasing, and the way going to the ceasing of decay and death—see, *The Book of the Kindred Sayings*, II, p.93; See *Kaṭha Upaniṣad*, 2.8 (*Ananyaprokte gatir atra nāsti*).

[28]*Mahāvagga,* p.67.

[29]T.W. Rhys Davids and W. Stede, *The Pāli English Dictionary,* p.96.

[30]Ibid., p.141.

merits of his disciple and place him on the right path.[31] Thus, according to the definition, the *Ācariya* was the teacher (*Śikṣa-guru*) and the *Upajjhāya* was the spiritual guide or preceptor.[32]

On the other hand N. Dutt states, 'It may be that he (*Ācariya*) gave the *nissayas,* prescribed the *Kammaṭṭhānas* for meditation to his disciple (*antevāsika*), in short, trained him up in the esoteric practices, while the *Upajjhāya* taught the three *piṭakas* and imparted the general instructions, in other words, the exoteric aspects of Buddhism.'[33] The position of the *Upādhyāya* was considered relatively more important of the two; for it is said that when the *Upādhyāya* and the *Ācārya* are together, *nissaya,* towards the latter ceases.[34] The order was, however, reverse in the brāhmaṇical system, where the *Upādhyāya* was a professional teacher while the *Ācārya*[35] was superior to him.[36] But regarding their duties and obligations there was apparently very little difference between them and in the absence of one, the other had to perform the functions of both.[37]

Epigraphic, literary evidence and the testimony of the Chinese pilgrims affirm that the tradition of the *Ācārya, Upādhyāya, antevāsika* and the *sadhivihārika* continued

---

[31]*Samantapāsādikā* (Nal. ed.), Vol.I, p.41. *('Ko ayaṃ tāta Upajjhāyo nāmā' ti. Vajjavajjaṃ disvācodetā sāretā maharaja ti... 'Ko ayaṃ tāta ācariyo nāmā' ti. Imasmiṃ Sāsane Sikkhitabbakadhammesu patiṭṭhāpetā mahārajā' ti).*

[32]A similar view is expressed by S. Dutt (*EBM.*, p.149) and Dipak Kumar Barua (op. cit., p.28).

[33]N. Dutt, *EMB.*, Vol. I, p.284. I-tsing (op. cit., pp.116, 118, 198) renders the term *ācārya* as 'the holder of rules', 'teacher of discipline', 'one who teaches pupils rules and ceremonies' and the term *Upādhyāya* as 'teacher of personal instruction', 'teacher in reading'. See, R.K. Mookerji, *Ancient Indian Education,* p.402. The above definition of *Ācārya* is also in accord with that described in the *Nirukta* 1.4. *'ācārya ācāraṃ grāhayati',* i.e. 'the *ācārya* makes (the students) understand traditional precepts or the proper course of conduct'.

[34]Vinaya Texts *(SBE.),* Vol.XIII, p.182, fn.2. See *Pācittiya Rule* 65.

[35]See, P.V. Kane, 'The meaning of Ācāryāh', *ABORI.*, Vol.XXIII, Pts.I-IV, 1942, Silver Jubilee Volume, p.206.

[36]*The laws of Manu* (SBE.), 11.145.

[37]*Vinaya Texts* (SBE.), Vol.XIII, Pt.I, p.178, fn.2.

unabated as time rolled by. The term *antevāsi* occurs in the minor rock inscriptions,[38] at Brahmagiri, Siddhapura and Jaṭinga-Rāmeśvara in the sense of a pupil but the term in its actual Buddhistic sense of a pupil living under the spiritual tutelage of a teacher in a *vihāra* occurs in the inscriptions ranging from 2nd-1st century BC. They are chiefly the Sonari Stūpa I Rail Inscription,[39] Sāñchī Buddhist Stūpa I Inscription,[40] Sañchī Buddhist Stūpa II Inscription,[41] Sārnāth Buddhist Inscription,[42] Kaṇheri Buddhist Cave Inscription,[43] Kuḍa Buddhist Cave Inscription,[44] Kuḍa Buddhist Tank Inscription,[45] Kondaṇe Cave Inscription,[46] Karle Buddhist Cave Inscription,[47] Bedsa Buddhist Cave Inscription,[48] Nasik Buddhist Cave Inscription,[49] Junnar Buddhist Cave Inscription,[50] Amāravati Buddhist Sculpture Inscription,[51] Amaravati Buddhist Pillar Inscription[52] and Amaravati Buddhist Stone Inscription.[53]

The term *Sadhivihārika* occurs in the inscriptions[54] in the sense of pupil, co-resident and fellow *bhikkhu*. The word *ācārya* has been used in the inscriptions of Aśoka[55] in a rather

---

[38]*CII.*, I, pp.176, 178-79, 180.

[39]*Atēvāsin*, *Lüders list*, Nos.154-55.

[40]*Aṁtēvāsin*, ibid., 303, 349.

[41]*Atēvāsinī*, ibid., 648.

[42]*Antēvāsikas*, ibid., 925.

[43]*Atēvāsinī*, ibid., 1006; *Aṁtēvāsin*, ibid., 1016.

[44]*Atēvāsin*, ibid., 1040, *Atēvāsinī*, No. 1041; *Ātivāsiṇi*, No.1060.

[45]*Aṁtivāsini*, ibid., No.1059.

[46]*Aṁtēvāsin*, ibid., No.1071, *Aṁtēvāsin*, ibid., No.1094.

[47]*Atēvāsini*, ibid., No.1107.

[48]*Aṁtēvāsin*, ibid., No.1110.

[49]*Aṁtēvāsini*, ibid., No.1128.

[50]*Aṁtēvāsin*, ibid., No.1171.

[51]*Ātēvāsini* No.1224, *Aṁtēvasika*, ibid., No.1233, *Ativāsini*, ibid., No.1251, *Atēvāsini*, ibid., Nos.1246, 1250.

[52]*Atavāsika*, ibid., No.1270.

[53]*Atevāsika*, *atêvāsini*, ibid., Nos.1280, 1286.

[54]*Saddhyēviharin* (ibid., Nos.918, 919) in Saheth-Maheth Buddhist Stone Inscription and Sārnāth Buddhist Inscription (ibid, No.925).

[55]*CII.*, I, pp.176, 178-79, 180.

general sense. It occurs frequently in the inscriptions[56] of the pre-Christian and Christian era. The term *Upādhyāya* alone occurs in a few inscriptions.[57] The term *Upadhyāyāchêras* along with *Saddhêvihārin* and *antêvāsikas* occurs in the Sarnath Buddhist Inscription of Kaniṣka.[58]

The *Milindapañho*[59] refers to the *ācārya* and the *antevāsika*. There is explicit reference to an *Ācārya* and an *Upādhyāyā* in the *Lalitavistara*.[60] Buddhist Mahāyāna *sūtras*, specially the *Larger Sukhāvati-Vyūha*[61] refer to *Ācāryopādhyāya* in the sense of masters and teachers and the *Saddharmapuṇḍarīka Sūtra*[62] mentions the *antevāsi*. The *Abhisamācārikā*[63] refers to *Ācārya, Upādhyāya,* as teachers and *sardhevihāri* and the *antevāsin* as pupils. The same terms occur in the *Visuddhimagga*[64] also.

It seems that the term *guru* came to be adopted from the Brāhmaṇical system of education. The Sārnāth Buddhist Stone Inscription refers to the dedication of a gift by a monk named Harigupta to his *guru*, mother and father.[65] The Ajanta Cave

---

[56]*Ācariya* in Sāñchi Stupa II Inscription on Steatite box No.1 outside lid (ibid., No.655), *Āchariya* in Kaṇheri Buddhist Cave Inscription (ibid., No.987) *Āchariya* in Amarāvati Buddhist Pillar Inscription (ibid., No.1230). See, D.C. Sircar, *Select Inscriptions,* Kalawān Copper Plate Inscription (Ācaryanaṁ), p.132; Sui Vihar Copper Plate Inscription of Kaniṣka I *(Ācarya),* p.140; Set-Mahet Stone Umbrella Staff Inscription of Kaniṣka I *(Ācaryanam)* p.144; Nāgārjunikonda Inscription of Virapurushadatta *(Ācariyanam),* p.232; Guṇaighar Copper Plate Inscription of Vainyagupta (Ācarya), p.341; Kūra Stone Inscription of the time of Toramana Shahi (*Ācarya*), p.424.

[57]*Upādhyāya* in Bodh Gaya Buddhist Image Inscription (*Lüders list*, No.952), *Traipiṭakōpaddhyāya* in Kaṇheri Buddhist Cave Inscription (ibid., No.989); *Uvajhāyini* in Amaravati Buddhist Stone Inscription (ibid., No.1286).

[58]Ibid., No.925.

[59]*Milindapañho* (ed.), pp.98-99, 308.

[60]*Lalitavistara* (BST.), pp.87, 88.

[61]*Buddhist Mahayana Sutras* (SBE.), Pt.II, p.25; See, *Śikṣāsamuccaya* (ed.), p.37.

[62]*Saddharmapuṇḍarīka Sūtram* (Rev.), p.18.

[63]*Abhisamācārikā,* pp.33-43.

[64]*Visuddhimagga* (ed.), pp.13, 64, 78, 82.

[65]*CII.*, III, p.281.

Inscription of the time of Hariṣena refers to the Buddha as *lokaguru.*[66] The terms *Upādhyāya* and *Ācārya (karmācārya)* continued in use as is reported by I-tsing. The former is used by him in the sense of a teacher of personal instruction and the latter in the sense of a teacher of discipline, rather 'one who teaches pupils rules and ceremonies'.[67] The word *Saddhi-vihārika* occurs in the sense of a pupil and co-resident.[68]

Teacher and Pupil: Mutual Relationship

The mutual relations between the teacher and the pupil is clearly stated in the Buddha's words: 'The Upājjhāya, Bhikkhus, ought to consider the Saddhivihārika as a son; the Saddhivihārika ought to consider the Upājjhāya as a father. Thus these two, united by mutual reverence, confidence and communion of life, will progress, advance and reach a high stage in this doctrine and discipline.'[69]

Apart from his studies and monastic duties, the *Saddhivihārika* was to act as a personal attendant of the *Upājjhāya.* The *Visuddhimagga*[70] recounts the daily duties of a pupil on the lines prescribed in the *Khandhakas.* The pupil had to rise betimes, offer him the teeth-cleanser, water and meal in the morning. He had also to accompany the teacher in his begging round. He was to supply him with drinking water, arrange for his bath, dry his robes clean the cells, etc.[71]

---

[66]D.C. Sircar, *Select Inscriptions,* p.454.

[67]J. Takakusu, op. cit., pp.96, 104, 106, 116-18.

[68]Ibid., pp.116, 197.

[69]*Mahāvagga,* pp.43, 58—*Upajjhāyo bhikkhave Saddhivihārikamhi puttacittaṃ upaṭṭhapessati, Saddhivihāriko upajjhāyamhi pitucittaṃ upaṭṭhapessati. Cullavagga,* pp.341-45. The relation was exactly the same as in the brāhmaṇical system between a *guru* and a *śiṣya.* See, *Sāṅkhyāyana Gṛhya Sūtra,* p.63; *Āsvalāyana Gṛhya Sūtra*, p.190. See, also G.K. Bhatt, 'Teacher-pupil relationship (in the context of Upaniṣadic literature)', *ABORI.*, Vol.LIV, Pts.I-IV, 1973, pp.173ff; V.S. Ramachandra Sastry, 'Teacher-pupil relation in the Gurukula system', *Prajñā,* Vol.XI, No.1, Oct.1965, pp.163ff.

[70]*The Path of Purification*, I, p.102.

[71]*Mahāvagga*, pp.44-46.

A slightly different routine is prescribed in the *Milindapañho*[72] where he is enjoined to 'rise early and betimes, sweep out the open space around the dagoba and having got ready the drinking water for the day's use and dressed himself and taken his bath, he should bow down in reverence before the dagoba and then pay visit to the senior bhikṣus, and, on his return, enter in due time into the chamber of solitude'.

The *Abhisamācārikā,*[73] a text belonging to the Lokottaravāda school, a branch of the Mahāsāṅghikas also refers to the duties of the pupil which commence with the daybreak. They include cleaning the *vihāra,* attending and waiting on the teacher and accompanying him on the begging round.

Menial work continued to be done by monks under the supervision of the *karmadāna* as reported by Hiuen-tsang.[74] But with the admittance of laity in the *Saṅgha* for secular education, such tasks were performed by them.[75] I-tsing gives details about the work of such monastic 'lay servants'.[76]

'This whole hearted devotion of the pupil to his teacher had its counterpart in the corresponding attitude and conduct of the teacher towards his pupil.'[77] As the *Milindapañho*[78] informs us, *the Upājjhāya* was expected to 'be never weary in giving exhortation and admonition and instruction and education, in rousing and inciting and gladdening and at the exposition of the faith'. The *Abhisamācārikā*[79] enjoins on the

---

[72]*The Questions of King Milinda*, Pt.I, pp.22, 25; Pt.II, pp.185, 280-81.

[73]*Abhisamācārikā,* pp.41ff. See, *Bodhisattvabhumi* (ed.), pp.164-65.

[74]T. Watters, op. cit., Pt.II, p.21.

[75]Fa-hien (J. Legge, op. cit., p.18) refers to them as attending at meals. Hiuen-tsang (S. Beal, *Life,* p.161) refers to them as attending on a venerable monk.

[76]J. Takakusu, op. cit., pp.36. 47, 64, 144, 145, 154.

[77]R.K. Mookerji, op. cit., p.404.

[78]*The Questions of King Milinda*, Pt.I, p.308. This is in accord with Buddha's words regarding the preceptor who 'ought to observe a strict conduct towards the pupil, afford spiritual help and furtherance to the pupil by teaching, by putting questions to him, by exhortation, by instruction'. See, *Mahāvagga,* p.48.

[79]*Abhisamācārikā*, pp.39ff.

teacher to instruct the disciple on doctrinal points and also to make him thoroughly understand the *Vinaya.*

A live picture of the deep and intimate relations that existed between the teacher and the taught in the 7th century AD is drawn by I-tsing.[80] What I-tsing observed of the relations, is on the lines of the *Vinaya* rules. The day began with the pupil rising early, and performing his morning chore. He visited the teacher, supplied him tooth-wood, water, washing basin and towel. He then went to worship the holy image. Thereafter he went to his teacher and after a proper salutation inquired about his health. Saluting other senior *bhikkhus* in the neighbouring rooms he retired to his cell for scriptural study.

I-tsing further reports, 'the following is also the manner in which a pupil waits on his teacher in India. He goes to his teacher at the first watch and at the last watch of the night. First the teacher bids him to sit down comfortably. Selecting some passages from the *Tripiṭakas* he gives a lesson in a way that suits circumstances and does not pass any fact or theory unexplained. He inspects his pupil's moral conduct and warns him of defects and transgressions;[81] whenever he finds his pupil faulty he makes him seek remedies and repent.

The pupil rubs the teacher's body, folds his clothes or sometimes sweeps the apartment and the yard. Then having examined water to see whether insects be in it, he gives it to the teacher. Thus, if there be anything to be done, he does all on behalf of his teacher. This is the manner in which one pays respect to one's superior. On the other hand, in case of a pupil's illness, his teacher himself nurses him, supplies all the

---

[80] J. Takakusu, op. cit., pp.116-17.

[81] For breach of duties, there was provision for punishment. If after the teacher's serious display of anger, the pupil begged pardon, he was to be pardoned. If the *Upājjhāya* did not do so he was to be guilty of committing the *dukkaṭa* offence. See, *Mahāvagga,* p.54; Gokuldas De, op. cit., p.28.

medicines needed, and pays attention to him as if he were his child.[82]

The basis of mutual relationship between the teacher and the taught was respect and reverence. A careful perusal of the Buddhist scriptures shows that the teacher occupies a revered position in the *Saṅgha*. Buddha himself enjoined high reverence for the teacher on the part of the disciples.[83] The teacher had to maintain a certain distance between himself and those he was going to teach.[84] His level is exalted, that of the learner is decidedly lower.[85] Treating the teacher with great respect is considered an essential requisite of proper conduct.[86] Dedication to the teacher is enjoined on the pupil, in the *Visuddhimagga*,[87] failing which he 'finds no footing in the dispensation, and he soon comes down to misconducting himself or to the lay state'. *The Saddharma Puṇḍarīka Sūtra*[88] states that the preachers of law and keepers of the *Sūtranta*

---

[82]J. Takakusu, op. cit., p.120. See, *Mahāvagga*, pp.48-51.

[83]*Mahāvagga*, p.44. Respect and reverence for the teacher (*Gurunam apachiti, gurunam suśrusha*) is enjoined in the 9th rock edict of Aśoka at Kalsi, Shahbazgarhi, Mansehra, Jaugada and 13th Rock Edict at Shabazgarhi and Kalsi. See, *CII.*, I, pp.37-38, 44, 61, 67, 78, 109.

[84]See, G.S.P. Misra, 'The Ideal of education in early Buddhism', *Journal of the Gujarat Research Society*, Vol.XXIX, Jan.1967, p.24. This is apparent from the trivial incident of the *'Pancavaggiya' bhikkhus* accosting the Buddha in a tone of familiarity as *''āvusa'* (friend) and the latter objecting to such an address, since he was now a Tathāgata, an arhat, a perfectly enlightened one. See, *Mahāvagga*, p.12.

[85]This was true literally also. The *Saddharma Puṇḍarīka* (SBE., pp.269-70) refers to the wise man (*pandita*) seated on an elevated pulpit delivering discourse to monks and nuns. This is in accordance with the *Sekiya* rule 69 (The *Pacittiya*, p.276) which lays down that one sitting on a low seat should not preach to one sitting on a higher seat. All this points to the respectful position of the teacher. A verse (96) in the 'Navāsuttaṁ' of the *Sutta Nipāta* also lays stress on this point—*Yasmā hi dhammaṁ puriso vijañña, Indaṁ vā naṁ devatā pūjayeyyā So pujito tasmiṁ pasannacitto; bahussuto pātukaroti dhammaṁ.*

[86]*Path of Purification*, I, p.19. See, *The Questions of King Milinda*, Pt.II, pp.333-34.

[87]*Path of Purification*, I, p.119.

[88]*The Saddharma Puṇḍarīka* (SBE.), pp.216-17.

(whether clergymen or lay devotees) 'must be saluted by all beings with joined hands, must be honoured, respected, worshipped, venerated, revered by Gods and men with flowers, incense, perfume, garlands, ointments, clothes, umbrellas, flags banners, musical instruments, with food soft and hard, with nourishment and drink, with vehicles, with heaps of choice and gorgeous jewels.'

Expression of reverence through offerings had become the practice in Fa-hien's time who refers to the same being done by the inmates of monasteries to the topes erected in honour of Sāriputra, Mahāmaudgalyāyana and Ānanda.[89] In Hiuen-tsang's time images of Buddha and patron saints were worshipped.[90] I-tsing meticulously reports the way in which respect was accorded to the superior. 'If one unavoidably comes near a superior, while chewing the tooth-wood, one should cover the mouth with the left hand'[91] and 'when the junior sees a senior he should quietly show respect and salute with the word "*vande*" (I salute) and the senior in accepting the salutation should say "*Ārogya*" (Health) holding his hands right in front'.[92]

Further, 'the priest in the presence of the holy image or when he approaches the honoured teachers (except in case of illness), should have his feet bare. He must always have his right shoulder bare and the left covered with his cloak, wearing no cap.'[93]

Respect, obedience and homage to teacher is enjoined in the Ugradattaparipṛcchā[94] and Sāgaramati *sūtra*.[95]

---

[89]J. Legge, op. cit., pp.44-45. The mention of 'Guru' first, even before mother and father by Harigupta, a Buddhist motik in the Sārnāth Stone Inscription ascribed roughly to the 5th century AD attests the superior position and prestige of the teacher in the eyes of the disciple. See, Fleet, *CII.*, III, p.281. A similar order occurs in the *Śikṣāsamuccaya* (ed.), p.151.

[90]T. Watters, op. cit., I, p.302.

[91]J. Takakusu, op. cit., p.33.

[92]Ibid., p.115.

[93]Ibid., p.22.

[94]*Śikṣāsamuccaya* (ed.), p.37.

[95]Ibid., pp.41-42.

Qualifications of a Teacher

The teacher who initiated the novice to his new birth[96] and supervised his conduct was to possess the requisite qualifications for the same. His own ability and range of knowledge was primary. With the liberalization of learning, encompassing a wide curriculum, the teachers were expected to have extensive knowledge.[97] The *Milindapañho*[98] is explicit in enumerating the qualities of a teacher. He should be 'a man modest, amiable, righteous, of beauty of character, learned in tradition and in the scriptures, lovable, venerable, worthy of reverence, a speaker of profitable things, meek, clever in admonition, in instruction and in education, able to arouse, to incite, to gladden'.

Further, a teacher must have these twenty-five virtues. 'He must always and without fail keep guard over his pupil. He must let him know what to cultivate, and what to avoid, about what he should be earnest and what he may neglect. He must instruct him as to sleep, and as to keeping himself in health and as to what food he may take and what reject. He should teach him discrimination (in food) and share with him all that is put as alms in his own bowl. He should encourage him, saying: 'Be not afraid. You will gain advantage (from what is taught here).' He should advise him as to the people whose company he should keep and as to the villages and *vihāras* he should frequent.

---

[96]The Brahmaṇical conception that true birth is birth to immortality and that the teacher who initiates the novice to his new birth shall be regarded as his father was taken up by the Buddhists. The novice entering the *Saṅgha* forsook his family name and became a 'son of Buddha' (*Sakyāputto*). This is reiterated in the *Nikāyas*. The *Bodhicaryāvatāra* (BST.), (Chap.1, v. 9) states that one is born in the *Buddha-kula*, the family of the Buddhas only after, the arising of the *bodhicitta*. One truly becomes a Buddha-son *(Sugatānaṁ suta)*.

[97]Initially the teacher was expected to master the *Dhamma* as set forth in the nine *aṅgas* of the canon. See, *Aṅguttara Nikāya,* III, p.74.

[98]*The Questions of King Milinda*, II, pp.292-93. This is quite in accord with the qualifications and virtues of a teacher as enunciated in the *Mahāvagga,* pp.68-70.

He should never indulge in foolish talk with him. When he sees any defect in him he should easily pardon it. He should be zealous, he should teach nothing partially, keep nothing secret and hold nothing back.[99] He should look upon him in his heart as a son, saying to himself: 'How can I keep him from going back?' He should determine in himself 'I will make him mighty'. He should love him, never desert him in necessity, never neglect him in anything he ought to do for him, always befriend him—so far as he can rightly do so—when he does wrong.'[100]

The *Saddharma Puṇḍarīka*[101] enjoins on the *bodhisattava,* who acts as a preacher, certain moral qualifications. He should be 'firm in his conduct and proper sphere, by being meek, patient, not rash, nor envious, when he sees the real character of the laws (or things)' while promulgating the *Dharma Paryāya.*

By I-tsing's time there were grades of teachers. One who became an *Upādhyaya* was to be a *Sthavira* and must have passed 'the full ten summer retreats'.[102] The *Karmācaryas* were to be fully acquainted with the *Vinaya,* 'being themselves pure'.[103]

The Concept of Teacher as Kalyāṇamitra

Buddhist texts frequently emphasize the necessity of a good spiritual friend (*kalyāṇamitra*). The term does not refer so much to good companions as to one's teacher, the spiritual adviser from whom one learns the *Dhamma* and who helps to win the ultimate goal of Buddhahood. The *Bodhicaryāvatāra* states that a *bodhisattva* should never give up the *kalyāṇa-*

---

[99]This is in conformity with Buddha's injunction that a teacher should be sincere in his efforts to reveal all that he knows to his pupil. His own statement that he had no *ācariyamutthi* explains it. See, *Dīgha Nikāya*, II, p.80; See also, G.S.P. Misra, *The Age of Vinaya,* p.151.

[100]*The Questions of King Milinda*, Pt.I, pp.142-43.

[101]*The Saddharma Puṇḍarīka* (SBE.), p.262.

[102]J. Takakusu, op. cit, p.104.

[103]Ibid., p.105.

mitra even for his own life because he practises the discipline of the *bodhisattva* and is skilled in the way of the Mahāyāna.[104]

The *bodhisattva* should obey the instructions of the *kalyāṇamitra* as a good son obeys his father. The Ugradatta-paripṛcchā'[105] *sūtra* states that he who teaches even a *gāthā* of four *padas* is a *kalyāṇamitra.* All Buddhas, lords, irreversible *bodhisattvasa* are termed *kalyāṇamitra.*[106] Even the six perfections are called good friends of a *bodhisattva.*[107] More so the very perfection of wisdom is identified with the teacher himself.[108] It is said that the *kalyāṇamitra* protects the *bodhisattva* from doing evil deeds, visiting pleasure resorts and from the wordly life.[109] So he should be worshipped for the sake of true knowledge (*paryupāsana-parijñānārtham*).

Mode of Instruction

The mode of imparting education in the Buddhist *vihāras can* best be known through a careful scrutiny of the way in which the founder imparted instruction to his disciples, through Buddhist scriptures and the testimony of Chinese travellers. That the Buddha had all the qualities of a skilful preacher is clear from the fact that he based his sermons keeping the listeners in view.[110] This point becomes more explicit in the

---

[104] *Bodhicaryāvatāra* (BST.), Chap.V, v.102—*Sadā kalyānamitraṁcha jivitārtho pi na tyajet. Bodhisattva vratadharaṁ mahāyānārthakovidaṁ.* The *Śikṣāsamuccaya* (ed., p.34) also has a similar advise *(Kalyāṇamitrānutsarajñāt).*

[105] *Śikṣāsamuccaya* (ed.), p.37.

[106] *Aṣṭasāhasrikā Prajñāpāramitā* (trans.), p.158; *The Large Sūtra* on *Perfect Wisdom* (trans.), pp.439-40.

[107] It is said that they are his teacher, they lead him to cognition, to understanding, to full enlightenment. See, *Aṣṭasāhasrikā Prajñāpāramitā*, p.158.

[108] 'The perfection of wisdom in particular should be regarded as a bodhisattva's good friend'—ibid., pp.54, 57, 158, 190; *The Large Sūtra on Perfect Wisdom,* p.283.

[109] '*Saṃbodhakāḥ kalyāṇamitrā akaraṇiyānām saṃnivārakāḥ pramadasthānāt niṣkāsayitārah saṃsārapurāt*'—*Śikṣāsamuccaya*, ed., p.35.

[110] 'I saw beings of little impurity, of much impurity, of keen or dull faculties, of good or bad conditions, easy or hard to teach, and some too I saw who perceived the danger and faults affecting a future life'—*Majjhima Nikāya*, I, pp.218-19.

Saddharma-Puṇḍarīka[111] where the lord says, 'I reveal the law in its multifariousness with regard to the inclinations and dispositions of creatures. I use different means to rouse each according to his own character.'

Ananda Coomaraswamy notes that he spoke in one manner to a group of disciples, who had already been familiar with his ideas, and in quiet another way to an audience of eighty thousand laymen who were sent to him to seek instruction. In this latter situation, he spoke in a much more popular style—'milk for babes'.[112]

The usual mode of delivery was the conversation method.[113] Parables,[114] similies, analogies drawn from experiences of day to day life were interspersed with wit, irony, humour,'[115] admonition,[116] analysis[116a] and

---

[111]*Saddharma Puṇḍarīka* (SBE.), pp.54, 122f. The *Śikṣāsamuccaya* (trans. p.63) enjoins on the *bodhisattva* to know first the bent of disposition in his fellowman and then preach the law according to their dispositions in due order. For Aśvaghosa's classification of human being on the basis of their intelligence, See, D.T. Suzuki (trans.), *Discourse on the Awakening of Faith in the Mahayana Literature*, p.51.

[112]Ananda Coomaraswamy, *Buddha and the Gospel of Buddhism*, pp.268-69.

[113]Matṛceṭa in his *Śatapañcāśatka* (ed., D.R. Shackleton Bailey, Section XII, v.127) praising the skill of the Buddha says, 'sometimes you spoke not even when questioned; sometimes you yourself accosted others and made converse; in another case you aroused desire and spoke (later): for you knew times and hearts': *'pṛṣṭenāpi kvacin noktam upetyāpi kathā kṛta tarṣayitvā paratroktaṃ kālāśayavidā tvayā'.*

[114]As the Buddha puts it 'for men of good understanding will generally readily enough catch the meaning of what is taught under the shape of a parable'—*Saddharma Puṇḍarīka* (SBE.), pp.72f, 99f, 119f, 129.

[115]*Buddhist Suttas* (SBE.), pp.175-76.

[116]On enquiring as to how Sakyamuni Buddha preaches Dharma, Vimalakirti says—'living beings of this world are pig headed and difficult to convert; hence the Buddha uses strong language to tame them ... Since the minds of those who are difficult to convert are like monkeys, various methods of preaching are devised to check them so that they can be entirely tamed. Like elephants and horses which cannot be tamed without whipping them until they feel pain and become easily managed, the stubborn of this world can be disciplined only with bitter and eager words'—*The Vimalakīrti Nirdeśa Sūtra* (trans.), pp.105-06.

[116a]The analytical method of Buddha is clearly evinced in the 'Anattapariyāya sutta' of the *Mahāvagga*. See also, G.S.P. Misra. 'logical and scientific method in early Buddhist texts', *JRAS.*, 1968, pp.54-64.

assertiveness[117] to make his sermons persuasive and effective.[118] To put it in Buddha's words 'by the aid of manifold interpretations and reasons; and by hundreds of arguments and illustrations, have I, in one way or another, gladdened all creatures. I utter both sutras and stanzas, legends, jatakas and prodigies, besides hundreds of introductions and curious parables.'[119]

All teaching was imparted by word of mouth and retained in the memory as is proved by the total lack of mention of any manuscript or writing material among the personal belongings of a monk listed in the *Vinaya Piṭaka.* A *Mahāvagga*[120] passage states that if at a certain place the monks do not know the *Pātimokkha,* one of them would go to a neighbouring *Saṅgha* and learn it there. In another passage[121] one reads of an *upāsaka* inviting a monk to hear him recite some important *suttanta* so that he may learn it and it may not be lost from his mind.

The very term *bahusutta* ('one who has heard much') used for an erudite *bhikkhu* suggests that knowledge was acquired chiefly through hearing. The pupil had to listen to and commit to memory the instruction imparted orally by the teacher.[122] The oral method of instruction was popular during 2nd-1st BC

---

[117]'Let one listen to this exalted sūtra avoiding all distractedness'—*Saddharma Puṇḍarika* (SBE.), p.223; *The Diamond Sūtra* (trans.), p.223.

[118]Matṛceṭa in his *Śatapañcāsatka* has praised Buddha's speech in many verses. To quote only a few—'*prāyeṇa madhuraṃ sarvam agatyā kiṃcid anyathā. Vākyaṃ tāvartha siddhyā tu sarvam eva subhāṣitam'* (Section VII, v.69); *'dṛṣṭārthatvād avitathaṃ niṣkleśatvād anākulam. Gamakaṃ, suprayuktatvāt trikalyāṇaṃ hi te vacaḥ'* (ibid., v.75).

[119]*Saddharma Puṇḍarīka* (SBE.), pp.44-45. N.H. Samtani ('Buddha: The Teacher Extraordinary' in Studies in Pali and Buddhism ed., p.341) recounts in details the qualities which made Buddha a supreme teacher (*anuttara-sattha*).

[120]*Mahāvagga,* p.121.

[121]Ibid., p.147.

[122]The discourse was to be 'heard, borne in mind, repeated out loud, pondered over in mind, well comprehended by (right) understanding'—*Middle Length Sayings*, Vol.III, p.159; *The Book of Gradual Sayings*, Vol.II, p.24; 'Those who hear, accept, penetrate, understand and comprehend are near to enlightenment'—*Saddharma Puṇḍarīka* (SBE.), p.221.

as is clear from the *Milindapañho.*[123] Nāgasena, the instructor of King Milinda tells us that he became the pupil of Dhammarakkhita of the Aśokārāma monastery at Pātaliputra and there from the mouth of his teacher, 'he learnt by heart the whole of the three baskets of 'the Buddha's word' in three months and after a single recital 'so far as the words were concerned', 'and in three months more he mastered the spirit'.

Fa-hien found the oral method of instruction prevalent in the Punjab region whereas writing was used in the eastern regions of India.[124] I-tsing refers to Pāṇini's *sūtras* and other grammatical works which had to be learnt by heart.[125] A passage of I-tsing[126] brings out the prevalent practice of learning. He states, 'there are two traditional ways in India of attaning to intellectual power; (a) committing to memory; (b) the alphabet fixes one's ideas. By this way, after a practice of ten days or a month, a student feels his thought rise like a fountain and can commit to memory whatever he has once learned. This is far from being a myth, for I myself have met such men.'

The oral method of teaching required reinforcement by the practice of frequent recitation of the texts and their chanting by the whole congregation in chorus on special occasions (*saṅgiti*). The recital and rehearsal in chorus of the *sūtra* is emphasized in the *Saddharma Puṇḍarika.*[127] Nāgasena learnt

[123]*The Questions of King Milinda*, Pt.I. p.28.

[124]J. Legge, op. cit., pp.98ff. The canon, both text and commentary was long reduced to writing in the reign of Vaṭṭagāmaṇi. See, *Mahāvaṁsa,* XXXIII-100-02; *Dipavaṁsa,* pp.20-21.

[125]J. Takakusu, op. cit., p.167.

[126]Ibid., p.183.

[127]*Saddharma Puṇḍarika* (SBE.), pp.220, 272. This tradition is recorded in the *Nikāyas.* See. 'Saṅgīti Suttanta', *Dīgha Nikāya.* The *Mahāvagga* (p.215) recounts the recitation of the Aṭṭhakavaggika by Soṇa. There is reference to *bhāṇakas* (reciters) in the Pāli canon, who memorized a portion of the *Tripiṭaka* and trained monks in the recitation, from memory of the text they had mastered. *Theras* were often termed as *Dīgha-bhāṇakas* or *Majjhima-bhāṇakas* after the *nikāya* in which they specialized. See, *The Questions of King Milinda*, II, p.231.

the *Abhidhamma,* through hearing and repetition.[128] Hearing and retaining in memory the *sūtra* is often emphasized in the Māhāyāna *sūtras.*[129]

Oral method continued even after the introduction of writing material as is clear from the *Saddharmapuṇḍarīka* which states, 'preach the law, whether he knows it by heart or has it in a book'.[130] Fa-hien[131] refers to monks who recite the *sūtras* and Hiuen-tsang[132] as late as the seventh century mentions the monks of Udyāna as being 'clever at reciting their books without penetrating their deep meaning'.

Besides recitation and chantings, other aids to memory like set words, fixed phrases, formularies, conventional descriptions in stereotyped terms and reiterative passage categories were used.

Kathās or debates on doctrines seem to have been an important mode of imparting education.[133] In a canonical legend,[134] two monks are referred to as holding an *abhidhamma kathā*, putting questions to one another, furnishing answers and not collapsing but gaining edification by their discussions. Buddha's mode of asking questions and counter-questions to explain or elucidate can be gleaned from the Mahāyana *sūtras.*[135]

---

[128]*The Questions of King Milinda*, I, pp.21, 172; II, p.95.

[129]*The Saddharma Puṇḍarīka* (SBE.), pp.214-15; *Aṣṭasāhasrikā Prajñāpāramitā,* pp.26, 34.

[130]*Saddharma Puṇḍarīka* (SBE.), p.268.

[131]J. Legge, op. cit., p.44.

[132]T. Watters, op. cit., I, p.226.

[133]As the Buddha advised: 'Let the wise put questions to one another, ask for reasons, talk the matter over, with or to their teacher, with or to their fellow disciples'—Rhys Davids, *Dialogues of the Buddha*, II, 225. The *Kathāvatthu,* among the books of the abhidhamma is 'an evidence of the liberty of thought allowed in the Order. All these discussions are in the form of questions and answers in the manner of a catechism with an imaginary opponent to argue with'—see, G.S.P. Misra, 'logical and scientific method in early Buddhist texts', *JRAS.*, 1968, p.61.

[134]'Mahāgosiṅga Sutta' *(Majjhima Nikāya)*, I, p.268 *'Dve bhikkhu abhidhammakathaṁ kathenti'.*

[135]*The Diamond Sutra,* pp.27-28; *Aṣṭasāhasrikā Prajñāpāramitrā,* p.6.

Right from the beginning the Buddhist method of teaching was not a monological process but rather a dialogical process where the teacher instructing the pupil 'in what pertains to the *Dhamma,* in what pertains to the *Vinaya,* in discussing or making others discuss, according to the *Dhamma,* a false doctrine that might arise'[136] was confronted by the student who was enjoined to 'combat by discussion any false doctrine that the teacher might take to or to get others to do it'.[137]

The Buddhist tradition of debate and discussion initiated by the founder was meant for a training in intellectual precision and clarity. But with the passage of time such personal goals were sacrificed in favour of intellectual conversion of non-Buddhists. Dialectics and logic were developed by the Mahāyāna schools and debates were conducted according to the formal rules codified in such texts as *Yogācāra-bhūmi-śāstra (Sapta-daśa-bhūmi śāstra).*[138]

Hiuen-tsang while referring to Nālandā reports: 'learning and discussing they found the day too short ... If among them were any who did not talk of the mysteries of the Tripiṭaka such persons, being ashamed, lived aloof.'[139] Discussion and debate occupied such a prominent place in the monk's curriculum that a person's ability was largely judged by his power to vanquish opponents in discussion. It was such men apparently who got royal appointments and whose names were 'as a reward written in white on their lofty gates'.[140]

The tutorial system of Buddha's time continued as late as 7th century AD for Hiuen-tsang[141] admits that the juniors and the seniors mutually helped each other to perfection. Hiuen-tsang himself was taught the *Yoga Śāstra* by Śilabhadra and he learnt many other works from Jayasena and others in the same manner.[142]

[136]*Mahāvagga*, pp.72-73.
[137]Ibid., p.46.
[138]See, R.K. Mookerji, op. cit., pp.453, 454.
[139]T. Watters, op. cit., II, p.165.
[140]J. Takakusu, op. cit., pp.176ff.
[141]T. Watters, loc. cit., II, p.165.
[142]S. Beal, *Life*, pp.153-57.

The lecture method was also popular at Nālandā side by side with the tutorial method.[143] Hwui Li writes, 'within the temple they arrange every day about 100 pulpits for preaching and the students attend these discourses without fail, even for a minute'.[144]

Medium of Instruction

Buddha taught his disciples in the popular dialect. 'He did not want to limit his teaching by the use of any single dialect and granted complete freedom to his followers to understand and preach his doctrine in their own speech.'[145] But this trend could not continue for long. Sanskrit became a subject of study and, as noted earlier, even Fa-hien spent three years at Patna learning Sanskrit.[146] 'This language was freely used for translation and composition by the *bhikkhus* 'as it was necessary in view of the situation that their learned opponents and critics whom they had to face and convince used the same language for literary purposes'.[147] The Sarvāstivādins and the Mahāyāna school of Buddhism had their classical texts in Sanskrit and not in any popular dialect. From I-tsing's account of Nālandā University's curriculum, it is clear that the study of Sanskrit was considered basic in order to grasp Buddhist or non-Buddhist *Sūtras* and *Śāstras*.

Curriculum

The initial course of study included instruction of sacred texts and doctrines imparted by the *Upādhyāya* and instructions in *Vinaya*. The Aṅguttara Nikāya[148] includes the nine *aṅgas* as

---

[143]I-tsing (J. Takakusu, op. cit., p.103) notes: 'The candidate begins to learn Vinaya-Piṭaka; he reads it day after day, and is examined every morning. Such is the way a teacher instructs in India.'

[144]S. Beal, op. cit., p.112.

[145]*Cullavaga,* pp.228-29 *(Anujānāmi bhikkhave, sakāya niruttiyā buddha-vacanaṁ pariyāpuṇitum).* For discussion, See, G.S.P. Misra, *The Age of Vinaya,* pp.137-38.

[146]J. Legge, op. cit., pp.98ff.

[147]G.S.P. Misra, op. cit., p.137.

[148]*Aṅguttara Nikāya,* II, pp.8, 113, 189, 197.

subjects of study. This is confirmed by the *Milindapañho*[149] also which includes, besides this, the study of the *Abhidhamma*. That grammer formed part of the curriculum is evident from inclusion of the *Niddesa,* a work consisting of interpretation, doctrinal teaching and in the verbal expositions, the beginnigs of grammar.

The *Abhidhamma* books and related works like the *Paṭisambhidāmagga* give other traces of its existence. 'It appears to be this system which is expressly referred to in the *Niddesa* and other places as the four kinds of analysis *(paṭisambhidā)*: the analysis of meanings *(attha),* of conditions *(dhamma),* of grammatical analysis *(nirutti),* and clearness of insight *(paṭibhāna).*'[150]

The Pāli language which was at first a living and spoken language became in course of centuries a learned language as Sanskrit. 'The fact of the *Niddesa* itself seems to show that this Pali was then a current language, but that *Nirutti,* grammatical analysis was becoming necessary for the interpretation of the texts.'[151] From the production of *kāvya* like the Buddhacarita in the 1st century AD one can infer that grammar was a fully developed study.

The courses of study had a theoretical as well as a practical aspect. These monasteries provided ample opportunities for education in the practical arts and crafts for their inmates. The very office of the *Navakammika*[152] (incharge of building operations and repair) presupposes knowledge of the size, form and object for which the apartments were to be utilized.

Bhikkhus were allowed 'the use of a loom and of shuttles, strings, tickets and all the apparatus belonging to a loom'.[153]

---

[149]*The Questions of King Milinda*, II, p.92.

[150]E.J. Thomas, 'Buddhist Education in Pali and Sanskrit School', *IHQ.*, Vol.2, No.3, Sept.1926, p.500.

[151]Ibid., p.502.

[152]*Cullavagga*, pp.268-69.

[153]Ibid., p.225.

They were expected to prepare their own robes and keep them in proper condition with the help of weaving appliances.[154]

The tradition of medical science which was developed and studied in the Buddhist epoch, formed a special subject of study in the Christian era. The *Mahāvagga*[155] and the *Cullavagga*[156] supply details of medical and surgical knowledge known to the monks. Besides the orthodox ruling on medicines, extra allowances were used and drugs supplied by the laity were stored. The cause, nature, progress and treatment and management of disease are discussed at length in the *Milindapañho*[157] which presupposes a knowledge of medicine and surgery in the monks.

Excavations at Kumrahar (near Patna) have unearthed in 1953 the remains of one monastery-cum-hospital named *Ārogyavihāra.* A terracotta sealing found in the monastic buildings belonging to the Gupta period (pd. IV-V, *c.* AD 300-600) reads *'Sri Ārogya Vihāre bhikṣu saṁghasya'* meaning, 'seal of the monastic community in a sanatorium monastery.[158] The legend *'Ārogya vihāre'* occurs on a potsherd from the same site.[159]

A Rajghat sealing with the legend *'Bhishakavihare therasa, bhikhu saghas'*[160] testifies to the existence of a Sthaviravādi *vihāra* at Sārnāth[161] which in all probability was famous among the people for its medical wing. The Rajghat

[154]Ibid., pp.204-06.

[155]*Mahāvagga*, Chap.VI.

[156]*Cullavagga*, p.224.

[157]*The Questions of King Milinda*, I, pp.68, 168, 191, 211, 240: II, pp.7, 109, 225. For types of medicines and their remedies. See, Meena V. Talim, 'Ancient Indian medicine according to Buddhist Sources', *Indica,* Vol.2, No.2, Sept.1965, pp.92-97. Classification of diseases occurs in the *Saddharma-puṇḍarika* (SBE.). p.130.

[158]See, Altekar and Mishra, *Report on Kumrahar Excavations,* 1951-55, pp.41, 103, Pl.XXXII, No.5.

[159]Ibid., p.107, Pl.XXXV. No.4.

[160]V.S. Agrawala, 'Clay sealing from Rajghat', *JNSI.*, XXIIII, 1961, p.409.

[161]K.K. Thaplyal, *Studies in Ancient Indian Seals,* pp.214-15.

sealing obviously belonged to a monastery which served as a hospital for monks of the Sthaviravāda sect whereas *Ārogya vihāra* (at Kumrahar) was a monastery-cum-sanatorium where *bhikshus* irrespective of their sects could stay and regain health.[162]

The central monastic establishment at Nagārjunikoṇḍa had also within its complex a building used as a hospital as appears from an inscription on one of the walls, viz., *Mukhya Jvarālaya* (main room for patients suffering from fever).[163]

All these evidences clearly postulate the knowledge of medical science among the monks and its inclusion in their curriculum.

With the rise of sects and sub-sects, knowledge of their respective scriptures also became essential. Fa-hien refers to students of Hināyana and students of Mahāyāna or to *bhikṣus* who pursue studies of both. A knowledge of brahmaṇical scriptures also became part of the curriculum. One hears of a brahman teacher Radhasāmi, a professor of Mahāyāna in a monastery at Pātaliputra.[164] A brahman teacher Manjuśrī was honoured by Mahāyāna *bhikṣuṣ*.[165] Sanskrit also became compulsory. Fa-hien learnt it for three years at Pataliputra in order to understand *Vinaya* rules.[166]

Monastic learning grew and expanded from century to century, branching off, with the growth of specialization and expertise, into different *śāstras* and *vidyās*.[167] Logic was developed in the Yogācāra system. 'Its growth in Buddhist learning and scholarship was stimulated by the fact that it was a potent intellectual instrument in public debates and discussions.[168]

---

[162]K.K. Thaplyal, op. cit., p.215. Nursing the sick is enjoined on all members of the Order. See, *Mahavagga*, pp.317-18.

[163]S. Dutt, *BMMI.*, p.134. See, P.R. Ramachandra Rao. *The Art of Nagarjunikonda*, p.25.

[164]J. Legge, op. cit., p.78.

[165]Ibid., p.79.

[166]Ibid., p.99.

[167]A.B. Keith, *History of Sanskrit Literature*, pp.404ff.

[168]S. Dutt, loc. cit., pp.404ff.

Copious information is supplied regarding the course of study at the primary and secondary level by Hiuen-tsang and I-tsing. Hiuen-tsang states that primary education in India started with a work called *Siddham* dealing with alphabets, vowels and consonants in twelve chapters. After mastering this course at the age of five the boy is introduced to the 'five sciences'.[169]

I-tsing[170] on the other hand reports that a boy started his education at the age of six years with a book called the *Siddhirastu'* containing 49 letters of the alphabet and 10,000 syllables. This was mastered within six months.

At the age of eight he studied the *sūtras* of Paṇini containing 100 *ślokas.* This could be repeated in eight months time. This was followed by the book on *Dhātu* dealing with verbal roots. After this at the age of ten, the book on the three *Khilas* dealing with cases and conjunctions and formation of words from root and suffix was mastered. This required three years diligent study. The *Vṛitti-sūtra,* a commentary on Paṇini's *sūtra*, was commenced at the age of fifteen and understood in five years. Thus grammatical study of Sanskrit language was preliminary to the study of higher subjects.

The curriculum at Nālandā is described thus: 'The priests, belonging to the convent, or strangers (residing there) (i.e. who came from outside and joined it) all study the Great Vehicle and also the works belonging to the eighteen sects, and not only so, but even ordinary (i.e. secular) works such as the *Vedas* and other books, the *hetuvidyā* (logic), *śabdavidyā* (grammar and philology), *cikitsāvidyā* (medicine), the works on magic *(Atharvaveda), sāṅkhya* (system of philosophy); besides these, they thoroughly investigate the miscellaneous works.'[171]

---

[169]T. Watters, op. cit., I, pp.154-58. The five Sciences are as follows—(a) *Śabdavidyā* or *vyākaraṇa,* (b) *Śilapasthānavidyā* or arts and crafts, (c) *Cikitsavidyā* or medicine, (d) *Heṭuvidyā* or *tarkaśāstra,* (e) *Ādhyātma-vidya* or spiritual science.

[170]J. Takakusu, op. cit., pp.170-76.

[171]S. Beal, *Life*, p.112.

Higher proficiency in grammar required the study of the *Chūrṇi*[172] (i.e. the *Mahābhāsya* or great commentary of Patañjali on Paṇini's *sūtras)* and the Bhartṛhari Śāstra,[173] a commentary on the former text.

Next came logic *(Hetuvidyā)* which required the knowledge of *Nyāya-dvāratarka-śāstra*[174] (introduction to logic) and also the *Vākya-padīya,*[175] a treatise on the inference and inductive arguments. Metaphysics and philosophy also received their due. Study of the *Abhidharmakośa*[176] and the *Peina*[177] (perhaps *Beda* or *Veda),* a work on philosophy formed part of the curriculum. All these texts were studied by both monks and laymen in order to covet the title of '*Bahuśruta*'.

Medicine *(cikitsavidyā)* seems to have been part of the curriculum of secondary education. I-tsing refers to a *sūtra* on medical science[178] and makes considerable mention of various forms of medical treatment.[179] He himself states that he made 'a successful study in medical science', of which course was not quite elementary, from the details he gives of it.

I-tsing also explains the reason for this regulation making medical study compulsory for all students, not excluding even the monks: 'Is it not a sad thing', he asks, 'that sickness prevents the pursuit of one's duty and vocation? ... Is it not beneficial if people can benefit others as well as themselves by the study of medicine'.[180]

---

[172]J. Takakusu, op. cit., p.178.

[173]Ibid.

[174]Ibid., p.177. This is one among the 8 *śāstras* assigned to Jina (ibid., pp.186-87) identified as Diṅnaga. See. T. Watters, op. cit., II, p.211.

[175]J. Takakusu, loc. cit., p.180.

[176]Ibid., pp.176-77. This also required the reading of six treatises on metaphysics belonging to the Sarvāstivāda school—ibid., p.187, fn.1.

[177]Ibid., p.180.

[178]J. Takakusu, loc. cit., p.131.

[179]Ibid., pp.127ff, 132ff, 222.

[180]Ibid., p.130.

The inclusion of *śilpasthānavidyā* in the list of studies shows that technical education with special reference to architecture, sculpture and painting was taught to the students.[181] We are told *of bhikṣus* being deputed to serve as 'building overseers' *(navakammika)*,[182] to take charge of building operation, on behalf of a lay-donor constructing a *vihāra* for purposes of the *Saṅgha.*

An inscription of Yasovarmadeva of 8th century AD found at Nālandā describes the monks as versed in the scriptures and arts *(āgamakalā vikhyātavidvajjanāḥ).*[183] The school of art at Nālandā was famous for the images and sculptures it produced in stone and mostly in metal or bronze.[184] These were connected with Mahāyāna Buddhism and its later developments known as Tantrayāna, Vajrayāna and Kalachakrayāna. Evidence of metalcasting is found in the series of furnaces, marking the temple site 13 at Nālandā.[185] Metal casting as a technique might have been highly developed at Nālandā and it is probable that it even formed part of the curriculum.[186]

The priests studied not only the five *vidyās* but all the *Vinaya* works and investigated the *sūtras* and *śāstras.*[187] Learning the *Āgamas* and investigating the *Nikāyas* also formed part of the curriculum.[188] Among the *śāstras,* the *Yogācara śāstra* was primary, followed by Asaṅga's eight *śāstras.*[189] Among the monastic recitations Matṛceṭa's hymns were a favourable item. The monks belonging to both Hīnayāna and Mahāyāna schools were required compulsorily

---

[181]T. Watters, op. cit., I, pp.155f.

[182]*Supra.*

[183]*MASI.*, No.66, p.169.

[184]R.K. Mookerji, op. cit., pp.582, 583.

[185]A. Ghosh, *Nalanda,* p.32.

[186]Ibid., p.39.

[187]J. Takakusu, op. cit., p.181.

[188]Ibid., p.187.

[189]Ibid., p.186.

to learn by heart, Matṛceṭa's two hymans, the *Sārdhaśataka-praśaṁṣā-gathā* (in 150 verses) and the other consisting of 400 *ślokas* on account of their educative value.[190] Another piece of standard literature was Nāgārjuna's *Suhṛllekha*[191] which contains exhortations in right living and enjoins respect and reverence for the *triratna.* It has two divisions-(a) accumulation of merit through the path of moral discipline, study and meditation and (b) accumulation of wisdom through realization of the lord's doctrine of inter-dependent origination. The former leads one away from desire for this life and desire for *saṁsara* as a whole while the latter leads one to the final enlightenment of a Buddha. As I-tsing puts it, 'Indian students learned the epistle in verse early in the course of their education, but the most devout made it their special object of study throughout their lives.'[192]

There was another work of similar character and equally famous. It was the *Jātakamālā* (the garland of birth stories) by Āryasūra.[193] The object of composing the *Jātakamālā* in verse was 'to teach the doctrine of universal salvation in a beautiful style agreeable to the popular mind and attractive to readers'.[194] Its popularity during the seventh century AD is proved by a historical anecdote recorded by I-tsing. King

---

[190]Ibid., pp.156-58. No other work of Matṛceṭa seems to have equalled the popularity of the *Śatapañcāśatka* (Hymn of 150 verses). In 1936 Rāhula Sāṃkṛtyāyana discovered a complete manuscript of the Hymn in the temple library of the Sa-skya monastery in Tibet. It consists of five palm leaves. It has been edited by K.P. Jayaswal and Rāhula Sāṁkṛtyāyana as 'The Adhyardha śataka of Mātṛceṭa'. See, *JBORS.*, Vol.XXIII, Pt.IV, Dec.1937, Appendix. See also, D.R. Shackleton Bailey (ed.), *The Śatapañcāśatka of Mātṛceṭa.*

[191]J. Takakusu, op. cit., pp.158-61. The Sanskrit text of the *Suhṛllekha* is no longer extant. There exist various editions of its Tibetan translation, three translations in Chinese and three earlier translations in English. For a recent translation into English from the Tibetan, See, Ven. Lozang Jamspal, Ven. Ngawang Samten Chophel, Peter Della Santina (trans.). *Nāgārjuna's Letter to King Gautamīputra.*

[192]J. Takakusu, loc. cit., p.162.

[193]Ibid.

[194]Ibid., p.163.

Harṣa Silāditya once commanded the poets and men of letters of his age to show their best compositions. The collection thus produced amounted to five hundred bundles and on examination it was found that most of them were based on *Jātakamālā*. Another work popularised by Harṣa and composed in verse by himself was the *Jimūtavāhana*.[195]

Another Buddhist work which was popularly studied in accompaniment with music and dance was *Sudāna*, a poetical song concerning the Viśvantara jātaka, composed by Chandradāsa.[196] Another popular work widely read or sung in India was the *Buddhacarita* of Asvaghoṣa.[197] Hiuen-tsang himself became a student of Nālandā *vihāra* for the study of *Yoga Śastra* in which the Nālandā chancellor, Śilabhadra, was the highest living authority.[198] His study of the *Yoga Śāstra* was followed by that of other subjects like *Nyāya*, *Hetuvidyā*, *Śabdavidyā* and the like, as also of the books of Brāhmaṇas, with the wide area of knowledge covered by them, including philological, legal, philosophical, astronomical subjects, and the Sanskrit grammar of Pāṇini.[199]

Among the works studied by him are specifically mentioned the *Nyāya-Anusāra-Śāstra,* a Sarvāstivādin Madhyamika Mahāyāna work, the *Śataśāstra* of Aryadeva, *Kośa, Vibhāshā, Shaṭpadābhidharma Śāstra* and the like. 'Thus he penetrated and examined completely all the collections of Buddhist books and also studied the sacred books of the brahmanas during five years."[200]

That astronomy formed part of the student's course of study is clear from the records of Hiuen-tsang's biographer who refers to a Nirgrantha graduate casting horoscope of

---

[195]Ibid., pp.163-64.

[196]Ibid., p.164. This was a new development in monastic life, taking into consideration the fact that dance and music were contrary to the norms prescribed for monks by the founder.

[197]Ibid., p.166.

[198]S. Beal, *Life*, p.107.

[199]Ibid., p.121.

[200]Ibid., p.125.

Hiuen-tsang.[201] He also states, 'the observatories seem to be lost in the vapours (of the morning clouds'[202] and 'from the windows one may see how the winds and clouds (produce new forms) and above the soaring eaves the conjunctions of the sun and moon (may be observed)'.[203]

Buddhism did not like Brahmaṇism favour extreme asceticism and bodily mortification. The care of bodily health was considered of importance for spiritual well being. We find that physical exercise was encouraged in the Buddhist monasteries of India and I-tsing tells us that, 'in India both priests and laymen are generally in the habit of taking walks, going backwards and forwards along a path, at suitable hours, and at their pleasure; they avoid noisy places. Firstly, it cures diseases and secondly, it helps to digest food. The walking hours are in the forenoon and late in the afternoon. They either go away (for a walk) from their monasteries, or stroll quietly along the corridors ... If anyone ... adopts this habit of walking he will keep his body well and thereby improve his religious merit.'[204]

From seventh century AD onwards Nālandā became a renowned centre of Tantric studies. The Nālandā copper plate of Devapāladeva (AD 810-50) states that 'Nālandā was an abode of bhikṣus and bodhisattvas well versed in tantras'.[205]

The range of subjects included in the curriculum points

---

[201]Ibid., p.166. The 'Mahavihāravāsins' of Theravāda-Vibhajyavāda sect residing in Dharana vihāra at Nagarjunikoṇḍa are described as adepts in reading the marks on the human body and fixing horoscopes. See, *IAR.*, 1955-56, pp.23-24.

[202]S. Beal, loc. cit., p.111.

[203]Ibid.

[204]J. Takakusu, op. cit., p.114. The *Vinaya* often speaks of monks preferring to walk up and down the *caṁkrama* (promenade) as an aid to meditation itself. Buddha had enumerated five advantages of an alley walk. 'It hardens one for travelling; it is good for striving; it is healthy; (its use) tends to good digestion after one has eaten and drunk, munched and crunched: the concentration won from (the thought of) an alley-walk lasts long'—see, *Book of the Gradual Sayings,* III, p.21.

[205]*EI.*, XVII, p.325.

to the fact that the traditional learning was progressively liberalized. Besides being seats of monk life and monk-culture, the *vihāras* became seats of secular learning also.

Specializations

The mode that was adopted for preserving and handing down the sayings and preachings of the Buddha to posterity was reciting them regularly and committing them to memory. Memorizing the different portions of the *Piṭaka* was entrusted to different sets of monks according to their mental proclivity. Each group memorized and specialized in its own section not simply as *bhāṇakas* but as expositors of the text. The existence of such specialists in the *āvāsas* is occasionally referred to in the early Pāli texts.[206] The *Cullavagga*[207] informs us that preceptors of allied subjects were given seats close to one another while those teaching different subjects were assigned seats in different cells.

Many terms occurring in the epigraphs of the pre-Christian and early Christian era signify specializations. They are *Pachanêkayika*[208] (master of the five *nikāyas*), *Sūtātikini,*[209]

---

[206]The *Mahāvagga* (p.188) relates that on one occasion the *Pavāraṇā* ceremony had to be cut short because the best part of the previous night had been sleeplessly spent by the monks in study and debate—some reciting the *Dhamma,* the *Suttantikas* propounding the *suttantas,* the *Vinaya-dharas* discussing the *Vinaya* and the *Dhamma-kathikas* conversing about the *Dhamma.* See, *Cullavagga,* p.255. Besides *Suttantikas* and *Vinayadharas* there were *Mātikadharas*—*'Bahussuto āgatāgamo dhammadharo vinayadharo mātikādharo'*—*Mahavagga,* pp.120, 368; *Cullavagga,* p.421; *Majjhima Nikāya,* I, p.274. The *Mātikādharas* were specialists in the *Abhidhamma Piṭaka.*

[207]Dabba Mallaputta made such an arrangement that the *bhikkhus* adopting the same mode of life *(sabhāga)* resided in the same place in order that specialists of different groups could recite, discuss or talk on their subjects. See *Cullavagga,* pp.154f. The *Aṅguttara Nikāya* (I, pp.24, 25, 26) provides a list of monks and nuns who occupied the topmost places in certain subjects.

[208]*Lüders list,* No.299 (Sāñchī Buddhist Stūpa I Inscription); ibid., 867. (Bharhut Buddhist Rail Inscription).

[209]Ibid., 319, 352 (Sāñchī Buddhist Stūpa I Inscription).

(versed in the *sūtrantas), Dhammakathika*[210] (preacher of the law), *Trêpiṭika,*[211] *Trêpiṭaka,*[212] *Peṭikin,*[213] (who knows the *Piṭakas), Vinaya dhara*[214] (master of *Vinaya). Traipiṭakôpād-dhyāya*[215] (a teacher of the *Tripiṭaka*) and *Mahavinayaṁ-dhara*[216] (great *Vinaya* teacher).

Literary data corroborate the epigraphic evidence. Some scholars specialized in *Avadānas* and were known as *Āvadānika* or *Avadānārthakovida.*[217] *The Suttantika-gaṇa* and the *Abhidhammika gaṇa* are referred in the *Visuddhimagga.*[218] The *Sumaṅgalavilāsinī*[219] names Upāli, Ānanda, Sāriputra, Mahakassapa, Anuruddha and their disciples as specialists in *Vinaya, Dīgha, Majjhima, Saṁyutta* and *Aṅguttara Nikāya* respectively. There were monks who were reputed for their proficiency in all the *Nikāyas.*[220] There were specialists in the Jātakas like Mahā-Paduma *thera* of Tulādhāra.[221]

Coming to the testimony of Chinese pilgrims one finds that Fa-hien[222] refers to the professors of the *Abhidharma, Vinaya* and the *Sūtras.* In course of time specialization in different versions of a particular wing of the canon had become quite marked in some of the monasteries as reported by Hiuen-

---

[210]Ibid., 347 (Sāñchī Buddhist Stūpa I Inscription); 949 (Bodh Gaya Buddhist Image Inscription); 1267 (Amarāvati Buddhist Pillar Inscription,). An inscription on a potsherd ascribed to 3-4th century AD reads—*Kathi ka kati Rahula* evidently suggesting Kati Rahula as a preacher of *Dhamma* or expounder of law. See, R. Subrahmanyam, op. cit., p.87.

[211]Ibid., 38 (Mathura Buddhist Image Inscription).

[212]Ibid., 918, 919 (Saheth Maheth Buddhist Stone Inscription); 925 (Sārnāth Buddhist Inscription, 927 (Sārnāth Buddhist Image Inscription).

[213]Ibid., 856 (Bharhut Buddhist Rail Inscription).

[214]Ibid., 949 (Bodh Gaya Buddhist Image Inscription); 1286 (Amarāvati Buddhist Stone Inscription).

[215]Ibid., 989 (Kaṇheri Buddhist Cave Inscription).

[216]Ibid., 1270 (Amarāvati Buddhist Pillar Inscription).

[217]*Avadānaśataka* (BST.), pp.272, 275.

[218]*The Path of Purification*, I, p.95.

[219]*Sumaṅgalavilāsinī* (Nal. ed.), I, pp.16-20.

[220]*Supra.*

[221]*Mahāvaṁsa*, XXXV.30.

[222]J. Legge, op. cit., pp.45-46, T. Watters, op. cit., I, p.302.

tsang.[223] The Purvaśaila and Avaraśaila monasteries were noted for their proficiency in *Abhidharma* works pertaining to the Māhasāṅghika school.[224] The Śrughna monastery near Sthaneśvara specialized in the teaching of Sautrantika literature, the study of which detained the pilgrim there.[225] The monastery of Udyāna is said to have specialized in magical exorcisms.[226]

Even the curriculum at Nālandā University, though emphasizing the study of *Vinaya* works, *sūtras* or *śāstras,* conducted specialized studies in grammar, logic, yoga and tantras. Thus it becomes clear that specialization in their respective branch of canon had already begun with the rise of different sects. It was a new development in monastic life though some monasteries as reported by the Chinese pilgrims were catholic enough to study different versions.

Monasteries as Centres o Popular Learning

It is true that 'Buddha was a spiritual teacher and it was the spiritual knowledge which he wanted to be available for each and everyone',[227] but with the gradual lapse of time Buddhist monasteries became centres for the dissemination not only of Buddhist teaching but also brahmanical studies and secular branches of learning. This was not something against the spirit of Buddhism for the 'Sigalovada sutta' of the *Dīghā Nikāya* emphasizes the fact that education and guidance of the laity is the duty devolving upon the monks. The *Milindapañho* is a fine example of how royal patrons like King Milinda resolved their doubts regarding *Dhamma* through learned monks like Nāgasena.

---

[223]In the monastery at Udyāna the course of studies comprised the five redactions of the *Vinaya* under the names of Dharmagupta, Mahīśāsaka, Kāśyapīya, Sarvāstivādin and Māhasaṁghika. See, T. Watters, op. cit., I, p.226.

[224]S . Beal, *Life*, p.137.

[225]Ibid., p.79.

[226]T. Watters, op. cit., I, p.226.

[227]G.S.P. Misra, *The Age of Vinaya*, p.147.

It is perhaps with the rise of Mahāyānism that religion and education were placed on a more popular basis and Buddhist monasteries began to undertake secular as well as religious education.[228] As L.M. Joshi puts it 'with the emergence of Mahāyāna, Buddhist education, scholasticism and literary activities received a tremendous impetus. Not only the doctrinal, disciplinary and sectarian problems of academic nature, but also secular arts and studies came within the scope of education and training of the bodhisattvas. Not only the monks, but the laity also came within the educational range of Buddhist monasteries.'[229]

The visit of Chinese scholars to study Pāli and Sanskrit and to secure copies of the sacred books of Buddhism shows that monasteries had become seats of popular learning. At the time of the visit of Fa-hien (AD 399-414) we find that the monasteries seem to have undertaken instruction of a more general kind than merely instructing those who joined the *Saṅgha*. While speaking of the Mahāyāna and Hinayāna monastery at Pātaliputra, by the side of the tope of Aśoka, he comments 'the rules of demeanour and the scholastic arrangements in them are worthy of observation. Samans (monks) of the highest virtue from all quarters, and students, inquirers wishing to find out truth and the grounds of it, all resort to these monasteries.'[230]

In a note of Fa-hien's reference to the 'scholastic arrangements' at Patna, James Legge[231] says: 'Why should there not have been schools in those monasteries in India as there were in China? Fa-hien himself grew up with other boys in a monastery; and no doubt had to "go to school". And the next

[228]As A.S. Altekar (*Education in Ancient India*, p.230) puts it, 'the Buddhist monks realized early that it was necessary to win public sympathy and support for the spread of Buddhism'.

[229]L.M. Joshi, op. cit., p.123.

[230]J . Legge, op. cit., pp.78-79.

[231]Ibid., p.78, fn.3.

sentence shows us there might be schools for more advanced students as well as for the Sramaneras.'

It seems reasonable to assume that by the time of Fa-hien the monasteries may have given some general instructions not only to young novices, but even to pupils who had no intention of joining the *Saṅgha.* But this cannot prove (in the absence of any other evidence) that such education included popular elementary instruction.

Hiuen-tsang[232] while referring to Nālandā says, '... foreign students come to the establishment to put an end to their doubts and then become celebrated, and those who stole the name (of Nālandā brother) were all treated with respect wherever they went'. The Ti-lo-shi-ka monastery near Pātaliputra and the monastery south of Kanchipura are described as places of rendezvous for the most eminent men of the country.[233] The education which I-tsing describes is education of a higher rather than of a popular type which was based on a profound study of Sanskrit grammar.

Commenting on the acquirement of secular education at Nālandā or Valabhi I-tsing says, '... to try the sharpness of their wit, they proceed to the king's court to lay down before it, the sharp weapon (of their abilities); there they present their schemes and show their (political) talent, seeking to be appointed in the practical government'.[234] He also tells us that after completing their course students could 'follow whatever occupation they like'.[235]

A passage further puts the matter more clearly. 'Those white-robed (laymen) who come to the residence of a priest, and read chiefly Buddhist scriptures with the intention that they may one day become tonsured and black-robed, are called "children" (mānava). Those who (coming to a priest)

[232]T. Watters, op. cit., II, p.165.
[233]Ibid., II, pp.105, 226.
[234]J. Takakusu, op. cit., p.177.
[235]Ibid., p.178.

want to learn secular literature only, without having any intention of quitting the world, are called "students" (brahmachāri). These two groups of persons (though residing in a monastery), have to subsist at their own expense. In the monasteries in India there are many "students" who are entrusted to *bhikkhus* and instructed by them in secular literature. On the one hand the "students" serve under priests as pages, on the other the instruction will lead to pious aspirations. It is, therefore very good to keep them, in as much as both sides are benefited in this way.'[236]

I-tsing quotes the example of Bhartṛhari who became a priest seven times joining intermittently the ranks of laity. 'At last he returned to the position of a lay devotee *(upāsaka)* and wearing a white garment continued to exalt and promote the true religion, being still in the monastery.'[237] It has been rightly suggested by A.S. Altekar[238] that, ancient India owed the rise of her temple colleges and organized public educational institutions to the influence of Buddhism. It is true that Buddhism placed both religion and education on a more popular basis than Brahmaṇism and thereby broke down the monopoly of higher learning which had been in the hands of the brahmaṇa teachers. This may have indirectly helped to increase the yearning for education amongst the laity. It cannot be denied that education provided in the *vihāras* by the monks had a sobering moral effect on the laity.

Monastic Universities

From times immemorial, India's contribution in the field of knowledge has been memorable. Among the great centres of learning that flourished during the Buddhist epoch the names

[236]Ibid., pp.105-06. F.E. Keay (*Ancient Indian Education*, p.104) points out that 'this practice also may have been influenced by the brahman schools which were open not only to young brahmans who were destined for the priestly office, but to others of the twice born castes as well'.

[237]J. Takakusu, op. cit., p.180.

[238]A.S. Altekar, op. cit., pp.231, 234.

of Valabhi, Nāgārjunikoṇḍa, Kanchipura, Nālandā, Vikramaśilā, Jaggaddala and Odantapurī are worth mentioning. Copious information is furnished by literature, archaeology and the testimony of Chinese pilgrims on Nālandā and Valabhi which fall within the purview of our study.

Nālandā[239]

The ruins of Nālandā have been unearthed near the village Bargaon, 55 miles south east of Patna in Bihar. It was famous even during the days of the Buddha as a prosperous township. Both the Buddha and Mahavira frequented this place.[240] It was here that Aśoka built a *vihāra* which served as the nucleus for the later university.[241]

The tradition of Nālandā as an educational centre grew up in stages and the first big effort towards founding a university was made during AD 440 by Kumaragupta.[242] He built numerous buildings round the central *Saṅghārāma* and this work was continued by his successors, Skandagupta, Purugupta and Narasimhagupta. Harṣa Śiladitya, the Maukhari kings and the Pālas contributed to the expansion and stabilization of this university.[243]

Nālandā was a vast educational complex. There were according to Hiuen tsang's biographer, 10,000 resident scholars.[244] Relying on this report R.K. Mookerji fixes the

---

[239]See, H.D. Sankalia, University of Nālandā; A.S. Altekar, *Education in Ancient India,* pp.260-72; S.K. Das, *The Educational System of the Ancient Hindus,* pp.357-72; R.K. Mookerji, 'The University of Nalanda', *JBRS.*, Vol.XXX, Pt.11, June 1944, pp.126-59.

[240]A. Ghosh, *Nalanda,* p.2; R.K. Mookerji, op. cit., p.556.

[241]Taranatha (trans.), *History of Buddhism in India*, p.101.

[242]Hiuen tsang names him as Śakraditya. See, T. Watters, op. cit, II, p.164. The name occurs on a seal discovered at Nālandā, See, *MASI.,* No.66, p.38.

[243]Rev. H. Heras, 'The Royal patrons of the University of Nalanda', *JBRS.*, Vol.XIV, 1928, pp.1-23; R.K. Mookerji, loc. cit., pp.562-63.

[244]S . Beal, *Life*, p.112. Hwui Li's information seems to be exaggerated. Hiuen-tsang simply observes that there were some thousands of brethren residing at the place. See, T. Watters, loc. cit., II, p.165.

number of teachers as 1,500 and students as 8,500.[245] At I-tsing's time there were 3,000 resident monks.[246] This vast university population was quite cosmopolitan in composition. It was not exclusively Indian. The reputation of Nālandā was not confined within the borders of India. Students from China, Japan, Korea, Mongolia, Tukhara came to Nālandā to quench their thirst for learning.[247] Hiuen-tsang himself was a resident student for five years and I-tsing for ten years. A student from Nālandā was held in high esteem throughout the country and even abroad.[248]

Trained scholars like Śantarakṣita, Padmasaṁbhava, Kamalaśīla, Kumārajīva and Paramārtha went to Tibet and China and contributed greatly to the dissemination of Indian culture. Among teachers the most eminent were Dharmapāla, Śīlabhadra, Chandrapāla, Guṇamati, Sthiramati, Prabhamitra, Jinamitra and Jñānachandra.[249] Even Nāgārjuna, Āryadeva, Rāhulbhadra, Asaṅga, Vasubandhu and Diṅnāga were associated with the Nālandā University.[250] The merit lies in Nālandā not only being the centre of all branches of higher knowledege but in 'collecting at one centre the available authorities on every subject of learning'.[251]

The Nālandā Stone Inscription of Māladā refers to Nālandā *mahāvihāra* as 'the pleasant abode of the learned and virtuous Saṃgha'; its inmates were 'erudite scholars, famous for their knowledge of the sacred lore (āgama) and the arts (kalā)'.[252] From the *Life*[253] we learn that in the philosophical conference

---

[245]R.K. Mookerji, op. cit., p.565.

[246]J . Takakusu, op. cit., pp.65, 154.

[247]S. Beal, op. cit., pp.xxvii-xxxvi.

[248]T. Watters, op. cit., II, p.165.

[249]Ibid., I-tsing (J. Takakusu, loc. cit., p.185) gratefully observes: 'I have been very glad that I have had an opportunity of acquiring knowledge personally from them, which I should otherwise have never possessed'.

[250]Taranatha, loc. cit., pp.106, 123, 131, 167, 171, 182.

[251]R.K. Mookerji, op. cit., p.567.

[252]*MASI.,* No. 66, pp.79, 81.

[253]S. Beal, loc. cit., p.177.

organized by Emperor Harṣa at Kannauj, 1,000 eminent monk scholars from Nālandā were present. Elsewhere, the same source tells us that there were 1,000 scholars at Nālandā who could explain twenty collections of the *sūtras śāstras*; five hundred scholars who could explain thirty collections and perhaps ten including the Master of the Law (i.e. Hiuen tsang) who could explain fifty collections but the Chancellor of the university, Śīlabhadra, was the person who had 'studied and understood the whole number'.[254]

Although the university was a centre of Mahāyāna Buddhism, it was in fact a temple of higher learning in all arts and letters known to the age. The curriculum was based on the traditional *sūtra* and *śāstra* study, but added the five *vidyās* or the practical study of liberal disciplines.[255]

The educational method was chiefly tutorial. Small goups of five or six students were under the care of a teacher. The students not only listened to the lectures of the most eminent monks (there were arrangements for a hundred lectures every day)[256] but engaged themselves in continual discussions. The art of formal disputation played a leading role in the educational system at Nālandā. As Hiuen tsang puts it, 'the brethren are often assembled for discussion to test intellectual capacity ... to reject the worthless and advance the intelligent. Those who bring forward (or according to some texts, estimate aright) fine points in philosophy, and give subtle principles their proper place, who are ornate in diction and acute in refined distinctions, ride richly caparisoned elephants preceded and followed by a host of attendants. But as for those to whom religious teaching has been offered in vain, who have been defeated in discussion, who are deficient in doctrine and redundant in speech, perverting the sense while keeping the language, the faces of such are promptly daubed with red and

[254]Ibid., p.112.

[255]*Supra*.

[256]S. Beal, loc. cit., p.112.

white clay, their bodies are covered with dirt, and they are driven out to the wilds or thrown into the ditches.'[257]

Sanskrit was the medium of instruction and the contribution of Nālandā to the development of Sanskrit literature is immense. The routine of every day life was regulated by a clepsydra.[258] The inmates of the monasteries had their own system of hierarchy based on scholarship.[259]

Nālandā University was essentially a postgraduate institution, although provision was made for primary and secondary education. Admission to the university was scrupulously restricted; rigorous oral entrance examination was conducted by the *dvarapaṇḍitas* (gate-professors), and not more than two or three out of ten could pass.[260] Only the most brilliant and accomplished of the students could hope to enter the portals of Nālandā. Once the student was admitted, he was in for discipline of a severe kind. Hiuen tsang notes that during the several hundreds of years it endured, Nālandā did not witness a single guilty rebellion.[261]

It is interesting to note that the general affairs of the university were administered by a democratic body of the students themselves. 'Inspite of its size and numbers, the affairs of the university, from the annual assignment of rooms to the trial and punishment of offences were administered on democratic principles by the entire body of students. The recognition of the principles that the cause of discipline among students is best promoted by boldly leaving it in their hands is in accordance with up-to-date pedogogic ideals.'[262] Funds and finances were also democratically managed though spending authority was invested in the executive's hands.[263]

---

[257]T. Watters, op. cit., I, p.162.

[258]J. Takakusu, op. cit., pp.145-46.

[259]*Supra.*

[260]T. Watters, loc. cit., II, p.165.

[261]S. Beal, op. cit., p.112.

[262]R.K. Mookerji, op. cit., p.570.

[263]R.K. Mookerji, 'The University of Nalanda', *JBRS.*, Vol.XXX, Pt.II, June 1944, p.132

The organizational structure of the university provided a framework of complex administration and authority needed to oversee the education of thousands of students in a wide variety of disciplines. At the head of the general administration was the abbot principal, assisted by two councils, one academic and the other administrative. The chief task of the academic council was to regulate admissions, fix syllabus and allot work to different teachers. It was also incharge of the library.[264] Construction and repairs of monastic abodes, distribution of food, clothes, medicines, allotment of rooms and assignment of monastic duties fell within the purview of the administrative council.[265] It was also incharge of finances and took steps to realize the revenue from monastic lands.

The needs of the students with regard to boarding, lodging, and clothing were looked after by the university. Towards the maintenance of this huge establishment went the revenue of about two hundred tax free villages.[266] The Nālandā University had no alternative but to take interest in promoting agriculture since it could not make daily purchases of the vast quantity of consumer goods required by its resident population.

An idea of the magnitude of problem of supplying the necessities of life at Nālandā can be gathered from the observations of the Chinese pilgrims. According to Hiuen-tsang who lived therefore six years (AD 635-640), the university's daily supply of food amounted to 'several hundred piculs of ordinary rice and several hundred catties in weight of butter and milk'.[267]

This large residential university had many colleges affiliated to it. This is clear from seals which have been

[264]The libraries of Nālandā were renowned for their collections which included works and copies of *sūtras* and *śāstras*. See, *Infra*.

[265]*Supra*, Chap.III.

[266]This is the number given by I-tsing (J. Takakusu. op. cit., p.65). Hiuen-tsang's biographer (S. Beal, op. cit., p.122) gives the number as 100. More villages may have been received in the time span between the two travellers.

[267]S. Beal, loc. cit., p.112.

unearthed.[268] The royal support and the public interest tendered the university self sufficient and a rewarding place of higher learning and research, until the 12th century, when the Muslim invaders led by Bhakhtiyar Khilji destroyed it completely. From the *Tabaqat-i-Nāṣiri*[269] we learn that the buildings were razed to the ground, the library was burnt and the monks were massacred.

It should be noted with pride that Nālandā, a seat of sacred and secular learning resorted to by both Buddhist monks and laymen and even by non-Buddhists aided in the diffusion of learning and culture in the country and abroad. It stood for intensive pursuit of higher knowledge, for tolerance and catholicity and for intellectual wisdom.

Valabhi

Valabhi situated on a strip of land eastward of the gulf of Cambay is identified with modern Wala in Kathiawar.[270] It was a reputed centre of religion and education and international trade and commerce in the 6th and 7th century AD. The spectacular growth of Valabhi both as a strong-hold of Buddhist faith and as a paramount centre of learning must be attributed mainly to the liberal patronage extended by the Maitraka kings.

According to the epigraphical sources, the earliest *vihāra* at Valabhi came into being through the religious aspirations of a great lady of the royal family. She was Duḍḍā, the niece of Dhruvasena I. This Maitraka king endowed in about AD 535 a number of villages for the maintenance of the monastery, which was known as 'Duḍḍā vihāra' after her.[271] This

[268]Academic seals were issued by the university of Nālandā described as a *mahāvihāra.* The subordinate institutions or colleges were called *vihāras* with their governing body described as *Saṅghas.* Each college had its own seal. See, R.K. Mookerji, 'The University of Nālandā,' *JBRS.*, Vol.XXX, Pt.II, June 1944, p.144.

[269]Elliot and Dowson, *History of India*, II, p.306. See also, S.C. Vidyabhusana, op. cit., p.516.

[270]A. Cunningham, *Ancient Geography of India*, p.317.

[271]*IA.*, IX, p.104; IV, pp.106-07.

monastery continued to receive generous support from the successors of Dhruvasena I for over a century and a half.[272]

Owing to its prominence it became a nucleus for other groups of monasteries and as such came to be known as 'Duḍḍā vihāra maṇḍala'. Later royal grants refer to it by this name or call it a *mahā-vihāra* which means a number of monasteries aggregated as one establishment.[273] Of the monasteries affiliated to the great monastery of Duḍḍā, one was 'Abhyantarikā vihāra' constructed by the venerable nun Mimmā who seems to have been related to the royal family of the Maitrakas, 'Bhaṭṭāraka vihāra' named after a Maitraka chief, 'Kakka vihāra' built by a merchant. Others were 'Buddhadāsa vihāra' 'Gohaka vihāra', 'Vimalgupta vihāra' and 'Sthiramati vihāra'.

Hiuen-tsang[274] records that not far from the city was a great monastery 'which was built by the arhat Āchāra (A-che-lo)'. This information is supplemented by a grant of Dharasena II in which he makes mention of 'Acarya Bhadanta Sthiramati who founded the vihāra of Sri Bappapada at Valabhi'.[275]

Another interesting feature of these monastic establishments was that some of them were set apart for the *bhikṣunīs*. A cluster of such *vihāras* for the nuns was headed by the 'Yakṣa Sūra vihāra' which took its name after its founder Yakṣa Sri.[276]

In the 7th century, Dharasena IV son-in-law of Emperor Harṣa was the greatest patron of this university.[277]

The details furnished by the epigraphical and literary sources relating to the importance of Valabhi as a seat of learning are substantiated and supplemented by the accounts

---

[272]Ibid., IV, pp.175-76, D.B. Diskalker, "Some Unpublished copper plates of the rulers of Valabhi', *JBBRAS.* (NS), I, 1925, pp.36, 37, 39, 40. For grants to Duḍḍā vihāra made by Maitraka rulers, See. S. Dutt, *BMMI.*, p.227.

[273]S. Dutt, loc. cit., p.226.

[274]T. Watters op. cit., II, p.247.

[275]*IA.*, VI, p.9.

[276]Krishna Kumari J. Virji, *Ancient History of Saurashtra*, p.173.

[277]Ibid., p.79.

of Hiuen-tsang and I-tsing. According to Hiuen-tsang there were at Valabhi about one hundred *Saṅghārāmas* and 6,000 monks. Most of its scholars studied the little vehicle.[278] Hwui li states that the dominant system studied in Valabhi was that of the Sammitiya school of Hinayāna.[279]

Hiuen-tsang's statement is supplemented by some Maitraka copper plate grants. The grants refer to the resident monk-community as '*Arya Bhikṣu-Saṅgha*' or as in Guhasena's grant, as '*Sakyarya Bhikṣu-Saṅgha*' of 18 schools (*nikāyas*).[280] Though Hīnayāna Buddhism seems to have prevailed in these monasteries, we find traces also of the existence side by side of Mahāyanā Buddhism. Dharasena IV made a grant to a monastery at the village of Yodhavaka, built by one Skandabhaṭṭa, the resident *Saṅgha* of which is described in the grant as '*Maha-nikāya-Ārya-Bhikṣu-Saṅgha*', where the expression, *mahā-nikāya* most probably means Mahāyānist.[281] The Bappāpādiya monastery must also have been a seat of Mahāyānist learning.[282]

The Buddhist *vihāras* at Valabhi constituted institutions of higher education wherein religious as well as secular studies were assiduously pursued. In other words they were not sectarian in the sphere of knowledge. They imparted education not only in the Buddhist religion, scriptures and philosophy but also taught the courses connected with the Vedic, Sāṁkhya and other systems. Secular subjects like law, grammar, astronomy and medicine, also found a place in their curriculum.[283]

---

[278]T. Watters, op. cit., II, p.206, 246.

[279]S. Beal, *Life*, p.159.

[280]*IA.*, IV, pp.175-76.

[281]*IA.*, I, pp.14, 45. See, H.D. Sankalia, *University of Nalanda* (p.180); D.B. Disalker, 'Buddhist Monasteries in Valabhi'. *Proceedings of the 7th All India Oriental Conference Report*, p.813. One cannot agree with Dr. Krishnakumari Virji's (op. cit., p.176) statement, in view of the evidences quoted above that 'in the 6th and 7th centuries, the chief form of religion must have been Mahāyānism in Valabhi'.

[282]S. Dutt, op. cit., p.266.

[283]R.K. Mookerji, op. cit., p.586.

I-tsing[284] compares Valabhi with Nālandā and states that scholars from all parts of India thronged to these two centres of learning to attain perfection in their studies. They used to reside there for 2 or 3 years and hold discussions on all possible and impossible doctrines. After gaining mastery in their subjects either at Valabhi or at Nālandā, scholars used to visit the courts of kings to prove their ability and propound their theories. They received land grants and were advanced to high ranks. Consequently the names of the eminent scholars of the universities were inscribed in glowing letters on its lofty gates.[285]

The University of Valabhi was equipped with an efficient library which was maintained and augmented by royal grants ear-marked for the purpose. The expression used in this context in a copper-plate grant of Guhasena I reads as—*'Saddharmasya pustakôpacayārtham',* i.e. for the acquisition of books on the sacred law.[286]

The fame of Valabhi is evident from the fact that two renowned scholars of this era, senior contemporaries of Hiuen-tsang, Gunamati and Sthiramati, who were disciples of Vasubandhu, after completing their studies at Nālandā and winning triumphs in many debates, finally settled at Valabhi to carry on their literary activities and to complete their philosophical studies uninterruptedly.[287]

Like Nālandā, Valabhi also was not exclusively a Buddhist monastic centre of learning. Parents deemed it a privilege to have their sons educated at Valabhi in preference to other centres of education. This is illustrated by an anecdote recorded in the *Kathāsaritasāgara.*[288] It narrates how a brahman named Vasudatta chose to send his son Viṣṇudatta

---

[284]J . Takakusu, op. cit., p.177.

[285]Ibid., p.178.

[286]*IA.*, VII, pp.67ff.

[287]T. Watters, op. cit., II, p.109.

[288]*Kathāsaritasāgara*, Taraṅga XXXII, 42-43 (*Sa viṣṇudatto vayasā Soḍasa-vatsaraḥ; gantuṁ pravavṛtte vidyāprāptaye valabhīpurīṁ*).

all the way from his native place Antarvedi in the Gangetic Doab to distant Valabhi for higher education.

The Maitraka capital, Valabhi, which was once a great centre of religion, learning, wealth and culture received a temporary setback with the Arab invasion in AD 775. It continued till the 12th century though not with the original fervour.[289]

Buddhist Libraries

The urge for disseminating knowledge among poeple and preserving it for posterity must have been strongly felt by Buddhist monk scholars and hence the establishment of libraries.[290] In the initial stages, though writing was well known, there is no mention of the manuscripts nor of reading or copying of the sacred texts. The possible explanation of this is that the *Tripiṭaka* was produced orally and handed down orally. Instead of libraries, it was the memory of the learned *bhikkhus* that served as the repository of literature.

Information about writing-material in Buddhist monasteries is very scarce. So far as the Buddhist traditions go, the Pāli canonical texts were committed to writing for the first time in the island of Ceylon during the reign of Vaṭṭagamaṇi in the 1st century BC.[291]

This receives support from a legend in the *Divyāvadāna* which makes a casual reference to the reading of the 'word of the Buddha' (*Buddha-vacāna*). The ladies of the house are said to peruse, after the day's household labours are over, the *Buddha vacana* by lamp light and take notes therefrom, for

---

[289]D.C. Apte, *Universities in Ancient India.* p.46.

[290]See, M. Ramarao, 'Libraries in Ancient and Medieval India', *JAHRS.*, Vol.VIII, Pt.IV, April 1934, pp.203-32.

[291]This event is thus commented in verse: 'The text of the three Piṭakas and the commentary thereon, the wise Bhikkhus of former times had handed down by word of mouth; The Bhikkhus of that time (i.e. the Ceylonese Bhikkhus in the reign of Vaṭṭagāmaṇi), perceiving how all beings decay and meeting together, wrote them down in books that the Dhamma might last long'—*Dipavaṁsa*, 20-21; *Mahāvaṁsa*, XXXIII.100-02.

which *bhūrja* (birch-bark) leaves, ink and pen as well as oil (for the lamp) and cotton (for the wick) are required.[292]

Early Buddhist literature refers to *paṇṇa* or *parṇa* (leaf) as a popular writing material.[293] According to a Buddhist tradition, the canon was written on palmyra leaves immediately after the Buddha's death.[294] Some of the earliest palmyra leaf manuscripts have been discovered outside India.[295] The oldest manuscript of Asvaghoṣa's writings discovered in Central Asia was on palm-leaf and belongs to 2nd century AD.

Among the earliest birch-bark manuscripts so far discovered, is the Khotan copy of the Prakrit *Dhammapada* written in the Kharoṣṭhi characters of about the 2nd or 3rd century AD and the manuscript of the Sanskrit Buddhist work *Saṁyuktā-gamasūtra* copied about the 4th century AD.

The practice of engraving texts on copper plates is also known. According to a tradition recorded by Hiuen-tsang, Kaniṣka caused the Buddhist religious texts to be engraved on copper plates.[296] There are also small Buddhist texts engraved on copper plaques or seals.[297]

Similarly the Kurram Casket Inscription[298] (*c.* AD 100) presents a text of the Sarvāstivāda sect in which the *Nidāna* formula explains only the *samudaya* aspect of *dukkha* while both the *samudaya* and *nirodha* aspects are brought out in the text of the *Pratityasamutpāda Sūtra* on the Gopalpur bricks.[299]

---

[292]*Divyāvadāna* (BST.), p.532: *'Ratraupradīpena Buddhiavacanaṁ paṭhanti; tatra bhurjena prayojanaṁ tailena masi rākalamayā tulena'*.

[293]R.B. Pandey, *Indian Paleography*, pp.68-69.

[294]S. Beal, op. cit., p.117.

[295]A.K. Biswas, 'Libraries in Buddhist Monasteries', *Indian Librarian*, Vol.17, No.2, Sept.1962, pp.105f.

[296]T. Watters, op. cit., I, p.271. See, the Kasia copper plate containing the *Nidānasūtra* in Sanskrit and deposited by a person in the local *Nirvaṇacaitya* (Bhandarkar's list, *EI.*, Vol.XIX-XXIII, No.1754).

[297]See, *IAR.*, 1954-56, Pl.XLIX; *Annual Report of Epigraphy*, 1956, No.B.120.

[298]*CII.*, Vol.II, Pt.I, p.155.

[299]*EI.*, Vol.21, Pt.V, p.195.

In two Brick Inscriptions from Nālandā[300] one finds an interesting Sanskrit text containing both the *ādi (desanā)* as well as the *vibhaṅga* of *Pratityasamutpāda.*

Texts inscribed on durable materials, though evidently of a votive character, lead us to believe that some such practice of collecting and preserving their texts in manuscript form must have been in existence which have not survived the ravages of time. A tiny copper casket inside the *stūpa* at Lauriya Nandangarh, revealed a long strip of a birch bark manuscript of about the 4th century AD. From the few words which have been deciphered, the manuscript appears to be a Buddhist text.[301]

Similarly, excavations at Gilgit revealed birch bark and a few paper manuscripts enshrined in a circular chamber inside a *stūpa.* They present Sanskrit texts, many of which are known only through the Chinese and Tibetan translations. The texts include a large number of *Sūtras, Prajñāpāramitā-Śāstra, Saddharma Puṇḍarīka* and the Sanskrit *Vinaya Piṭaka* of the Mulasarvāstivādins.[302]

The Mahāyānic texts[303] regard reading, copying, keeping or collecting in a volume, preserving and storing away the copy as meritorious. This seems to suggest that they were available in the *vihāras.*

The Chinese pilgrim Fa-hien made copies of Buddhist sacred works at Patna.[304] In a Mahāyanā monastery at Pātaliputra he found a copy of the *Vinaya* containing the Mahāsaṅgika rules.[305] He got a transcript of the rules in six or seven thousand *gāthas,* being the Sarvāstivāda rules. He got the *Saṃyuktabhidharmahṛidaya (śāstra)* containing about six or seven thousand *gāthās.* He also got a *sūtra* of two thousand

[300]*EI.*, XXIV, pp.21ff; *MASI.*, No.66, p.75.

[301]Debala Mitra, op. cit., p.85.

[302]Ibid., p.113. For further details see, M.S. Kaul Shastri, 'Report on the Gilgit Excavation in 1938', *QJMS.*, Vol.XXX, No.1, July 1939, pp.1-12.

[303]*Saddharma Puṇḍarīka* (SBE.), pp.218, 220, 268, 272, 336ff, 367, 389: *The Diamond Sutra,* pp.55-56, 77; *Aṣṭa Sāhasrikā Prajñāpāramitā,* pp.22, 25, 26, 34; *The Large Sūtra on Perfect Wisdom*, p.236.

[304]J. Legge, op. cit., pp.98ff.

[305]Ibid., p.98.

five hundred gāthas; one chapter of the *Parinirvāṇa-Vaipulya Sūtra* of about five hundred *gāthas* and the Mahāsāṅghika *Abhidharma.*[306]

Hiuen-tsang in his sojourn refers to the Jetavana monastery with its libraries and reading rooms. 'The libraries were richly furnished, not only with orthodox literature but also with Vedic and other non-Buddhistic works, and with treatises on the arts and sciences taught in India at the time.'[307]

That libraries had become an indispensable part of the monastic establishment is clear from Hiuen-tsang's further references. In Kashmir, King Jayasena gave him twenty clerks to copy out manuscripts.[308] In the Śvetapura monastery at Vaiśāli the pilgrim obtained a copy of the *Bodhisattva Piṭaka.*[309] In the Purvaśaila and Aparaśaila monasteries he spent a few months for the study of *Abhidhamma* works. In the Kānchipura monastery[310] the pilgrim discussed *Yoga* texts with many Ceylonese monks who came there on hearing its fame. He refers to many monasteries inhabited by scholars who composed various treatises. This presupposes the existence of some such collections.

As to the scriptures, the Master brought 224 Mahāyāna Sūtras, 192 Mahāyāna Śāstras, 14 texts of the Tripiṭaka of the Sthavira school, 15 texts of the Tripiṭaka of the Mahasaṅghika school, 15 texts of the Tripiṭaka of the Sammatiya school, 22 of the Mahiśāsaka school, 17 of the Kāśyapiya school, 42 of the Dharmagupta school, 67 of the Sarvāstivādin school, 36 Hetuvidyā Śāstras, 13 Śabdavidyā Śāstras, making a total of 520 cases including 657 volumes.[311]

---

[306]Ibid., p.99.

[307]T. Watters, op. cit., I, p.386. S.N. Chakravorti (Libraries in Ancient Times with Special Reference to India', *Indian Librarian*, Vol.9, No.2, Sept.1954, p.53) wrongly mentions the name of Fa-hien in connection with the description of Jetavana vihāra with its libraries and reading rooms.

[308]T. Watters, loc. cit., I, p.259.

[309]Ibid., II, p.80.

[310]Ibid., II, p.227.

[311]*Bhikshu* Thich Minh Chau, *Hsuang Tsang, the Pilgrim and Scholar*, pp.47-48; Chou Hsiang-Kuang, *Indo Chinese Relations, A History of Chinese Buddhism*, p.262.

Hiuen-tsang saw at Valabhi 'some 100 Saṅghāramas with about 600 priests'. This monastery-complex was also equipped with a library as is clear from one of the copper plate grants of Maitraka kings which provides for the purchase of religious books for the monastery.[312] *(Saddharmasya pustakôpachayārtham).*

I-tsing collected some 400 Sanskrit texts, amounting to 5,00,000 *ślokas.*[313] While referring to arrangements after the death of *a bhikkhu,* he states that the scriptures and their commentaries should not be parted with, but be kept in a library to be read by the members of the Order. Non-Buddhistic books are to be sold.[314]

The Nālandā University had a grand library situated in a special area known as *'Dharmaganja'* (Mart of Religion) housed in three separate buildings known as *Ratnasāgara, Ratnadadhi* and *Ratnāraṇjaka.* Of these Ratnasāgara, which was a nine storeyed building, specialized in the collection of rare sacred works such as the *Prajñāpāramitā Sūtra* and Tantrika books like *Samaja Guhya* and the like.[315]

Besides the professional copyists there were monks who considered copying of sacred books a religious duty. One could find at Nālandā that in several monks cells, an adjacent cell—too small to live in—was occasionally provided. Perhaps it was intended for the safe keeping of manuscripts borrowed for private study.[316]

There are epigraphic records which show that financial arrangement was made for the preservation of the rich collections of the Nālandā Library. An inscription relates how the famous king of Java and Sumatra, Balputradeva by name, had a monastery built at Nālandā and also requested his friend, King Devapāla of Bengal, to make a grant of five villages for

---

[312]Buhler, 'Guhasena's grant of V.S.240', *IA.*, VII, pp.61f.

[313]J. Takakusu, op. cit., p.XVII.

[314]Ibid., p.192.

[315]H.D. Sankalia, op. cit., pp.72-73; S. Dutt, *BMMI.*, p.343.

[316]S. Dutt, loc. cit., p.337.

the maintenance of the monastery and expenditure of adding to its library, manuscripts copied for the purpose[317] (*Dharmaratnasya lekhanārtham*).

This celebrated library became victim of the barbaric destructive activity of the Muslim invaders. The Tibetan sources[318] give a vague description of the destruction. 'After the Turushka raiders had made incursions in Nalanda, the caityas, the library buildings were repaired by a sage named Mudita bhadra. Soon after this, Kukutasidha, minister of the King of Magadha erected a temple at Nalanda and while religious sermons were being delivered there, two very indigent Tirthika mendicants appeared. Some naughty young novice monks in disdain threw washing water on them. This made them very angry. After propitiating the sun for 12 years, they performed a yajña (fire sacrifice) and threw living embers and ashes from the sacrificial pit into the Buddhist temples. This produced a great conflagration which consumed Ratnadadhi.'

The library tradition was carried well in the Odantapuri, Vikramaśila, Somapura and Jagaddala *vihāras*.[319]

Female Education

Facts do not warrant the position taken up by Buddhist Philosophy that 'all things are neither male nor female' or 'though they appear in female form, they are fundamentally not women or as Sariputra puts it 'the form of a woman neither exists nor is non-existent'.[320] Reality affirms that women who were admitted to the *Saṅgha* by the Buddha after much hesitation, did not, as time went by, enjoy the same academic and spiritual benefits as their male counterparts. Nevertheless, the Pāli canon furnishes information regarding nuns who

[317] *EI.*, Vol. XVII, p.310. See also *IA.*, XXI, pp.257-58.

[318] See, S.C. Vidyabhusana, op. cit., pp.515-16.

[319] Dipak Kumar Barua, op. cit., pp.135, 159-60, 165, 175.

[320] *Vimalakīrti Nirdeśa Sūtra* (trans.), pp.78-79.

achieved eminence both academic and spiritual,[321] though paradoxically passages occur where they are looked down upon in general intelligence.[322]

Epigraphic records give scattered reference to nuns in contrast to the *bhikkhus* who are referred as *Aya (Ārya), bhadaṃta, bhayaṃta.* On the uprights of the Bodh Gayā railing Kuraṅgi is honoured as Ayā Kuraṅgi.[323] The term *bhadantī*[324] and *therī*[325] occur once. There is reference to senior nuns having junior nuns as their disciples, e.g. Dhammadevā, Mulā, Bodhi and Asalhamita were antevāsinīs of Mitasiri,[326] Goda, Padumanika and Bodhi[327] respectively.

In some Sāñchi Votive Inscriptions the nun Avisinā is called *Sutātikini*,[328] which may denote either one well versed in the *Sutta-piṭaka* or a female member of the Sautrantika school.[329] That nuns received education from monks is clear from the evidence of Bhikkhunī Buddhamitra,[330] pupil of Bhikkbu Bala and Sarpila of Thera Vijaya.[331]

Bhikkhunī Dhanavati[332] is praised as one who knew the

---

[321]Dhammadinnā *(Aṅguttara Nikāya*, I. p.26; *Therīgāthā,* PTS., XII) and Sukkā (*Saṁyutta Nikāya*, I, p.214; *Therīgāthā*, XXXIV) as preachers; Proficient in the rules of discipline was Paṭacāra *(Aṅguttara Nikaya*, I, p.25; *Therigāthā,* XLVII); Other noteworthy names are those of Bhaddā Kapilanī (Therigāthā XXXVII), Bhaddā Kuṇḍalakesa *(Aṅguttara Nikāya,* I, p.26; *Therigāthā,* XLVI), Uppalavaṇṇā (ibid., I, p.25; ibid., LXIV), Nanduttarā *(Therīgāthā,* XLII), Sakula (ibid., XLIV) and Bhaddā Kaccānā *(Aṅguttara Nikāya*, I, p.26).

[322]*Supra.*

[323]*Lüders list*, Nos.939-42.

[324]Ibid., 1240 (Amarāvati Buddhist Sculpture Inscription).

[325]Ibid., 1006. (Kaṇhêri Buddhist Cave Inscription).

[326]Ibid., 573 (Sāñchī Buddhist Stupa II Inscription).

[327]Ibid., 1041 (Kuḍā Buddhist Cave Inscripton).

[328]Ibid., 319, 352 (Sāñchī Buddhist Stupa II Inscription).

[329]Dr. Bannerjea takes it in the sense of a sect. See, J.N. Bannerjea, 'Schools of Buddhism in early Indian Inscriptions', *IHQ.*, Vol.XXIV, No.4, 1948, pp.255-56; See also Ajay Mitra Shastri, op. cit., p.144.

[330]In the records of the Kushana period, Buddhamitra is described as one proficient in the 3 *Piṭakas* (*Trêpiṭikā)*, see, *EI.*, VIII, pp.173-79, 18lf; ibid., XXIV, pp.210-12; *Lüders list*, No.38.

[331]*Lüders list*, No.1060 (Kuḍā Buddhist Cave Inscription).

[332]Ibid., 38.

Tripiṭaka (Trepiṭika) and introduced as the female pupil *(antevāsinā)* of the Bhikkhu Bala who himself was a master of the three *Piṭakas (Trepiṭika)* in the Mathura Inscription assigned to the reign of Huvishka. In two records of Amarāvati the *bhikkhunis* are introduced as the resident female pupils of two *theras,* Buddharakhita of the Thera Bhadanta Budharakhita[333] and Nandā of the Arahata *(arhat)* Ayira (*arya*) Buddharakhita.[334]

Though the Mahāyana *sūtras* are depicted as being delivered to a mixed congregation of monks and nuns, still the general trend in them points to the conclusion that women were considered spiritually and intellectually inferior to men.[335] The actual position of nuns becomes clear from the fact that the Chinese pilgrims, while delineating details of academic life, specifically refer to *bhikkhus* with academic brilliance but are silent about nuns. The paucity of information, coupled with the fact that archaeological references to nunneries are rare, it may be assumed that their number went on decreasing and they did not enjoy the same position as before.

Foreign Students

The names of foreign monk scholars[336] is interwoven with the history of Buddhism. They, from time to time, facing the perils of the route, came to India in quest of authentic Buddhist texts and to pay reverence to the sacred relics. Fa-hien[337] who came by the land route had as his object the collection of *Vinaya* works. Hiuen-tsang[338] spent sixteen years in travels and studied in many Central Asian and Indian Buddhist Centres.

Shortly after him arrived I-tsing[339] who spent ten years in

[333]Ibid., 1250.

[334]Ibid., 1280.

[335]*Supra.*

[336]See, T.N. Ramachandran, 'Buddhist India and the rest of the world', *JAHRS.*, Vol.XVIII, July 1947-April 1948, Pts.I-IV, pp.1-25.

[337]J. Legge, op. cit., pp.10, 98-99.

[338]Chou Hsiang Kuang, op. cit., pp.251-63.

[339]J. Takakusu, op. cit., Intd., p.xxxiii.

eastern Indian monasteries, especially at Nālandā and specialized in the *Vinaya* and the Sanskrit grammar. I-tsing in his memoirs[340] refers to pilgrims who visited India and studied in monasteries. The most prominent among them are the following—Hiuen-Chiu (Indian name Prakaśamati) gained proficiency in Sanskrit literature at Jalandhara. He stayed four years at Mahābodhi *vihāra* and three years at Nālandā.

Taou-hi also called Śrideva visited the Mahābodhi *vihāra* and stayed for some years at Nālandā where he studied Mahāyānic texts and copied some four hundred chapters of *sūtras* and *śāstras*. Sse-pin was well versed in 'the Sanskrit forms of magic incantation'. Aryavarman, a native of Korea stayed at Nālandā, copying out many *sūtras*. Hiuen-Ta'i and Hiuen-hau, both Koreans, visited the Mahābodhi *vihāra*.

Buddhadharma, a Tokhārian studied at Nālandā where I-tsing saw him. Taou-Sing, called Chandradeva in Sanskrit, visited Nālandā, though he studied the Hīnayāna *Tripiṭaka* in a monastery situated twelve stages eastwards from Nālandā. Tung procured a Sanskrit copy of the Fā -hwa (Lotus of the Good Law) from mid-India.

Tang, a priest of the Mahāyāna school stayed at Tamralipti for twelve years where he perfected himself in Sanskrit. Taou-lin called Śilaprabha in Sanskrit spent three years at Tamralipti learning the Sanskrit language and studied the *Kośa* at Nālandā.

Hiuen-ta, learned Sanskrit and practised the *śabda-śāstra* at Tamralipti for one year and stayed at Nālandā for ten years. Wou-Hing studied the *Yoga, Kośa* and other works at Nālandā.

Nālandā was thus truly an international university. 'Races belonging to different climates, habits and languages were drawn together, not in the clash of arms, not in conflict of exploitation, but in harmony of life, in amity and peace.'[341]

---

[340]See, S. Beal, op. cit., Intd., pp.xxxvii-xli; see also, H.D. Sankalia, op. cit., pp.227-29.

[341]H.D. Sankalia, op. cit., p.237.

CHAPTER 5

Monasteries and the Social Context

There seems to be a tendency among certain scholars to interpret Buddhism entirely on monastic lines and to argue that it encourages the householders to renounce the mundane life and to adopt the life of a recluse.[1] Another charge, which is essentially related to the first, is that it is mystical and asocial.[2] It is further contended that it does not contain systematic teachings regarding society, and its attitude towards society is negative.[3] In the same vein follows E. Conze's remark that 'there is almost no Buddhist ritual or ceremony in which a layman may participate'.[4]

It is true that Buddha maintained that the life of a monk is pure, open and free in comparison to the life of a householder which is impure and obstructs spiritual progress (*sambādho gharāvāso rajapatho abbhokāso pabbajjā, nayidaṃ sukharaṃ agāraṃ ajjhāvasatā ekantaparipuṇṇaṃ ekantaparisuddhaṃ saṅkhalikhitaṃ brahmacariyaṃ carituṃ*).[5] It cannot be denied that Buddha's offer to mankind was to point the way which led to a higher life—higher than household, higher than society.

---

[1]N. Dutt, *EMB.*, II, p.208; Anukul Chandra Banerjee. 'Laity in Buddhism', *Journal of the Assam Historical Research Society*, Vol.XIV, 1960. p.18; See, Paul Dahlke, *Buddhist Essays*, pp.134-35.

[2]See, Max Weber, *The Religion of India: The Sociology of Hinduism and Buddhism*, pp.204ff,

[3]Y. Krishnan ('The Transformation of the Buddhist Saṅgha', *VIJ.*, Vol.13, 1975, p.136) commenting on the *bhikkhus* states that 'they had no social function to perform'.

[4]E. Conze, *Buddhism: its Essence and Development*, pp.85-86.

[5]*Majjhima Nikāya*, I, p.344; II, p.55.

D.D. Kosambi has rightly pointed out, that 'this was the most social of all religions', that its doctrine continued to spread 'because it was eminently fitted to the needs of a rapidly evolving society'.[6] Therefore as Trevor Ling puts it, 'to understand Buddhism apart from its social dimension is futile'.[7]

G.S.P. Misra makes the point more explicit when he observes that 'Buddha and his disciples had renounced the worldly society in favour of a spiritual society which the Buddhist *Saṅgha* stood for, but this did not mark their apathetic or indifferent attitude towards the former; renunciation of the worldly society was only a spiritual contingency'.[8]

For the transmission of ethical and spiritual values, cherished by the *Saṅgha,* to the surrounding society, contact and intercourse was essential. As Trevor Ling puts it 'equally essential is the faithful practice of the contemplative life, if what is transmitted is to be worth transmitting and it to have an ennobling effect'.[9] It cannot be denied that the *Saṅgha* gave direction of values to society deemed absolutely essential for the well being of all.

An interesting feature of Mahāyānic Buddhism is its changed outlook towards the world. Unlike the Hīnayānic Buddhism which emphasized that worldly life was full of snares, and had to be escaped from, Mahāyānism laid stress on developing a *state of mind;* rather an *attitude* which aims at total purification of consciousness, thereby identifying *Saṁsara* with *Nirvāṇa.*

---

[6]D.D. Kosambi, *The Culture and Civilization of India,* pp.106, 114. B.G. Gokhale (*Buddhism and Aśoka*, preface, p.iv) also states 'Buddhism apart from being an ethico-religious creed was a social movement of the first magnitude'.

[7]Trevor Ling, *The Buddha*, p.149.

[8]G.S.P. Misra, 'The Buddhist Conception of Social Change and the Buddhist Social Ethics', *Indica*, Vol.15, No.2, 1978, p.72.

[9]Trevor Ling, *Buddha, Marx and God*, p.57.

Saṅgha and Laity: A Symbiotic Relationship

The relation between the *Saṅgha* and society has been an interesting and complex issue at the same time. The *Saṅgha,* though an institution away and above society, could not exist without maintaining a proper reciprocity. Both the *Saṅgha* and the laity were intrinsically related to each other. The earliest guidelines for the mutual relationship between the two, though detailed in the 'Sigalovada sutta' of the *Dīgha Nikāya.*[10] finds mention in texts like the *Milindapañho* and the *Mahāvastu.*

The close identification of spiritual and social interests between the *Saṅgha* and the laity is very succinctly expressed by Nāgasena when he enumerates the ten qualities of an ideal layman: '[He] suffers like pain and feels like joy as the Order does. He takes the Doctrine (Dhamma) as his master. He delights in giving so far as he is able to give. On seeing the religion (Dhamma) of the conqueror decay, he does his best to revive it. He holds right views. Having no passion for excitement, he runs not after any other teacher his life long. He keeps guard over himself in thought and deed. He delights in peace, is a lover of peace. He feels no jealousy, and walks not in religion in a quarrelsome spirit. He takes his refuge in the Buddha, he takes his refuge in the Doctrine, he takes his refuge in the Order.'[11]

The Laity (Upāsakas) were expected to be well disposed towards the *bhikkhus* by regarding them in high esteem, receiving them with honour,[12] treating them with loving kindness, in body, speech and mind and by ministering to their needs.[13]

---

[10] *Digha Nikāya,* III, pp.139ff; See, G.S.P. Misra, *The Age of Vinaya,* p.129.

[11] *The Questions of King Milinda,* I, pp.143-44.

[12] Respect was shown in the form of prostration (*abhivādana*), salutation (*añjalikaraṇa*), rising from seat to welcome them (*pratyutthāna*) and waiting upon them *(vaiyāvṛtta).* See, *Mahāvastu,* I, p.247.

[13] Ibid., I, p.41.

The *bhikkhus* as custodians of the moral and spiritual values of society and as living examples and symbols of the higher life of meditation and holy conduct were expected to fulfil their obligations towards the laity in the following manner:

(a) To restrain the laity from performing bad acts (*pāpā nivārenti*);
(b) To admonish and advice them to do good (*kalyāne nivesati*);
(c) To be compassionate towards them (*kalyānena manasā anukampanti*);
(d) To instruct them in the doctrine which had not been heard by them before (*assutam sāveti*);
(e) To clear doubts concerning things about which they have heard (*sutam pariyodapeti*);
(f) To point or reveal the path to heaven (*saggassa maggam ācikkhanti*).[14]

Walpola Rahula quoting from a Sinhalese text *Saddharmālaṅkāraya* sums up the association and interdependence between the *Saṅgha* and the laity thus: '*Gihīnam upakarontānaṃ niccaṃ āmisadānato karotha dhammadānena tesaṃ paccupakārakaṃ*'—'Render help in return by spiritual gifts to lay people who always support you with material gifts'.[15]

Thus the *bhikkhus* standing for a way of life set apart from that of the householder, nevertheless had to have regular transactions with the laity.

Place of the Laity in the Buddhist Order

In its proper theoretic framework, the term *Saṅgha* signifies technically the *bhikkhus* and *bhikkhunis* only.[16] But taking

---

[14] *Infra.*

[15] Walpola Rahula, op. cit., p.194.

[16] H. Oldenberg (op. cit., p.162) points out 'the monks alone not the lay adherents, are exclusively members of the church' H. Kern (op. cit., p.72) also maintains that 'the laity was but an accessory of monastic institution'.

Buddhism as a scheme of culture and a path of spiritual progress, the laity (*upāsakas* and *upāsikas*) who took refuge in the sacred triad were as much members of the *Saṅgha* as the monks and nuns.[17]

The term *upāsaka* denotes a pious Buddhist,[18] a devout layman[19] who has deep faith in Buddhism and has taken refuge in the triple gem.[20] As Trevor Ling puts it, 'those who acknowledged the Buddha and wished to prepare themselves, as laymen, for eventual admission into the Order, were known as adherents or Upāsakas'.[21]

Another synonymous term for a lay devotee *(upāsaka)* is *gihi (gihiṁ)*.[22] Being householders they are clearly distinguished from the *pravrājita* in being described as clad in white robes[23] but are nevertheless designated as *ariya-sāvakas,* i.e. disciples of the noble ones.[24]

The Mahāsāṅghikas and, later on, the Mahāyānists included in their community not only *bhikkhus* and *bhikkhunis* but also *upāsakas* and *upāsikas*.[25] Since the layman also is

---

[17]L.M. Joshi, 'Social Perspective of Buddhist Soteriology', *Religion and Society*, Vol.XVIII, No.3, Sept.1971, pp.60-61.

[18]Walpola Rahula, loc. cit., pp.140fn.

[19]R.C. Childers, *Dictionary of the Pali Language*, pp.531-32.

[20]O. Frankfuter, *Handbook of Pāli, Being an Elementary Grammar, a Chrestomathy, and a Glossary*, p.158.

[21]Trevor Ling, *A History of Religion, East and West*, p.90.

[22]*Milindapañho* (ed.), pp.238, 241, 251, 249, 259, 342. The term *gṛhapati* occurs frequently in the Pāli Canon, the *Divyāvadāna* and the *Avadānaśataka.*

[23]Ibid., p.238 (*gihi odatavasano*); See, *Majjhima Nikāya*, III, p.350.

[24]*Milindapañho* (ed.), p.342.

[25]Though Hiuen tsang (T. Watters, op. cit., II, pp.159-60) confuses between the accounts of the first and second councils and wrongly assumes that the Mahāsāṅghika tradition originated at the time of the first council still he records the following tradition: 'Those Brethren, arhats and others, some myriads in number, who were not admitted to Kāsyapa's council assembled here. They said among themselves—"While Ju-lai was living we all had one teacher now he is dead we are put aside as strangers; to requite Buddha's kindness we must compile a canon." So the common brethren and Arhats united and drew up a fivefold canon of Sutras, Vinaya, Abhidharma, Miscellaneous and Dhāranis; this was called the "Great Congregation's Collection" because Arhats and common brethren formed the assembly by which it was drawn up'.

involved in the sufferings and as originally divine and endowed with spiritual potentialities the discourses of the Lord are addressed to them as well.[26] This liberal attitude of the Mahāyānists can be understood only in view of their changed outlook and understanding of the world. They did not conceive the world as evil and hence to be renounced. They seem to have taken cue from early Buddhism where Buddha praises certain householder *upāsakas* for their spiritual attainments.[27]

The question now is that if the *upāsakas* were part and parcel of the community, rather, the partakers of the spiritual heritage, why is a distinction made between actions associated with the *saṁsaric* realm of rebirth and suffering and actions associated with the *nibbanic* experience of release and freedom? That raises the fundamental issue, whether Buddha's teaching was of common validity for householders and recluses alike?[28]

Aśoka's edicts which seek to exemplify the *Dhamma* for laity, emphasize actions on their part which lead to heaven.[29] Nagārjuna's letter to king Gautamīputra[30] distinguishes two aspects of *Dharma,* namely, lay and monkish, the practice of the former resulting in heaven and the latter resulting in liberation.

This makes Kenneth J. Saunders observe: 'From the first Buddhism claimed to be not only a Middle Path but also a twofold Path. It offered a way between the extremes of austerity and of self indulgence; the way of the monk, the

---

[26]*Saddharma Puṇḍarīka* (SBE.), p.7; *Aṣṭasāhasrikā Prajñāpāramitā*, p.22.

[27]*Aṅguttara Nikāya,* III, pp.148-49.

[28]Such a distinction in discourses emerges in the *Nikāyas* also. For example in the *Majjhima Nikāya* (III, p.350) Sariputta tells the ill Anāthapiṇḍika that such *Dhamma* talk is not revealed to white-clothed housefolk but to those who have left the world.

[29]*Infra.*

[30]*Nagārjuna's letter to King Gautamīputra* (trans.), p.4.

eightfold Path to nirvāṇa; for the layman, rebirth in a better state through almsgiving and morality.'[31]

The issue can be resolved by analysing the founder's attitude towards the same as gleaned from Mahāyānic texts. Lord Buddha maintains absolute impartiality so far as social distinctions were concerned when he says, 'I am inexorable, bear no love nor hatred towards any one, and proclaim the law to all creatures without distinction, to the one as well as the other'[32] but, making a distinction in the mental capacities of his followers, utters, 'I reveal the law in its multifariousness with regard to the inclinations and dispositions of creatures. I use different means to rouse each according to his own character[33] . . . 'I speak according to their reach and faculty; by means of various meanings I accommodate my view.'[34]

The above attitude can best be intepreted in Mrs. Rhys Davids' words who claims that 'there was no such external distinction in the religious fitṇess of the "man". Man was not first lay or monk; he was a "man" first and last. There were, of course, different stages in the man's becoming: he is fit or not fit, ready or not ready for this or that in religious "training".[35]

A gradation of men and their actions finds a classic exposition in the *Saundarānanda Kavya* where Buddha tells Nanda that 'the lowest class of men undertake action for this world only, the next class both for this world and the world above, the middle men for results in the here-after only and the man of superior character for freedom from rebirth'.[36] But the

---

[31]Kenneth J. Saunders 'Buddhist Monasticism and its Fruits', *AP.*, Vol.X, No.5, May 1939, p.230. *Contra.*, Mrs. Rhys Davids *(A Manual of Buddhism,* p.302) observes, 'the primal gospel preached was not dual but specialized set of values emerging out of and top of the unitary primal message'.

[32]*Saddharma Puṇḍarīka* (SBE.), p.124. See *Bhagavad Gītā IX.29.*

[33]Ibid., p.54.

[34]Ibid., p.122.

[35]Mrs. Rhys Davids, loc. cit., p.301.

[36]*Saundarānanda*, XVIII.55.

best among these is one who desires to teach this tranquillity to others.[37]

Thus 'Buddhism has no clear cut twofold standard of morality, one for laymen and one for religious orders or priests; such differences as are recognized are of levels of attainment, the transition from one level to another being gradual and imperceptible rather than clear or distinct. The overall structure is one of progression through a continnum.'[38]

Norms for the Laity

(I) FAITH

Faith in the Buddha, *Dhamma* and *Saṅgha* was a basic prerequisite for one who had set out on the spiritual way.[39] *Upāsakas* were expected to be devoted towards the doctrine (*śāsane śraddhā prasanno*) and loyal to the triple gem (*Buddha-dharma-Saṅgha-maṅgalo*).[40] Buddha spoke of *śraddhā* as the first necessary condition for receiving religious instruction.[41]

Major Buddhist texts contain a eulogy of faith. It makes men cross the ocean of continual becomings.[42] It breaks up the five hindrances—lust, malice, mental sloth, spiritual pride and doubt and leads to tranquillity and makes the person thereby aspire for the final attainments.[43]

Faith is called the most excellent of all possessions.[44] While exhorting Nanda, Buddha in the *Saundarānanda*

---

[37]Ibid., XVIII.56.

[38]Trevor Ling, *The Buddha*, p.197.

[39]*Majjhima Nikāya*, II, p.23, pp.23, 439; *Saṁyutta Nikāya,* IV, p.291; *Dhammapada*, v.333; *Sutta Nipāta*, v.184 (Āḷavakasutta), etc.

[40]*Mahāvastu*, I, p.31.

[41]*Lalitavistara* (BST.), p.293.

[42]*The Questions of King Milinda*, II, p.55. *See, Sutta Nipāta,* (Āḷavakasutta) v. 186 (*Saddhāya tarati oghaṁ).*

[43]*The Questions of King Milinda*, I, pp.54, 55. See The 'Janavasabha Suttanta' of the *Dīgha Nikāya* (*Dialogues of the Buddha*, SBB., II, p.251) which also speaks of the attainment of insight through unwavering faith.

[44]*Saundarānanda* (trans.), v.24.

Kavya says that it is faith which governs conduct and leads to the deathless stage.[45] 'Therefore take head to cherish this shoot of faith; for as it grows the law grows, as a tree grows with the growth of its root'.[46]

Faith receives its best exposition in the hands of Śantideva who calls it the guide, mother, producer, protector and increaser of all virtues.[47] It 'expels desire, helps cross the stream, shows the city of bliss, it is a hand to grasp happiness, gives joy in renunciation, gives delight in the Law of Jina, reveals the path of Supreme deliverance, faith has the seed of virtues, it causes the tree of wisdom to grow'.[48]

It is faith which produces the thought of enlightenment as a consequence of which a person is born in Buddha-kula, walks in perfection, worships the Buddhas and embraces the Great Vehicle.[49]

It is to be emphasized that Mahāyānism with its ideal of 'universal salvation' *(sarva-mukti)* tried to make the *Dharma* accessible if not intelligible to the laity. For this it realized that the path of wisdom could not be feasible for all. They therefore offered the easy way of faith or *bhakti* to the populace.

Faith *(śraddhā)* which had meant confidence in the truth of religion in early Buddhism was supplanted by devotion *(bhakti)* and reliance on the grace of saviours in the form of Buddhas and *Bodhisattvas.*[50] The *Bodhisattvas* were thus chosen for worship and adoration in order to satisfy the needs of the devout and pious Buddhists.[51]

The saviours were expected to promote virtues, bestow material benefits and provide conditions for the attainment of

---

[45]Ibid., XIII.10.

[46]Ibid., XII.41.

[47]*Śikṣāsamuccaya* (ed.), p.2.

[48]Ibid. (trans.), p.3.

[49]Ibid. (ed.), p.4.

[50]*Supra.*

[51]Hardayal, op. cit., p.35. He is of the opinion that the idea of *bhakti* associated with the worship of Buddhas and *Bodhisattvas* grew and flourished among the Buddhists and was not borrowed from Hinduism. See, ibid., p.33.

enlightenment in a future life.[52] A sincere heart and belief, unaware of the merit of its sincerity was all that was needed on the part of the lay followers.[53]

(II) MORALITY (*ŚĪLA*)

Morality is the second quality which is to be possessed by all. In the absence of *sīla* a person (whether *bhikkhu or upāsaka*) cannot be regarded as a disciple of Buddha.[54] The general principles of morality recommended for the lay people are the five precepts *(pañca-śila)*.[55] They are spoken as the *Śikṣāpadas* of an *upāsaka*.[56] A lay Buddhist promised to observe these five precepts immediately after declaring his faith in the three jewels.[57] For the pious the precepts on particular occasions could be extended to eight[58] or ten.[59]

Another line of development in the *upāsaka sīla* can be gleaned faintly through Aśoka's edicts and more fully in

---

[52]E. Conze, op. cit., pp.152-54.

[53]Surrender in faith, without reservation, to the Buddhas and *Bodhisattvas* on the part of the devotee is best expressed by Śantideva in his *Bodhicaryāvatāra* (trans. Chap.II, v.9) as 'through devotion (bhakti) I go into servitude'.

[54]*Mahāvastu*, II, p.324; *Saundarānanda*, XIII.19.

[55]*Mahāvastu*, I, p.270. In the Pali canon the five *sīlas* are: *pāṇātipātā veramaṇi, adinnādānā veramaṇi, kāmesumicchācārā veramaṇi, musāvādā veramaṇi and surāmerayamajjapamādaṭṭhānā veramaṇi.* See, *Saṁyutta Nikāya*, II, pp.58-59; *Aṅguttara Nikāya*, II p.70; III, pp.345, 450; Dialogues of Buddha, I, p.182; *Sutta Nipāta* (Dhammikasuttaṁ), vv.174-81: *Vimānavatthu,* pp.43, 45, 51. The five precepts originally formed part of the ten *śikṣāpadas* enjoined on the novices who entered the *Saṅgha.*

[56]*Avadānaśataka* (BST.), p.152.

[57]Ibid., pp.133, 144.

[58]Laymen could observe the precepts on *uposatha* days. See, *Book of Gradual Sayings*, I, pp.191; II, pp.107, 231, 240; III, pp.26, 129, 150f, 153ff, 199, 303; IV, p.4, 149, 169, 170, 179, 190, 245, 260, 273, 299, 304; V, pp.59ff, 124f. The *Aṭṭha sīla* was of two kinds—(a) periodical *(Kālapariyanta sīla)* and (b) Life long *(Āpāṇakoṭika sīla)* and constituted a form of temporary rununciation. See, *Path of Purification*, I, p.12.

[59]The *Dasa śila* (10 precepts) were laid down for the *Śāmaneras* and the pious *upāsakas.* The *Mahāvastu* (I, p.274) refers to Ghaṭikara, the potter, who observed the ten precepts.

certain Buddhist texts. In Pillar Edict II[60] (Delhi-Topra) Aśoka includes within morality—few sins *(āpāsinave),* many virtuous deeds *(bahu kayāne),* compassion (*dayā*), liberality (*dāne*), truthfulness *(sache)* and purity *(sachaye).* It should be noted that a part of the five *Śikṣāpadas* is included here, the only difference being that instead of the negative approach, emphasis is laid on inculcation of positive virtues which finds its culmination in Mahāyāna lay ethics.

The *Mahāvastu* presents two varying lists emphasizing ten right ways of behaviour. The first list[61] includes abstention from taking life, stealing, sensual pleasures, intoxicating liquor, lying, slander, idle chatter, ignorance, ill-will, and wrong belief. The second list[62] includes abstention from killing, stealing, sensual pleasures, falsehood, frivolous talk, malevolence, heresy, treachery, cruelty and covetousness.

Nāgārjuna's letter to King Gautamīputra[63] explicitly refers to the practise of ten virtuous deeds through body, voice and mind[64] by avoiding ten non-virtuous actions: three of body—killing, stealing, sexual misconduct; four of voice—lying, slander, malicious speech, idle speech; three of mind—covetousness, malevolence and erroneous views.

Morality is not just the extermination of *rāga* and *dveṣa.* It includes positive virtues such as generosity, mercy, self control, ardour, forbearance, fortitude, humility, modesty, conscientiousness, politeness and purity.[65] It is only in the *Bodhisattvabhūmi*[66] that the precept of morality in its developed form occurs. It divides *śīla* into three categories—

---

[60]*CII.*, I, p.121.

[61]*Mahāvastu*, II, p.96.

[62]Ibid., I, p.85.

[63]*Nagārjuna's Letter to King Gautamīputra* (trans.), p.5. See, *Path of Purification*, I, p.49.

[64]Such a tripartite arrangement of precepts under body, speech and mind occurs in the *Book of the Gradual Sayings*, I, pp.88ff, 95, 97, 99, 105, 121f, 135, 139, 249; II, pp.139, 163f, 234, 238, 242; III, pp.2, 99, 102, 115, 195, 208, 250, 254, 274f, 311; IV, pp.24ff, 48, 72, 119f, 126, 131, 241.

[65]*Jātakamālā* (BST.), p.217; *Lalitavistara* (BST.), p.162.

[66]*Bodhisattvabhūmi* (ed.), pp.96ff.

(a) *Saṁvara śīla* which could be followed by practising the 'ten ways of meritorious actions';

(b) *Kuśala-dharma-saṅgrāhaka śīla* which is conducive to the accumulation of merit;

(c) *Sattva-kriyā śila* which consists in rendering service to the living beings.

Thus virtues of moral behaviour which lie scattered throughout the entire Pāli Canon were gradually systematised by the Mahāyānists and were definitely influenced by the dual positive virtues of *karuṇā* and *maitrī*. The emphasis on the former which constitutes the very base on which the laity could train his heart and make his wisdom grow and eventually attain *nirvāṇa*, was carried to its extreme by a strange doctrine evolved by the Mahāyānists that a *bodhisattva* may violate any or all of the precepts of *śīla* if he is moved by compassion.[67] A sin arising from passion is declared to be no sin if it is for the good of creatures.[68]

'This doctrine' remarks Hardayal 'must have originated on account of three circumstances. These keen thinkers must have realized that no ethical laws can be universally and eternally valid, and that the ordinary social code must break down under certain circumstances. They attached such exaggerated importance to mercy and compassion that they began to take a short sighted view of ethical obligation. They thought that the immediate relief of pain and suffering outweighed the permanent loss inflicted on the individual and on society by the deliberate violation of the great moral principles.'[69]

---

[67]*Bodhicaryāvatāra* (BST.), Chap.V, v.84.

[68]*Śikṣāsamuccaya* (trans.), pp.163-65.

[69]Hardayal, op. cit., p.207. *Contra.*, A.B. Keith *(Buddhist Philosophy in India and Ceylon*, p.297) observes that 'the permission given to the Bodhisattva to sin in the cause of compassion is rather a glorification of the merits of compassion than an invitation to violate the moral law.'

It is also probable that the later Mahayanists in order to condone the moral laxity of monks[70] used the motive of *karuṇā* as a pretext or justification and allowed them to transgress the social code.

(III) LISTENING TO THE DHARMA

'Hearing Dhamma, is of much service to remembering Dhamma. Whosoever should not hear that Dhamma could not remember that Dhamma; but if he hears Dhamma, then he remembers Dhamma, therefore hearing Dhamma is of much service to remembering Dhamma.'[71] These words of Buddha point to the importance of listening to the *Dhamma* on the part of Buddhist householders.

The faculty of wisdom could be acquired only by hearing the *Dhamma*.[72] The laity heard the discourses on feast days[73] or after invitation of a meal offered to the *Saṅgha*.[74] But by the beginning of the Christian era with the growth of popular education in the monasteries, the lay followers visited the monasteries regularly to hear the sermons.

Besides terrestrial blessings assured to the lay devotees who were regular in attending the sermon, the *Saddharma Puṇḍarīka* states that hearing the *sūtra* will lead to perfect enlightenment.[75]

---

[70]Passages of the *Rāṣṭrapāla-paripṛcchā* (pp.28-33) contain a prophecy regarding the future decadence of the monks who are presented as completely devoid of virtues, morally lax, occupied with abject occupations, seductors, slaves of desires, indulging in worldly talks, neglecting meditation and study, rich like householders, slaves of covetousness, indulging in calumny thereby causing the noble doctrine to fall into ruin.

[71]*Middle Length Sayings*, II, p.364; *Majjhima Nikāya*, II, p.439.

[72]See, *Mahāvastu*, II, p.76; III, p.370. The *Śikṣāsamuccaya* (trans., p.184) observes that wisdom comes to one who hears the *Dhamma*.

[73]*Supra*.

[74]*Avadānaśataka* (BST.), pp.64, 66, etc.; *Divyāvadāna* (BST.), pp.28, 51, 54, 61, etc.

[75]*Saddharma Puṇḍarīka* (SBE.), pp.214-15, 221.

(IV) *DĀNA*

Wherever the ways of acquiring merit are enumerated for the *upāsakas, dāna* (charity) invariably finds the first place. The unsurpassable power of giving, gifts and liberality find mention in all Buddhist texts.[76] Devout householders are therefore known as *dānapati* and *dāyaka.*[77] The virtue of *dāna* is emphasized in Hindu scriptures also.[78] The motives, methods and merits of giving are explained in many passages of the Pāli Canon.[79] The Mahāyānists emphasized it as one of the *pāramitas* to be practised by the *bodhisattva.*

Liberality as a virtue is extolled in the Aśokan Edicts.[80] The quality of 'giving without miserliness, the giving itself, the effort one makes in giving, the gift itself and the joy one has for the practice of giving' is stressed by Nagārjuna in his letter to King Gautamīputra.[81] Further, 'knowing that wealth is unstable and devoid of essence, rightly bestow gifts upon monks, brahmans, the poor and friends; so for the next life there is no more excellent a kinsman than giving'.[82]

Among the recipients of *dāna,* Aśoka mentions two categories,[83] viz., gifts to Brahmaṇas and Śramaṇas and liberality to friends, acquaintances and relatives. The *Mahāvastu*[84] list includes Brahmaṇas, recluses (Śramaṇas), blind,

---

[76]*Infra.*

[77]*Avadānaśataka* (BST.), pp.119, 129, etc.; *Abhisamācārikā*, pp.1, 127; *Bodhisattvabhūmi* (ed.), p.85.

[78]*Chāṇḍogya Upaniṣad* 11.23.1; *Bṛahadaraṇyaka Upaniṣad* VI.2.16.

[79]*Aṅguttara Nikāya*, I, p.14; II, pp.306, 307; III, pp.198, 199-200, 336-37, 338, 340, 342; IV, pp.35-36; *Dīgha Nikāya*, II, p.263; *Saṁyutta Nikāya*, I. p.90; *Sutta Nipāta* (Māgha sutta); *Itivuttaka*, Chap.26, *Vimānavattu* and *Petavatthu.*

[80]*CII.*, I, PE., II, VII; RE., III, VIII, IX, XI. *Dhammadāna* is considered the best *dāna* amongst all—RE., XI. See, *Dhammapada*, v.354.

[81]*Nāgārjuna's letter to king Gauramīputra* (trans.), p.4.

[82]Ibid., p.5.

[83]*CII.*, I, RE., III, VIII, IX, XI.

[84]*Mahāvastu*, II, pp.76-77; III, p.404.

helpless, poor and the destitute. The *Jātakamālā*[85] mentions Śramaṇas, Brahmaṇas; friends and relatives; needy, poor, sick and helpless. The *Śikṣāsamuccaya*[86] presents a comprehensive list which includes the following in a descending order, namely—Buddhas and *bodhisattvas,* man who supports Buddha's teaching, disciples and *pratyekabuddhas,* mother and father, teachers and preceptors, poor mendicants and beggars.

It is interesting to note that in nearly all the texts the Śramaṇas and Brahmaṇas are given precedence over other categories and among the two the Buddhist monks are held superior.[87] They are held as supreme fields of merit and worthy recipients of meritorious giving.[88] In the *Śatapañcāśatka*[89] of *Mātṛceṭa*, Buddha and his saints are conceived as fields (*satkṣetram*) in which meritorious deeds are sown, issuing in a crop of rewards. The *Arya Saṅgha* is spoken as the unsurpassable field of merit in the *Jātakamālā.*[90] The *Śikṣāsamuccaya*[91] makes it clear that it is more meritorious to give to a monk than to a pious layman or an ordinary person.

The *Vimānavatthu* stories teach that the householders can become dwellers of celestial mansions through certain acts of piety such as *dāna* (liberal gifts of food and drink and other requisites to the Buddha and the Order), *vihāradāna*, *bhikkhādāna* (alms giving), etc. By offering food, medicines, robes and dwelling places, they could enter heavens and enjoy wealth, health and social status on earth.

---

[85]*Jātakamālā* (BST.), pp.16, 110, 228; See *Divyāvadāna* (BST.), pp.55, 253; *Avadānaśataka* (BST.), pp.4, 89, 110, 114, 116, 128.

[86]*Śikṣāsamuccaya* (trans.), pp.30, 86.

[87]*See, Dīgha Nikāya*, II, p.263; *Aṅguttara Nikāya*, III, pp.338, 339, 340.

[88]*Vimānavatthu* (SBB.), p.11.

[89]*Śatapañcāśatka* of Matṛceṭa (ed.), v.99.

[90]*Jātakamālā* (BST.), p.18; See *Avadānaśataka* (BST.), p.73.

[91]*Śikṣāsamuccya* (trans.), p.89.

The extent and kinds of endowments made to the *Saṅgha* can be gleaned from the *Milindapañho*[92] where it is said that 'When faith arises in their hearts some give food to those worthy of gifts and some give clothes and some give bedding and some give dwellings and some give mats or robes and some give slave girls or slaves and some give fields or premises and some give bipeds or quadrupeds and some give a hundred or a thousand and some give the kingdom itself and some give away even their own life.'

The *Saddharma Puṇḍarīka*[93] in the words of the Lord says: 'Let him, during eight thousand *kotis* of complete aeons, continue giving alms repeatedly to Buddhas and disciples; regaling pratyekabuddhas and *kotis* of Bodhisattvas by giving meat, food and drink, clothing and lodging; let him build on earth refuges and monasteries[94] of sandalwood, and pleasant convent gardens provided with walks.'

The *Jātakamālā*,[95] *Avadānaśataka*,[96] *Divyāvadāna*[97] and *Śikṣāsamuccaya*[98] are replete with instances of the members of royal family and the *bodhisattvas* giving 'food, drinks, medicines, couches, seats, gardens, houses, villages, towns, perfumes, garlands, ointments, silver, gold, elephants, horses, chariots, clothes, corn, gems, ornaments, musical instruments, men-servants and maid servants' etc.

A *bodhisattva* is asked to give whatever he possesses to the extent of his limbs, life, wife, children or his merit.[99]

---

[92]*The Questions of King Milinda*, II, pp.121-22.

[93]*Saddharma Puṇḍarīka* (SBE.), p.318.

[94]The *Milindapañho* (*The Questions of King Milinda*, II, p.3) in the same strain says 'let therefore the wiseman, regarding his own weal. Have pleasant dwelling places built, and lodge their learned men'.

[95]*Jātakamālā* (BST.), pp.8-9.

[96]*Avadānaśataka* (BST.), p.139.

[97]*Divyāvadāna* (BST.), pp.180, 426.

[98]*Śikṣāsamuccaya* (trans.), pp.29-31. Compare *Jātaka* stories (Nos.499, 547) of Kings Śivi and Vessantara.

[99]Ibid., pp.23-24, 26-36.

A classification of *dāna* categories occurs in the *Bodhisattvabhūmi*[100] which is as follows:

(a) *Svabhāva-dāna*—giving away things including spiritual gains;
(b) *Sarva-dāna*—giving away unlimited and unrestricted gifts;
(c) *Duṣkara-dāna*—giving away gifts beyond a *bodhisattva's* capacity as also objects dear to him;
(d) *Sarvato mukhaṁ-dāna*—giving away to all including friends and relatives;
(e) *Satpuruṣa-dāna*—giving to saintly persons;
(f) *Sarvākāraṁ-dāna*—giving frequently, at all times and all sorts of objects;
(g) *Vighātārthikaṁ-dāna*—giving to persons who could not procure what they wanted;
(h) *Ihāmutra-sukhaṁ dāna*—gifts of material objects for happiness in this life and gift of spiritual instructions for happiness in future lives;
(i) *Visuddha dāna*—giving without slightest self-interest.

The *Saṅgha* concealed its economic interests by devising the strange doctrine that the merit of a charitable deed depends on the spiritual status of the recipient and not on the greatness of his need or the nature of service rendered by the donor. 'This teaching throws a lurid light on the sub-conscious psychology of the monks, who depended for their subsistence on the alms of the laity.'[101]

But there were sects like the Rājagirikas and Siddhattikas who maintained that *dāna* is [not the gift but] the mental state.[102] The Vetulyakas asserted that the Order does not accept gifts,[103] nor does it purify (causes to fructify) the gifts.[104] It neither enjoys, eats nor drinks[105] and so it should not

---

100 *Bodhisattvabhūmi* (ed.), Chap.IX (Danapaṭala).

101 Hardayal, op. cit., p.174.

102 *Points of Controversy* (PTS.), VII.4.

103 Ibid., XVII.6.

104 Ibid., XVII.7.

105 Ibid., XVII.8.

be said that a thing given to the Order brings great reward.[106] The Madhyamikas elaborated on this doctrine and considered mind control to be superior to *dāna-paramitā*. For all that a person experiences in the phenomenal and relative world in only illusion and illusion is something imagined or fabricated by the *citta*.[107]

However, such an intellectual exposition failed to impress the ordinary devoted householders who continued to offer charity with the earnest hope of acquiring merit.

(V) BRAHMA VIHĀRAS

The more advanced householders *(bodhisattvas)* were required to practice the four sublime states of mental development leading to *ceto-vimutti*.[108] They were not practices in action; their prime purpose was purification of mind.[109] The *Brahma vihāras* are not specifically Buddhistic. But they came to assume great importance in Mahāyānism. The *Mahāvastu* exalts the *Brahma vihāras* to such an extent that it promises *nirvāṇa* to the person who practices them.[110]

Maitrī (Pali *Mettā*)

Maitrī, the first among the *Brahma vihāras* is translated as loving kindness, friendliness, benevolence, amity and goodwill. It is mentioned and extolled more frequently in the Pāli Canon than *karuṇā*.[111] It is a virtue which promotes

---

[106]Ibid., XVII.9.

[107]*Bodhicaryāvatāra* (trans.), Intd., p.50.

[108]*Dīgha Nikāya*, III, pp.62, 235f, 250f, 254.

[109]As G.S.P. Misra ('A Study of Philanthropy in Early Buddhist Ethics', *Indica,* Vol.18, No.2, Sept. 1981, p.78) puts it 'The Brahma-Vihāras are not only the objects of meditation (*samādhi*) or the states of mind (*citta*) but they are also the ethical virtues (*sīla*) which should be practised by one who has chosen to walk on the right path. They are, thus, on the one hand, stages of spiritual and metaphysical development and, on the other, they present the very best of social ideals.'

[110]*Mahāvastu*, III, pp.422-23.

[111]*Khuddaka Paṭha,* (Metta sutta); *Aṅguttara Nikāya*, I, p.169, III, p.270; *Sutta Nipāta* (Khaggavisāṇasutta), v.73, (Māgha sutta), v.106; *Psalms of the Brethren,* vv.645-49.

welfare.[112] It is manifested as the removal of annoyance. Its proximate cause is seeing lovableness in beings. It succeeds when it makes ill will subside and it fails when it produces (selfish) affection.[113]

Maitrī is a form of personal discipline[114] unfolded through meditation in four stages[115], viz., (a) towards oneself (b) one's friend (c) a person towards whom one is neutral and (d) an enemy. This feeling can be extended in all ten directions towards all beings and creatures without distinction.[116]

This 'unlimited friendliness' is interpreted by Buddhaghosa as meaning that a man should identify himself (*attatāya*) with all (*sabbesu*).[117] 'As I myself wish to be happy and have an aversion to suffering, as I wish to live and do not wish to die, so also do other beings wish for the same.'[118]

It may appear surprising that in a religion which exalts monastic life, friendliness which is a basis of social relations should figure so prominently. In fact, practice of *maitrī* purports to cultivate a spiritual disposition of mind which, when put in application, can provide a base for healthy social relationship. This brings about detachment and aloofness.

Karuṇā and Muditā

The second and the third *Brahma vihāras* are an outcome of *Maitrī*. *Maitrī* as shown above purifies the heart by removing hatred and ill will. Compassion is a virtue that makes people

---

[112]*Avadānaśataka* (BST.), pp.15, 27; *Śikṣāsamuccaya* (trans.), p.204.

[113]*Path of Purification*, I, p.344.

[114]Among the benefits of the practice of *metta* as enumerated in the *Milindapañho* (*The Questions of King Milinda*, I, p.279) there is no mention of its effect on society or family. The practiser sleeps pleasantly, wakes up fresh, undisturbed by anxious dreams, is dear to men and gods who watch over him, is not harmed by fire, poison or sword, becomes easily tranquillised, his countenance is calm, undismayed he meets death and is reborn in the Brahma world. See also *Book of the Gradual Sayings*, IV, p.103.

[115]*Path of Purification*, I, pp.322f.

[116]Ibid., p.335.

[117]Ibid., p.334.

[118]Ibid., p.323.

sensitive to the misery of others. Though the concept appears in early Buddhism, it achieved its greatest importance in Mahāyānism.

Aśoka's view of compassion as revealed from his rock and pillar inscriptions was revulsion from the cruelties of war and conquest and exaltation of the sanctity of animal life.[119] In Mahāyāna Buddhism, compassion becomes the chief characteristic of the *bodhisattva*[120] and is defined in the words of the Lord as 'the unsurpassed resolute intention to further the well being and welfare of all beings at all times'.[121]

Karuṇā can only be realized when one considers the other as equal to oneself (*parātma-samatā*) and practices the substitution of others for oneself (*parātma-parivartana*).[122]

It can be understood on two levels—

(a) Seeking enlightenment (supreme wisdom) for the sake of saving all creatures ;[123]

(b) Resolving to suffer the agonies in order to lead all beings to perfect enlightenment.[124]

---

[119]*CII.*, I, RE., I, III, IV, XI; PE., V.

[120]*Mahāvastu*, I, p.61; II, p.312; *Lalitavistara* (BST.), pp.112, 130, 203, 254; *Avadānaśataka* (BST.), pp.84, 94; *Śikṣāsamuccaya* (trans.), pp.8, 180, 219, 262.

[121]*The Large Sutra on Perfect Wisdom,* p.656.

[122]*Mahāvastu*, III, p.385; *Bodhicaryāvatāra* (trans.), Chap.VIII, vv.90f; *Śikṣāsamuccaya* (trans.), p.3—'Since I and my fellow-men abhor pain and fear alike, what distinction can I rightly make for self, that I should preserve it and not another'—Karika 1.

[123]*The Large Sutra on Perfect Wisdom,* p.611; *Śikṣāsamuccaya* (trans.), p.115. Buddha is depicted as unwilling to teach the *Dhamma* immediately after enlightenment. It was compassion coupled with Brahma's request which made him reveal the *Dhamma* to people. See, *Mahāvagga,* p.9. The *Jātakas* (T.W. Rhys Davids, *Buddhist Birth Stories)* meant for the edification of the laity also show that it was *karuṇā* which made the future Buddha endure sufferings for the sake of acquiring ominscient wisdom whereby he could save both men and gods.

[124]For the sake of the weal of every single being will I roast in the hells for aeons countless as the sands of the Ganges, until that being has been established in the Buddha cognition'—*The Large Sutra on Perfect Wisdom,* p.168. See, *Bodhicaryāvatāra* (trans.). Chap.III, vv.12, 16.

Muditā (sympathetic joy) is feeling glad about the prosperous condition of others and experiencing happiness in their happiness. Its chief characteristics are joy, faith, freedom from despondency, craving, jealousy and hostility.

Upekṣā

It is the cultivation of a mental state of equanimity under all circumstances which produces a state of undisturbed calm within oneself. This can be developed in two ways, namely—

(a) Seeing all beings as equal *(sama-bhāva)*;[125]

(b) To ignore the effect which others have on oneself.[126]

This is the highest state when a person becomes a disinterested spectator of the worldly scene. He is unperturbed by events over which he cannot have control.[127]

Thus the *Brahma vihāras* though apparently concerned with the social world of living beings are in reality stages which enable the *bodhisattva* to withdraw from the social world and take the final step towards salvation. On the level of the ordinary faith follower at least the first three *vihāras* could be cultivated as social and ethical virtues.

Ideology of Merit

A Buddhist lay disciple was given systematic instruction not only on charity, morality, heaven and the path but also merit and its fruition.[128] Merit in Buddhism is to be understood as that quality which either guarantees a happier life in the future or alternatively increases the scope of spiritual opportunities

---

[125]*Path of Purification*, I, p.344.

[126]Ibid., p.347.

[127]Ibid., p.348.

[128]Making merit and reaping its reward was mere layman's creed—not that of a genuine bhikkhu, who by entering on the Path had renounced heavenly goals'—see, *Book of the Kindred Sayings*, I, p.231, fn.2. See also *Dīgha Nikāya*, II, pp.35-36; *Majjhima Nikāya*, II, pp.52,393; *Mahāvastu*, III, p.246.

and achievements.[129] It is laying the foundation for a future period. The increase or merit is considered to be the root of all increase.[130]

The ideology of merit can be understood on two levels,[131] viz., (a) The ordinary or worldly and (b) the supramundane. On the first level, the spiritually less endowed faith followers were advised to acquire merit through faith, *dāna,* moral behaviour, revering the relics, Buddhas and *bodhisattvas* and through reading, writing, hearing and believing the *Sūtras.*[132]

E. Conze[133] explains this point succinctly when he states that 'it has always been the tactics of the Buddhist to weaken the possessive instincts of the spiritually less endowed members of the community by withdrawing them from such objects as wealth and family and directing them instead towards one aim and object, i.e. the acquisition of merit. But that, of course, is good enough only on a fairly low spiritual level. At higher stages one will have to turn also against this form of possessiveness, one will have to be willing to give up one's store of merit for the sake of happiness of others. The Mahāyāna drew this conclusion and expected its followers to endow other beings with their own merit or as the scriptures put it, 'to turn over, or dedicate, their merit to the enlightenment of all beings'.

On the highest level, to aim at merit in the truly Mahāyānic sense is to diminish it. It is only aiminig at emptiness which brings infinite reward. Buddhahood infact is not something real, actually existing condition produced as a result of the merit gained from giving or other perfections.

---

[129]For verily has it been said in the *Mahāvastu* (III, p.45) that, 'blessed is the fruit of merits; the wish of the meritorious prospers. Speedily does he attain perfect peace, utter release'.

[130]*Śikṣāsamuccaya* (trans.), p.145.

[131]Buddhist tradition itself distinguishes two classes of people, the ordinary worldlings (*pṛthagjana*) and the 'saints' (*āryajana*).

[132]*Supra.*

[133]E. Conze, op. cit., p.149.

Faith,[134] *dāna*,[134A] morality, worship of relics[135] and reverence of Buddhas and *bodhisattvas*[136] lead to the acquisition of merit[137] which can be classified as follows—

[134]For a discussion on the importance of faith as a prerequisite to attaining the goal, See, J.T. Ergardt, *Faith and Knowledge in Early Buddhism.*

[134A]Commenting on the extravagant generosity of King Śivi and Vessantara as enumerated in the Jātaka Stories, J.G. Jones (*Tales and Teachings of the Buddha*, p.134) says, 'One is compelled to say that at this immensely popular point, the Jātaka tales are moving very markedly in the direction of the Mahāyāna, where the quality of sacrificial self-giving, often in the most extravagant terms, is one of the most emphasized of the bodhisattva's qualities. This Mahāyānist extravaganza is also, as we have noted, a return to a very popular Hindu theme, though a departure from the "middle way" of canonical Theravāda, in that it turns giving, into a mechanism for merit-making which is essentially a substitute for the rejected vedic sacrifies. Giving becomes almost like gambling; the higher the stakes, the higher the potential winnings—though the Jātakas assure us that there is really no gamble involved. By sheer karmic necessity, giving must have its reward. The canonical view is that giving is a means to an end, the means by which the Sangha can be nourished and maintained, but that it should not be allowed to get out of hand. The monk must constantly be on guard against being corrupted by the generosity of merit-seeking donors; the donor must never forget that his is the inferior position. To receive is more blessed than to give since one's highest good depends on one's willingness to forsake all worldly possessions and oneself depend on the generosity of others. The magnification of heroic giving into an end in itself, a supreme expression of spiritual eminence, is a clear distortion of the canonical teaching.'

[135]Ritual worship varied from simple bowing and reverential salutation (*abhipradakṣinaṃ karoti*) of the *stūpa*, offering flowers, garlands, perfumes, flags and banners, precious jewels, music, to carrying brick to the shrine, cleaning and removing withered flowers. See, *The Questions of King Milinda*, I, pp.148-49; *Saddharma Puṇḍarīka* (ed.), pp.37ff. *Mahāvastu,* II, pp.329, 331, 332, 339, 343, 345, 347, 348, 351, 352; *Divyāvadāna* (BST.), pp.304-05, 426; *Śikṣā-samuccaya* (trans.), pp.270ff.

[136]Detailed exposition of the worship of Buddhas and *bodhisattvas* occurs in the *Larger Sukhavati Vyūha* (Buddhist Mahayana Sutras, SBE., Pt.II, p.49). Honouring *bodhisattvas* meant houring all Buddhas. See, *Śikṣāsamuccaya* (trans.), pp.88-89.

[137]*Vimānavatthu* (SBB.), p.2; *Mahāvastu*, I, p.247; II, pp.76-77, 324, 325, 328, 329-32, 345, 347-48, 351-52; III, p.300: *Divyāvadāna* (BST.), p.278; *Avadāna-śataka* (BST.), p.141; *Jātakamālā* (BST.), p.160; *Śikṣāsamuccaya* (trans.), pp.270ff, 278.

(a) Virtuous disposition encompassing mindfulness, truthfulness, joy, amiability, confidence, freedom from envy etc.
(b) Physiognomical advantages in the form of physical strength, fair complexion, freedom from physical handicaps, clear voice, marks of excellence, etc.
(c) Earthly sovereignty in the form of righteous universal ruler.
(d) Celestial sovereignty and prosperity as Sakra, Lord of Devas and Brahma.
(e) Acquisition of super human powers.
(f) Rebirth in heaven
(g) Secular benefits in the form of wealth, affluence, fame, social status, enjoyment of pure food, safety against evils and longevity.

Greater merit in the form of terrestrial and spiritual benefits (supreme enlightenment) were assured to the laity who read, recited, copied, heard, kept in memory or worshipped the Mahāyāna *Sūtras*.[138] But the merit of the devotee of perfect wisdom is said to be immeasurable, incalculable, inconceivable, incomparable, illimitable,[139] because from the perfection of wisdom the all-knowledge of the Tathagata has come forth.[140] But this knowledge was limited to the very advanced householders because of its incomprehensibility.[141]

Merit versus Karman

The concept of merit is essentially related to the theory of *karman.* Buddhist ethics may be understood as an intuitionist ethics in that in ethical evaluation of any act it lays great

---

[138]*Saddharma Puṇḍarīka* (SBE.), pp.220, 221, 328f, 336f, 388, 389.

[139]*Aṣṭasāhasrikā Prajñāpāramitā* (trans.), pp.22, 23, 24-25, 26-27, 28-29, 35-36; *The Large Sutra on Perfect Wisdom* (trans.), pp.234, 248, 249, 282, 308, 406; *Vajracchedikā* (*Buddhist Mahayana Sutras*, SBE.), pp.119, 123-24.

[140]*Aṣṭasāhasrikā Prajñāpāramitā,* p.27. Perfection of wisdom is the mother and genetrix of the Tathagatas. See, *The Diamond Sutra* (trans.), pp.41-42.

[141]*Vajracchedikā* (SBE., Pt.II), p.130.

emphasis on the intention of the doer.[142] The *Milindapañho*[143] which elaborates the doctrine of *karman* makes it clear that good works *(kuśala karman)* have a happy result and lead to *sagga* (heaven) and evil works *(akuśala karman)* have an unhappy result and lead to *niraya* (purgatory).[144] *Puṇya* (merit) results automatically from righteous action.

Two trends are visible in Mahāyāna literature namely the gradual exaltation of *puṇya* and annulment of *karmas* through devious means. As shown earlier, in the early Mahāyānistic literature *puṇya* was only a means of securing happy rebirths and gaining other advantages.[145] But gradually the idea gained ground that *puṇya* itself could lead to enlightenment. Śanti-deva[146] goes to the extent of substituting 'transfer of *puṇya*' for the perfection of wisdom as the final goal of a *bodhi-sattva's* career.

Secondly the original Buddhist doctrine that the stock of good works *(kuśalamūla)* performed in this world *(avara-mātraka)* will bear fruit in the next was superseded by the doctrine that salvation could be obtained by mere repetition of the name of Amitābha. Efficacy of prayer and not *kuśala karma* results in birth in the Buddha country of Tathāgata Amitāyus. For it has been stated specifically in the *Smaller Sukhāvati Vyūha*,[147] 'beings are not born in that Buddha country of the Tathagata Amitāyus as a reward and result of good works performed in this present life. No, whatever son or daughter of a family shall hear the name of the blessed Amitāyus, the Tathagata and having heard it, shall keep it in mind, and with thoughts undisturbed shall keep it in mind for

[142]'*Cetanāhaṃ bhikkhave kammaṃ vedāmi;cetayitvā kammaṃ karoti kāyena vācāya manasā*'—*Aṅguttara Nikāya*, III, p.120.

[143]*The Questions of King Milinda*, I, pp.32-33, 71, 191, 263; II, pp.145, 163-64.

[144]Ibid., I, p.283. S. Tachibana (*The Ethics of Buddhism*, pp.207-08) discerns a direct causal relationship between the quality of one's motives and soteriological achievements.

[145]*Supra.*

[146]*Śikṣāsamuccaya* (trans.), p.34.

[147]*Buddhist Mahayana Sutras* (SBE.), Pt.II, pp.98-99, 101.

one, two, three, four, five, six or seven nights—When that son or daughter of a family comes to die, then that Amitāyus, the Tathagata, surrounded by an assembly of disciples and followed by a host of *bodhisattvas* will stand before them at their hour of death and they will depart this life with tranquil minds.'

'After their death they will be born in the world Sukhāvati, in the Buddha country of the same Amitāyus, the Tathāgata. Therefore, then, O Sāriputra, having perceived this cause and effect, I with reference say thus, every son and every daughter of a family ought with their whole mind to make fervent prayer for that Buddha country.' And further 'Whatever evil deeds these beings, have done in a former birth, deeds that must lead to suffering, those deeds these beings owing to their being overcome, after they have seen the law, will destroy, and they will obtain the knowledge of Buddha.'[148]

Similarly in the *Amitāyur-Dhyāna-Sūtra*[149] it has been laid down that meditation on Bodhisattva Avalokiteśvara will remove the obstacle that is raised by *karma* and will expiate the sins which would involve them in births and deaths for numberless *kalpas.* Annulment of *karmas* was also possible through hearing, reading, reciting, bearing in mind or expounding the *Sutra.*[150]

The climax of this concept can be seen in the *Bodhicaryāvatāra*[151] where the devotee adopts an attitude of self-abasement by acknowledging all his shortcomings before Buddhas and *bodhisattvas* and for fear of *karmic* consequences, beseeching them to have pity on him.

In the words of Marion Matics, 'the act of worship, the act of confession, the act of taking refuge, are themselves the causes of great effects. On the plane of relativity they carry karmic potency, they are seeds of merit which must germinate

[148] *Vajracchedikā* (SBE.), Pt.II, p.131.
[149] *Buddhist Mahayana Sutras* (SBE.), Pt.II, p.183.
[150] *Diamond Sutra* (trans.), p.56.
[151] *Bodhicaryāvatāra* (trans.), Chap.II, vv.32-36.

into good fruit, and so when he says, 'I by-pass former sin', he really modifies the effect of previous action by the intervention of present action. On the plane of partial non-phenomenality, wherein there is complete equality of every self (parātmasamatā), all of the merit of the Bodhisattva is interchangeable with the demerit of anyone else, and all sins decisively are by-passed; and on the plane of absolute non-phenomenality, Nirvāṇa and saṁsāra are identical, the world of appearance is illusion and karma is another fraud.'[152]

Transfer of Merit (Puṇya Pariṇāmanā)

The belief which seems at first sight to run counter to the *karman* theory is the transfer of merit. According to the old and approved doctrine of Buddhism, merit or demerit produced by a person's actions *(karma)* is strictly personal.[153] It is also imperishable.

In the *Nāgasena-bhikṣu sūtra*,[154] the Chinese version of the *Milindapañho,* Na-hsien (Nāgasena) asks, 'If a man infringes the law and is punished, can the non-guilty replace him?' The king replies: 'This cannot be'. The Syāmaka Jataka in the *Mahāvastu*[155] states that it is not possible 'to evade the results of deeds committed by oneself' and that 'neither weeping nor mourning for him (Syāmaka) can ensure his escape from the results of the deeds he has himself committed'. The inexorability of the doctrine of *karman* is illustrated by many stories in the *Avadānaśataka.*[156] Men are driven into the cycles of existence through their own actions.[157]

---

[152]*Bodhicaryāvatāra* (trans.), Intd., p.40.

[153]*Dīgha Nikāya* (ed., N.K. Bhagwat) I, pp.78-79, *Saṁyutta Nikāya,* III, p.280; *Aṅguttara Nikāya*, IV, pp.339-40; *Majjhima Nikāya*, II, p.64: III. p.280.

[154]Thich Minh Chau, *Milindapañho and Nāgasena-bhikṣu sūtra, A Comparative Study*, p.60.

[155]*Mahāvastu*, II, pp.205, 213.

[156]*Avadānaśataka* (BST.), pp.34, 37, 39ff, 42, 46, 48, 50, 53.

[157]*Saundarānanda*, XV.31.

In later Pāli writings, the conception of transfer of merit is adumbrated. This conception suggests that a man can transfer to others the merit of any good deed he has done, still he would only increase himself in merit. The stress is laid on the latter part of the proposition but the existence of the former conception is clearly indicated for it is stated in the *Milinda-pañho* that 'if even through a hundred years, O king, a man were to keep on transferring to others (the merit of) any good he had done, the more he gave it away the more would his goodness grow and he would still be able to share it with whomsoever he would'.[158]

This idea was developed to its logical conclusion by the Māhāyānists as it was well suited to the *bodhisattva's* ideal of welfare of all sentient beings inspired by the feeling of *karuṇā* and *maitrī* towards all.[159] Hardayal[160] is of the view that the Mahāyāna owed its teaching of *pariṇāmanā* partly to the influence of Hinduism.

Even if partial influence of Hinduism is admitted it cannot be denied that the Mahāyānists provided the theory with a rationale. In the Mahāyāna *sūtras, pariṇāmanā* is of two kinds[161]—

(a) Application of the merit of a good deed for his own enlightenment by the *bodhisattva* and

---

[158]*The Questions of king Milinda*, II, pp.155-56. Buddhaghośa at the end of VIśuddhimagga *(Path of purification*, II, p.836) makes a similar wish:

> 'What store of merit has been gained by me
> Desiring establishment in this Good Law ...
> By the power of that store of merit
> May every being prosper happily ...'

[159]The same notion is hinted at in abundance in the epigraphs of the Christian era where the donor expresses his pious wish—'*Sarva hita sukhartham*' while making donations to the *Saṅgha.*

[160]Hardayal, op. cit., p.191.

[161]*Bodhisattvabhūmi* (ed.), Chap.III *(Svaparārthapaṭala);* See also, *Śikṣāsamuccaya* (trans.), pp.166-67.

(b) Application of his merit for the welfare and spiritual progress of all creatures.[162]

Between the two, the latter is considered more commendable. It is expressed by the *bodhisattva's* resolution thus: 'By this root of good may I become a rest of all beings to keep them away from all the mass of pain: may I become the protector of all beings by setting them free from sin: may I become a shelter for all beings to save them from all fear: may I become a path for all beings that they may go in every place: may I become a refuge for all beings that they may attain peace in the infinite meditation: may I become a light to all beings by showing knowledge without darkness: may I become a fire for all beings by driving away the darkness and gloom of ignorance: may I become a radiance for all beings by establishing infinite purity: may I become the guide for all beings by bringing them into the interpretation of the law surpassing thought: may I be a leader for all beings by bringing them to the elements of knowledge revealed.'[163]

Saṅgha, Society and the State

The process of individual liberation is linked up with the general welfare of society, an orderly society operating under a state. According to the Buddhist view of the state, righteousness is the essence of kingship and it is the king who shapes the moral stature of his subjects.[164] The Buddhist

---

[162]Ibid., pp.178, 213; *The Large Sutra on Perfect Wisdom*, p.268; *Śikṣāsamuccaya* (trans.), pp.32, 36, 204f; *Bodhicaryāvatāra* (trans.), Chap.X.

[163]*Śikṣāsamuccaya* (trans.), pp.32, 36, 204f.

[164]See, *Book of the Gradual Sayings* (II, pp.84f) where it is said that the goodness or badness of the king affects the state, gods and even the weather. J.G. Jones (op. cit., p.118) speaking in the same connection states that 'in the righteous state, the righteous individual would be a natural outcrop and the monk would be seen, not as an isolated segment of society, but as the man who had risen to the top of a ferment of righteousness which ran right through society. He in turn would be seen as leavening the rest of the lump. It was along these lines, at least in theory, that empire of Aśoka, the first great Indian empire, was conducted.'

Saṅgha tried to influence the actions of the state and induce the rulers to live up to the ideal of the state they were laying down upon.[165] Kingship and polity were thus infused with Buddhist meaning.[166]

"The Buddhist Conception' writes S.J. Tambiah 'makes the unversalistic assertion that dharma (in its manifold aspect as cosmic law that regulates the world totality and the truth embodied in the Buddha's teachings that show the path to liberation) is the absolutely encompassing norm and that the code of kingship embodying righteousness (dharma) has its source in this dharma and is ideally a concrete manifestation of it in the conduct of worldly affairs.'[167]

The early Buddhist conception of righteousness is related to the concept of world ruler (*Cakkavattī*).[168] He is described as the emperor over the four quarters of the earth, righteous in himself, ruling righteously, pursuing the path of ten virtues

---

[165]U.N. Ghoshal (*A History of Indian Political Ideas*, p.69) observes that 'the most important contribution of the early Buddhist canonists to the store of our ancient political thought consists in their "total" application of the principle of righteousness to the branches of the king's internal and foreign administration'.

[166]B.G. Gokhale ('Dhamma as a political concept in Early Buddhism', *JIH.*, Vol.46, August 1968, Pt.II, p.255) opines that 'the taming of political power constantly exercised their minds and they saw a solution to the problem through their theory of Dhamma'.

[167]S.J. Tambiah, *World Conqueror and World Renouncer,* p.40.

[168]The status of *Cakkavattī* (world ruler) was equated with that of the Tathagata. Many passages occur in the Pāli canon where a parallelism is drawn between the two. In the *Book of the Gradual Sayings* (I, p.71) it is said that two beings appear in the world for the health of many, for the good of Gods and men—the perfect awakened one and the *Cakkavatti* or universal sovereign. In the 'Mahāparinibbāna Suttanta' of the *Dīgha Nikāya* it is said that both deserve erection of relics on their bodies after their demise. See also, Lakkana Suttanta' and 'Cakkavattī-Sihanada-Suttanta' of the *Dīgha Nikāya.* For a detailed account of the Buddhist conception of kingship. See, B.G. Gokhale. 'Dhammiko Dhammaraja. A Study in Buddhist Constitutional Concepts', *Indica,* Silver jubilee commemoration volume, 1953, pp.161-65; B.G. Gokhale, 'Early Buddhist Kingship', *JAS.*, Vol.XXVI, No.1, 1966, pp.15-22; B.G. Gokhale, 'Dhamma as a Political Concept in Early Buddhism', *JIH.*, Vol.46, Aug. 1968, Pt.II, pp.249-61; B.G. Gokhale, 'The Early Buddhist View of the State', *JAOS.*, Vol.89, 1969, pp.731-38; U.N.G. 'Principles of the King's Righteousness', *Mahabodhi,* Vol.86, Nos.11-12, Nov.-Dec.1972, pp.296-301; U.N. Ghoshal, op. cit., Chaps.4, 11, 19.

and possessed of seven jewels.[169] Though the *Cakkavattī* and the Tathagata are held in esteem yet a distinction between the two has been made in many Buddhist texts. The former is designated as lord of earth and possessed of the treasure of jewels while the latter is Lord of the law, possessing the treasure of wisdom.[170] Spiritual sovereignty is highlighted in comparison to temporal sovereignty in the *Buddhacarita*.[171]

The theory and norm of *Cakkavattī* and the righteous ruler originally conceived by the Theravādins was developed by the Mahāyānists with a slight variation. With the development of the *Bodhisattva* ideal, kings were identified as *bodhisattvas*.[172] Just as a *bodhisattva* considered it his duty to work for the liberation of beings similarly the emperor felt it obligatory for himself to promote the people's welfare.[173]

The *bodhisattvas* are portrayed as rulers of Buddha fields in the *Large Sutra*[174] but contrasted with the universal monarch on account of their non-attachment to *saṁsāra*.[175]

---

[169] *Mahāvastu*, I, pp.41, 85; II, p.301.

[170] *Saddharma Puṇḍarīka* (SBE.), pp.274-75.

[171] *Buddhacarita* (trans.), pp.131-33. That the two ideals could not be combined is clear from Aśvaghosa's statement that 'as for the tradition that kings obtained final emancipation while remaining in their homes this is not the case. How can the dharma of salvation in which quietude predominates be reconciled with the dharma of kings in which severity of action predominates? If a king delights in quietude his kingdom collapses; if his mind turns to his kingdom, his quietude is ruined. For quietude and severity are incompatible, like the union of water which is cold, with fire which is hot' (Ibid., p.133).

[172] *Mahāvastu*, I, pp.41f, 84.

[173] Commenting on this Bikkhu Telwatte Rahula (*A Critical Study of the Mahavastu*, p.176) says, 'bearing in mind the fact that so much stress has been laid on the virtuous conduct and righteous rule of the *Cakravartin*, it may seem reasonable to infer that it was mainly by way of a means to guide and inspire the contemporary rulers towards a more humanitarian outlook that such enthusiastic elaborations of the advent of a righteous ruler (*dhārmikodharmarāja)* found their way into the Buddhist scripture in a legendary attire'.

A vague hint is given by Buddhaghoṣa in the *Visuddhimagga (Path of Purification*, I, p.460) where he says that since the Bodhisattva (Buddha himself) promoted other's good (*rañjeti*) righteously and equitably he was a king (*rājā*).

[174] *The Large Sutra on Perfect Wisdom* (trans.), p.176.

[175] Ibid., p.652.

Concretization of the Buddhist Ideal of State-Authority: Āśoka—A Dhammika Dhammarāja

Pāli chronicles and legends portray Aśoka as a *Dhammika Dhammarāja,* the builder of many *stūpas,* defender of Theravādin Buddhism as given in the account of the third council and as a propagator of Buddhism in India and abroad.[176] His edicts portray him as a righteous monarch, founder of a socio-moral order, propounder of a system of piety and duty who tried to provide conditions for a virtuous society in which the *Sangha* and its *Dhamma* could flourish.[177]

The Mauryan Emperor Aśoka made an attempt to combine in his person the ideal of the *Cakkavattī Dhammika Dhammarāja*[178] as portrayed in the Pāli Canon. He seems to have emulated an already set precedent of Buddha who, as a *Cakkavattī Dhammika Dhammarāja,* rules justly and righteously and resorts to use of force of his world conquest, abandoning the rod or sword only when his conquests are complete.[179] Aśoka too sought to renounce force (violence), espoused *ahiṁsa* and advocated *Dhammavijaya* only after accomplishing conquest and empire building.[180]

---

[176]*Supra.*

[177]*Infra.*

[178]S. Dutt, *BMMI.*, p.112. There occurs a prophecy of Buddha regarding Aśoka appearing as a *Cakkavattī Dhammika Dhammarāja* in the *Divyāvadāna* (BST.), pp.87-88; A Brahmi Inscription from Salihundam ascribed on paleographical grounds to the 2nd century AD reads *'Dhamma (mā) Raño Asokasirino'* of the Dharmarāja Asokasri—see, R. Subrahmanyam, op. cit., pp.121-22. In the early Buddhist literature this epithet is applied both to the Buddha and to a *Cakravartin.* It is not improbable that an ancient tradition current in the locality ascribed this epithet to Aśoka. Aśoka is represented as a *Dvipacakravartin,* i.e. Lord of the entire Jambudvipa in the *Samantapāsādikā* (I, p.84). Suddhodana is called *Dharma Cakravarti* in *Buddhacarita* (trans., p.28, fn.40).

[179]*Book of the Gradual Sayings*, IV, p.54,

[180]Kalinga Rock Edict XIII. Romila Thapar (*Aśoka and the Decline of the Mauryas*, p.168) comments that 'with the conquest of Kalinga the consolidation of the empire was complete' and that 'there was now no opposing power within the empire'.

Another similarity[181] can be traced in Aśoka's measure towards the people of outlying regions (even as far as places where kings of Syria, Egypt and Macedonia ruled) who were conquered through *Dhamma.*[182] Aśoka expresses his attruistic motives thus: "This alone is my wish with reference to the borderers, that they may learn that Devanampriya ... that they may not be afraid of me, but may have confidence in me; that they may obtain only happiness from me, not misery; that they may learn thus, that Devanampriya will forgive them what can be forgiven, that they may be induced by me to practise morality and that they may attain happiness in this world and in the other world.'[183]

There is no discussion of the doctrinal tenets of the religion still the contents of the edicts have a distinct Buddhistic flavour.[184]

---

[181]See, 'Cakkavatti Sīhanāda Sutta' of the *Dīgha Nikāya.* Even the *Mahāvastu* (I, p.41; III, p.106) pictures the Bodhisattva as a king ruling over the four continents which he had won not by violence but by righteousness.

[182]RE., II, V and XIII (Girnar. Kalsi, Shahbazgarhi, Mansehra, Dhauli).

[183]Separate Dhauli RE., II. *Contra.*, RE., XIII where Aśoka threatens the forest people that if they did not adopt his new way of life, he had the power to punish them despite his repentance.

[184]B.M. Barua (*Aśoka and his Inscriptions*, Pt.II, Chap.IV) admits that even the linguistic phraising has Buddhist parallels.

Though S. Dutt (*BMMI.*, p.110) states that 'from all these edicts discovered so far the figure of Emperor Aśoka as an enthusiast and propagandist for Buddhism scarcely emerges and (ibid., p.112) that the edicts 'show decidedly greater concern on the emperor's part with the Dhamma of his own conception than with the Dhamma founded by the Buddha and postulated by monks in scripture' still he admits that Aśoka's edicts had 'so imbibed the inner spirit of Buddhism—its charity and human heartedness, its sensitiveness to suffering, whether of men and animals, its message of peace and goodwill to all—that it breathes ineffably through the phraseology of his multi-purpose edicts' (ibid., p.110). Elsewhere (ibid., p.111) Dutt says that Aśoka's dharma shows 'the culture of fundamental social and ethical virtues' tinged by the emperor's Buddhist faith. See also. D.R. Bhandarkar, *Aśoka,* p.65; R.K. Mookerji, *Aśoka,* pp.60f.

For example, the ban against the slaughter of animals,[185] the 'grant of life to living creatures, two-footed and four-footed as well as birds and animals',[186] the *dhamma-yatras* of the king,[187] the appointment of *Dhamma-mahamatras*,[188] visit to Buddha's birth place and enlightenment,[189] following the 'middle path' in the administration of justice,[190] recommendation of certain texts for the *Saṅgha* members and the lay followers[191]—all these measures show definite Buddhistic flavour.

It is true that Aśoka's emphasis on virtues is not similar to the ethos of monks but still it was the ethos of lay Buddhism which could flourish in a just society. The principles of duty inculcated by Aśoka for the ordinary lay person is as follows:

(a) Respectful attention to parents *(mātari pitari susrūsā)*;[192]

(b) towards teachers and preceptors[193] (*guru susrūsā);*

(c) towards high personages (*agabhutasusrūsā*);[194]

(d) towards seniors or men of experience (*thaira susrūsā*,[195] *vudha-susrūsā*)[196] following their advice and waiting upon

---

[185]RE., I, XI; PE., V.

This is in confirmity with the portrayal of the ideal Buddhist ruler in the 'Cakkavatti Sihanada Sutta' of the *Dīgha Nikaya* who would provide righteous ward and protection (*rakkhāvaraṇaguttiṁ*) not only to his human subjects but to all other beings in his territory including the beasts of the forest and the birds of the air (*migapakkhisu*).

[186]RE., II: Girnar, Kalsi, Shahbazgarhi, Mansehra, Dhauli; PE., II: Delhi Topra, Delhi Mirath, Allahabad Kosam, Lauriya-Araraj, Lauriya Nandangarh, Rampurva (*Dupada chatupadesu pakhivālichalesu vividhe me anugahe kaṭe āpāna dākhināve).*

[187]RE., VIII.

[188]RE., III, V; PE., I, VII.

[189]Rummindei Pillar Edict.

[190]Ist SRE., at Jaugada and Dhauli.

[191]Calcutta Bairat Rock Inscription.

[192]RE., III, XI; PE., VII.

[193]RE., IX, XIII (Girnar, Kalsi, Shahbazgarhi, Mansehra).

[194]RE., XIII (Mansehra).

[195]RE., IV (Girnar).

[196]RE., IV (Dhauli).

them (*vayomahālakānaṃ anupatipati*,[197] *thairānaṁ vudhānaṁ dasane*);[198]

(e) towards Śramaṇas and Brahmaṇas;[199]

(f) towards friends;[200]

(g) slaves and servants;[201]

(h) non-slaughter;[202]

Further, the idea of mutual obligation in the discharge of duties by the householders is suggested by him thus—'This should be propounded by a father or a son or a brother or a husband (master) or a friend, associate or relative or even by neighbours. This is good, this should be done.'[203] 'This has a clear resonance with the Sigalovada sutta of the *Dīgha Nikāya.*

Even the aims in practising *Dhamma,* viz., 'happiness either in this world or in the next',[204] the production of merit in this world and to an unlimited degree in the next world,[205] the gaining of heaven[206] are what the ordinary householder is shown as aspiring for in the Buddhist texts.

Righteousness of *Dhamma* was implemented by the exercise of political authority. With Aśoka the supreme duty was doing good to the whole world—'*Katavyamate hi me sarvalokahitam*: *nāsti hi kaṁmataraṁ sarvalokahitātpā*,[207] since all men were like his progeny.[208]

Aśoka's principle of *uṭṭhāna* or *parākrama* (strenous exertion) sought its fulfillment through *atthasantiraṇa*—

---

[197]PE., VII (Delhi Topra).

[198]RE., VIII (Girnar).

[199]RE., III (Girnar), XI; PE., VII.

[200]RE., III (Girnar), XI.

[201]RE., IX (Girnar), XI; PE., VII.

[202]RE., III, IV, XI (Girnar, Kalsi, Shahbazgarhi, Mansehra).

[203]RE., IX (Girnar), XI.

[204]RE., XIII; PE., I; SRE., II (Dhauli).

[205]RE., XI.

[206]RE., IX.

[207]RE., VI (Girnar, Kalsi).
PE., VI (Delhi Topra).

[208]I and II SRE., (Dhauli).

'prompt dispatch of state business'.[209] He sought to promote righteousness through twofold[210] means, namely moral persuasion and state propagation of *Dhamma* through official machinery. His works of public utility were also part of the drive.

Aśoka also made a systematic effort to maintain the purity and solidarity of the Buddhist *Saṅgha.* As patron of Buddhism and head of the state he expressed his stern disapproval of schism in the Buddhist *Saṅgha* and threatened the schismatics with expulsion from the Order.[211] He empowered the laity and his state officials to act as sentinels of *Saṅgha's* unity.[212]

As leader of the empire in which the *Saṅgha* was physically located he proceeds to advice the *Saṅgha* members and the laity regarding texts which they should hear and reflect upon.[213] 'This shows nothing but his special regard for Buddhism.'[214]

Endowments

The original *Vinaya* rule that a *bhikkhu* should not dig or tell another to dig the earth became obsolete with the growth of monastic life. For the maintenance and upkeep of the Buddhist monastic establishments, regular endowments both in cash and kind became a prerequisite and were supplied throughout history by royal patrons, government officials and rich trading class. Donations of the laity were considered as *deyadhamma* (meritorious gift)—a term which occurs frequently in inscription recording their gifts to the *Saṅgha* as well as in literature. Such *dāna* was usually for the greater good of all (*Sarvasatvānaṁ hita sukhāye*, or *Sarvasatvanaṁ sukhārthaṁ*).

---

[209]RE., VI (Girnar, Kalsi, Shahbazgarhi, Mansehra, Dhauli).

[210]PE., VII (Delhi Topra).

[211]'Kauśāmbi, Sāñchi, Sārnāth Pillar Edict.

[212]Sārnāth Pillar Edict.

[213]Calcutta—Bairat Rock Inscription.

[214]B.K. Majumdar, 'Aśoka and the Buddhist Church', *JIH.*, Vol.LIV, Pt.II, Aug. 1976, p.271; See, G.S.P. Misra, *Development of Buddhist Ethics*, pp.112-17.

Aśoka, as already noticed before, was an active patron of the Buddhist faith and is known as the builder of *stūpas* all over the country.[215] Gifts were given to the monastic Order both by the *bhikkhus* and *bhikkhunis* as well as laity in the Suṅga period as is clear from the illustrations and labels at Bharhut, Sāñchī, Bodhgaya, and Sārnāth.[216]

This was followed by a glorious period of Buddhist architecture during which a large number of *Caitya* halls and *leṇas* were excavated in western India for different sects.[217] Foreign trade and rise of guilds in the first and second century AD provided the impetus for such large scale donations.[218] Most of the Buddhist rock cut establishments in western India were built during the time of the early Sātvāhana kings who happened to be staunch followers of Brahmaṇism. The credit for earliest land grants goes to the Sātvāhanas.[219]

The Śaka King Mahākṣatrapa Rājula and his queen[220] gave ample benefactions to the *Saṅgḥa* at Mathura. Patika the Kṣatrapa gave a *Saṅghārāma* in the town of Taxila. The endowments of Ushavadatta, the son-in-law of Nahapāna are well known. Rudrasena, I, the descendent of Caṣṭana built a monastery at Junagarh.[221]

Mathura was an important seat of Buddhism in the Kushāna age with King Kaniṣka as its active supporter. The Buddhist establishment at Nāgārjunikoṇḍa flourished under the Ikṣavakus. Vīrapuruṣadatta made a permanent endowment (*akshaya-nīvika*) in the form of village to one of the religious

---

[215]*Supra.*

[216]K.G. Goswami, 'Buddhism in the Sunga Period', *IHQ.*, Vol.32, Nos.2-3, 1956, pp.211-22.

[217]For details, See, K. Gopalachari, *Early History of the Andhra Country*, pp.123-25; K. Satyanarayana, *A Study of the History and Culture of the Andhras*, Vol.1, Chap.III.

[218]C.K. Gairola, 'Western Indian Guilds and International Trade in Ancient India', *JMSUB.*, Vol.XIV, No.1, April 1965, pp.1-13.

[219]R.S. Sharma, 'A Survey of Land System in Ancient India from *c.* 200 BC to AD 650', *JBRS.*, Vol.XLIV, Pts.III-IV, Sept.-Dec.1958, p.226.

[220]*CII.*, II, I, p.48.

[221]*EI.*, Vol.28, p.128.

establishment at Nāgārjunikoṇḍa probably to the Aparamahāvanaśailas.[222] Rudradhara-bhaṭṭārikā, the wife of Vīrapuruṣadatta was equally a staunch Buddhist. She got a monastery constructed called 'Devi vihara' for masters of the Bahusutiya sect.[223] Kodabalisiri consecrated to the masters of the Mahiśāsaka school a monastery and a *Caitya.*[224] The son and successor of Vīrapuruṣadatta, Ehuvula Sāntamula II erected a *vihāra.*

Fa-hien,[225] visiting India in the 5th century, noticed the Buddhist monasteries and the assets held by them. He states that 'the kings of the various countries and heads of the Vaiśyas built viharas for the priests and endowed them with fields, houses, gardens, and orchards, along with the resident populations and their cattle, the grants being engraved on plates of metal, so that afterwards they were handed down from king to king, without anyone daring to annul them, and they remain even to the present time'.

The state of things as recorded in Fa-hien's account continued even in 7th century AD as is illustrated in the development of Nālandā University. According to Hiuen tsang,[226] 'this monastery was originally a mango garden of the Śreṣṭhin Āmra. It was bought by 500 merchants for ten koṭi of gold coins and presented by them to the Buddha'. The monasteries were built successively by Śakraditya (Kumaragupta I) and his successors Buddhagupta, Tathagatagupta and Baladitya.

Regarding the remittance of revenues at Nālandā, Hiuen tsang[227] says, 'the king of the country respects and honours the priests, and has remitted the revenues of about 100 villages for the endowment of the convent. Two hundred householders in

---

[222]*EI.*, Vol.34, pp.210-12.

[223]K. Gopalachari, op. cit., p.148.

[224]Ibid.

[225]J. Legge, op. cit., p.43.

[226]T. Watters, op. cit., II, pp.164-65; S. Beal, op. cit., p.110.

[227]S. Beal, op. cit., pp.112-13.

these villages, day by day, contribute several hundred piculs of ordinary rice, and several hundred catties in weight of butter and milk. Hence the students here, being so abundantly supplied, do not require to ask for the four requisites'.

I-tsing who visited India in the 7th century AD observed that 'Indian monasteries possess special allotments of land'.[228] About the monastery at Nālandā in particular he states—'the land in its possession contains more than 200 villages. They have been bestowed upon the monastery by kings of many generations'.[229] Among the royal patrons[230] of Nālandā *vihāra* during our period mention may be made of Emperor Harṣavardhana, Pūraṇavarman of Magadha, Bhāskaravarman of Kāmarūpa and King Aṃsuvarman of Nepal in the seventh century AD.

Lavish endowments were made by the Maitrakas of Valabhi in the 6th and 7th century.[231] Harṣavardhana constructed one of the largest monasteries at Nālandā and built the boundary wall round the whole establishment.[232] He offered the revenue of 800 large towns in Orissa for the scholar Jayasena.[233] His charities at Prayāga are well known. In the session attended by Hiuen-tsang at Prayāga, Harṣa had invited 10,000 Buddhist monks, each of whom received 100 gold pieces, one pearl, one cotton garment, sumptuous meals, flowers and perfumes.[234]

Donors

An analysis of the list of donors, mostly lay worshippers *(upāsakās* and *upāsikās),* makes it clear that it was cosmopolitan in character. It includes the following—

---

[228] J. Takakusu, op. cit., p.193.

[229] Ibid., p.65.

[230] H. Heras, 'The Royal Patrons of the University of Nalanda'. *JBORS.*, XIV, Pt.I, March 1928, pp.13-20.

[231] Krishna Kumari Virji, op. cit., pp.172-73.

[232] T. Watters, op. cit., II, 165.

[233] S . Beal, op. cit., p.154.

[234] Ibid., pp.184-187.

(a) Kings, prince *(kumāra)* and their relatives;[235]

(b) Feudatories *(mahābhojas* and the *mahāraṭhis* with their relatives and servants);[236]

(c) Royal officials:

  (1) Amacas[237] *(amātyas,* ministers);

  (2) *Heraṇikas*[238] (treasurers);

  (3) *Rājalipikara*[239] (royal scribe),

(d) Trading and professional classes—

  (1) *Vānija*[240] *(vaṇika),* negamas,[241] sathavāhas;[242]

  (2) *Mālakāras*[243] (gardeners);

  (3) *Kamāras*[244] (blacksmiths);

  (4) *Maṇikāras*[245] (jewellers);

---

[235]*Lüders list,* Nos.1072—Mahāḍ Buddhist Cave Inscription; 1099—Kārle Buddhist Cave Inscription of Ushavadata; 1105—Kārle Buddhist Cave Inscription of Gautamiputra Satakarṇi; 1123—Nāsik Buddhist Cave Inscription of the time of Vasisthiputra Sri Pulumavi, Ibid., 1124, 1125, 1126—Nāsik Buddhist Cave Inscription of Gautamiputra Satkarṇi; 1131—Nāsik Buddhist Cave Inscription of Ushavadatta; Sāñchī Stone Inscription of Chandragupta II—*CII.*, III, pp.31-32.

[236]*Lüders list,* Nos.1079—Bhājā Buddhist Cistern Inscription: 1088—Karle Buddhist Lion Pillar Inscription; 1037—Kuda Buddhist Cave Inscription.

[237]*Lüders list,* Nos.994—Kāṇherī Buddhist Inscription of the time of Vasisthiputra pulumavi; 1174—Junnar Buddhist Cave Inscription of the time of Nahapana; 1141—Nāsik Buddhist Cave Inscription of the time of Kanha of Sātavāhana family.

[238]*Lüders list,* Nos.996—Kāṇherī Buddhist Tank Inscription; 1033—Kānherī Buddhist Stone Inscription; 1179—Junnar Buddhist Cave Inscription.

[239]Ibid., No.271—Sāñchi Buddhist Stupa I Inscription.

[240]Ibid.. Nos.269, 320, 355—Sāñchi Buddhist Stupa I Inscription; 987—Kāṇherī Buddhist Cave Inscription of the time of Gautamiputra: 1198—Ajantā Cave Inscription.

[241]Ibid., Nos.995—Kāṇherī Buddhist Tank Inscription: 999, 1000, 1001—Kāṇherī Buddhist Cave Inscription; 1024—Ibid., of the time of Gautamiputra Satkarṇi, 1127, 1139—Nāsik Buddhist Cave Inscription of the time of Gautamiputra Satakarni.

[242]Ibid., Nos.1062, 1066—Kuda Buddhist Cave Inscription.

[243]Ibid., Nos.1051, 1061—Kuda Buddhist Cave and Tank Inscription.

[244]Ibid., 1032—Kāṇherī Detached Rock Inscription.

[245]Ibid., 1005—Kāṇherī Buddhist Cave Inscription.

(5) *Suvarṇakāras*[246](goldsmiths);
(6) *Lohavāṇiyas*[247] (iron-mongers),
(7) *Vānika*[248] (musician);
(8) *Sotika*[249] (weaver);
(9) *Āvêsanin*[250] (artisan);
(10) *Vaḍhakin*[251] (carpenter);
(11) *Seṭhin* [252] (banker);
(12) *Rupakāraka*[253] (sculptor);
(13) *Veja*[254] (physician);
(14) *Gaṁdhika*[255] (perfumer);
(15) *Chaṁmakara*[256] (leather worker),
(16) *Sêla-vaḍhakin*[257] (stone masons);
(17) *Miṭhika*[258] (polisher);
(18) *Dhaṁñika*[259] (corn dealers);
(19) *Lekhaka*[260] (clerk);
(20) *Rajuka*[261] (surveyor);

---

[246]Ibid., Nos.986—Kāṇherī Buddhist Cave Inscription; 1177—Junnar Buddhist Cistern Inscription.

[247]Ibid., No.1055—Kuda Buddhist Cave Inscription.

[248]Ibid., Nos.280, 532—Sāñchī Buddhist Stupa I Inscription.

[249]Ibid., No.331—Sāñchi Buddhist Stupa I Inscription.

[250]Ibid., Nos.346; 1202—Jagayyapêṭa Buddhist Pillar Inscription.

[251]Ibid., Nos.495—Sāñchi Buddhist Stūpa I Inscription; 1092—Kārle Buddhist Pillar Inscription.

[252]Ibid., Nos.248, 339, 363, 379, 470—Sāñchī Buddhist Stupa I Inscription; 1056, 1064—Kuda Buddhist Tank Inscription; 1075—Kol Buddhist Cave Inscription; 1087—Kārle Buddhist Cave Inscription.

[253]Ibid., No.345—Sāñchī Buddhist Stupa I Inscription.

[254]Ibid., No.1048—Kuda Buddhist Cave Inscription.

[255]Ibid., No.1090—Kārle Buddhist Cave Inscription.

[256]Ibid., Appendix 1273—Amarāvati Buddhist Sculpture Inscription.

[257]Reference to the term *Sêla-Kaṁmaṁta* (stonework) occurs in the Bharhut Buddhist Inscription—Ibid., No.687. The term *Sêla-vadhakin* occurs in Kāṇherī Buddhist Cave Inscription—Ibid., No.967.

[258]Ibid., No.987.

[259]Ibid., No.1180—Junnar Buddhist Cave Inscription.

[260]Ibid., No.209—Sāñchī Buddhist Stupa I Inscription.

[261]Ibid., No.416.

(e) *General*

(1) The four *Varṇas* (Brahmaṇas,[262] Kshtriyas,[263] Vaiśyas[264] and Śudras[265]);

(2) Sakas,[266] Yavanas[267];

(3) Gahapatis[268] (householders);

(4) *Kamika*[269] (labourers);

(5) *Dāsakas*[270] (fishermen);

(f) Buddhist religieux:

Bhikkhus,[271] *pavajitas*,[272] *theras*,[273] *ācāryas*.[274] Donations were made not only by single individuals families but also by corporate groups[275] such as a whole town *(dharmanigama* or *gāma)* or a guild *(seṇi)*.

---

[262]Ibid., Nos.1035—Mahakal Cave Inscription; 1050—Kuda Buddhist Cave Inscription, etc.

[263]Ibid., No.987—Kāṇherī Buddhist Cave Inscription of the time of Gautamiputra Satkarṇi.

[264]Ibid.

[265]Ibid., No.1151—Junnar Buddhist Cave Inscription.

[266]Ibid., Nos.1148—Nāsik Buddhist Cave Inscription; 1149—Nāsik Buddhist Cistern Inscription; 1162—Junnar Buddhist Cave Inscription.

[267]Ibid., Nos.1093, 1096—Kārle Buddhist Pillar Inscription; 1154, 1156, 1182—Junnar Buddhist Cave Inscription.

[268]Ibid., Nos.1001—Kāṇherī Buddhist Cave Inscription of the time of Svami Sakasena; 1056, 1062—Kuda Buddhist Tank Inscription; 1120—Nanāghāt Cistern Inscription of the time of Vasisthiputra pulumavi; 1121—Śailārwādi Buddhist Cave Inscription; 1127—Nāsik Buddhist Cave Inscription; 1121, 1147—Nāsik Buddhist Cave Inscription of the time Vasisthiputra Pulumavi; 1170—Junnar Buddhist Cave Inscription.

[269]Ibid., No.181—Sāñchī Buddhist Stupa I Inscription.

[270]Ibid., No.1129—Nāsik Buddhist Cave Inscription.

[271]Ibid., Nos.990—Kāṇherī Buddhist Image Inscription; 1046, 1047—Kuda Buddhist Cave Inscription; 1101, 1102—Kārle Buddhist Cave Inscription.

[272]Ibid., Nos.999, 1016—Kāṇherī Buddhist Cave Inscription; 1108—Karle Buddhist Cave Inscription.

[273]Ibid., No.1089—Kārle Buddhist Cave Inscription.

[274]Ibid., No.992—Kāṇherī Buddhist Cave Inscription.

[275]Ibid., Nos.1142—Nāsik Buddhist Cave Inscription; 1153, 1180—Junnar Buddhist Cave Inscription.

Women Donors

(1) Queen;[276]
(2) Queen mother;[277]
(3) Daughter of raja;[278]
(4) Daughters of royal ministers;[279]
(5) Daughters of *mahābhojas*[280] and *mahārathis;*[281]
(6) Wives of treasures,[282] *mahasenāpatis*[283] and royal physicians;[284]
(7) Wives of *sarthavahas,*[285] *sethins,*[286] *hālakiyas,*[287] brahmaṇas.[288]
(8) Wives or daughters and sisters of *gahapatis.*[289]
(9) Nuns *(theris),*[290] *pavayitikas*[291], *bhikkunis,*[292] *atevāsinis.*[293]

---

[276]*Supra.*

[277]*Lüders list,* No.1123—Nāsik Buddhist Cave Inscription of the time of Vasisthiputra Pulumavi.

[278]Ibid., No.1132 of the time of Ushavadatta.

[279]Ibid., Nos.1141; 1053—Kuda Buddhist Cave Inscription.

[280]Ibid., Nos.1054; 1111—Bedsā Buddhist Cistern Inscription.

[281]Ibid., No.1021—Kāṇherī Buddhist Cave Inscription.

[282]Ibid., No.993.

[283]Ibid., No.1146—Nāsik Buddhist Cave Inscription.

[284]Ibid., No.1192—Pitalkhora Buddhist Cave Inscription.

[285]Ibid., No.1065—Kuda Buddhist Cave Inscription.

[286]Ibid., Nos.206, 207, 423—Sāñchī Buddhist Stupa I Inscription.

[287]Ibid., Nos.1084—Bhajā Buddhist Cave Inscriptions; 1121—Śailarwāḍi Buddhist Cave Inscription.

[288]Ibid., No.1050—Kuda Buddhist Cave Inscription.

[289]Ibid., Nos.1018—Kāṇherī Buddhist Cave Inscription; 1043—Kuda Buddhist Cave Inscription; 1073—Kol Buddhist Cave Inscription: 1091—Karle Buddhist Pillar Inscription; Mathura Stone Image Inscription of Gupta Era 135—*CII.*, III, p.263.

[290]*Lüders list,* No.1006—Kuda Buddhist Cave Inscription.

[291]Ibid., Nos.1020—Kāṇherī Buddhist Cave Inscription; 1041, 1060—Kuda Buddhist Cave Inscription; 1128—Nasik Buddhist Cave Inscription.

[292]Ibid., Nos.1014—Kāṇherī Buddhist Cave Inscription: 1098, 1104—Karle Buddhist Cave Inscription.

[293]Ibid., No.1107—Kārle Buddhist Cave Inscription.

Forms of Donations

Donations offered to the Buddhist *Saṅgha* were meant to meet the needs of the monks—individual as well as corporate. The various donations can be classified as follows—

(I) (a) *Vihāras* or *Saṅghārāmas*[294]

(b) Complete caves mentioned as *Guhā, Leṇa, Selaghara,* donated at Kāṇherī,[295] Kuda,[296] Mahad,[297] Kol,[298] Kārle,[299] Kondane,[300] Bedsā,[301] Nāsik,[302] Junnar,[303] Karhad[304] and Pitalkhora.[305]

(c) Two-celled cave (*bigabha leṇa*) donated at Junnar[306] and Kāṇherī.[307]

(d) Four-celled cave (*catugabha leṇa*) at Nāsik.[308]

(e) Five-celled cave *(paṁcagabha leṇa*) at Junnar.[309]

(f) Seven-celled cave *(satagabha leṃa*) at Junnar.[310]

(g) Nine-celled cave (*navagabha leṇa*) at Kārle.[311]

(h) Single-celled mentioned as *ovaraka* or *gabha* were

---

[294]*Viharas* or *Saṅghārāmas* were donated by kings, royal officials, kshatrapas, and rich merchant classes throughout history.

[295]*Lüders list,* Nos.959, 992, 997, 998, 1000, 1001, 1005, 1007, 1008, 1010, 1012, 1016, 1017, 1018, 1024, 1026. 1027.

[296]Ibid., Nos.1037-46, 1051-55,1062.

[297]Ibid., No.1072.

[298]Ibid., Nos.1075, 1077.

[299]Ibid., Nos.1087, 1108

[300]Ibid., No.1071.

[301]Ibid., No.1109.

[302]Ibid., Nos.1128, 1129, 1130.

[303]Ibid., Nos.1152, 1155, 1172, 1175.

[304]Ibid., No.1184.

[305]Ibid., Nos.1189-93.

[306]Ibid., No.1169.

[307]Ibid., No.998.

[308]Ibid., No.1127.

[309]Ibid., No.1157.

[310]Ibid., No.1180.

[311]Ibid., No.1106.

made at Kāṇherī,[312] Kuda,[313] Ajantā,[314] Nāsik[315] and Bhājā.[316]

(II) Gifts of *Caitya*-caves or halls mentioned as *'Cetiya-ghara' 'Caitya', 'Cetiakodhi';* these were made at Kāṇherī,[317] Kuda,[318] Mahad,[319] Nāsik,[320] Junnar,[321] Kuda,[322] Shelawardi.[323] A *bodhisattva* chapel was donated at Taxila.[324]

(III) Halls *(maṭapas-koḍhi)* dinning halls or refectories *(bhôjan chātu sālā* or *bhojana maṭapa),* reception halls *(upaṭhana sālā)* were donated at Kāṇherī,[325] Junnar[326] and Kārle.[327]

(IV) Water-cisterns, water-halls, tanks, wells, etc., mentioned as *pāṇiyaka, pāṇiya-bhajana, poḍhi, pāniya-poḍhi, saṇāna-podhi, nhāna poḍhi, vāpi, taḍāka, prapa* were donated at Kāṇherī,[328] Kuda,[329] Mahad,[330] Bhājā,[331] Nāsik,[332] Junnar,[333] Kārle,[334] Bedsā[335] and Tor Ḍherai.[336]

---

[312]Ibid., Nos.988, 1018.
[313]Ibid., No.1058.
[314]Ibid., No.1198.
[315]Ibid., Nos.1127, 1132.
[316]Ibid., No.1078.
[317]Ibid., Nos.987, 988.
[318]Ibid., No.1058.
[319]Ibid., No.1072.
[320]Ibid., No.1140.
[321]Ibid., Nos.1153, 1179, 1183.
[322]Ibid., Nos.1050, 1073.
[323]*EI.*, XXVIII, p.77.
[324]Peshawar Museum inscription of year 168—*CII.*, II, Pt.I, p.77.
[325]*Lüders list*, Nos.998, 988, 1007.
[326]Ibid., Nos.1174, 1182.
[327]Ibid., No.1106.
[328]Ibid., Nos.986, 994-98, 1000, 1006, 1007, 1013, 1014, 1016, 1018.
[329]Ibid., Nos.1039, 1041, 1056, 1061, 1064.
[330]Ibid., No.1072.
[331]Ibid., No.1079.
[332]Ibid., Nos.1140, 1148, 1149.
[333]Ibid., Nos.1150, 1152, 1154, 1155, 1173, 1180, 1176.
[334]Ibid., No.1107.
[335]Ibid., No.1111.
[336]Tor Ḍherai Inscription—*CII.*, II, I, p.176,

(V) Frontages of caves mentioned as *'ghara-mukha'*, *'gabhadāra'* were donated at Junnar,[337] Kārle[338] and Ajantā.[339]

(VI) Verandahs or a passage or path mentioned by the words *'cakama' (caṁkrama)* and *'patha'* were donated at Kāṇherī[340] and Mahad.[341]

(VII) (a) *Stūpas*[342]as such or for enshrining Buddha image.

(b) *Stūpas* in the form of memorials to the mortal remains of reputed Buddhist teachers were donated at Bhājā,[343] Bedsā[344] and Kāṇherī.[345]

(VIII) Miscellaneous objects:

(a) Images of Buddhas and Bodhisattvas at Mathura,[346] Deoria[347] Sahêṭh-Mahêṭh,[348] Sār-nāth,[349] Bodh Gaya,[350] Kuda,[351] and Kāṇherī.[352]

(b) Figures of elephants *(hathin)* at Kārle.[353]

(c) *Yakṣa (Yakha)* at Nāsik.[354]

(d) Two pair of flgures[355] at Kārle.

337*Lüders list*, No.1156.

338Ibid., Nos.1090, 1092.

339Ibid., No.1197.

340Ibid., Nos.998, 1032, 1033.

341Ibid., No.1072.

342Taxila Meridarkh Inscription—*CII.*, II, I, p.5; Taxila Vase Inscription—Ibid., p.87.

343*Lüders list*, Nos.1080-83, 1085.

344Ibid., No.1110.

345Ibid., No.993.

346Ibid., Nos.38, 43, 138, 146-49. Also, Mathura Stone Inscription of year 135-*CII.*, III, p.263.

347Ibid., No.911.

348Ibid., Nos.918, 919.

349Ibid., No.925.

350Ibid., No.950.

351Ibid., No.1047.

352Ibid., Nos.989, 990.

353Ibid., No.1089.

354Ibid., No.1143.

355Ibid., No.1101.

(e) Stone benches and seats mentioned as '*āsana-peḍhikā*' and '*sata* (?)' at, Kāṇherī.[356]

(f) Rail or *Vedikā* (*veika, veyika*) at Mathura,[357] Sonari,[358] Kārle,[359] Nāsik[360] and Amarāvati.[361]

(g) Wheel of enlightemnent (*Dharmacakra*) at Amarāvati.[362]

(h) Foot prints at Amarāvati.[363]

(i) Slab *(paṭa)* at Amarāvati.[364]

(j) Umbrella (*chhātra*) at Sahêth-Mahêth,[365] Sārnāth,[366] and Amarāvati.[367]

(k) Staff (*daṇḍa*) at Sahêth-Mahêth[368]

(l) *Vajrāsana* (Lion seat) at Bodhgaya[369] and Amarāvati.[370]

(m) Ghee lamps (*Pradipa*) at Bodhgaya,[371] Sārnāth[372] Taxila.[373]

(n) *Caitya* slabs at Amarāvati.[374]

(o) Caskets at Bhaṭṭiprôlu.[375]

356Ibid., Nos.985, 998.

357Ibid., No.125.

358Ibid., Nos.154, 155.

359Ibid., Nos.1089, 1103, 1104.

360Ibid., No.1143.

361Ibid., No.1216.

362J. Burgess, *The Buddhist Stupas of Amaravati and Jagayyapeta*, p.100.

363*Lüders list*, Nos.1209, 1219, 1225.

364Ibid., Nos.1213, 1215, 1216, 1226. Slab with footprints (*padukapaṭa*) at Amaravati—Ibid., No.1217.

365Ibid., Nos.918, 919.

366Ibid., No.925.

367Ibid., No.1276.

368*Lüders list*, Nos.918, 919.

369Ibid., No.950.

370Ibid., No.1223.

371Ibid., No.950.

372Ibid., Nos.1430, 1431, 1448.

373Dharmarajika Vihara Inscription at Taxila—*CII.*, II, I, p.90.

374Ibid., No.1225.

375Ibid., Nos.1330, 1338.

(p) Crystal boxes at Bhaṭṭiprôlu.[376]
(q) Pillars (*thabha*) at Bharhut,[377] Sāñchī[378] and Jamalgarhi.[379]
(r) Pillar for lamps (*divatha* [*bha*]) at Amarāvati.[380]
(s) Base of pillar (*kuṁbhaka*) at Mathura.[381]
(t) Entrance pillars at Jagayyapêṭa.[382]
(u) Caitya pillars at Amarāvati.[383]
(v) Lion pillars at Karle.[384]
(w) Arches (*toraṇa*) at Mathura[385] and Bharhut.[386]
(x) Coping stone (*unisa*) at Bharhut[387] and Amarāvati.[388]
(y) Base stone (*ālabana*) at Sārnāth.[389]
(z) Upright slabs (*udhapaṭa*) at Amarāvati.[390]
(za) Vase at Wardak.[391]
(zb) Jars at Palaṭu Ḍheri.[392]
(zc) Copper ladle at Taxila[393] and Bedadi.[394]

(IX) Donation of fields and villages are recorded in the

---

[376]Ibid.

[377]Ibid., Nos.712, 715, 716-21, 729, 758-59, 762-63, 766-68, 772, 733, 782, 798, 778-79, 792, 796, 799, 800, 803-04, 805.

[378]Ibid., Nos.585, 589, 611.

[379]Jamalgarhi Pilaster Base Inscription—*CII.*, II, I, p.115.

[380]*Lüders list*, No.1244 (*divakhaṁbha*).

[381]Ibid., Nos.40, 61, 62, 64, 122, 129, 139, 144, Appendix 1410-16.

[382]Ibid., No.1202.

[383]Ibid., Nos.1210, 1229.

[384]Ibid., No.1088.

[385]Ibid., No.125.

[386]Ibid., Nos.687, 688, 689.

[387]Ibid., No.690.

[388]Ibid., Nos.1221, 1225.

[389]Ibid., No.1423.

[390]Ibid., Appendix Nos.1235, 1243, 1262, 1271, 1272.

[391]Wardak Vase Inscription of year 51—*CII.*, II. I, p.170.

[392]Pālāṭu Ḍheri Jars Inscription—Ibid, pp.121-22.

[393]Taxila Copper Ladle Inscription—Ibid., p.88.

[394]Bedadi Copper Ladle Inscription—Ibid., p.89.

inscriptions at Kāṇherī,[395] Kārle,[396] Nāsik,[397] Junnar,[398] Mahad[399] and Sāñchī.[400] Donation of town occurs in an inscription at Bharhut.[401]

(X) Monetary Donation may be divided into two broad classes—

---

[395]*Lüders list*, Nos.1000 Endowment of a field in the village for the support of and repairs of the porch (*meṭapa*) and the *pavāḍa* (?) monks; 1024 (Endowment with) money and fields of a half-*paṇa*-owner (*ādha paṇa khetiya*) in the village of Magalathāna (Maṅgalasthana). Also Nos.1158, 1163, 1164, 1166, 1167.

[396]Ibid., Nos.1100 (Gift of a village (*gāma*) to the community (*sagha*) *of* Valūraka lena; 1105 (gift of the village of Karajaka in the Māmāla district (āhāra) on the northern road as monk's land (*bhikhu* hala) to the *pavajita bhikhus* dwelling in the Vāluraka *lena* for the support of the Mahasāṅghikas.

[397]Ibid., Nos.1123 (for the embellishment of the cave, the queen's grandson, lord of Dakshiṇāpatha granted the village of Piśāchipadraka on the S.W. side of amount Trirasmi); 1124 (gift of the village Sālmalipadra on the eastern road in the Gôvadhana āhara to the *bhikkhus* of the *nikāya* of Bhadrāyaṇiyas dwelling in the dêvilena, in exchange for the village of Sudarśana on the southern road in the Gôvadhana āhara formerly given to the same monks for repairs of the cave); 1125 (conferring of a field in the village of Aparakakhaḍiya up to the present time enjoyed by Ṛshabhadatta, on the Trairśmika? ascetics (*pavajita*); 1126 (gift of a field within the boundaries of the town (*nagara*) to the Trairaśmika monks instead of a field at the village of Kakhaḍi formerly given); 1130 (gift of a field in western kaṇhahini to this cave for providing clothes to the *bhikkhus*); 1131 (donation of a field to the *bhikhusagha* of the 4 Quarters); 1142 (gift of the village of Dhambhika of Nāsikakas).

[398]Ibid., No.1158 (Gift of a certain field in the village of Puvānada by Palapa and investment of the income from the field with the school of the Apajitas); 1163 (in the village of Mahāveja, a field for the planting of Jambu trees entrusted to the holy assembly (? Sidhjaṇa) of the Aparajitas; to the east of Mount Mānamukaḍa, another field for a plantation of palmyra trees; within the boundaries of the town (*nagarasimaṇ*) a third field for sāla trees (?); 1164 (a field for the planting of mango trees); 1166 (in the village of Valāhaka a field for the plantation of Karanja trees; another field in the village of Sêuraka); 1167 (a field in western (? āvarila) Vasarikhaḍaka. A field in western (? āvarila)—in western (? avarila)—a field for the plantation of Jambu trees. A field in the village of Koḍaka.

[399]Ibid., No.1073.

[400]Ibid., Nos.195, 571, 625. Also Sāñchī Stone Inscription of Chandragupta II of the year 93—*CII.*, III, pp.31-32.

[401]*Lüders list*, No.705.

(a) Payment by the donor of the cost of some part of the construction such as pillar or repairs as at Kāṇherī.[402] Payment could also be made for feeding *bhikṣus* and maintaining lamps.[403]

(b) Perpetual endowments *(akṣayanīvi)* in the form of money deposited either with the *Saṅgha* or with the various guilds out of which or from the interest of which, the needs of the monks were to be met, are recorded in the inscriptions at Kāṇherī,[404] Nāsik,[405] Junnar,[406] Mahad[407] and Nāgārjunikoṇḍa.[408]

(XI) Miscellaneous donations such as coconut trees, etc., recorded in the inscriptions at Nāsik.[409]

Household Life Contrasted with Monastic Life: Exaltation of the Monastic Ideal

A survey of the entire Buddhist literature makes it clear that

---

[402]Ibid., No.1000.

[403]Sāñchī Stone Inscription of Gupta Era 93—*CII.*, III, pp.31-32; Sāñchī Stone Inscription of Gupta Era 131—ibid., p.261.

[404]*Lüders list,* Nos.998, 999, 1006, 1007, 1016, 1024.

[405]Ibid., Nos.1133 (endowment of money to the *catuddisa Saṅgha.* Money was invested in two weaver's guilds (srêṇi, kôlikanikaya at Govardhana): 1135, 1137, (money was invested with the guilds of the potters (? kularika), the workers fabricating hydraulic engines (*ôdayaṁtrika*), the oil millers (*tilapishaka*); 1139 (gift of cloth money to the *pavaita* (ascetic).

[406]Ibid., Nos.1152, 1155, 1165 (investment of money with the *sêṇi* (guild) of bamboo-workers (*vasakara*) and the *sêṇ*i of braziers (*kāsākara*).

[407]Ibid., No.1073 (endowments of certain fields (*chheta*) situated below the *caves*).

[408]Certain fragmentary inscriptions from Nāgārjunikoṇḍa refer to the perpetual endowment (*akṣaya-nivikā*) in the form of village to one of the religious establishments at Nāgārjunikoṇḍa—probably of the Aparamahā-vanaśailas. The same inscription refers to a second endowment whose money amounting to 150 *dināri-māsakas* was deposited with a kulika, 'the chief or head of a guild. See, *EI*, XXXIV, pp.210-11.

[409]Ibid., No.1133.

monastic life is viewed as the superior state.[410] One has, therefore, to agree with Frithjof Schuon's remark that 'the spiritual edifice of Buddhism has at its base a message of renunciation'.[411] Though Mahāyānism made an attempt to place the laity on the same footing as the members of the *Saṅgha,* still it is clear from a careful perusal of the entire Buddhist literature that monastic celibacy and seclusion are highlighted and domestic life is considered an inferior state,[412] a life incompatible with the practice of the entire set of *pāramitās*[413] and the attainment of *Bodhi.*

The *Milindapañho* referring to the householder's state as the lower state[414] says—'that if a layman, a disciple of the faith, who has entered upon the excellent way, should attain to

---

[410]The Pāli Canon is replete with such instances. To quote only a few:

(a) 'Monks, there are two pleasures. What two? That of home, and that of home leaving—Of these two pleasures that of home-leaving has the pre-eminence'—(*Book of the Gradual Sayings*, I, p.74);

(b) Ānanda (*Dīgha Nikāya*, I, p.171) and Kassapa (*Book of the Kindred Sayings*, II, p.148) seem to utter the same statements when they remark that household life is congested dirty abode and the life of a monk is free like the open sky;

(c) The *Sutta Nipāta* praises homelessness in comparison to secular society which binds men to its pleasures, where happiness is temporary and deliverance is impossible—*Aṭṭhānataṁ Saṁgaṇikāratassa yam phassaye sāmayikaṁ vimuttim* (Khaggavisāṇa sutta', v.54); *'Sango eso parittamettha sokhyaṁ appassādo dukkhamettha bhiyyo'* (ibid., v.61); *'Santhavāto bhavaṁ jātaṁ niketā jāyate rajo, aṁketaṁ asanthavaṁ etaṁ ve munidassanaṁ* ('Muni sutta', v.209):

(d) Therefore stresses the *Dhammapada* (v.290) that if by forsaking a lesser happiness one may behold a great happiness, let the wise man renounce the lesser considering the geater—*'mattā-sukhapariccāgā passe ce vipulaṁ sukham caje mattā-sukhaṁ dhiro sampassaṁ vipulaṁ sukham'*.

[411]Frithjof Schuon, *In the Tracks of Buddhism,* pp.117-18.

[412]Hardayal, op. cit., p.223.

[413]The *Bodhisattvabhūmi* (ed., Chap.XIII) mentions both laymen and monks in connection with the first four pāramitas, but it does not refer to the layman in the Chapter on *dhyāna.*

[414]*The Questions of King Milinda*, II, p.63.

the realization of Arhatship one of the two results must happen to him, and there is no other—he must either die away on that very day, or taken upon himself the condition of a *bhikkhu*. For immovable, O King, is that state of renunciation, glorious and most exalted—I mean the condition of being a member of the Order'[415] and further, 'But nevertheless, O King, it is the recluse who is the Lord and master of the fruit of renunciation and renunciation of the world, O King, is full of gains, many and immeasurable are its advantages, its profit no one can calculate.'[416]

In the *Saddharma Puṇḍarīka,* Buddha says that he had imparted training to *bodhisattvas* who were continuously engaged in studies and concentration of thoughts and who avoided contact with worldly objects, applied energy and were fond of solitude.[417] The *bodhisattvas* are enjoined to remain away from females and householders and to approach them only for teaching purposes.[418]

The *Mahāvastu,* by stressing the futility and vanity of sensual pleasures,[419] stresses 'going forth'. 'Those who are devoted to endeavour, their minds intent on what is good, those who have withdrawn from the world as Gotama taught them, win the highest gain, pass to immortality and with their hearts liberated enjoy complete bliss.[420]

Even the *Suhṛllekha*,[421] written by Nagarjuna to king Gautamiputra, emphasizes the production of revulsion for *Saṁsāra* which is impermanent and without essence. Renunciation is essential in order to practice *Dharma* with the thought of attaining liberation. The *Jātakamālā* distinctly

---

[415]Ibid., I, p.233.

[416]Ibid., II, p.58.

[417]*Saddharma Puṇḍarīka Sūtra* (BST.), p.185.

[418]Ibid., p.166.

[419]*Mahāvastu*, II, pp.212, 303; III, p.417.

[420]Ibid., I, p.244.

[421]*Nāgārjuna's letter to king Gautamīputra* (trans.), pp.38ff.

favour monastic life. Kṣāntivādin[422] and Ayogṛha[423] think that virtue cannot proliferate in home life—a life associated with love of pleasure, jealously, anger and pride. Agastya[424] condemns the householder's life as undesirable. In the Aputra-Jātaka,[425] Aryasūra admits that a layman in order to earn wealth could neglect certain moral precepts. A home is always infested with the serpents named sensuality, pride and infatuation.

The Large Sūtra on Perfect Wisdom makes a distinction between foolish common people who lean on duality and become attached to conditioned things[426] while the *bodhisattvas* though firmly anchored in society, stand in void, because they have well attended to the emptiness of the essential original nature.[427] Such *bodhisattvas* are neither delighted by gain nor dejected by loss, pleasure and pain are alike to them. They who thus are not attracted by the things of the world, are said to know the void.

The *Bodhisattvabhūmi*,[428] while making a distinction between *gṛhi* (lay) and *pravrajita* (recluse) *bodhisattvas,* exalts the latter's status. He is described as one who is *parimukta,* celibate, knower of *Bodhipakṣya dharmas,* welcomes and follows rules and practices. The *Daśabhūmika Sūtra*[429] states that a *bodhisattva* becomes a monk in the very first stage of his career.

The *Śikṣāsamuccaya* enjoins on the *bodhisattva* to renounce the world in all existences.[430] He is asked to shun society since pride laughter and wranglings are found in

---

422 *Jātakamālā* (BST.), p.189.
423 Ibid., p.239.
424 Ibid., p.36.
425 Ibid., pp.111-13.
426 *The Large Sūtra on Perfect Wisdom*, pp.531, 592
427 Ibid., pp.14, 399.
428 *Bodhisattvabhūmi* (ed.), p.213.
429 Quoted, Hardayal, op. cit., pp.222, 285-86.
430 *Śikṣāsamuccaya* (trans.), p.15.

society.[431] 'No son nor daughter has he [the true Bodhisattva], nor no wife; no friend has he, no troop of kinsmen; he has neither man-servant nor maid-servant nor any to exercise lordship over: therefore make no strife when once ye have forsaken the world.'[432]

'If he desires to bring to nought all hindrances of action, be must delight in the absence of society, living in the remote parts of the forest.'[433] The 'Akshyamati Sutra' mentions avoiding society and rejoicing in solitude[434] among conditions conductive to 'inward peace': The same *sūtra*[435] emphasizes avoiding society in order to accomplish righteousness.

Praising forest seclusion, the 'Candrapradipa Sūtra' states:[436] 'Never indeed shall one obtain the supreme and highest wisdom if he follows his lusts, with attachment to sons and wife and follows the household life which he ought to loathe. They who avoid lust like a fire of cowdung, without attachment to sons and wife, and terrified flee from the household life; not hard to get for them is that highest wisdom ...'

It is thus clear from the fore going passages that household life was considered culpable. Perfection was possible by rejecting societal relations and only in the framework of monastic renunciation. In a sense, spiritual life was identified with monastic life.

---

[432]Ibid., p.113.
[433]Ibid., p.114.
[434]Ibid., p.118.
[435]Ibid., p.186.
[436]Ibid., p.188.

CHAPTER 6

Existing Monastic Remains: Form and Structure

Ravages of time and men have destroyed most of the monasteries of India. The foundations of some of them have been unearthed by archaeologists. Much scholarly work has been done on monastic architecture. Here an attempt is made to study the three important structures inevitably associated with the monastic complex namely—the residential *vihāra* with its essential adjuncts, the *stūpa* and the *caityagṛha*. The entire development of the monastic establishment was influenced by several factors such as lay patronage and ideological set up of the various sects.

Structural Vihāras

Excavations at different sites have shown that a monastery site was rarely abandoned. The original structure got buried under layers of successive construction.[1] Hardly any vestiges of monasteries of BC centuries have been discovered so far. The earliest beginnings can be seen in the second monastery at Kumrahar which included a long hall (21.5m × 9.2m) with a series of rooms on its east and west.[2] Archaeological

[1]Sārnāth has yielded a monastic complex ascribed to Gupta times. But under this foundation are ruins of Kushāna buildings. The first beginnings might have been in BC centuries as is clear from the Pillar Inscription of Aśoka addressed to the monk community regarding measures to be taken against monks or nuns who create schism. Similarly Kusinagara, has yielded brick structures round the smaller *stūpa* near the *Mahāparinirvāṇa* shrine.

[2]*IAR.*, 1953-54, p.10.

excavation has laid bare a quadrangular brick monastery at Lumbini with an array of cells on four sides of the courtyard. This was adjacent to ruined brick structures which were possibly bases of small brick *stūpas*.[3]

Similarly the site of Piprahwa has disclosed a few monastic structures. Near the *stūpa* was a quadrangular brick monastery with small cells on four sides of a courtyard. Another large brick monastery (45.5m × 41.5m) with an entrance porch on the west facing the *stūpa,* based on a similar pattern, was found to the east-north-east of the *stūpa*.[4] It has yielded coins of early Kushāna kings besides iron objects.

Four groups of *Saṅghārāmas,* south east of the Dharmarājikā *sūpa,* reveal a pattern of evolution of the *Saṅghārāma* in the first-second century AD.[5] There is a marked tendency to separate the main *stūpa* from the residential quarters of the monks. In the monastery (Site C), the living cells are found on three sides of the quadrangle, the fourth side was either left bare or was occupied by a *stūpa* shrine for the private use of monks. The hall of Assembly and other adjuncts were probably outside the monastery and might have been built of perishable materials.

In the more developed monastery (Site B) the private shrine is in the middle of one of the sides of the quadrangle, but the living cells are restricted to two sides and the fourth side is occupied by an assembly hall, a common room and another *stūpa* shrine. The main *stūpa* is still in the open facing the entrance to the monastery as it was on Sites A and C.

A further development is noticed at Site D. The three sides of the monastic quadrangle are occupied by cells and the fourth by an assembly hall and other chambers. On this site (D1) the main *stūpa* appears to have stood in a court of its own. In the other group (D2) the *stūpa* stood in the middle of

---

[3]Debala Mitra, op. cit., pp.59-60.

[4]Ibid., p.81.

[5]J. Marshall, *Taxila*, I, pp.320-21.

the court with row of cells on three sides and an assembly hall and other adjuncts on the fourth side.

The final step in the evolution of the *Saṅghārāma* took place in the 4th-5th century AD when the *caityagṛha* became a very essential feature. Gradually, as at Jaulian,[6] the living area came to be sharply demarcated from the court of public worship. The cult *stūpa* was placed in a quadrangle with image shrines around it. 'The hall of Assembly, the refectory, kitchen, etc., were grouped outside the monastic quadrangle.

The *vihāra* discovered near the Dharmarājikā *stūpa* is of prime importance. This consisted 'of several square courts open to the sky and encompassed by rows of cells in two storeys, with verandahs in front; and it was provided no doubt with a hall of assembly, refectory and kitchens. The monastery was destroyed and rebuilt on several occasions, but most of the remains now visible belong to early medieval period.'[7] This indicates that by the first-second century AD a type and pattern of *vihāra* construction had emerged. It was also the pattern on which the *leṇa* monasteries of the BC centuries were built which shows that such a plan must have gradually evolved by the Christian era.

Excavations conducted at Kauśāmbī have laid bare the remains of the Ghoṣitārāmā[8] continuously occupied from *c.* 6th century BC to 6th century AD. The massive *stūpa* was surrounded by chapels for monks. The courtyard also exposed a number of small *stūpas*.[9] Available evidence shows that it had been built towards the close of the 2nd century AD and continued in existence till the third quarter of the 6th century AD.

---

[6]J. Marshall, op. cit., I, pp.379f.

[7]J. Marshall, *A Guide to Taxila*, p.53.

[8]Like the Jivakāmravana monastery at Rajgir, the Ghoṣitārāma at Kauśāmbī also yielded an elliptical structure made of brick. See, H. Sarkar, 'Elliptical Structures in Ancient India', *Journal of the Asiatic Society*, Vol.VII, Nos.1-2, 1965, p.85. For a similar structure at Saheth-Maheth, See, *ASIAR.*, 1907-08, pp.108-09.

[9]*IAR.*, 1954-55, p.16, for details, See, G.R. Sharma, *Excavations at Kauśāmbī*.

In its ultimate form the monastery consisted of a square quadrangle lined with cells, with a verandah on the inner side enclosing the main *stūpa* and several other subsidiary *stūpas,* the whole establishment being enclosed by a boundary wall.[10]

Similar monastic units, either three winged or four winged, can be seen at Nāgārjunikoṇḍa.[11] Here each monastic establishment was complete in itself and contained a *vihāra* or dwelling place, an apsidal temple and a *stūpa.* On plan, the *vihāra* consisted of a rectangular open courtyard enclosed by a brick wall. In the centre was a square stone paved hall with a wooden roof supported by stone pillars. All around the enclosure abutting on to the outer walls was a row of cells for the monks often with a verandah in front. Some of the cells were used as storerooms, a few as shrines and there was usually one large room which served as a refectory.[12]

The site of Devnimori[13] yielded a 11.4m square monastery (with 3 phases—the earliest going to 3rd century AD) situated to the south of the *stūpa.* It had 8 cells on each of the four sides with a brick paved courtyard in the centre. The central cell on the southern side had a stone-paved floor and a platform of moulded bricks, suggesting a shrine. On the western side of the courtyard was a small platform, probably to serve as a stage.[14]

---

[10]Ibid., 1955-56, p.20.

[11]Ibid., 1954-55, p.22 (Sites III, VI); 1955-56, p.24 (Sites V, XI, XIII, XXV, XV); 1956-57, p.37; 1957-58, p.8; 1958-59, p.8.

[12]*MASI.*, No.54, p.9. In Monastery 2 at Nāgārjunikoṇḍa was excavated a room with a stone seat all around and a big stone table outside the doorway. It is presumed that it was a refectory. On its southern side are two cells or store rooms, a kitchen and a small lavatory in the north corner of the enclosure. *Stūpa* 4 stood close to the monastery. See, ibid., p.10; *ASIAR.*, 1928-29, pp.102-03 (Monastery Nos.1, 2). See also, ibid., 1926-27, pp.158, 160.

[13]*IAR.*, 1959-60, p.21; 1960-61, p.9. See also, R.N. Mehta and S.N. Chowdhary, *Excavation at Devnimori*, pp.34-45.

[14]Built over the verandah platform, it is termed as the *Vyakhayāna-Pitha* by archaeologists. See, R.N. Mehta and S.N. Chowdhary, loc. cit., p.44. This was probably used for reading the *sūtras* after the worship of the *stūpas* and other ceremonial meetings. See also. J. Takakusu, op. cit., pp.152-54.

Kaveripattinam revealed a *vihāra* consisting of five square rooms and a common verandah. The cells are 3.5m square laid in the south east and north west direction. The walls are built of bricks 42cm × 24cm × 10cm. The main building is ascribed to 4th-5th century AD with reconstruction at a later date.[15] Similar monastic structure were exposed successively.[16] A brick structure south of the *vihāra* appears to be a broad hall contemporary with the *vihāra*.[17] The discovery of a Buddhist monastery confirms the literary evidence found in Tamil epics such as the Silappadikaram and Manimekhalai, which mention that Kaveripattinam was an important centre of Buddhist faith.

Another example of a *catuḥsāla saṅghārāma* is at Sārnāth (Monastery V) which contains an open courtyard 15.25m square, a series of cells (2.60m × 2.45m) on four sides and a well in the centre of the court. In front of the cells inside the court was a verandah supported on pillars. The central room on the inner side was the entrance chamber. In front of it is the portico and two guard rooms.[18]

The remains at Nālandā comprise a continuous range of monasteries along the east side, a corresponding range of detached *stūpas* along the west and a couple of connecting monasteries bounding the area on the south. Down the centre of the area runs an approach avenue, entered upon from the north. The period embraced by the ruins is between 6th-12th century AD and the outstanding characteristic of the site is the remarkable succession of structures that have been built and rebuilt on the ruins of earlier ones. The typical monastery is planned round a square courtyard, which is enclosed by a colonnaded verandah backed in turn by the cells. In the centre of one side is located the main shrine and immediately opposite it, the entrance gateway.

---

[15] *IAR.*, 1964-65, p.24.
[16] Ibid., 1965-66, p.24.
[17] Ibid., 1972-73, p.32.
[18] *ASIAR.*, 1904-05, pp.59ff; 1906-07, pp.68f; 1907-08, pp.43f.

From the foregoing description it follows that monasteries gradually evolved as self contained units with two or more storeys, enclosed by high walls with no openings except the entrance. These monasteries were quadrilateral on plan with cells flanking the central courtyard. Cavities existing in the walls afford ample evidence to show that the cells were originally fitted with doors, presumably of wood.

The cells of the upper level monastery (Site 1) at Nālandā are built with recess to contain beds for the monks, a feature which is absent in the earlier monasteries.[19] They were often provided with niches for keeping lamps.[20] The open courtyard had sometimes a central *maṇḍapa* resting on pillars as at Nāgārjunikoṇḍa (Sites 2, 3, 32A).[21] One of the cells, often the one facing the gateway was the shrine,[22] containing a *stūpa* or an image for the worship by the inmates and another would contain the staircase to reach the upper storey.

Attached to each *vihāra* were, besides the assembly hall, a refectory, kitchen, store-room and a bath. These adjuncts were sometimes outside the main complex but they were connected with it by a door as at the sites of Taxila[23] and Kasia.[24] Covered drains were provided under the verandah and one of the cells. On either side of the entrance were introduced two projecting pylon like structures as at Nālandā, Taxila[25] and Kasia.[26] The

---

[19]A. Ghosh, *Nalanda*, p.22. Monastery No.2 at Ratnagiri has brick built beds which have one of its end raised to serve the purpose of a pillow. The *vihāra* at Saheth-Maheth (*ASIAR.*, 1907-08, p.120) contains only one cell which is furnished with a bed in the form of a brick work bench raised on the southern side to serve as a pillow. This might have been the apartment of an *Upādhyāya* or *Ācarya*.

[20]*ASIAR.*, 1915-16, p.11 (Taxila); 1907-08, p.56 (Sārnāth).

[21]H. Sarkar and B.N. Misra, *Nagarjunikoṇḍa*, p.38.

[22]*ASIAR.*, 1906-07, pp.48-49 (Kasia); 1907-08, p.119 (Saheth-Maheth).

[23]Initially no kitchen accommodation was provided in the *vihāra* but by Kushāna times, kitchen and sculleries became necessary adjuncts and were placed either at the back or on the side of monasteries as at Jaulian, Mohra Moradu, Giri and Bhamala, See, *ASIAR*, 1915-16, p.27; 1927-28, p.56: 1930-34, p.153; *MASI.*, No.7. pp.15-19; J. Marshall, *Taxila*, I, pp.343-44, 360-62, 379, 394.

[24]*ASIAR.*, 1906-07, pp.46-47 (Monastery N-O).

[25]Ibid., 1915-16, p.11.

[26]Ibid., 1904-05, p.56; 1906-07, pp.51-52.

later monasteries were not different in plan from the earlier ones save in elaboration and ornamentation of the *caityagṛha*. The *caityagṛha* came to occupy a position in the centre of the open courtyard as at Mainamati and Somapura.

Rock Cut Caves

The history of rock cut caves from simple *vassā* retreats to multistoreyed *leṇas* is varied and interesting. The earliest habitats were simple cells scooped out of rocks with no amenities as at Jivadan-*Virar*,[27] a few miles from Sopara and Tulja Leṇa (Junnar).[28] Their well dressed surface reminds one of earlier rock-cut examples of Mauryan times. Similarly the Bayan and Pangoraria[29] complex (district Sehore) have revealed several rock shelters with nearby *stūpa* complexes. Hinayāna establishments in the form of rock cut caves and brick constructions of 3rd-2nd BC have been found at and near Pauni (Vidarbha).[30]

With the gradual increase in the number of monks and the pious patronage of the lay-followers, the cells were provided with a front wall having a doorway. With the growth of monastic life, a hall for holding congregational services was added, preceded by a verandah. Structural amenties in the form of stone benches, stone beds and cisterns were provided in the *leṇas*. The ideological growth of the Order and the liberal donations resulted in the decoration and embellishments of the *leṇas*.

A residential cave had normally two parts:

(A) A Hall, behind a narrow porch or verandah was meant for congregation. This was generally square or oblong on plan but was in rare instances as at Bedsa, apsidal.[31] It was frequently astylar but in two pre-Christian

---

[27]S. Nagraju, *Buddhist Architecture of Western India*, pp.130ff.

[28]Ibid., pp.134, 136, 137 (Caves 1, 6, 7, 13, 14).

[29]*IAR.*, 1975-76, pp.29-30.

[30]S.B. Deo and J.P. Joshi, *Pauni Excavations*, p.7.

[31]James Fergusson, *A History of India and Eastern Architecture*, Vol.I, p.179, S. Nagaraju, op. cit., p.111.

vihāras, at Kondane[32] and Pitalkhora,[33] pillars were introduced. A further development is noticed in the addition of a pillared verandah (*caṅkama*) of which ornamental examples are provided by three caves of the 2nd Century AD at Nasik[34] and Ganesa Leṇa at Junnar,[35] the earliest being the one at Kondane.[36]

(B) Dormitory cells (called *Garbha* or *Ovaraka)* which opened into the hall. The number of monks' cells in a cave varied from two to twenty.

The oldest cells had one or two fixed rock beds, some of which were provided with rock pillows. The cell was semi dark inside since the only aperture was the door. Amenities in the form of niches in the wall for holding lamps, a rod to hang clothes on, are indicated by existing mortice holes. The hinge holes of the door can be seen in many caves.

At a later stage, the construction of the cells was improved. The doors were provided with some sort of ornamental work on the outside as at Nasik[37] and Ajanta.[38] The walls of the hall were sculpted and small Buddha images provided in the niches. Stone benches were placed in the verandah facing its rear walls. The backs of these stone benches were usually decorated with carved floral and other designs. The approach to a cave was thus made more spectacular.

Grace was combined with utility as seen at Ajanta caves[39] which consist of a pillared hall with cells on three sides, the cell on the back side opposite the entrance being converted into a shrine-chamber. In some caves subsidiary shrines were

---

[32]Vidya Dehejia, *Early Buddhist Rock Temples*, p.92.

[33]Ibid.

[34]Ibid., *ASWI.*, Vol.IV, p.31, S. Nagaraju, op. cit., p.259.

[35]Vidya Dehejia, 'Early Buddhist Caves at Junnar', AA., Vols.31, 1969, p.164; Fergusson and Burgess, *Cave Temples of India*, p.253.

[36]Fergusson and Burgess, loc. cit., p.222.

[37]Ibid., p.267.

[38]*ASWI.*, Vol.IV, pp.49, 50.

[39]Debala Mitra, op. cit., p.176.

scooped out at the back of the hall or on the two sides. Paintings embellished the walls and ceilings of the verandah, hall and shrine.[40]

A characteristic feature of every cave is the existence of cisterns called *poḍhis*[41] in inscriptions, often donated by the laity. Certain additional features as the existence of a refectory, a kitchen are seen in some of the caves as at Junnar.[42] Most of the caves are single storeyed. Cave 6 at Ajanta is double storeyed while Caves 11 and 12 at Ellora are three storeyed.

M.K. Dhavalikar, while discussing at length the different stages in the evolution of rock-cut caves of western India from *Hinayānism* to *Mahāyānism,* has pointed out that 'the Hinayanists preferred to have the shrine and the residence separated from each other whereas the Mahayanists, save for a few exceptions, combined both the elements and made arrangements for the residence of monks in the shrine itself by providing cells in the side walls. In other words, in the Mahayanic caves we find the caitya and the vihara combined together.'[43]

Stūpa

The Early Buddhist literature is replete with details of a *Saṅghārāma* and its essential adjuncts.[44] But none of the texts anterior to the time of Aśoka say anything about the building or cult of stūpa. Though eight, *stūpas* were built over Buddha's relics, the impetus to the *stūpa* cult was given by Aśoka from whose time onwards the *stūpa* became an object of marked veneration and an emblem of Buddhist faith.

---

[40]Vidya Dehejia, *Early Buddhist Rock Temples*, pp.124-26; Fergusson and Burgess, op. cit., p.285.

[41]*Infra*.

[42]*ASWI.*, Vol.IV, p.32. Dinning halls (*Bhojansālā*) are referred to in some donatory inscriptions at Kāṇherī and Junnar. See, *Lüders list*, Nos.998, 1182.

[43]M.K. Dhavalikar, 'Evolution of the Buddhist Rock-cut shrines of western India', *JASB.* (n.s.), Vols.45-46, 1970-71, p.52.

[44]*Supra*.

Thus before the beginning of the Christian era the *stūpa* became an essential and significant adjunct of monasteries and hence of monastic life. Originally an earthern tumulus,[45] a *stūpa* (synonymous with the term *caitya)* came to connote, in the practice of Buddhism any funerary memorial of the Buddha or a distinguished personage.[46] The simple dome was an adaptation of a pre-Buddhist grave mound[47] with one essential difference. The Buddhist *stūpas* were not always erected over the remains of the dead.

Stūpas were *śaririka* if erected over the corporeal relics of the Buddha but there arose gradually the practice of enshrining the relics of his chief disciples and distinguished monks. *Pāribhogika stūpas* were built over objects believed to have been used by the Buddha like his begging bowl, etc. *Uddeśika stūpas* commemorated the spots sanctified by important incidents of Buddha's life.

---

[45]The term *stūpa* (Pali *Thupa)* derived from the root *stūp* ('to heap') meant mounds. See, C.B. Pande, *Mauryan Art*, p.39.

[46]The four persons worthy of a cairn are—a Tathāgata, a *pratyekabuddha,* a true hearer of Tathāgata and a king of kings—'Mahāparinibbāna Suttanta', *Dīgha Nikāya*, II, p.110.

[47]S. Pant *(The Origin and Development of Stupa Architecture,* Chap.IV) has discussed in detail the views of scholars like Coomaraswamy, Hermann Goetz, B.M. Barua, J. Marshall, J. Fergusson who accept the burial tumulus theory of the origin of *stūpa.* V.S. Agrawala (*Indian Art*, p.120) traces its origin from the Hiraṇya *stūpa* and co-relates the *Yupa* (sacrificial pillar) with the *stūpa* (ibid., pp.121-22). D.C. Sircar ('Hiraṇya stupa in Vedic literature'. *JAHRS.,* Vol.XXXV, 1975-76, pp.145-46) has put forth arguments to show that Agrawala's theory is based on a misunderstanding of Ṛgveda hyman (X.149). G. Yazdani (op. cit., Vol.II, Pt.X, p.724) is of the opinion that 'the form of the *stūpa* as a burial mound seems to have been adopted from the hemispherical tumuli of the Scythians, or from the megalithic tombs (cairns) of the aboriginal inhabitants of the Deccan and south India, for such tombs are found in great abundance there'. But J. Przyluski ('The Harmika and the Origin of the Buddhist *Stūpas*', *IHQ.*, Vol.XI, 1935, pp.205-06) takes note of the pre-Buddhist sepulchral mounds near the villages of Lauriya and Pakhri and concludes that every element of the *stūpa* existed already in pre-Buddhist India.

For the laity who wanted some concrete form of worship the *stūpa* became an object of supreme veneration.[48] Worship and erection of a *stūpa* was considered an act of profound merit.[49] 'To worship and circumambulate it, was not a mere emotional satisfaction but a spiritual gain—a gain so great and enduring, that it availed the worshipper till his final nirvāna.'[50]

The practice[51] thus arose of donating numerous votive *stūpas* of miniature size which were installed around large Buddhist *stūpas* or temples. This is clear from a ring of miniature *stūpas* around the Dharmarājikā at Taxila.[52] Certain monasteries here, which belonged to the orthodox community had establishments without or with few miniature *stūpas*[53] while one establishment[54] abounded with such donations.

This liberal attitude of certain sects towards the laity who it was believed could win spiritual attainment without renouncing the world or adhering to strict monastic rules, was an attempt to gain popularity among the masses. Similar

---

[48]S. Dutt (*BMMI.*, pp.183-86) considers *stūpa pujā* as a product of lay mind which found place in the monk made canon as a lay ritual and was invested with a sacramental character. The monk mind which conceived the *stūpa* as a memorial had to accede to the popular conception of the *stūpa* as a symbol of divine presence.

[49]'... And whosoever shall there place garland or perfumes or paint, or make salutation there, or become in its presence calm in heart—that shall long be to them for a profit and joy'—'Mahaparinibbana Suttanta', *Dīgha Nikāya* (SBB.), pp.156, 183. 'A wise man who perceives that only by inner faith in the Holy One is the way to heaven found, will therefore bring offerings to the Thupa'—*Mahāvaṁsa,* XXX.43. For various kinds of offerings to the *stūpa,* see, *Avadānaśataka* (BST.), pp.156-57, 158, 160, 162, 164, 166, 168, 169, 172, 174, 177.

[50]See *Mahāvastu*, II, p.329; *Saddharma Puṇḍarīka* (BST.), p.159. For efficacy of the worship of *stūpa* see, 'Avalokana sutra' of *Śikṣāsamuccaya,* (trans.), pp.270-76.

[51]H. Sarkar (op. cit., p.57) is of the opinion that the Buddhist *Saṅghas* might have given the lead in the introduction of miniature *stūpas,* which subsequently became an important item of gift by the lay worshippers.

[52]*ASIAR.*, 1912-13, p.11; 1914-15, pp.4-5.

[53]See, H. Sarkar, loc. cit., Table II, p.58.

[54]Ibid.

attempt was made by the Aparamahavanaśailyas and the Caityakas at Nāgārjunikoṇḍa where Sites 2, 6, 9, 15, 23, 38, 106 and 108 have yielded miniature *stūpaa.*[55] Votive *stūpas* have been unearthed at various other sites such as Salihundam,[56] Devnimori,[57] Sārnāth,[58] Bodhgaya,[59] Nālandā[60] and Ratnagiri.[61]

An ensemble as great as the *stūpa* evidently erected for popular and ceremonial worship such as at Sāñchī, Taxila, Sārnāth and Amarāvati caused the development of other ancillaries—prominently the *vihāra.*[62] It became in course of time an essential adjunct of the monastic complex and found its place within the precincts of the *vihāra,* usually in the *caityagṛha.*

Structural Parts and Associated Symbolism

The hemispherical *stūpa* which was a crystallization of the mound of earth, utilizing different ground plans evolved the following essential features—

(1) A hemispherical dome (*aṇḍa*) which varied in dimension, proportion and ornamentation in accordance with lay patronage and ideology of the sects.

(2) Raising of the dome on the ground or on a platform (*meḍhī*).

(3) A *harmikā,* square, cubical or rectangular in shape was placed above the dome.

---

[55]Ibid., p.83

[56]*IAR.,* 1953-54, p.12.

[57]Ibid., 1961-62, p.13.

[58]*ASIAR.,* 1903-04, p.71.

[59]Debala Mitra, op. cit., p.62.

[60]A. Ghosh, op. cit., pp.17, 30, 31 (Main Temple Sites 3, 12, 13).

[61]Debala Mitra loc. cit., pp.227, 228.

[62]From the inscriptions *in situ,* the chronology of the construction of the various appendages of the *Mahāvihāra* at Nāgājunikoṇḍa become clear. From that it appears that the *Āvasatha, Mahācaitya, Maṇḍapa* and the *Caityagṛha* followed respectively. See, S.K. Dikshit. 'A Guide to Nagarjunakonda', *JAHRS.,* Vol.XXII, 1952-54, p.115. This was also the case with several *guha* settlements in western India where the residential caves were excavated followed by *Caityagṛhas* and *Maṇḍapas.*

(4) *Chhatrāvalī* or *chhatra* was the rod having parasols.
(5) In some *stūpas,* a relic chamber containing the reliquary.
(6) The *Madhyameḍhī* or second *meḍhī* on the berm.
(7) *Pradakṣiṇa patha* for circumambulation.
(8) *Vedikas* (railings), *toraṇas* (gateways) and *sopāna* (staircase).
(9) *Āyāka stambhas* with platforms—a feature prominently found in the Andhra *stūpas.*

These architectural features were invested with philosophical meaning.[63] The hemispherical *aṇḍa* became suggestive of the original creative power, the source of universe. The *chhatra* was the abstract form of the Bodhi tree as well as the symbol of spiritual sovereignty. The four *toraṇas* came to symbolize the four directions opening the message of the Enlightened One to the four quarters of the world. Another interpretation ascribes the eastern gateway to the Buddha's birth, the southern to his enlightenment, the western to his setting in motion the wheel of law and the northern to his *nirvāṇa.* It is also assumed that the four gates are aligned to sunrise, zenith, sunset and nadir in view of the *pradakṣiṇā patha* meant for circumambulation in the direction of the sun's course.

The earliest Buddhist *stūpas* were built of layers of piled up mud as at Vaiśāli.[64] The layers were separated from one

---

[63]See, Mulk Raj Anand, 'Reflections on the house, the stupa, the temple, the mosque, the mausoleum and the town plan from the earliest time till today (Being notes on the Social and spatial imagination in Indian architecture), *Marg,* Vol.XVII, No.1, Dec.1963, p.16. Satish Grover (The Architecture of India, Buddhist and Hindu, p.42) takes the hemisphere as symbolical of the 'dome of heaven' or 'the fixed cosmic structure', the *harmika* as the 'heaven of 33 Gods' and the *chhatra* as the 'world axix'. For a fanciful interpretation based on the Hindu cosmological concept of *Triloka,* See, K. Ramavarma Raja. 'The Buddhist Stūpa: A Comparitive Study', *QJMS.*, Vol.XXI, No.2, Oct.1930, pp.106-07.

[64]B.P. Sinha and Sita Ram Roy, *Vaiśāli Excavations,* pp.4, 5, 17f. Another *stūpa* roughly assigned to the 5th-4th century BC was excavated at Piprahwa. For details, see, K.M. Srivastava, 'Buddha's lost town of Kapilavastu identified', *VIJ.*, Vol.XV, Pt.1, March 1977, pp.97-98.

another by kankar and cloddy clay. Originally built in the 5th century BC the *stūpa* received four brick enlargements. The most interesting feature of this *stūpa* is the projections at four cardinal directions,[65] prototypes of the *āyakas* of the lower Krishna Valley.[66]

The definitely dated *stūpas* are ascribed to Aśoka who disseminated the *stūpa* cult. He seems to have used this symbol as a mass medium of appeal. The *stūpa* within the later enlargements of *Stūpa* 1 at Sāñchī and the Dharmarājikā at Sārnāth are ascribed to him. The former was made of burnt bricks (40cm × 25cm × 7.5cm) in mud mortar crowned by a *chhatra* of chunar sandstone.[67]

The Suṅgas gave a new vision and dimension to *stūpa* architecture as represented at Sāñchī[68] and Bharhut.[69] The low hemisphere of the Aśokan age was enlarged, stone railings were provided and monumental *toraṇas* erected. The plain architecture of the early *stūpas* received progressive embellishment of figure sculptures. The railings were engraved in low relief with geometrical and floral motifs. *Jātaka* tales were profusely illustrated and Buddha was represented symbolically.

The *stūpa* complex at Pauni (Vidarbha) ascribed to the Mauryan-Suṅga period represents a transitional phase in *stūpa* construction. The dome of the *stūpa* at Jagannātha Ṭekḍi[70] is constructed in a box type technique, i.e. rectangular boxes,

---

[65]Ibid., p.21.

[66]The *Āyakapaṭas* in Andhra are decorated with fine beautifully carved stone pillars of imposing height placed upon them with a terrace behind them going all round the *stūpa*. Both these features are absent in connection with the *āyakapaṭas* of the *stūpa* at Vaiśāli (ibid., p.19).

[67]Debala Mitra, *Sāñchi*, p.16.

[68]For excellent details, See, J. Marshall, *The Monuments of Sanchi*; F.C. Maisey, *Sanchi and its Remains*; V.S. Agrawala, *Indian Art*, pp.148f; *ASIAR.*, 1913-14, pp.2f.

[69]B.M. Barua, *Barhut;* A. Cunningham. *The Stupa of Bharhut*; V.S. Agrawala, *Indian Art*, pp.128-47,

[70]S.B. Deo and J.P. Joshi, op. cit., pp.25f.

2m in length and 1m in breadth were filled with clay and brick bats so as to reduce the load of the dome on the base which was made of a circular platform of bricks comprising brick bats and compact light brown clay. Repairs and additions were made to it in the early centuries of the Christian era. The Chāṇḍakapur Ṭekḍi *stūpa*[71] has utilized an ingenious technique. The dome appears externally to be of fired bricks though inside it were alternate receding tiers of clay bricks and fired bricks. The painted pot reliquary containing human bones, in a *kuṇḍa* like construction with a wooden *yaṣṭi* nearby is entirely a new feature.

At Taxila, two methods[72] were utilized to raise the height of the *stūpas* namely the introduction of recessed terraces by the adoption of the square plinth in place of the circular one as early as the beginning of the Christian era. The second method was of elevating the dome on a very high drum.

The Dharmarājikā *stūpa,* as its name[73] indicates was built by Aśoka to enshrine the body relics of Buddha. The core is built of rough rubble masonry, strengthened by sixteen walls radiating irregularly from the centre.[74] The first addition was made in the Kushāna period when the solid core of the *stūpa* was replaced by a wheel shaped plan. The second enlargement was made in the fifth, sixth century AD by the addition of a *pradakṣiṇā patha* and erection of four gateways in four cardinal directions. The *stūpa* face was decorated with ornamental bands over the berm and niches for the images of Buddha and his attendants. In the third enlargement which took place in the 7th century AD the *pradakṣiṇā patha* was

---

[71]Ibid., pp.94f.

[72]J. Marshall, op. cit., I, p.233, H. Sarkar, op. cit., p.65.

[73]Aśoka is referred to as a *Dharmarāja* in the *Divyāvadāna* (BST., p.87) and on the basis of this Vogel takes Dharmarājikā to mean a *stūpa* erected by Aśoka, the *Dharmarāja*. See, *ASIAR.,* 1903-04, p.223. Konow basing his information again on the *Divyāvadāna* (p.279) that Aśoka was called *Dharmarāja* because he had erected Dharmarājikās, infers that Dharmarājikā denotes a *stūpa* erected over the relics of the Buddha who was a *Dharmarāja*. See, *EI.*, II, p.75.

[74]J. Marshall, op. cit., p.236.

filled up and access to the *stūpa* was provided by placing four staircases. Later additions continued till the 12th century AD.

The Dhamekh[75] *stūpa* at Sārnāth is roughly ascribed to the Gupta Period. This *stūpa* has a substantial core of mud and bricks[76] and is faced with a solid envelope of stone masonry, which, however is manifestly a later addition. It is an example of a cylindrical double domed *stūpa,* a technique copied from the Bhallar and Jandial *stūpas* and is provided with eight niches for the pedestal of a seated Buddha.

Various forms of plan or construction which is seen in *stūpas,* of northern India seem to have been followed in the Krishna Valley. The *stūpa* at Bhattiprolu[77] is akin in structural pattern to the *stūpas* of northern India. This is built of bricks, the central portion of the base being wheel shaped. This was the beginning of a new constructional technique in south, a technique followed at Piprahwa,[78] Taxila,[79] Peshawar,[80] Sanghol[81] and Kasia.[82]

In the Ghaṇṭasāla *stūpa,*[83] mud, rubble and stone was utilized in between the radiating walls. This provided a strong inner structure over which the superstructure was constructed. The image of the Buddha had not come up on the face of the *stūpa.* At Jaggayapeta,[84] the *stūpa* has an outer brick casing

---

[75]This was an *Uddesika stūpa* which might have been raised by Aśoka to mark the site where Buddha preached his law for the first time to the five monks. D.R. Sahni rendered the name Dhamekh as *Dharmekshā* in Sanskrit, i.e., the *stūpa* marking the cogitation of Buddha about his *Dharma.* See, V.S. Agrawala, *Sarnath,* p.10.

[76]Ibid., p.11.

[77]A. Rea, *South Indian Buddhist Antiquities,* p.1.

[78]H. Sarkar, op. cit., p.88.

[79]Ibid., p.64.

[80]*ASIAR,* 1908-09, p.48.

[81]Hari Mitra Sharma, 'A Buddhist Stupa from Sanghol', *VIJ.,* Vol.XIII, Nos.1-2, Mar.-Sept.1975, pp.302-03; *IAR.,* 1971-72. p.39.

[82]*ASIAR.,* 1910-11, p.64.

[83]Ibid., K.R. Subrahmanyam, *Buddhist Remains in Andhra,* p.17.

[84]Jas Burgess, *The Buddhist Stupas of Amaravati and Jaggayyapeṭa,* pp.107, 108.

with an interior packing formed of 'layers of earth about 2 feet thick, over each of which was laid a close flooring of very large bricks closely fitted together'.

At the four cardinal points, a rectangular platform, of the same height as the drum, projected outwards and served as an altar for the floral offerings[85] presented to the shrine by the pious devotees. This was a distinctive feature of the Andhra *stūpas* and is unknown in northern India. In the larger and more important *stūpas*[86] each platform supported a group of five stone pillars, which in the inscriptions are called *āyaka-khambhas* but the platforms on which the pillars stand are not mentioned in the inscriptions. Even the *āyaka* platforms are not peculiar in Andhra Pradesh. Excavations at Vaiśāli[87] have brought to light, remains of a *stūpa* with such platforms. H. Sarkar is of the opinion that the *stūpas* with wheel base and with *āyaka*-platforms discovered at or near Vaiśāli 'may vaguely be ascribed to the spread of the Mahāsāṅghikas, who had their original stronghold at Vaiśāli and from whose doctrines the Sailas (including the Aparamahāvinaseliyas) derived theirs'.[88]

The most elaborate of this series of southern *stūpas* seems to be the one at Amarāvati,[89] on the southern banks of the Krishna river. The nucleus of this *stūpa* which goes back to Aśokan times was of bricks and earth.[90] Encasing in limestone slabs took place during the reign of the Satvahanas. The railings, casing slabs, *āryaka*-platforms and five *āryaka*-pillars were added at a later date.[91]

---

[85]The *Mahāvaṁsa* (XXX.51, 56) refers to the three and ten flower terraces *(pupphādhānattyāni)* where flowers were offered by the laity. The *Saddharma Puṇḍarika* (BST., p.278) also refers to the *pushpagrahanivedika.*

[86]*Infra.*

[87]*IAR.*, 1957-58, p.10.

[88]H. Sarkar, op. cit., p.90.

[89]For details see, Jas Burgess, op. cit.

[90]*IAR.*, 1973-74, p.4.

[91]Jas Burgess, op. cit., pp.112-13.

It is generally believed that the Caityakas, a sub-division of the Mahāsāṅghikas, were responsible for the construction of this *mahācaitya.*[92] The appearance of Buddha image in front of the *āryaka* platforms shows Mahāyānic influence. Marble has been used for plinth, drum and lower portion of the dome which is adorned with richly carved marble slabs. The upper part of the dome is covered with thick plaster coating.

The bas-reliefs portraying *stūpas* and the actual remains of such structures unearthed, show that two kinds of *stūpas* existed at Nāgārjunikoṇḍa in the 2nd-3rd century AD. One was a plain simple structure built of brick and plaster, while the other was profusely decorated from top to bottom. The *stūpas* of many sizes (ranging in diameter from 6m to 3.18m) from small mounds to the *mahācaitya*[93] were nearly of one essential design[94]—in horizontal section, a precise geometrical orientation of concentric bricks (50cm × 25cm × 7.5cm) in the form of a wheel[95] *(cakra)* with a tyre and spokes[96] radiating from a central hub, square in the smaller and circular in the larger *stūpas.*

---

[92]*ASIAR.,* Southern Circle, Madras, 1918-19, pp.21, 22.

[93]The Mahācaitya at Nāgārjunikoṇḍa was a *śāririka stūpa* for it disclosed a reliquary including a tooth relic and the inscription alludes to it as the *dhātu* or bodily remains of the Buddha—*Saṁma Saṁbudhasa dhatuvara-parigahita.* See, Inscription B2, B4—*EI.*, XX, p.18.

[94]Contrary to this the Mahāvihāravāsins at site 38 chose the mode of solid construction of the *stūpa* instead of the wheel shaped pattern. Site 108 revealed a *stūpa* with the arrangement of bricks in the centre in the shape of a *svastika,* a form repeated at Site 59 and Site 20. This pattern may have been due to some ideological consideration. See, H. Sarkar and B.N. Mishra, op. cit., p.36.

[95]The wheel shaped pattern for the larger *stūpas* was perhaps motivated by considerations of structural stability and economy. 'The wheel shaped plan' remark H. Sarkar and B.N. Mishra (loc. cit., p.42) 'was not only an improvement over an earlier building tradition but also a successful attempt at transforming an idea, a sacred Buddhist symbol into an architectural entity'.

[96]H. Sarkar (op. cit., pp.85-87) is of the opinion that the number of spokes was subservient to the dimensions of the *stūpa.* But he does not rule out the possibility of the numbers being symbolic representations of particular episodes of Buddha's life or of aspects of his teachings. The spokes varied from 4, 6, 8 to 10. See *IAR.*, 1954-55, pp.22, 23; 1955-56, pp.24, 25.

The open spaces between the radiating walls which formed the spokes were filled in with earth. At the four cardinal points were the *āyaka* platforms supporting five *āyaka* pillars.[97] The *mahāstūpa* was probably surrounded by a stone railing as evidenced by socketed pillars from the site. It was embellished in stone and stucco. It was built with the adjacent *mahāvihāra* and *caityagṛha* for the sake of the Aparamahavanaśailyas.[98]

Rock Cut Stūpas of the West Coast

The Rock cut *stūpas* of the west coast, mostly enshrined in *caityas,* differ architecturally from their structural counterparts in being essentially monolithic. The railing lost its importance here and was retained simply as a decorative motif on the berm. The middle terrace and the stairway leading to it become conspicuous by their absence. Here the aisles and nave serve the purpose of the *pradakṣiṇā patha.*

The *stūpas* assigned to the Hīnayānic phase are found at Sana, Mahad, Bhājā, Kondane, Ganeṣa lena group and Caves IX and X at Ajantā. The lithic technique though in the process of development is marked by the following features—

(a) A marked tendency towards elongation of the dome by erecting it on a cylindrical drum of moderate height.
(b) In some the dome and drum are devoid of decoration but others have the rail pattern around the upper edge of the drum.
(c) Almost all the *stūpas* in Hīnayānic *caityas* are equipped with sockets cut in the dome which were utilized as reliquaries.

With the introduction of the Buddha image, a mean was struck between reverence of the *stūpa* and exclusive worship

---

[97]The five *āyaka* pillars might symbolize the five principle incidents in the life of Buddha—the Nativity, Renunciation, Enlightenment, First Sermon and *Nirvaṇa.* See, S.K. Dikshit, 'A Guide to Nagarjunikonda', *JAHRS.,* Vol.XXII, 1952-54, p.124; P.R. Ramachandra Rao, *The Art Nagarjunikonda*, p.19.

[98]P.R. Ramachandra Rao, loc. cit., p.12.

of the Buddha image. Hence images of Buddha appear on *stūpas* enshrined within niches. Mahāyānic *stūpas* (Caves XIX, XXVI at Ajantā) were carved with the image of the Buddha to such prominence that the Buddha literally overshadowed the *stūpa*.

Mahāyānic *stūpas* are imposing and overlaid with a wealth of detail. The emphasis is placed on the elevated platform and the projections in the middle on each side, forming the base. The tendency towards elaboration, elongation and ornamentation were signs of a sectarian influence.

Caityagṛha

The *caityagṛha*[99] does not find mention in the scriptures among the requirements of a monk settlement. 'Evidently it arose from the idea of providing a convenient shelter to the devotees, where he might perform his worship without being handicapped by weather.'[100] Circumambulation was provided for, in a *caityagṛha* through the pillared aisles.[101] Before the introduction of images the *stūpa* was the chief focus of devotion. It was retained in Hīnayānic monasteries at Bhājā, Nāsik, Kāṇherī, Pitalkhora and Ajantā (Caves 9 and 10).

Archaeological evidence shows that in the 3rd century AD both the image and *stūpa* worship was recognized and the

---

[99]Regarding the etymology of the term I-tsing (J. Takakusu, op. cit., p.121) remarks '... when the Great teacher, the world honoured, entered into Nirvana, and men and gods assembled together, to burn his remains in the fire, people brought their all kinds of perfumes until they made a great pile, which was called citi, meaning 'piling'. Derived from this we have afterwards the name of caitya. But there are other explanations of this word: firstly because it is thought that all virtues of the world-honoured are deposited together (or collected, cit) here; secondly, because it is formed by piling up bricks or earth. The meaning of this word has been thus clearly handed down. Another name for it is stupa, the meaning being the same as caitya'.

[100]Debala Mitra, op. cit., p.41.

[101]At Nāgārjunikoṇḍa the *pradakṣiṇā patha* is a sort of conventional requirement, symbolizing the observance of circumambulation but is too narrow to be traversed.

choice was left on the worshipper. The evidence comes from Nāgārjunikoṇḍa[102] and some west Indian cave monasteries. In several *guhās,* as at Ajantā, Nāsik and Ellora, a compromise is effected by engraving an image on the *stūpa* itself or recessing the image into it.

With the advent of Mahāyānism, image worship became a concomitant of *bhakti.* I-tsing remarks that every monastery has its holy image which is enshrined in a specific temple.[103] This is bathed every morning and offered incense and flowers.[104] Thus the image or *stūpa* as cult object found its place in the *caityagṛha* making the latter an inseparable part of a monastic complex. The *caityagṛhas* may be broadly classified into three kinds according to their ground-plans, namely, (i) Circular, (ii) Apsidal and (iii) Quadrilateral.

Circular Structural Shrines

It cannot be doubted that the circular plan with a domical roof was the original plan as represented in the early reliefs of Bharhut, Sāñchī and Amarāvati. Bairāṭ[105] in Rajasthan has yielded a structural temple built of brick and timber, of which only parts survive. Around the *stūpa* was constructed a circular wall made of 'panels of brick work alternating with octagonal columns of wood'. Similar brick-built circular *stūpa*-chapel was unearthed at Salihundam,[106] district Srikākulam, Andhra Pradesh, belonging to the second-first century BC.

---

[102] *Infra.*

[103] J. Takakusu, op. cit., p.113.

[104] Ibid., pp.147f, 152. I-tsing's information is amply corroborated by literary evidence. The *Abhisamācārikā* (p.204) refers to the Dipavārika's duty of lighting lamps in the shrine dedicated to the Buddha as part of the *caitya puja.* Worship of Buddhas and Bodhisattvas is delineated in the *Bodhicaryāvatāra* (BST., Chap.II, vv.10-25).

[105] D.R. Sahni, Archaeological Remains and Excavations at *Bairāṭ,* pp.28-32.

[106] *IAR.,* 1953-54, p.11.

Rock-Cut Shrines

The earliest example of the circular form of religious building, though dedicated to the Ājivikas, is the Sudamā cave in the Barābar hills. This consists of two apartments of which the outer one is rectangular, and beyond this at the back and separated from it by a solid wall with a narrow passage connecting the two, there is an empty circular chamber in the place usually occupied by the votive *caitya.*[107]

The Tulja Leṇa group at Junnar resembles the circular temple at Bairāṭ. Here the *stūpa* is encircled by a row of twelve plain octagonal stone columns, above which riṣes a domed roof.[108] This feature is absent both at Guntupalli, Andhra Pradesh as well at Kondavite near Bombay. The Guntupalli cave, datable to the second century BC has in front, a vestibule of roughly crescentic ground plan. A thin wall separates it from the circular shrine having a ribbed vaulted roof. At Kondavite, the circular plan is similar to that of Guntupalli, but here a narrow opening connects the *stūpa* shrine with the rectangular vestibule.[109] In other words the cave-temple at Kondavite follows a ground plan very similar to the Sudamā cave. Circular *stūpa* shrines occur at Bhājā and Bedsā also.[110]

Apsidal Shrines

The Apsidal *caityagṛhas* in India may be. roughly divided into three main groups, viz., apse in the form of a (i) semi-circle, (ii) an octagon and (iii) apse formed by a row of pillars within an oblong plan. The largest number of structures and caves fall within the first group. Of the semi-circular type, the Cave 13 of Pitalkhora stands as a unique example with a much

---

[107]S.P. Gupta, op. cit., p.190.

[108]Vidya Dehejia, 'Early Buddhist Caves at Junnar', *AA.*, Vol.31, Nos.2-3, 1969, pp.149-150.

[109]Fergusson and Burgess, *Cave Temples of India,* p.360.

[110]Ibid., pp.228-31.

pronounced circular end.[111] Octagonal apse was confined only to Temple 1_3 at Taxila,[112] while Cave 10 from Ajantā[113] and Cave 4 from Aurangābād[114] have apse formed by a row of pillars within a rectangular ground-plan.

Structural Shrines

The most noteworthy feature regarding apsidal shrines in the structural group was that they represented only a subsidiary building in the whole of the monastic establishment. Here the main object of veneration was an open-air *stūpa* which was later transformed into remarkable proportions. The structural apsidal shrines claim slight chronological priority over the rock-cut ones on the basis of archaeological records.

Temple 40 at Sāñchī[115] and an apsidal structure from Sārnāth[116] are attributed to the later Mauryan period. The remains of a rubble built *caityagṛha* at Rajgir discovered below the Muniyar Math[117] is likely to go back to the same period. Both at Sāñchī and Sārnāth, the ruins of apsidal shrines were unearthed close to an Aśokan column and the Temple 40 at Sāñchī[118] had entrance on its longer side like that of the Sudamā and other Mauryan caves.

A unique contribution of Taxila to the development of apsidal shrines was the use of octagonal apse. In case of Dharmarājikā,[119] the interior of the apse was octagonal whereas Kalawān[120] consisted of an octagonal shrine with an antechamber in front.

---

[111]M.N. Deshpande, 'The Rock-cut caves of Pitalkhora', *AI.*, No. 15, 1959, pp.66-79.

[112]*ASIAR.*, 1912-13, p.17; J. Marshall, op. cit., I, pp.254-55.

[113]Debala Mitra, *Ajanta,* p.41.

[114]Owen C. Kail, *Buddhist Cave Temples of India*, p.126.

[115]Marshall and Foucher, *Monuments of Sanchi*, I, pp.66f.

[116]*ASIAR.,* 1914-15, p.109.

[117]Ibid., 1905-06, pp.105f.

[118]Ibid., 1913-14, p.29.

[119]Ibid., 1912-13, p.17; J. Marshall, *Taxila*, I, pp.254-55.

[120]*ASIAR.,* 1930-34, p.161; J. Marshall, loc. cit., I, p.326.

The *caityagṛhas* at Nāgārjunikoṇḍa[121] built on a platform, either apsidal or oblong, present a single hall with the side opposite the entrance semicircular. Towards the apse end is the votive *stūpa.* Often there are two structures, one containing the image of the Buddha and the other a *stūpa* as at site 4 and site 32A at Nāgārjunikoṇḍa and Salihundam.[122]

Rock Cut Shrines

Unlike the structural *caityagṛhas* the rock-cut apsidal shrines form the primary edifice in a Buddhist establishment. They were in the beginning faithful replicas of the structural ones of timber[123] not only in general form and detail but also in the actual use of wooden accessories some of which, like beams and rafters of the ceiling, appear redundant. In fact, the wooden beams or their remnants are still to be found in the caves of Bhājā, Ajantā (Cave 9), Pitalkhorā and Kārle.

The *caityagṛha* at Bhājā[124] has twenty seven pillars running along the entire length of the apsidal hall and around the votive *caitya*, thus dividing it into a central nave and two side aisles. The pillars are plain octagonal shafts, a little over 3.3m in height, and support the barrel-vaulted roof on a framework of curved ribs, originally of wooden construction. The votive *caitya* is placed near the back end, and the entrance just opposite to it. Along the entire width of the facade extends the rail pattern which is imitated from wood.[125]

Of approximately the same style and pattern are the ruined *caitya*-hall at Kondāne, the *caitya* cave at Pitalkhorā in Khandesh and also one of the early *caitya* halls (Cave 10) at Ajanta.[126] These three caves may be considered to be

---

[121]*IAR.*, 1957-58, pp.8-9; H. Sarkar and B.N. Mishra, op. cit., pp.33, 38.

[122]*IAR.*, 1953-54, p.11.

[123]V.S. Agrawala, *Indian Art,* pp.187, 190.

[124]Fergusson and Burgess, *Cave Temples of India,* pp.223ff.

[125]Benjamin Rowland, *The Art and Architecture of India* (*Buddhist, Hindu, Jain*), p.71.

[126]Debala Mitra, op. cit., p.147.

contemporary to the Bhājā *caitya* shrine or very nearly so. These four represent the oldest specimens of their class in western India and may be dated in the 1st half of the second century BC.[127]

Caityas following the apsidal plan were excavated at Budh Leṇa—Manmodi hill at Junnar.[128] Here the right side pillars are roughly hewn, the right aisle is partly completed and the half arched ceiling has taken definite shape—a feature indicative of an early date. The *caitya* arch on the facade retains the classic shape seen on other western *caityas,* but is no longer functional, as it has not been cut through and is of solid stone, hence termed 'blind arch'.

The caitya-shrine at Bedsā[129] has a curved roof supported by twenty-six pillars, which are really meant to lend beauty to the hall. At the farther end of the sanctuary is the *caitya.* There is space round the *stūpa* for circumambulation by the devotees. The facade of the *caitya* cave is rather unique, the like of which is not found in the other Buddhist caves in India, with the typical *caitya* window over the main entrance.

The facade of the cave is cut out vertically from a sloping rock leaving two rugged fronts of rock about 7.5m high on either side, forming a sort of walled way 1.8m wide and 12m long. This peculiar frontage was seemingly excavated to afford some privacy to the inmates, probably Buddhist nuns.

Quadrilateral Shrines

The *stūpas* in India were sometimes housed inside the quadrilateral chapels. In the archaeological records the *caitya-gṛhas* at Kuda appear to be the earliest among the quadrilateral *stūpa*-shrines, followed closely by the *stūpa*-shrine A 14 of the Kalawān monastery at Taxila, ascribable to the latter half of the first century AD.

---

[127]V.S. Agrawala, op. cit., p.188.

[128]Vidya Dehejia, op. cit., pp.151-52.

[129]M. Lalitha Rao, 'Buddhist Cave Temples of Bedsa', *The Hindu*, 9 June 1968, Column 4.

The entire Ganga Yamuna Doab and the east coast seems to have been devoid of such *caitya-gṛhas*. Later extension of this form appears in central India at Bāgh[130] and Dhamnār.[131] But its occurrence at Kuda, Mahad, Karad,[132] Sailarwadi, Junnar, Kāṇherī[133] etc., clearly suggest western India as the focal point of this type of *stūpa*-shrines.

Structural

The *caityagṛha* of Kalawān[134] monastery consists of an octagonal cella and a squarish antechamber connected by a passage. A unique feature observed at Taxila was the occurrence of the quadrangular shrines within the monastic enclosures. Such shrines came from Chir Topes B and C, and probably at Mohra-Maradu, but each of these establishments has its principal *stūpa* as well.

Rock-Cut

Quadrilateral rock-cut shrines are mostly without pillars since the size of the shrines itself are comparatively smaller. At Kuda,[135] the caves comprised a cella and a vestibule, the latter built on pillars varying in number from two to four. Cave 9 at Ajantā has also a square end like some of the Junnar caves, with a flat roof over the two aisles, but not over the nave which is vaulted as usual.

Thus the Buddhist *caityagṛha* in evolving a standardized plan underwent some notable changes which may be briefly summed up as follows:

---

[130]John Anderson, 'Bagh Caves: Historical and Descriptive Analysis'. *Marg*, Vol.XXV, No.3, June 1974, pp.21, 24.

[131]Fergusson and Burgess. op. cit., pp.393-95.

[132]*ASWI.*, Vol.IV, Pls.VIII-X for Kuda, Mahad and Karad.

[133]Fergusson and Burgess, loc. cit., Pls.V, XVIII, LIII for Sailarwadi, Junnar and Kanheri.

[134]J. Marshall, op. cit., I, p.326.

[135]Fergusson and Burgess, op. cit., pp.204-09.

(A) The wooden frontage of the *caityagṛha* was replaced entirely by stone and became conspicuous with variegated ornamentation like Cave 9 at Ajanta and Cave 18 at Nāsik.

(B) The *caitya* arch on the facade, in due course of time, lost its functional aspect of admitting light into the otherwise dark, cool and sombre recesses and became a traditional motif.

(C) The rigorously plain hall (*maṇḍapa*) with simple octagonal pillars gave way to pillars and pilasters with ghata bases and capitals, lavishly decorated with carvings.

The typical developed plan of a *caityagṛha* consists of a long rectangular hall, rounded at the rear end and divided into a nave, an apse and two side aisles. The aisles are separated from the nave by pillars, and the apse contains, in place of the altar, a solid *stūpa* or Buddha image as the votive object. The aisles are continued round the apse, thus providing for circumambulation (*pradakṣiṇā*). The nave is usually opposite the votive object and over it appears a huge arched window shaped like a horse-shoe, dominating the entire scheme of the facade.[136]

Taking the above plan and general design of a Buddhist *caityagṛha*, scholars have pointed out, its undeniable resemblance to the Graeco-Roman basilica, a type of structure which was being evolved in Europe at about the same time.[137] But inspite of this similarity and their almost contemporaneous emergence, it is extremely unlikely that the two forms were in any way related.

E.B. Havell on the other hand has pointed out that 'the necessity of providing accommodation for both classes (the

---

[136]V.S. Agrawala, op. cit., p.190.

[137]Percy Brown, *Indian Architecture* (Buddhist and Hindu Periods), p.25; Vincent Smith, *A History of Fine Art in India and Ceylon*, p.19.

bhikkhus and the *upāsakas)* meeting together at stated times, in Buddhist places of worship, dictated the structural arrangements of the *caityagṛha*—the elements of its structure grew together by a natural creative process'.[138]

This leads to an assumption of an independent evolution of such shrines in India, from a primitive beginning, though a certain impetus from outside might have been a precondition for the introduction of such apsidal shrines, since India was not a closed door all through her history.[139]

[138]E.B. Havell, *The Ancient and Medieval Architecture of India: A Study of Indo-Aryan Civilization*, pp.65-66.

[139]Inscriptions from Kārle, Junnar and Nāsik clearly reveal that the Yavanas and the Sakas participated in the construction of these cave temples. See, *ASWI.*, Vol.IV, pp.82-116.

Bibliography

Original Sources

(1) BUDDHIST

Abhidharmakośa, ed., Rahula Sankrityayana, Varanasi, 1932.

—— *and Bhāṣya* of Acharya Vasubandhu with Sphutārtha commentary of Ācārya Yaśomitra, critically ed., by Dwarikadas Shastri, Pt.1, 1st edn., Varanasi, 1970; Pt.IV, Varanasi, 1973.

Abhisamācārikā (Bhikṣuprakīrnaka), ed., B. Jinananda, Tibetan Sanskrit Works Series, K.P. Jayaswal Research Institute, Patna, 1969.

Abhisamayālaṅkara, ed., E. Conze, Intro., and trans., from original text with Sanskrit Tibetan Index, Serie Orientale Roma VI, Roma, Is. MEO, 1954.

Amitāyur-dhyānasūtra, trans., J. Takakusu in Buddhist Mahayana Sutras, SBE., Vol.XLIX, Pt.II, London, 1894.

Aṅguttara Nikāya, ed., Bhikshu Jagdish Kashyap, 4 Vols., Nālandā-Devanāgarī-Pāli Series, Pāli Publication Board, Nalanda, 1960.

——, trans., as *The Book of the Gradual Sayings*, 5 Vols., PTS., Luzac and Co., Ltd., London, 1951, 1952, 1955.

Aṣṭasāhasrikā Prajñāpāramitā, trans., E. Conze, Bibliotheca Indica, Works No.284, Asiatic Society, Calcutta, 1958.

Aṭṭhasālinī, trans., as *The Expositor by Pe Maung Tin*, ed., and revised by Mrs. Rhys Davids, 2 Vols., rep., Luzac tnd Co., London, 1958.

Avadānaśataka, ed., P.L. Vaidya, BST., No.19, Mithila Vidyapitha, Darbhanga, 1958.

Bhikṣunī-Vinaya: Manual of Discipline for Buddhist Nuns, ed., Gustav Roth, K.P. Jayaswal Research Institute, Patna, 1970.

Bodhicaryāvatāra with Pañjikā, ed., P.L. Vaidya, BST., No.12, Mithila Vidyapitha, Darbhanga, 1960.

——, trans., as *Entering the Path of Enlightenment*, by Marion L. Matics, George Allen and Unwin Ltd., London, 1971.

Bodhisattvabhūmi, ed., N. Dutt, Tibetan Sanskrit Works Series Vol.VII, K.P. Jayaswal Research Institute, Patna, 1966.

Buddhacarita (Acts of the Buddha), Complete Sanskrit text with English translation by E.H. Johnston, rep., Delhi, 1972.

——, trans., E.B. Cowell in Buddhist Mahayana Sutras, SBE., Vol.XLIX, Pt.1, Oxford University Press, London, 1894.

Buddhism in Translations, trans., Henry Clarke Warren, Vol.III (Harvard Oriental Series), Harvard University Press, Cambridge, 1896.

Buddhist Suttas, trans., Rhys Davids, SBE., Vol.XI, rep., Motilal Banarsidass, Delhi, 1965.

Bu-ston's History of Buddhism, trans., E. Obermiller, 2 Vols., Heidelberg, 1931-32.

Cullavagga, ed., Bhikshu Jagdish Kashyap, Nālandā-Devanāgarī-Pāli-Series, Pāli Publication Board, Nalanda, 1956.

Dhammapada, ed., Jagdish Kashyap in Khuddaka Nikāya, Vol.I, Nālandā-Devanāgarī-Pāli-Series, Pāli Publication Board, Nalanda, 1959.

——, by S. Radhakrishnan, Oxford University Press, 1966.

Dharmasaṅgraha, ed., P.L. Vaidya in Mahāyāna Sūtra Saṅgraha, BST., No.17, Pt.1, Darbhanga, 1961.

Dīgha Nikāya, ed., Jagdish Kashyap, 3 Vols., Nālandā-Devanāgarī-Pāli-Series, Pāli Publication Board, Nalanda, 1958.

——, trans., as Dialogues of the Buddha by T.W. and C.A.F. Rhys Davids, 3 parts, SBB., Oxford University Press, London, 1923, 1938, 1921.

——, ed., N.K. Bhagwat, Vol.I, 1st edn., Devanāgarī Pāli Text Series, No.8, Bombay University Publication, Bombay, 1942.

Dīpavaṁsa, ed., and trans., by H. Oldenberg, Williams and Norgate, London,1879.

Divyāvadāna, ed., P.L. Vaidya, BST., No.20, Mithila Vidyapitha, Darbhanga, 1959.

Gilgit Manuscripts, ed., N. Dutt with the assistance of Vidyavridhi Shivnath Sastri, Vol.III, Pt.II, Kashmir, 1942; Vol.III, Pt.III, Kashmir, 1943; Vol.III, Pt.IV, Calcutta, 1950.

Itivuttaka, ed., Jagdish Kashyap in Khuddaka Nikāya, Vol.I, Nālandā-Devanāgarī-Pāli-Series, Pāli Publication Board, Nalanda, 1959.

Jātakamālā by Āryaśūra, ed., P.L. Vaidya, BST., No.21, Mithila Vidyapitha, Darbhanga, 1959.

Jātakas, trans., T.W. Rhys Davids as Buddhist Birth Stories, George Routledge and Sons, London, 1925.

Jātaka Stories, ed., E.B. Cowell, Vols.I-IV, PTS., rep., Luzac and Co. Ltd., London, 1957.

Kathāvatthu, trans., by Shwe Zan Aung and Mrs. C.A.F. Rhys Davids, as Points of Controversy or Subjects of Discourse, rep., PTS., Luzac and Co. Ltd., London, 1960.

——, *Aṭṭthakathā* (Pañcappakaraṇa Aṭṭhakathā), Vol.II, ed., Mahesh Tiwary, Nava Nalanda Mahavihara, Patna, 1971.

Karaṇḍavyūha, ed., P.L. Vaidya in Mahayana Sutra Saṅgraha, BST., No.17, Pt.1, Darbhanga, 1961.

Khuddakapāṭha, ed., Jagdish Kashyap in *Khuddaka Nikāya*, Vol.I, Nālandā-Devanāgarī-Pāli-Series, Pāli Publication Board, Nalanda, 1959.

Latitavistara, ed., P.L. Vaidya, BST., No.1, Mithila Vidyapitha, Darbhanga, 1958.

Large Sutra on Perfect Wisdom (with the divisions of the Abhisamayālaṅkāra) trans., E. Conze, 1st Indian edn., Motilal Banarsidass, Delhi, 1976.

Larger Sukhāvati Sūtra, trans., F. Max Müller in Buddhist Mahayana Sutras, SBE., Vol.XLIX, Pt.II, Oxford University Press, London,1894.

(The) Life of Hiuen-Tsiang by the Shaman Hwui Li, trans., by S. Beal, 2nd edn., Munshiram Manoharlal, Delhi, 1973.

Madhyānta Vibhaṅga (Discourse on discrimination between middle and extremes) ascribed to Bodhisattva Maitreya, commented by Vasubandhu and Sthiramati, trans., from the Sanskrit by Th. Stcherbatsky, Soviet Indology Series, No.5, Indian Studies Past and Present, Calcutta, 1971.

Mahāvagga, ed., Jagdish Kashyap, Nālandā-Devanāgarī-Pāli-Series, Pāli Publication Board, Nalanda, 1956.

Mahāvaṁsa or The Great Chronicle of Ceylon, ed., and trans., in English by W. Geiger, PTS., Oxford University Press, London, 1934.

Mahāvastu, trans., J. J. Jones, SBB., Vols.XVI, XVIII, XIX, Luzac and Co. Ltd., London, 1949, 1952, 1956.

Mahāyānasūtrālaṅkāra, ed., S. Bagchi, BST., No.13, Mithila Vidyapitha, Darbhanga, 1970.

Mahāyānasūtrasaṅgraha, ed., P.L. Vaidya, 2 Vols., BST., Nos.17-18, Mithila Vidyapitha, Darbhanga, 1961, 1964.

Mahāyānaviṁśaka of Nāgārjuna, ed., and trans., V. Bhattacharya, Visva Bharati Studies, No.1, Calcutta, 1931.

Majjhima Nikāya, ed., Jagdish Kashyap, 3 Vols., Nālandā-Devanāgarī-Pāli-Series, Pāli Publication Board, Nalanda, 1958.

——, trans., as the Middle Length Sayings, by I.B. Horner, 3 Vols., PTS., Luzac and Co. Ltd., London, 1954, 1957, 1959.

Milindapañho, ed., R.D. Vadekar, 1st edn., Bombay University Publications, Devanāgari-Pāli Texts Series, No.7, Bombay, 1940.

——, trans., from the Pali as the Questions of King Milinda, by T.W. Rhys Davids, SBE., Vols.XXXV, XXXVI, 1st published, Dover Publications Inc, New York, 1963.

Mūlasarvāstivāda Vinayavastu, ed., S. Bagchi, BST., No.16, Pt.1, Darbhanga, 1967.

On Yuan Chwang's Travels in India (AD 629-45), trans., by T. Watters, 1st Indian edn., Munshiram Manoharlal, Delhi, 1961.

Pācittiya (Bhikkhu Vibhaṅga and Bhikkhuni Vibhaṅga) ed., Jagdish Kashyap, Pt.II, Nālandā-Devanagarī-Pāli-Series, Pāli Publication Board, Nalanda, 1958.

Papañcasudanī (Commentary on the Majjhima Nikāya), ed., J.H. Woods and D. Kosambi, Vol.II, London, 1928.

Pārājika (Bhikkhu-Vibhaṅga), ed., Jagdish Kashyap, Pt.I, Nālandā-Devanāgarī-Pāli-Series, Pāli Publication Board, Nalanda, 1958.

Prātimokṣa-Sūtram, ed., Anantlal Thakur, Tibetan Sanskrit Work Series, No.16, K.P. Jayaswal Research Institute, Patna, 1975.

—— (Mūlasarvāstivāda), ed., Anukul Chandra Banerjee, Calcutta Oriental Press, 1954.

Rāṣṭrapāla-paripṛcchā, Sūtra Du Mahāyāna, Publie par, L. Finot, Mouton and Co., 'S-Gravenhage, The Hague, 1957.

(A) Record of the Buddhist Religion as practised in India and the Malay Archipelago (AD 671-95) by I-tsing, trans., by J. Takakusu, rep., Munshiram Manoharlal, Delhi, 1966.

Saddharma Puṇḍarīka Sūtra, ed., P.L. Vaidya, BST., No.6, Mithila Vidyapitha, Darbhanga, 1960.

——, trans., H. Kern, SBE., Vol.XXI, rep., Motilal Banarsidass, Delhi, 1965.

——, *Sūtram*, revd. edn., N. Dutt, Asiatic Society, Calcutta, 1953.

Samantapāsādikā, Commentary on the Vinaya Pitaka, ed., Birbal Sharma, Vol.I, Nava Nalanda Mahavihara, Patna, 1964, Vol.II, (Pārājika and Pācittiya), Nava Nalanda Mahavihara, Patna, 1965.

——, Commentary on the Vinaya Piṭaka by Buddhaghosa, ed., J. Takakusu and Makoto Nagai, Vol.VI, PTS., London, 1947.

Saṁyutta Nikāya, ed., Jagdish Kashyap, 4 Vols., Nālandā-Devanāgarī-Pāli-Series, Pāli Publication Board, Nalanda, 1959.

——, trans., by Mrs. Rhys Davids and F.L. Woodward, as the Book of Kindred Sayings, 5 vols., PTS., Luzac and Co. Ltd., London, 1950, 1952, 1954, 1956.

Śatapañcāśatka of Mātṛceṭa, Sanskrit Text, Tibetan translation and commentary and Chinese translation, ed., D.R. Shackleton Bailey with an introduction, English translation and notes, Cambridge University Press, 1951.

Saundarānanda (or Nanda the fair), trans., E.H. Johnston, Punjab University Oriental Publishing, No.14, Oxford University Press, London,1932.

Śikṣāṣamuccaya of Śantideva, ed., Cecil Bendall, rep., Mouton and Co., 'S. Gravenhage, The Hague, 1957.

——, trans., from the Sanskrit by Cecil Bendall and W.H.D. Rouse, rep., Motilal Banarsidass, Delhi, 1981.

Smaller Sukhāvati Sutra, trans., F. Max Müller in Buddhist Mahayana Sutras, SBE., Vol.XLIX, Pt.II, Oxford University Press, London, 1894.

Suhṛllekha, trans., as Nāgārjuna's letter to King Gautamīputra by Ven. Lozang Jamspal, Ven Ngawang Samten Chopel, Peter Della Santina, with explanatory notes based on Tibetan commentaries, 1st edn., Motilal Banarsidass, Delhi, 1978.

Sumaṅgalavilāsinī (Dīgha Nikāya), ed., Mahesh Tiwari, Vol.I, Nalanda, 1974.

Sutta Nipāta, ed., Jagdish Kashyap in *Khuddaka Nikāya,* Vol.I, Nālandā-Devanāgarī-Pāli-Series, Pāli Publication Board, Nalanda, 1959.

Tarānātha's History of Buddhism in India, trans., from the Tibetan by Lama Chimpa and Alaka Chattopadhyaya, Indian Institute of Advanced Studies, Simla, 1970.

Theragāthā, trans., as Psalms of the Brethren by Mrs. Rhys Davids in Psalms of the Early Buddhists, PTS., London, 1951.

Therīgāthā, trans., as Psalms of the Sisters by Mrs. Rhys Davids in Psalms of the Early Buddhists, PTS., London, 1948.

(The) Travels of Fa-hien, A Record of Buddhistic kingdoms, being an account of the Chinese monk Fa-hien of his travels in India and Ceylon (AD 399-414) in search of the Buddhist Books of Discipline, trans., by J. Legge, 2nd Indian rep., Orient Publishers, Delhi, 1972.

Travels of Fa-hien and Sung-Yun, (AD 400 to AD 518) by S. Beal, 2nd edn., London, 1964.

Vajracchedikā, trans., J. Takakusu in Buddhist Mahayana Texts, SBE., Vol.XLIX, Pt.II, Oxford University Press, London, 1894.

——, trans., as the *Diamond Sūtra* by E. Conze, Buddhist Wisdom Books, George Allen and Unwin Ltd., London, 1958.

Vimalakīrti Nirdeśa Sūtra, trans., Charles Luk, 1st published, The Clear Light Series, Shambala Publications, Berkeley and London, 1972.

Vimānavatthu and Petavatthu, trans., as The Stories of the Mansions and Stories of the Departed by J. Kennedy and Henry S. Gehman, in the Minor Anthologies of the Pali Canon, SBB., Series, Pt.IV, London, 1942.

Vinaya Piṭaka, ed., H. Oldenberg and T.W. Rhys Davids as Vinaya Texts, SBE., Vol.XIII, XVII, XX, 3 Pts., rep., Motilal Banarsidass, 1974, 1975.

——, trans., into English by Miss I.B. Horner as Book of the Discipline, SBB., Vols.X, XI, XIII, XIX, XX.

Visuddhimagga, ed., Dharmananda Kosambi, Bharatiya Vidya Series, Vol.I, Bharatiya Vidya Bhawan, Bombay, 1940.

——, trans., as the Path of Purification by Bhikkhu Ñyāṇamoli, 2 Vols., Shambala Publications, Berkeley and London, 1976.

(2) NON-BUDDHIST

Ācārāṅga Sūtra, trans., into English by H. Jacobi in Jaina Sutras, Pt.I, SBE., Vol.XXII, rep., Motilal Banarsidass, Delhi, 1964.

Āruṇeyopaniṣad, ed., by T.R.C. Dikshit in the Samnyāsa Upanishads, Adyar Library and Research Centre, 1966.

Āśvalāyana Gṛhyasūtra, trans., by H. Oldenberg in the Grihya-Sūtras, SBE., Vol.XXIX, Pt.I, rep., Motilal Banarsidass, 1964.

Atharvaveda, trans., by M. Bloomfield in Hymns of the Atharvaveda, SBE., Vol.XLII, Oxford, 1897.

Baudhāyana Dharmasūtra, trans., by G. Bühler in the Sacred Laws of the Aryas, SBE., Vol.XIV, Pt.I, rep., Motilal Banarsidass, Delhi, 1965.

Bhagvadgītā, trans., by K.K. Telang, SBE., Vol.VIII, Oxford, 1908.

Bṛhādaraṇyaka Upaniṣad, ed., and trans., by S. Radhakrishnan in the Principal Upaniṣads, 1st published, George Allen and Unwin Ltd., London, 1953.

Chāndogya Upaniṣad, ed., and trans., by S. Radhkrishnan in the Principal Upaniṣads, 1st published, George Allen and Unwin Ltd., London, 1953.

Gautama Dharmasūtra, trans., by G. Buhler in The Sacred Laws of the Aryas, SBE., Vol.II, Pt.I, rep., Motilal Banarsidass, 1965.

Harṣacarita of Bāṇabhaṭṭa, trans., by Jagannath Pathak, Chowkhamba Vidyabhavan, Varanasi, 1972.

Īśa Upaniṣad, ed., and trans., by S. Radhakrishnan in the Principal Upaniṣads, 1st published, George Allen and Unwin Ltd., London,1953.

Jābāla Upaniṣad, ed., and trans., by S. Radhakrishnan in The Principal Upaniṣads, 1st published, George Allen and Unwin Ltd., London, 1953.

Kaivalya Upaniṣad, ed., and trans., by S. Radhakrishnan in The Principal Upaniṣads, 1st published, George Allen and Unwin Ltd., London, 1953.

Kaṭha Upaniṣad, ed., and trans., by S. Radhakrishnan in The Principal Upaniṣads, 1st published, George Allen and Unwin Ltd., London,1953.

Kaṭharudropaniṣad, ed., by T.R.C. Dikshit in the Samnyāsa Upanishads, Adyar Library and Research Centre, 1966.

Kathāsaritsāgara of Somadevabhatta, ed., by Pt. Durgaprasad and Kaśinath Pandurang Paras, Revised by Vasudev Laxman Śastri Pansikar, 4th edn., Bombay, 1930.

Maitrī Upaniṣad, ed., and trans., by S. Radhakrishnan in The Principal Upaniṣads, 1st published, George Allen and Unwin Ltd., London,1953.

Manu Smṛti with the 'Manubhāṣya' of Medhātithi, ed., by Mahāmahopādhyāya Gaṅgānātha Jha, Bibliotheca Indica No.256, Vol.II, Royal Asiatic Society, Calcutta, 1939.

——, trans., by G. Bühler in the Laws of Manu, SBE., Vol.XXV, Oxford, 1886.

Muṇḍaka Upaniṣad, ed., and trans., by S. Radhakrishnan in The Principal Upaniṣads, Ist published, George Allen and Unwin Ltd., London, 1953.

Nāradaparivrājakopaniṣad, ed., by T.R.C. Dikshit in The Samnyāsa Upanishads, Adyar Library and Research Centre, 1966.

Nāradīya Manusaṁhitā, with the Bhāṣya of Bhavasvāmin, ed., by K. Sambaśiva Śastri, Trivandrum Sanskrit Series, No.XCVII, Trivandrum, 1929.

Nirukta, ed., Shivnarayan Śastri, 1st edn., Indological Book House, Delhi, 1972.

Ṛgveda, trans., by R.T.H. Griffith in the Hymns of the Ṛgveda, 2 Vols., Benares, 1896-97.

Sāmaveda, trans., by R.T.H. Griffith in the Hymns of the Samaveda, Benares, 1907.

Sāṅkhyāyana Gṛhyasutra, trans., by H. Oldenberg, SBE., Vol.XXIX, Pt.I, rep., Motilal Banarsidass, Delhi, 1964.

Śatapatha Brāhmaṇa, trans., by Julius Eggeling, SBE., Vol.XII, Pt.I, rep., Motilal Banarsidass, Delhi, 1963.

Śvetāśvatāra Upaniṣad, ed., and trans., by S. Radhakrishnan in The Principal Upaniṣads, lst published, George Allen and Unwin Ltd., London, 1953.

Uttarādhyayana Sūtra, trans., into English by H. Jacobi in Jaina Sūtras, Pt.II, SBE., Vol.XLV, Oxford, 1895.

Vasiṣṭha Dharmaśāstra, trans., by G. Buhler in the Sacred Laws of the Aryas, SBE., Vol.XIV, Pt.II, rep. Motilal Banarsidass, Delhi, 1965.

Vedānta Sūtras, with the commentary by Saṅkarācārya, trans., by George Thibaut, SBE., Vol.XXIV, Pt.I, rep., Motilal Banarsidass, Delhi, 1962.

Secondary Sources

Adhikaram, E.W., *Early History of Buddhism in Ceylon*, 2nd impression, M.D. Gunasena and Co. Ltd., Colombo, 1953.

Agrawala, V.S., *India as known to Pāṇini,* Varanasi, 1963.

——, *Indian Art (A History of Indian Art from the earliest times to the 3rd century AD)*, Varanasi, 1965.

——, *Sarnath*, 3rd edn., Delhi, 1980.

Altekar, A.S., *Education in Ancient India*, 5th edn., Varanasi, 1957.

Altekar, A.S. and Mishra, V.K., *Report on Kumrahar Excavations, 1951-55*, K.P. Jayaswal Research Institute, Patna, Historical Research Series, Vol.III, Patna, 1959.

Apte, D.G., *Universities in Ancient India*, Baroda.

Banerjee, Anukul Chandra, *Sarvāstivāda Literature*, Firma K.L. Mukhopadhyay, Calcutta, 1957.

Bareau, A., *Les Premiers Conciles bouddhiques*, Presses Universitaires de France, Paris, 1955.

Barua, B.M., *Aśoka and his Inscriptions*, 2nd edn., New Age Publishers Ltd., Calcutta, 1955.

——, *Barhut,* Vols.I, II, Calcutta 1934; III, Calcutta, 1937.

Barua, B.M. and G.N. Sinha, *Barhut Inscriptions*, Calcutta, 1926.

Barua, Dipak Kumar, *Viharas in Ancient India* (A Survey of Buddhist Monasteries), Indian Publications, Calcutta, 1969.

Basham, A.L., *The Wonder that was India*, London, 1954.

Bhagat, M.G., *Ancient Indian Asceticism*, Munshiram Manoharlal, Delhi, 1976.

Bhagvat, Durga, *Early Buddhist Jurisprudence*, Oriental Book Agency, Poona, 1939.

Bhandarkar, D.R., *Aśoka* (in Hindi), Delhi, 1960.

Bhargava, Dayanand, *Jaina Ethics*, 1st edn., Motilal Banirsidass, Delhi, 1968.

Bhattacharyya, B., *The Indian Buddhist Iconography*, revd. edn., Firma, K.L. Mukhopadhyay, Calcutta, 1958.

Bhattasali, N.K., *Iconography of Buddhist and Brahmanical Sculptures in the Dacca Museum*, Dacca, 1929.

Brown, Percy, *Indian Architecture* (Buddhist and Hindu Period), 3rd revd. edn., Bombay, 1956.

Burgess, J., *Notes on Amaravati Stupa*, Indological Book House, Delhi, 1972.

——, *The Buddhist Stupas of Amaravati and Jagayyapeta, ASSI.*, Vol.I, Indological Book House, Varanasi, 1970.

Burgess, J. and Indraji, *Bhagwanlal, Inscriptions from the Cave Temples of Western India with Descriptive Notes*, 1st rep., Indian India, Delhi, 1976.

Chakraborti, Haripada, *Asceticism in Ancient India in Brahmanical,* Buddhist, Jaina and Ajivika Societies (From the Earliest Times to the Period of Saṅkarāchārya), Punthi Pustak, Calcutta, 1973.

——, *Early Brahmi Records in India (c.300 BC–c.AD 300)*, An Analytical Study: Social, Economic, Religious and Administrative, Sanskrit Pustak Bhandar, Calcutta, 1974.

Chang, Kun, A *Comparative Study of the Kaṭhinavastu,* Indo Iranian Monographs I, Mouton and Co. S'. Gravenhage, The Hague, 1957.

Chau, Thich Minh, *Hsuang Tsang,* the Pilgrim and Scholar, Bihar, 1963.

——, *Miliandapañha and Nāgasena Bhikshu Sūtra*, a Comparative Study, Firma K.L. Mukhopādhyay, Calcutta, 1964.

Coomaraswamy, A., *Buddha and the Gospel of Buddhism*, 1st Indian edn., Munshiram Manoharlal, Delhi, 1974.

Conze, E., *Buddhism, Its Essence and Development*, 2nd edn., Oxford, 1953.

——, *Buddhist Meditation*, George Allen and Unwin Ltd., London, 1956.

——, *Buddhist Thought in India*, 1st published, George Allen and Unwin Ltd., London, 1962.

Cunningham, A., *Ancient Geography of India*, rep., Indological Book House, Varanasi, 1963.

——, *The Stupa of Bharhut*, rep., Varanasi, 1962.

Dahlke, Paul, *Buddhist Essays*, trans., from the German by Bhikkhu Sīlācāra, Macmillan and Co. Ltd., London, 1948.

Das, A.C., *Rigvedic India*, Calcutta, 1927.

Das, S.K., *The Educational System of the Ancient Hindus*, Calcutta, 1930.

De, Gokuldas, *Democracy in the Early Buddhist Saṅgha*, Calcutta, 1955.

Dehejia, Vidya, *Early Buddhist Rock Temples*, Thames and Hudson Ltd., London, 1972.

Deo, S.B., *History of Jaina Monachism from Inscriptions and Literature*, Poona, 1956.

Deo, S.B., and Joshi, J.P., *Pauni Excavations (1969-70)*, Nagpur, 1972.

Deussen, Paul, *The Philosophy of the Upaniṣads*, English trans., by A.S. Geden, Oriental Publishers, Delhi, 1972.

Dorjee, Prema, *Stupa and its technology: a Tibeto-Buddhist perspective*, Motilal Banarsidass, Delhi, 2001.

Dube, S.N., *Cross Currents in Early Buddhism*, Manohar Publications, Delhi, 1980.

Dumont, Louis, *Religion, Politics and History in India*, Collected papers in Indian Sociology, Mouton Publishers, Paris, 1970.

Dutt, N., *Aspects of Mahayana Buddhism and its Relation to Hinayana*, Luzac and Co., London, 1930.

——, *Buddhist Sects in India*, 2nd edn., Motilal Banarsidass, Delhi, 1978.

——, *Early Monastic Buddhism*, Vol.I, Calcutta, 1941, Vol.II, Calcutta, 1945.

Dutt, S., *Buddhist Monks and Monasteries of India, Their History and their Contribution to Indian Culture*, George Allen and Unwin Ltd., London, 1962.

——, *Early Buddhist Monachism*, 1st revd. Indian edn., Asia Publishing House, Delhi, 1960.

——, *The Buddha and Five After Centuries*, Sahitya Samsad, Calcutta, 1978.

Elder, Joseph. W. (ed.), *Chapters in Indian Civilization*, 2 Vols., Dubuque, Iowa: Kendall Hunt Publishers, 1970.

Elliot, H.M. and J. Dowson, *The History of India as told by its own historians*, Vol.II, London, 1869.

Ergardt, Jan. T., *Faith and Knowledge in Early Buddhism*, Leiden, E.J. Brill, 1977.

Fergusson, J., *A History of Indian and Eastern Architecture*, Vol.I, rep., Delhi, 1967.

Fergusson, J., and J. Burgess, *The Cave Temples of India*, rep., Orient Books Rep. Corporation, Delhi, 1969.

Fleet J.F., *Corpus Inscriptionum Indicarum* (Inscriptions of the Early Guptas and their Successors), Vol.III, Indological Book House, Varanasi, 1963.

Foucher, A., *The Life of the Buddha*, trans., S.B. Boas, Connecticut, U.S.A., 1963.

Frankfuter, O., *Handbook of Pali,* being an elementary grammar, a chrestomathy and a glossary, 1883.

Frauwallner, E., *The Earliest Vinaya and the Beginnings Buddhist Literature*, Serie Orientale Roma VIII, Roma, Is. M.E.O., 1956.

Gajrani, S., *Ancient Buddhist Monasteries: India and Nepal*, D.K. Publishers, Delhi, 1998.

Ghosh, A., *Nalanda*, 5th edn., Delhi, 1965.

Ghoshal, U.N., A *History of Indian Political Ideas*, Oxford University Press, London, 1959.

Ghurye, G.S., *Indian Sadhus*, Bombay, 1953.

Gnoli Raniero, (ed.), *The Gilgit Ms. of the Sayanāsanavastu of the Adhikaraṇa Vastu*. Being the 15th and 16th section of the Vinaya of Mulasarvastivādin, Rome: Instituto Italiano per il Medio ed Estremo Oriente, 1978.

Gokhale, B.G., *Buddhism and Aśoka*, Baroda, 1958.

Gopalachari, K., *Early History of the Andhra Country*, 2nd edn., University of Madras, 1976.

Goyal, S.R., A *History of Indian Buddhism*, 1st edn., Kusumanjali Prakashan, Meerut, 1987.

Grover, Satish, *The Architecture of India*, Buddhist and Hindu, Vikas Publishing House Pvt. Ltd., Delhi, 1980.

Grunwedel, A., *Buddhist Art in India*, trans., from the German by A.L. Gibson, revised and enlarged by J. Burgess, 2nd edn., Sushil Gupta, Spain, Santiago De Compostela, 1965.

Gupta, S.P., *The Roots of Indian Art*, Mauryan and late Mauryan, B.R. Publishing Corporation, Delhi, 1980.

Gupte, R.S., *Inconography of the Hindus, Buddhists and Jains*, 1st published, D.B. Taraporevala sons and Co. Pvt. Ltd., Bombay, 1972.

Hardayal, *The Bodhisattva Doctrine in Buddhist Sanskrit Literature*, rep., Motilal Banaridass, Delhi, 1975.

Havell, E.B., *The Ancient and Medieval Architecture of India: A Study of Indo-Aryan Civilization*, rep., Delhi, 1972.

Hofinger, M., *Étude sur le concile de Vaiśāli*, Louvain, 1946.

Holt, John, C., Discipline: *The Canonical Buddhism of the Vinaya Piṭaka*, 1st edn., Motilal Banarsidass, Delhi, 1981.

Hopkins, Thomas, *The Hindu Religious Tradition*, Dickenson Publishing Company Inc., 1970.

Horner, I.B., *Women under Primitive Buddhism*, George Routledge and Sons Ltd., London, 1930.

Hsiang-kuang, Chou, *Indo Chinese Relations, A History of Chinese Buddhism*, Indo Chinese Literature Publications, Allahabad, 1955.

Hultzsch, E., *Corpus Inscriptionum Indicarum* (Inscriptions of Aśoka), Vol.I, Indological Book House, Delhi, 1969.

Iyer, A.V.T., *Indian Architecture*, Book II, Madras.

Jones, J.G., *Tales and Teachings of the Buddha* (The Jataka Stories in Relation to the Pāli Canon), George Allen and Unwin Ltd., London, 1979.

Joshi, L.M., *Studies in the Buddhistic Culture of India* (During the 7th-8th century AD), 2nd revd. edn., Motilal Banarsidass, Delhi, 1977.

Kail, Owen C., *Buddhist Cave Temples of India*, 1st published, D.B. Taraporevala sons and Co. Pvt. Ltd., Bombay, 1975.

Kalupahana, David J., *Buddhist Philosophy, A Historical Analysis*, University Press of Hawaii, Honolulu, 1976.

Kane, P.V., *History of Dharmaśāstra*, Vol.II, Pt.II, Poona, 1941.

Keay, F.E., *Ancient Indian Education* (An Inquiry into its Origin, Development and Ideals), rep., Cosmo Publications, Delhi, 1980.

Keith, A.B., A *History of Sanskrit Literature*, Oxford University Press, London,1928.

——, *Buddhist Philosophy in India and Ceylon*, Chowkhamba Sanskrit Studies Vol.XXVI, Varanasi, 1963.

Kern, H., *Manual of Indian Buddhism*, Indological Book House, Varanasi, 1972.

Kitagawa, Joseph, *Religions of the East*, Westminster Press, Philadelphia, 1960.

Konow, Sten, *Corpus Inscriptionum Indicarum* (Kharoshṭhi Inscriptions), Vol.II, Pt.I, Indological Book House, Varanasi, 1963.

Kosambi, D.D., *The Culture and Civilization of Ancient India in Historical Outline*, 2nd rep., Vikas Publishing House, Delhi, 1975.

Lamotte, E., *Histoire du Bouddhisme Indien des origines à l' ère Śaka*, Louvain, 1958.

Lannoy, R., *The Speaking Tree* (A Study of Indian Culture and Society), Oxford University Press, London, 1971.

Law, B.C. *Mahavira: His Life and Teachings*, London, 1937.

Ling, Trevor, A *History of Religion,* East and West, New York, 1968.

——, Buddha, *Marx and God,* New York, 1966.

——, *The Buddha: Buddhist Civilization in India and Ceylon*, Pelican Books, New York, 1976.

Maisey, F.C., *Sanchi and its Remains*, Delhi, 1972.

Marshall, J., *A Guide to Taxila*, Delhi, 1936.

——, *Mohenjodaro and the Indus Valley Civilization*, I, London, 1931.

——, *Taxila*, Vol.I (Structural Remains), Motilal Banarsidass, Delhi, 1975.

Marshall J. and A. Foucher, *The Monuments of Sanchi* (ed.), N.G. Majumdar, 3 Vols., Delhi, 1940.

McCrindle, J.W., *Ancient India as described by Megasthenes and Arrian*, Calcutta, 1960.

Mehta, R.N. and S.N. Chowdhary, *Excavations at Devnimori*, M.S. University Archaeology Series, No.8, Baroda, 1966.

Mirashi, V.V., *Corpus Inscriptionum Indicarum* (Inscriptions of the Vakatakas), Vol.V, Ootacamund, 1963.

Misra, G.S.P., *The Age of Vinaya*, Munshiram Manoharlal, Delhi, 1972.

——, *Development of Buddhist Ethics*, Munshiram Manoharlal, Delhi, 1984.

Mitra, Debala, *Buddhist Monuments*, rep., Sahitya Samsad, Calcutta, 1980.

——, *Sanchi*, 4th edn., Delhi, 1978.

——, *Ajanta*, 7th edn., Delhi, 1974.

Mookerji, R.K., *Ancient Indian Education* (Brahmanical and Buddhist), rep., Motilal Banarsidass, Delhi, 1974.

——, *Aśoka*, Delhi, 1962.

Nagaraja Rao, M.S. (ed.), *Madhu* (Recent Researches in Indian Archaeology and Art History), Agam Kala Prakashan, Delhi, 1981.

Nagaraju, S., *Buddhist Architecture of Western India*, Agam Kala Prakashan, Delhi, 1981.

Narain, A.K. (ed.), *Studies in Pali and Buddhism*, A Homage volume to the memory of Bhikkhu Jagdish Kashyap, B.R. Publishing Corporation, Delhi, 1979.

Narendradeva, Acharya, *Bauddha Dharma Darśana*, Bihar Rāṣtra Bhāṣā Pariṣad, Patna, 1956.

Obermiller, E., *Analysis of the Abhisamayālaṃkara*, Fasc. 1, Luzac and Co., London, 1933.

Oldenberg, H., *Buddha, His Life, His Doctrines, His Order*, trans., William Hoey, Indological Book House, Delhi, 1971.

Olivelle, Patrick, *The Origin and Early Development of Buddhist Monachism*, M.D. Gunasena and Co. Ltd., Colombo, 1974.

Pachow, W., A *Comparative Study of the Pratitmokṣa on the basis of its Chinese, Tibetan, Sanskrit and Pali versions*, The Sino Indian Cultural Society, Shantiniketan, 1955.

Pande, C.B., *Mauryan Art*, Varanasi, 1982.

Pande, G.C., *Bauddha Dharma ke Vikāsa ka Itihāsa*, 2nd edn., Hindi Samiti, Lucknow, 1976.

——, *Śramaṇa Tradition, Its History and Contribution to Indian Culture*, L.D. Institute of Indology, Ahmedabad, 1978.

——, *Studies in the Origins of Buddhism*, 2nd revd. edn., Motilal Banarsidass, Delhi, 1974.

——, *Studies in Mahāyāna*, 1st edn., Central Institute of Higher Tibetan Studies, Sarnath, Varanasi, 1993.

Pandey, R.B., *Indian Palaeography*, Pt.I, Motilal Banarsidass, Delhi, 1952.

——, *Historical and Literary Inscriptions*, Chowkhamba Sanskrit Studies, Vol.XXIII, Varanasi, 1962.

Pant, Sushila, *The Origin and Development of Stupa Architecture*, Bharata Manisha Research Series: 8, Varanasi, 1976.

Poussin, Louis de La Vaillée, *The Buddhist Councils*, K.P. Bagchi and Co., Calcutta, 1976.

Prebish, Charles (ed.), *Buddhism, A Modern Perspective*, 2nd printing, The Pennsylvania State University Press, London, 1978.

——, *Buddhist Monastic Discipline*, The Sanskrit Prātimoksa Sūtras of the Mahāsāṃghikas and Mūlasarvāstivādins, The Pennsylvania State University Press, London, 1975.

Przyluski, J., *Le Concile de Rājagṛha*, Paris, 1926-28.

Radhakrishnan, S., *The Principal Upanisads*, 1st published, George Allen and Unwin Ltd., London, 1953.

Rahula, Telwatte, *A Critical Study of the Mahavastu*, 1st edn., Motilal Banarsidass, Delhi, 1978.

Ramachandra Rao, P.R., *The Art of Nāgārjunikonda,* Madras, 1956.

Rea, A., *South Indian Buddhist Antiquities,* Indological Book House, Varanasi, 1969.

Rhys Davids (Mrs.), *A Manual of Buddhism for Advanced Students,* 1st Indian edn., Oriental Book Rep. Corporation, Delhi, 1978.

Rhys Davids, C.A.F., *The Birth of Indian Psychology and its Development in Buddhism,* Luzac and Co., London, 1936.

Rhys Davids, T.W., *Buddhism,* London, 1889.

Robertson, Alec, *The Triple Gem and the Uposatha*, Apothecaries Co., Colombo, 1971.

Rockhill, W.W. (trans.), *The Life of the Buddha and the Early History of his Order*, Popular Edition, London, 1884.

Rosen, Valentina (ed. and trans.), *Der Vinayavibhaṅga Zum Bhikṣu Pratimokṣa Der Sarvastivadins*, Vol.II of Sanskrittexte aus den Turfanfunden, Berlin: Deutsche Akademie der Wissenschaften zu Berlin Institut für Orientforschung, 1959.

Rowland, Benjamin, *The Art and Architecture of India,* Buddhist, Hindu, Jain, London, 1953.

Sahni, D.R., *Archaeological Remains and Excavations at Bairāṭ,* Jaipur.

Sarkar, H., *Studies in Early Buddhist Architecture,* Munshiram Manoharlal, Delhi, 1966.

Sarkar, H., and B.N. Mishra, *Nagarjunikonda,* 3rd edn., Delhi, 1980.

Sankalia, H.D., *The Nalanda University,* Oriental Publishers, Delhi, 1972.

Satyanarayana, K., A *Study of the History and Culture of the Andhras: From Stone Age to Feudalism,* Vol.I, People's Publishing House, Delhi, 1975.

Schuon, Frithjof, *In the Tracks of Buddhism,* trans., from the French by Marco Pallis, George Allen and Unwin Ltd., London, 1968.

Sen, A.C., *Aśoka's Edicts,* Institute of Indology Series No.7, Calcutta, 1956.

Sharma, G.R., *Excavations at Kauśāmbī,* Allahabad 1960.

Shastri, Ajay Mitra, *An Outline of Early Buddhism* (A Historical Survey of Buddhology, Buddhist schools and *Saṅghas* mainly based on the study of pre-Gupta Inscriptions), Indological Book House, Varanasi, 1965.

Singh, M.M., *Life in North-Eastern India in Pre-Mauryan Times*, Delhi, 1967.

Sinha, B.P. and S.R. Roy, *Vaiśāli Excavations*, Directorate of Archaeology and Museum, Patna, 1969.

Sircar, D.C. (ed.), *Select Inscriptions bearing on Indian history and civilization (6th BC to AD 6th)*, Vol.I, 2nd revd. and enlr. edn., Calcutta, 1965.

Smith, Vincent, *A History of fine art in India and Ceylon*, London, 1911.

Stcherbatsky, Th., *Buddhist Logic*, Vol.I, lst published, Dover Publications, New York, 1962.

Stevenson, Sinclair, *The Heart of Jainism*, rep., Delhi, 1970.

Subrahmanian, K.R., *Buddhist Remains in Andhra and the History of the Andhra between AD 225 and 610*, Madras, 1932.

Subrahmanyam, R., Salihundam—*A Buddhist site in Andhra Pradesh*, A.P. Government Archaeological Series No.17, Hyderabad, 1964.

Suzuki, D.T. (trans.), *Discourse on the Awakening of Faith in the Mahayana Literature,* Chicago, 1900.

——, *Studies in the Laṅkavatara Sutra,* rep., Routedge and Kegan Paul, London, 1968.

Tachibana, S., *The Ethics of Buddhism*, Oxford University Press, London, 1926; rev. edn., Harper and Row, New York, 1975.

Takakusu, J., *Essentials of Buddhist Philosophy*, 3rd edn., Office Appliance Co., Honolulu, 1956.

Tambiah, S.J., *World Conqueror and World Renouncer: A Study of Buddhism and Polity in Thailand against a Historical Background,* 1st paperback edn., Cambridge University Press, London,1977.

Thapar, Romila, *Ancient Indian Social History, Some Interpretations*, Orient Longman Ltd., Delhi, 1978.

——, *Aśoka and the Docline of the Mauryas*, Oxford University Press, London, 1961.

Thaplyal, K.K., *Studies in Ancient Indian Seals* (A Study of North Indian Seals and Sealings from 3rd Century BC to mid-seventh century AD), 1st edn., Akhil Bharatiya Sanskrit Parishad, Lucknow, 1972.

Thomas, E.J., *The History of Buddhist Thought*, 2nd edn., Routledge and Kegan Paul Ltd., London, 1951.

Vidyabhusana, S.C., *History of Indian Logic*, Calcutta, 1921.

——, *History of Medieval School of Indian Logic*, 2nd edn., Calcutta, 1977.

Virji, Krishna Kumari J., *Ancient History of Saurashtra* (Being a Study of the Maitrakas of Valabhi, V to VIII centuries AD), Konkan Institute of Arts and Sciences, Bombay, 1955.

Venkata Ramanan, K., *Nāgārjuna's Philosophy as Presented in the Mahā-prajñāpāramitā Śāstra*, 1st Indian edn., Bharatiya Vidya Prakaṣhan, Varanasi, 1971.

Vogel, J. Ph., *A Catalogue of the Archaeological Museum of Mathura*, Indological Book House, Varanasi, 1971.

Waldschmidt, Ernst (ed. and trans.), *Bruchstücke des Bhikṣuni Prātimokṣa der Sarvastivadins*, Vol.III of Kleinere Sanskrittexte Leipzig: Deutsche Morgenländischen Gesellschaft in Komission bei F.A. Brockhaus, 1926.

Walpola, Rahula, *History of Buddhism in Ceylon: The Anuradhpura Period* (*3rd century BC–10th century AC*), 2nd edn., M.D. Gunasena and Co. Ltd., Colombo, 1966.

Warder, A.K. *Indian Buddhism*, 1st edn., Motilal Banarsidass, Delhi, 1970.

Weber, Max, *The Religion of India: The Sociology of Hinduism and Buddhism*, Illinois, 1958.

Yazdani, G., *The Early History of the Deccan*, Vol.II, Ist Indian edn., Oriental Books Rep. Corporation, Delhi, 1982.

Journals, Memoirs, Periodicals, Proceedings, and Reports

Ancient India.
Annals of the Bhandarkar Oriental Research Institute.
Annual Report of Epigraphy.
Annual Report of the Archaeological Survey of India.
Archaeological Survey of Western India.
Artibus Asiae.
Aryan Path.
Asia Major.
Bhāratī.
Bhāratīya Vidyā.
Bulletin de l'École Francaise d'extrême Orient.
East and West.
Epigraphia Indica.
History of Religions.
Indian Antiquary.
Indian Archaeology—A Review.
Indian Historical Quarterly.
Indian Librarian.
Indica.
Indological Studies.
Jijñāsā.
Journal Asiatique.
Journal of Asian Studies.
Journal of Indian History.
Journal of the American Oriental Society.
Journal of the Andhra Historical Research Society.
Journal of the Asiatic Society Bombay.
Journal of the Asiatic Society, Calcutta.
Journal of the Assam Research Society.
Journal of the Bihar and Orissa Research Society.
Journal of the Bihar Research Society.
Journal of the Bombay Branch of the Royal Asiatic Society.

Journal of the Department of Letters.
Journal of the Ganganath Jha Research Institute.
Journal of the Gujarat Research, Society.
Journal of the Maharaj Sayajirao, Univervity of Baroda.
Journal of the Numismatic Society of India.
Journal of the Oriental Institute, Baroda.
Journal of the Oriental Research, Madras.
Journal of the Royal Asiatic Society.
Journal of the University of Bombay.
Mahābodhi.
Marg.
Mélanges Chinois et bouddhiques.
Memoirs of the Archaeological Survey of India.
Prajñā.
Proceedings of the 7th All India Oriental Conference Report.
Quarterly Journal of the Mythic Society.
Religion and Society.
Times of India, Annual.
The Hindu.
Visvabharati Annals.
Vishveshvaranand Indological Journal.
Wiener Zeitschrift für die Kunde Südund Ostasiens.

Catalogues, Dictionaries, Encyclopaedias and Other Works of Reference

A Catalogue of the Chinese translation of the Buddhist Tripitaka—Bunyu Nanjio.
Buddhist Hybrid Sanskrit Dictionary, Vol.II—F. Edgerton.
Dictionary of Early Buddhist Monastic Terms—C.S. Upasak.
Dictionary of the Pali Language—R.C. Childers.
Encyclopaedia of Buddhism—G.P. Malasekara.
Encyclopaedia of Hindu Architecture—P.K. Acharya, Manasara Series, Vol.VII.
Encyclopaedia of Religion and Ethics, ed., James Hastings, New York, 1908-55.
Pali English Dictionary, ed., Rhys Davids and Stede, PTS.
A Sanskrit English Dictionary—Monier Williams.
Taishô-shinshu-daizôkyô, ed., Takakusu and Watanabe.
Vedic Index of Names and subjects—Macdonell and Keith.

Index